GW00456672

Chancellors of the Exchequer

First Edition

1

Editor: Jamie Steel

Other titles by Ben Steel:

A 300 Year Concise History of British Prime Ministers 1721 - 2021

Dear Rajesh

all the very best for the next
step in your career. Hope this
serves as a fitting souvenir!

kindest Regards
Kawalveer
February 2022.

Ben Steel

The Role of the United Kingdom Chancellor of the Exchequer:

The Chancellor of the Exchequer is the government's chief finance minister and one of the most senior members of the Cabinet. The Chancellor is responsible for setting levels of taxation and public spending across the UK announcing changes to these each year in the annual Budget statement (the word Budget comes from the French 'bougette', a small bag/wallet). The Chancellor of the Exchequer has overall responsibility for HM Treasury.

The term Exchequer was named after a table used to perform calculations for taxes and goods in the medieval period. The name "Exchequer" then came to refer to the twice yearly meetings held at Easter and Michaelmas, at which government financial business was transacted and an audit held of sheriffs' returns. The department or office was a state in medieval England charged with the collection and management of the royal revenue and judicial determination of all revenue causes. In the 18th and early 19th centuries, it was common for the Prime Minister also to serve as Chancellor of the Exchequer if he sat in the Commons; the last Chancellor who was simultaneously Prime Minister and Chancellor of the Exchequer was Stanley Baldwin in 1923. Indeed the first 'de facto' Prime Minister, Robert Walpole was the first Chancellor of the Exchequer from 1715 to 1717 before becoming simultaneously Chancellor and Prime Minister in 1721. The first Budget appears to date back to 1733 when Britain experienced a so-called Excise Crisis. The Prime Minister at the time, Robert Walpole, planned to shift the burden of paying taxes away from the wealthy landed gentry and on to the "consumer" or common person. The holder of the office of Chancellor of the Exchequer as the Second Lord, has their official residence in 11 Downing Street in London, next door to the residence of the First Lord of the Treasury (a title that has for many years been held by the Prime Minister), who resides in 10 Downing Street. While in the past both houses were private residences, today they serve as interlinked offices, with the occupant living in an apartment made from attic rooms, previously resided in by servants. Since 1827, the Chancellor has always simultaneously held the office of Second Lord of the Treasury, when that person has not also been the Prime Minister. One part of the Chancellor's key roles involves the framing of the annual year Budget. As of 2017, the first is the Autumn Budget, also known as Budget Day which forecasts government spending in the next financial year and also announces new financial measures. The second is a Spring Statement, also known as a 'mini-Budget'. The Chancellor traditionally carries his Budget speech to the House of Commons in a particular red Despatch Box. The original Budget briefcase was first used by William Ewart Gladstone in 1853, and continued in use until 1965, when James Callaghan was the first Chancellor to break with tradition when he used a newer box. Prior to Gladstone, a generic red Despatch Box of varying design and specification was used. In March 2008, Alistair Darling reverted to using the original Budget briefcase, and his successor, George Osborne, continued this tradition for his first Budget, before announcing that it would be retired due to its fragile condition. The Chancellor of the Exchequer is the only member of the House of Commons allowed to drink alcohol in the chamber, according to an historic ritual which allows them their choice of drink when they are delivering their Budget speech at the despatch box. Benjamin Disraeli liked to sink a brandy with water while his great rival William Gladstone enjoyed the unusual tipple of a sherry with a beaten egg. Ken Clarke enjoyed a whisky while Nigel Lawson favoured a spritzer and Geoffrey Howe was partial to a gin and tonic. 2019 was the first year in recent history without a Budget statement, Sajid Javid had been due to deliver a Budget in November 2019, but a General Election was called and a new Budget was set for March 2020. No year in the 20th century passed without at least one Budget, and the same was true of the 21st century until 2019. Taxes have been around since medieval times when taxation was introduced as a system to raise money for royal and government expenses. Land taxes were the main source of income in addition to custom duties and fees to mint coins. The most important tax of the Anglo Saxon period was the 'danegold', which was a kind of medieval insurance policy to protect against Viking raiders from ransacking land. Before the United Kingdom formed on 1 May 1707, many taxes were introduced, these included; King John introducing an export tax on wool in 1203, King Edward I introducing a wine tax in 1275 and a Poor Law tax was established in 1572. In 1628 Parliament passed a Petition of Right, which prohibited the use of taxes without it passing through Parliament. After the Great Fire of London in 1666, Charles II introduced Coal Tax Acts in 1667 and 1670, to help repair the damage to the City of London, the laws were later repealed in 1889. The Chancellor of the Exchequer delivers his Budget statement to Members of Parliament in the House of Commons. The first part of the statement typically begins with a review of the nation's finances and the economic situation. The statement then moves on to proposals for taxation. The longest continues Budget speech by a Chancellor was four hours 45 minutes by William Gladstone in 1853, and the shortest ever Budget speech was by Benjamin Disraeli's in 1867, which lasted 45 minutes. By tradition the Chairman of Ways and Means (Deputy Speaker) chairs the Budget debates rather than the Speaker of the House, and traditionally the Leader of the Opposition, rather than the Shadow Chancellor replies to the Budget Speech. The Budget is usually followed by four days of debate on the Budget Resolutions, these are the tax measures announced in the Budget. Each day of debate covers a different policy area such as health, education and defence. The Shadow Chancellor makes his response the day after the Budget statement during the Budget debates. Budget Resolutions can come into effect immediately if the House of Commons agrees to them at the end of the four days of debate but they require the Finance Bill to give them permanent legal effect.

Contents   Page

Page

William Pitt the Younger
1759 - 1806 (46 years old) Whig/Tory

Chancellor of the Exchequer:
3 stints
10 July 1782 - 31 March 1783
(8 months and 22 days)
19 December 1783 - 1 January 1801
(17 years and 14 days)
10 May 1804 - 23 January 1806
(1 year, 8 months and 14 days)
Born
28 May 1759, Hayes Place, near Hayes Kent
Died
23 January 1806, aged 46, Putney Heath, London
Title: Lord Warden of the Cinque Ports

Constituencies Represented as MP:
Appleby 1781 - 1784
Cambridge University 1784 - 1806

Other Official Offices held:
Leader of the House of Commons 1783 - 1801 and 1804 - 1806
Prime Minister 1783 - 1801 and 1804 - 1806

Prime Minister served with as Chancellor:
William Petty and Himself

Education: Pembroke College, Cambridge.

William Pitt the Younger, (28 May 1759 – 23 January 1806) was an important British Tory statesman (although he referred to himself as an 'Independent Whig') of the late eighteenth and early nineteenth centuries. He was Chancellor of the Exchequer on three separate occasions and was Chancellor for all of his time as Prime Minister. Pitt became the youngest Prime Minister of Great Britain in 1783 at the age of 24 and the first Prime Minister of Great Britain and Ireland as of January 1801. He left office in March 1801, but served as Prime Minister again from 1804 until his death in 1806.

Born at Hayes Place in the village of Hayes, Kent, William Pitt, was the second son of William Pitt, 1st Earl of Chatham. To avoid

STATUE OF PITT AT
PEMBROKE COLLEGE

confusion, the names Pitt the Younger and Pitt the Elder were used. He was from a political family on both sides, along with his Prime Minister father, his mother, Hester Grenville, was sister to former Prime Minister George Grenville. Suffering from occasional poor health as a boy, Pitt was educated at home by the Reverend Edward Wilson, described as an intelligent child, he quickly became proficient in both Latin and Greek. He was admitted to Pembroke College, Cambridge, on 26 April 1773, a month before his fourteenth birthday, where he studied political philosophy, classics, mathematics, trigonometry, chemistry and history.

While at Cambridge, Pitt befriended the young William Wilberforce (later the leader of the movement to abolish the slave trade) who became a lifelong friend and political ally in Parliament. Pitt who was continually plagued by poor health, took advantage of a little-used privilege available only to the sons of noblemen, and chose to graduate without having to pass examinations. He then went on to acquire a legal education at Lincoln's Inn and was called to the bar in the summer of 1780. During the General Elections on 9 September 1780, at the age of 21, Pitt contested the University of Cambridge seat but lost, coming last out of five candidates with 142 votes (277 to 247, 206 and 150). Still intent on entering Parliament, Pitt who was unable to afford the expense of standing for Parliament himself, was able to embark on a political career through the influence of Sir James Lowther, who secured his election as an Independent Whig for Appleby in a By-election in 1781. In Parliament, the youthful Pitt cast aside his tendency to be withdrawn in public, and in 1782 aged 23, he was appointed Chancellor of the Exchequer (after three others had turned down the position). The following years were marked by the battle between George III and the radical Charles Fox, whom the King detested. Matters deteriorated when Fox forged an alliance with the previously loyal Lord North. The two men defeated the government and King George was forced to ask them to take control, with Fox becoming Pitt's lifelong political rival. In December 1783, George III dismissed the Lord North/Fox ministry that had succeeded Petty's government, and it was to the 24-year-old Pitt that the King turned to serve as both Prime Minister and Chancellor. At 24, Pitt was the youngest man to become Prime Minister, a record that still stands today. Although he faced immediate defeat in Parliament he refused to resign, and George III was prepared to abdicate rather than let Fox in again. Therefore in 1784, Parliament was dissolved for a General Election on 3 April 1784, in which Pitt won the Cambridge University seat as a 'Non Partisan' (two seats available) with 351 votes (against 299, 278 and 181). Pitt's government worked to restore public finances which had been severely strained, and he introduced 'The Brick Tax' in 1784, as a means of helping to pay for the wars being fought in the American Colonies. Tax was paid at the rates of 4 shilling per thousand bricks (the tax was later abolished in 1850 as it was regarded as a detrimental tax to industrial development). Pitt imposed other new taxes - including Britain's first income tax, and he reduced both smuggling and frauds, while simplifying customs and excise duties. In 1785, he introduced a bill to remove the representation of thirty-six rotten boroughs (a rotten borough was able to elect an MP despite having very few voters, the choice of MP typically being in the

hands of one person or family). Pitt also tried to extend the electoral franchise to allow more individuals, but this was abandoned after a parliamentary defeat. Among Pitt's initiatives were financial and administrative reforms which had the intention of improving efficiency and eliminating corrupt practices. In 1786, Pitt made a serious attempt to reduce the national debt through the creation of a sinking fund (setting aside money for the gradual repayment of a debt).

STATUE OF PITT IN GEORGE STREET EDINBURGH

In 1788, Pitt faced a major crisis when King George fell victim to a mysterious illness, which at the time was classed as "madness" but was down to the physical and genetic blood disorder called 'porphyria' (the 1994 film The Madness of King George was based on this period). With the King incapacitated, Parliament had to look to appoint a regent to rule in his place. All factions agreed that the only viable candidate was the King's eldest son, Prince George, Prince of Wales. The Prince, however, was a supporter of Charles Fox, and had the Prince come to power, it is most likely that he would have dismissed Pitt. Parliament spent months debating legal technicalities relating to the regency and fortunately for Pitt, the King recovered in February 1789, just after a Regency Bill had been introduced and passed in the House of Commons. At the 1790 General Election, which ran from 16 June until 28 July, Pitt was re-elected as a Tory in the Cambridge seat with 510 votes (against 483 and 207), 92 of the 314 constituencies (29 per cent) were contested, an increase of five on the figure for 1784. Roughly the figures in Parliament consisted of 558 Members, of which 340 might be classed as government, 183 opposition, and 35 independent or doubtful. The French Revolution remained a great concern in the early 1790's, and in 1793 the French finally declared war on

William Pitt the Younger

Britain. The wartime situation made it difficult for Pitt to pursue his administrative reforms, and financial restraints forced Pitt into a series of recourses to raise the vast sums necessary to sustain the war effort. In the General Election of 1796, which ran from 25 May to 29 June, Pitt was again returned as a Tory in the Cambridge seat unopposed. In 1797, in an attempt to generate more revenue for the country, Pitt imposed yet another tax – the clock tax. The clock tax required a payment of five shillings on every clock, even within a private home, two shillings and sixpence on pocket-watches of silver or other metal, and ten shillings on those of gold. This proved immensely unpopular and was scrapped after only nine months. In Pitt's December 1798 Budget, he introduced Britain's first income tax as a temporary measure in the hope of raising £10 million to pay for weapons and equipment in preparation for the Napoleonic Wars (implemented in 1799, £6 million was raised, worth over £700m in 2020). Pitt oversaw a major triumph with the Act of Union of 1800, which saw the United Kingdom of Britain and Ireland come into being on 1 January 1801, with the Irish Parliament being closed down. But with opposition from the King to his supplementary proposals for Catholic emancipation and state provision for Catholic and Dissenting

clergy, it resulted in Pitt resigning on February 3, 1801. Although now physically failing, Pitt was re-elected unopposed in the Cambridge University seat and in May 1804, he returned to head a second ministry, albeit weaker in its basis than his first. Pitt saw Nelson's victory at Trafalgar in 1805, which provided a welcome and rare moment of success in his continental war strategy.

Unfortunately the exhausted premier had to witness Napoleon's decisive victory at Austerlitz before he died of suspected liver failure at his house on Putney Heath on the morning of 23 January 1806, aged only forty-six years old, and exactly twenty-five years to the day after he had first entered the House of Commons. Pitt had been unmarried and left no children.

Interesting Pitt the Younger facts:

Pitt's attempts during his tenure as Prime Minister to cope with the dementia of King George III are portrayed by Julian Wadham in the 1994 film *The Madness of King George*.

Pitt made his maiden speech in Parliament in March 1782.

Pitt was known for his fondness and heavy consumption of port wine, which was linked to his premature death of liver failure.

The Pitt River, is in British Columbia, Canada.

Chancellors of the Exchequer – A Concise History

Pitt is caricatured as a boy Prime Minister in the third series of the television comedy *Blackadder*.

In a series of prime ministerial biographies, the program *Number 10* was produced by Yorkshire Television and Pitt was portrayed by Jeremy Brett.

The 2006 film *Amazing Grace*, with Benedict Cumberbatch in the role of Pitt depicts his close friendship with William Wilberforce who was the leading abolitionist in Parliament.

At 23, Pitt is still the youngest person ever to become Chancellor of the Exchequer and at 24 the youngest Prime Minister.

On 27 May 1798, Pitt fought a duel with Foxite MP George Tierney on Putney Common, London, in which neither man was injured, Pitt wrote to his mother saying "the business concluded without anything unpleasant to either party".

Robert Donat portrays Pitt in the 1942 biopic *The Young Mr. Pitt*, which chronicles the historical events of Pitt's life.

Probate was obtained in 1821 by Pitt's executors, sixteen years after his death, it afforded a surplus of some £7600 (worth £697,511 in 2020), but this followed public provision of £40,000 which had been used to settle his debts in 1806. £40,000 in 1806 is approx. worth £3,671,111 in 2020.

Former Conservative leader, William Hague wrote a bestselling biography of Pitt in 2005.

Pitt's final words, as recorded by his nephew James Stanhope, who was at his deathbed, were "Oh, my country! How I leave my country!"

Henry Addington
1757 - 1844 (86 years old) Tory

Chancellor of the Exchequer:
17 March 1801 – 10 March 1804
(3 years 1 month and 24 days)

Born
30 May 1757, Holborn, London

Died
15 February 1844, aged 86, London

Title: 1st Viscount Sidmouth

Constituency Represented as MP:
Devizes 1784 - 1805

Other Official Offices held:
Speaker of the House of Commons 1789 - 1801
Prime Minister 1801 - 1804
First Lord of the Treasury 1801 - 1804
Leader of the House of Commons 1801 - 1804
Lord President of the Council 1805, 1806 - 1807 and 1812
Lord Privy Seal 1806
Home Secretary 1812 - 1822

Prime Minister served with as Chancellor:
Himself

Education:
Brasenose College, Oxford.

Henry Addington, 1st Viscount Sidmouth, (30 May 1757 – 15 February 1844) was the Chancellor of the Exchequer as well as being Prime Minister from March 1801 to May 1804. He replaced William Pitt the Younger, who left office on March 14, 1801, after which the King chose Addington, who was an uncompromising Anglican, as opposed to Pitt whose position was favouring Roman Catholic emancipation. Addington is best known for obtaining the Treaty of Amiens in 1802, but the peace only lasted a year and he struggled to cope with the problems of the Napoleonic Wars.

Henry Addington was the first British Prime Minister to emerge from the middle classes. He was born on 30 May 1757, the fourth child and eldest son of Anthony Addington a leading physician and his wife Mary. Addington senior was the physician to William Pitt the Elder, which resulted with Henry becoming friends with William Pitt the Younger. Addington first studied at Cheam School and later at Reading School, Winchester College and Brasenose College, Oxford. He then went on to study law at Lincoln's Inn, eventually becoming a barrister in 1784.

Later in 1784, when Pitt the Younger called his first election, he suggested to Addington that he should enter politics, and with Pitt's help, Addington secured a seat in the House of Commons as a member for Devizes in Wiltshire. Addington continued to represent Devizes for the following twenty-one years until he accepted a peerage in 1805. By 1789, Pitt had made Addington Speaker of the House, a move which was commended by the King. The King and Addington opposed Pitt's plans in 1801 for Catholic emancipation, and although they tried, they couldn't get him to change his mind, resulting in the King asking Addington to form his own ministry. Pitt however remained in support when Addington became Prime Minister and Chancellor of the Exchequer in March 1801. Addington's first Cabinet was noted for including three future Prime Ministers; Spencer Perceval, Robert

Jenkinson and William Cavendish-Bentinck. Once in office, Addington's first speech as Prime Minister was on 25 March 1801, when he announced that his government would be seeking peace with France. Addington's declaration of the pursuit of peace, was not least on the grounds that further military conflict was financially unaffordable. Addington produced two peacetime

HENRY ADDINGTON

Budgets in April and December 1802. The key problem was the heavy expense of the army, and outstanding war costs as the armed forces were slowly reduced. There was also the public expectation that taxation would be lowered, especially the income tax and Addington had to raise an even larger loan to cover expenditure in 1802. In 1803, Addington again proposed to borrow to cover the deficit, but also declared himself satisfied that existing taxes would be sufficient to service this new loan. Pitt, however, took strong exception to his second Budget and was absent when it was presented. Pitt feared that borrowing on such a scale would produce a repetition of the slow strangling of the 'system of credit' that had occurred in 1793 to 1794.

Addington had more faith in the expansionary effects of peace and, indeed, greater confidence in Britain's overall economic strength. Addington consolidated the sinking funds and indirect taxes, removing public service expenses such as public buildings and colonial and diplomatic establishments from the civil list, while paying off the King and the Prince of Wales's debts. Above all Addington could claim to have made the first 'Budget speech', in April 1802. Addington's domestic reforms doubled the efficiency of the Income tax. By early 1803, Britain's financial and diplomatic positions had recovered sufficiently to allow Addington to declare war on France (Addington making the declaration in the Commons wearing military uniform), but the administration was attacked in Parliament by Pitt, who eventually declared open opposition to Addington's ministry. In 1803, for the first time, deduction of income tax at source was introduced by Addington.

COAT OF ARMS
VISCOUNT SIDMOUTH

At this time, the amount charged was reduced from the original rate of 10 per cent on incomes in excess of £60 per annum, but the earnings threshold was widened to double the size of the liable population. Although the King stood by him, it was not enough because Addington did not have a strong enough hold on the two houses of Parliament. By May 1804, partisan criticism of Addington's war policies provided the pretext for a parliamentary coup by the three major factions; Grenvillite, Foxites and Pittites who had decided that they should replace Addington's ministry, which resulted in Addington resigning on 10 May 1804. Addington, was invited back into Cabinet in 1805 in Pitt's second administration as Lord President of the Council, and was given a peerage as Viscount Sidmouth (county of Devon). After Pitt's death in 1806, Addington served in William Grenville's ministry as Lord Privy Seal, and in 1812, Robert Jenkinson (Lord Liverpool) offered him the role of Home Secretary which he accepted. Addington continued as Home Secretary throughout the years of economic distress and radical political activity that marked the period after the battle of Waterloo in 1815. He held the post of Home Secretary for over ten years, until Robert Peel took over in

1822. Addington remained in the Cabinet as Minister without Portfolio for the next two years, before moving on to the House of

Lords. Addington's achievement as premier during a difficult period of international conflict has been underrated, having rose to the premiership from a family background which was in the lesser gentry and professions. Addington died in London on 15 February 1844, at the age of 86, and was buried in the churchyard at St Mary the Virgin Mortlake, now in Greater London.

DR ANTHONY ADDINGTON AND HIS SON HENRY ADDINGTON'S PLAQUE IN READING

Interesting Henry Addington facts:

On 19 September 1781, Addington married Ursula Mary Hammond the daughter and coheir of Leonard Hammond of Cheam. Henry and Ursula were to have six children, two sons and four daughters. After the death of Ursula in 1811, Addington married again in 1823 to Marianne Townsend.

In 1802, Addington accepted an honorary position as vice-president for life on the Court of Governors of London's Foundling Hospital for abandoned babies.

Addington was described as "Honest but unimaginative and inflexibly Conservative".

George Canning coined the famous spiteful quote about Pitt and Addington by saying "Pitt is to Addington As London is to Paddington".

Henry Petty-Fitzmaurice
1780 - 1863 (82 years old) Whig

Chancellor of the Exchequer:
5 February 1806 –
26 March 1807
(1 year, 1 month and 22 days)
Born
2 July 1780, London

Died
31 January 1863, aged 82, Calne, Wiltshire

Title: 3rd Marquess of Lansdowne

Constituencies Represented as MP:
Calne 1802 - 1806
Cambridge University 1806 - 1807
Camelford 1807 - 1809

Other Official Offices held:
Secretary of State for the Home Department 1827 - 1828
Lord President of the Council 1830 - 1834, 1835 - 1841 and 1846 - 1852
Leader of the House of Lords 1846 - 1852
Lord Lieutenant of Wiltshire 1827 - 1863
Senior Privy Councillor 1851 - 1863

Prime Minister served with as Chancellor:
William Wyndham Grenville (Lord Grenville)

Education:
Trinity College, Cambridge.

Henry Petty-Fitzmaurice, 3rd Marquess of Lansdowne, (2 July 1780 – 31 January 1863), known as **Lord Henry Petty** from 1784 to 1809, was an MP for Calne, Cambridge and Camelford, who served notably as Home Secretary and Chancellor of the Exchequer, as well as serving three times as Lord President of the Council.

Petty was the son of Prime Minister William Petty, the first Marquess of Lansdowne (known as the Earl of Shelbourne). He was born on 2 July 1780 at Lansdowne House, Berkeley Square, London, to Petty senior's second wife, Lady Louisa Fitzpatrick. He attended Westminster school with a political career in mind from 1793 to 1796. While at Westminster school Petty was a regular visitor to the House of Commons to watch debates, and where he was further guided towards a political future. After Westminster Petty's father sent him to Edinburgh University (1796 to 1798) rather than Oxford, to study under Professor Dugald Stewart, from whom he formed a lot of his political ideas. After Edinburgh, he continued on to Trinity College, Cambridge in 1798, graduating with an M.A. degree in 1801.

After leaving Cambridge, Petty went on a Grand Tour of Europe, and while still abroad, at the age of 22, he was returned by his father as a Whig MP for Calne (Wiltshire) on 7 July 1802. On returning to England he entered the House of Commons as an MP, making his maiden speech in 1804. Petty's father died in 1805, leaving him extensive lands in co. Kerry and an income which contemporaries put at £5000 a year (worth approx. £440,000 in 2020). Petty's half-brother John Petty the second Marquess of Lansdowne (from William's first marriage) died on 15 November 1809. John had been an MP in his father's old seat in Wycombe (1786 – 1802) and was a member in the House of Lords, but upon his death, Henry took his seat in the Lords on 23 January 1810. In Parliament, Petty was gaining the attention of both party leaders (William Pitt the Younger and Charles James

Fox) but after rejecting an offer as a subordinate from Pitt, Petty attached himself to Fox instead. After the death of Pitt on 23 January 1806, William Wyndham Grenville formed the Ministry of 'All the Talents' in which, on 5 February at the age of 25, Petty became Chancellor of the Exchequer. With Pitt's death, Petty resigned his seat at Calne on 24 January 1806, and won Pitt's vacated University of Cambridge seat on 7 February 1806, beating fellow Whig John Spencer by 331 votes to 145. Petty was then returned unopposed in the October-November 1806 General

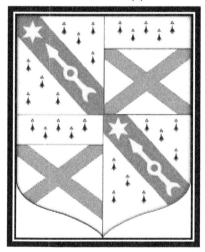

HOUSE OF FITZMAURICE

Election. In Petty's first Budget on 28 March 1806, against strong opposition, he raised property tax from six and a half percent to ten percent and continued the Whig campaigns for economy in public expenditure and the fight against official corruption. On 29 January 1807, Petty introduced a new financial plan to sustain expenditure on the war, embodied in his second Budget on 4 March 1807. This involved the redemption of public loans over fourteen years, but it was thought fundamentally unsound and was abandoned by the following government. Petty was a strong supporter of the ministry's moves to improve the position of Catholics in the army, which led to its dismissal by George III on 24 March 1807, resulting in Petty leaving the post of Chancellor on 26 March 1807. Petty was then defeated in his Cambridge seat over the Catholic issue, when on 8 May 1807, he finished fourth and last with 265 votes against fellow Whig George FitzRoy who won with 324 votes, with the two Tory candidates Vicary Gibbs being elected with 312 votes and future Prime Minister Henry Temple finishing third with 310 votes. Petty was then brought in as the second member for Camelford (Cornwall) by the Duke of Bedford on 11 May 1807. In 1810 when Petty became Marquess of Lansdowne, he continued to play an active part as one of the Whig leaders from the Lords. Petty (Lansdowne as he was now known), spent years of Whig opposition in championing causes which were to stay with him throughout his career; the ending of the slave trade and the removal of discriminatory legislation against dissenters, Catholics and Jews. He was also particularly

interested in the big financial questions, foreign affairs, and law reform. On succeeding his cousin as fourth Earl of Kerry in 1818, Petty added the family's original surname of Fitzmaurice to his own. Throughout the 1820's, Petty and his followers refused to take full office until King George IV's opposition to installing pro-Catholics in the Irish government could be overcome, but he initially joined the government without portfolio on 20 May 1827, when he eventually took up the post which was always intended for him as

BUST OF HENRY PETTY IN WESTMINSTER ABBEY

Home Secretary, on 16 July 1827. By then Prime Minister George Canning was mortally ill, and it fell to Petty to convey the news of his death on 8 August 1827 to the King. King George was not prepared to countenance the idea of a Whig Prime Minister and sent instead for Frederick Robinson (Viscount Goderich), Petty agreed to continue in office, but at the start of 1828, Robinson's administration finally collapsed and damaged Petty's political standing. When the Whigs finally returned to power in November 1830, Earl Grey offered to stand aside if Petty wished to be Prime Minister, but Petty refused the offer. The recurrence and rejection of similar offers characterised the second half of Petty's political life, with Petty also turning down the post of Foreign Secretary and instead settling for that of Lord President of the Council (22 November 1830), a position he was to hold over three periods until February 1852. Petty, upon reaching his seventies, had

HENRY PETTY

already made clear his desire to stand down from his offices, when he announced the government's resignation to the Lords on 23 February 1852, he also signalled his own effective retirement from public life, stating "I think the time has arrived when I may reasonably dispense with a constant, or… compulsory attendance upon the proceedings of this House". On 21 January 1863 Petty, who, though still active, had grown increasingly deaf and frail, fell on the terrace at Bowood House (Calne) and cut his head. His strength slowly failed and he died on 31 January at Bowood, where he was buried on 7 February 1863, aged 82. Petty's second son (Henry) succeeded him as Marquess of Lansdowne.

Interesting Henry Petty-Fitzmaurice facts:

Petty chaired the inaugural meeting of the London Statistical Society and was its first president (1834–1836), he later served a second term (1842–1844).

Petty married Lady Louisa Emma Fox-Strangways, daughter of Henry Thomas, second Earl of Ilchester on 30 March 1808, they had three children (two boys and a girl). Petty's eldest son, the Earl of Kerry, had predeceased him (d.1836) and he was succeeded in the marquessate by his eldest surviving son Henry.

Petty made his last speech in the Lord's on 4 March 1861.

Petty was a connoisseur and an avid collector of the arts. He assembled a large collection of paintings (including many by Reynolds), watercolours, and drawings, becoming a trustee of the British Museum in 1827, the National Gallery in 1834, and the National Portrait Gallery in 1856. He was appointed to the royal commission for promoting the fine arts in 1841.

Petty has a memorial bust in the North West tower chapel in the nave of Westminster Abbey. The bust is by the sculptor Sir J. Edgar Boehm.

Lord Byron wrote about Petty and Lord Palmerston's rivalry in his first volume of poetry 'Hours of Idleness' published in 1807:

One on his power and place depends,
The other on the Lord knows what,
Each to some eloquence pretends,
Though neither will convince by that.

Petty's grandson Henry Petty-FitzMaurice, 5th Marquess of Lansdowne, became a distinguished Liberal Unionist statesman, he was the Foreign Secretary from 1895 to 1900 and the Leader of the House of Lords from 1903 to 1905.

Petty social influence and political moderation made him one of the most powerful Whig statesmen of his time; he was frequently consulted by Queen Victoria on matters of moment, and his long official experience made his counsel invaluable to his party.

Petty's wealth at death was given as 'under £300,000' which would be worth approx. over £38 million in 2020.

Petty succeeded the Duke of Wellington as the Leader of the House of Lords in July 1846.

Spencer Perceval
1762 - 1812 (49 years old) Whig

Chancellor of the Exchequer:
26 March 1807 –
11 May 1812 (5 years 1 month and 49 days)
Born
1 November 1762, Audley Square, London

Died
11 May 1812, aged 49, in the Lobby of the House of Commons

Title: None

Constituency Represented as MP:
Northampton 1796 - 1812

Other Official Offices held:
Solicitor General for England and Wales 1801 - 1802
Attorney General for England and Wales 1802 - 1806
Chancellor of the Duchy of Lancaster 1807 - 1812
Leader of the House of Commons 1807 - 1812
Prime Minister 1809 - 1812

Prime Minister served with as Chancellor:
William Cavendish-Bentinck and Himself

Education:
Trinity College, Cambridge.

Spencer Perceval, (1 November 1762 – 11 May 1812) was a British Tory statesman who served as Chancellor of the Exchequer (from 1807) and then jointly as Prime Minister (from 1809), until his assassination in May 1812. Perceval is the only British Chancellor/Prime Minister to have been murdered.

Spencer Perceval was born in Audley Square, Mayfair London on 1 November 1762, he was the second son of the second marriage to the second Earl of Egmont (which made him a man of comparatively slender means) and his wife Catherine. Perceval was educated at Harrow School from 1774 and then from 1780 at Trinity College, Cambridge, where he associated with others who shared his Anglican evangelicalism, which later marked him out among his political peers. Perceval took an honorary MA in 1782, and then studied Law at Lincoln's Inn in 1783, before practising as a barrister on the Midland circuit.

Perceval turned his attention to politics in 1791, publishing two anonymous pamphlets, the first in favour of continuing the impeachment of Warren Hastings (the first Governor-General of Bengal) and the second offering advice for those who wished to resist radicalism. In 1796, he became a *King's Counsel,* and in the same year of 1796, at the age of 33, Perceval was elected unopposed as MP for Northampton in a By-election. Perceval went on to represent Northampton until his death 16 years later. In the following General Elections of 1802, 1806 and 1807, Perceval was again returned unopposed on each occasion. In the House of Commons, Perceval became a strong supporter of William Pitt and the Tory group, and in August 1798 he was appointed Solicitor to the Ordinance, and the following year he was appointed Solicitor-General to the Queen. From 1801, he served Prime Minister Henry Addington as Solicitor General and then Attorney

General, he was Pitt's chief law officer in the Commons during a series of important political trials (he prosecuted the revolutionary Colonel Edward Despard who was executed for high treason in 1803 after being accused of plotting both the seizure of the Tower of London and the assassination of George III, known as the 'Despard Plot'). When King George III dismissed William Grenville's ministry in March 1807, Perceval, who was an ardent

opponent of Catholic emancipation, initially declined the offer to become Chancellor, but changed his mind, becoming Chancellor of the Exchequer and the Chancellor of the Duchy of Lancaster on 16 March 1807. As Chancellor, Perceval had to raise money to finance the war against Napoleon. This he managed to do in his Budgets of 1808 and 1809 without increasing taxes, instead raising loans at reasonable rates and making economies. As leader of the House of Commons,

STATUE OF SPENCER PERCEVAL
GUILDHALL NORTHAMPTON

Perceval had to deal with a strong opposition which challenged the government over the conduct of the war, Catholic emancipation, corruption, and Parliamentary reform. After the Prime Minister, Cavendis-Bentnick, suffered a stroke in August 1809 and was unable to carry on, Perceval was recommended to the King by the Cabinet on 30 September 1809 for the role of Prime Minister, which he accepted while continuing as the unpaid Chancellor of the Exchequer. Against expectations, Perceval skilfully kept his government afloat for three years despite a severe economic downturn and the continuing war with Napoleon. His government introduced repressive methods against the Luddites (The Luddites were a secret oath-based organisation of English textile workers in the 19th century, a radical faction which destroyed textile machinery as a form of protest). This included the Frame-Breaking Act (Criminal Damage) which made the destruction of machines a capital offence.

On 11 May 1812 at the height of his power, Spencer Perceval entered the House of Commons at around 5pm to an inquiry into

the Orders in Council, that had placed embargoes upon French trade. The Commons wasn't very busy with around 60 of the 658 members present, and as Perceval entered the lobby a number of people were gathered around. No one had noticed a quiet man named John Bellingham walk calmly towards Perceval and

ASSASSINATION OF SPENCER PERCEVAL MAY 1812

from a short distance, he drew his pistol from a specially designed pocket in his overcoat and shot Perceval in the chest. The sound of the gunshot inside the chamber was intense and a thick smell of gunpowder filled the air. Perceval was carried to an adjoining room but was pronounced dead within a short time. Bellingham was restrained, claiming he had shot the Prime Minister for what he saw as the unjust refusal of the government to assist him when he was wrongly imprisoned in Russia, and subsequently not paid any compensation.

On 16 May 1812, Perceval was given a private funeral at his wife's request and was buried in Lord Egmont's family vault at St Luke's, Charlton, near to his birthplace.
Bellingham was hanged for murder on 18 May 1812.

The Commons met the following day and voted that Perceval's wife, Jane Perceval, should receive £2,000 per annum (worth approx. £145,000 in 2020) and granted £50,000 (worth approx. £3,600,000 in 2020) to his family.

Interesting Spencer Perceval facts:

Spencer Perceval is the only Chancellor/Prime Minister in history to be assassinated, he received the accolade of a monument in Westminster Abbey.

Perceval is the only MP for Northampton to have held the office of Prime Minister.

Perceval was assassinated 6 months before his 50th birthday and left a wife (Jane) and 12 children. In July 2014, a memorial plaque was unveiled in St Stephen's Hall of the Houses of Parliament, close to where he was killed.

Author Denis Gray wrote a biography on Spencer Perceval entitled: Spencer Perceval: The Evangelical Prime Minister 1762-1812 in 1963.

As well as the monument in Westminster Abbey, further monuments to honour Perceval were erected in Northampton and Lincoln's Inn.

Perceval's final words were said to be "Oh, I have been murdered."

There have been three books written about Perceval's assassination, one by Mollie Gillen, one by David Hanrahan, and one by Andro Linklater titled 'Why Spencer Perceval Had to Die'.

Perceval's grandson, Spencer Walpole was a successfully published historian and wrote a biography of Perceval in 1874 titled: *The Life of the Rt. Hon. Spencer Perceval, Including His Correspondence with Numerous Distinguished Persons.*

A green plaque was unveiled on 3 October 2009 by Liz Perceval, the great great great great grand-daughter of Spencer Perceval at All Saints Church, the Spencer Perceval Memorial Church and the site of Elm Grove, Perceval's home. It was jointly sponsored by Ealing Civic Society with All Saints Church and the John and Ruth Howard Charitable Trust.

Short in height, Perceval's nickname was 'Little P'.

The Conservative MP Henry Bellingham who represented North West Norfolk from 1983 - 1997 and 2001 – 2019, is said to be a direct descendent of Perceval's assassin, John Bellingham.

Bellingham was tried at the Old Bailey and was found guilty. The judge gave the punishment: "That you be taken from hence...to a place of execution, where you shall be hanged by the neck until you be dead; your body to be dissected and anatomised." Bellingham was executed on 18 May 1812 and his body was dissected in entirety at The Royal College of Surgeons by Sir William Clift. Bellingham's skull remains there to the present.

The name of Perceval's children were: John Thomas, Jane, Isabella, Spencer, Dudley Montague, Michael Henry, Maria, Henry, Louise, Frederick James, Frances Perceval, Frederica Elizabeth and Ernest Augustas.

Nicholas Vansittart
1766 - 1851 (82 years old) Tory

Chancellor of the Exchequer:
12 May 1812 –
31 January 1823 (10 years 8 months and 20 days)
Born
29 April 1766, Bloomsbury, Middlesex

Died
8 February 1851, aged 84, Kent

Title: 1st Baron Bexley

Constituencies Represented as MP:
Hastings 1796 - 1802
Old Sarum 1802 - 1812
Helston 1806 - 1807
East Grinstead 1812
Harwich 1812 - 1823

Other Official Offices held:
Secretary to the Treasury (junior) 1801 - 1802
Secretary to the Treasury (senior) 1802 - 1804 and 1806 - 1807
Chief Secretary for Ireland 1805
Chancellor of the Duchy of Lancaster 1823 - 1828

Prime Minister served with as Chancellor:
Robert Jenkinson (Lord Liverpool)

Education:
Christ Church, Oxford.

Nicholas Vansittart, 1st Baron Bexley, (29 April 1766 – 8 February 1851) was an English Tory politician, who served as Chancellor of the Exchequer for over ten years between 1812 and 1823.

Nicholas Vansittart was born on 29 April 1766, in Old Burlington Street, London. He was the fifth and youngest son of Henry Vansittart (1732-1770) the governor of Bengal and his wife Emilia, daughter of Nicholas Morse, governor of Madras. In 1770 after the loss of his father at sea, Nicholas was placed under the guardianship of his uncles, Sir Robert Palk and Arthur Vansittart. He was educated at Mr. Gilpin's school at Cheam, and at Christ Church, Oxford, where he matriculated on 29 March 1784, graduating with a B.A. in 1787 and an M.A. 1791. Vansittart was a student at Lincoln's Inn from April 1788, and he was called to the bar in May 1791, going on the northern circuit for about a year, but never fully devoting himself to law.

Vansittart instead turned to politics, and he proved himself a useful pamphleteer in support of William Pitt the Younger's government. In 1793, he published 'Reflections on the Propriety of an Immediate Peace,' in which he maintained the necessity for the war, and the folly of trusting to an uncertain peace. He was elected to the House of Commons as a Tory MP for Hastings (second member) in May 1796, and in March 1801 he was appointed joint Secretary of the Treasury, an office he held with credit until the resignation of the Henry Addington (Lord Sidmouth) ministry in 1804. In January 1805, Vansittart was appointed by Pitt the Younger as Secretary for Ireland and was admitted as a member of the Privy Council on 14 January. His stint as Secretary for Ireland was short lived as he stepped down in September 1805. Following the death of Pitt in 1806, Vansittart again became Secretary to the Treasury, in William Wyndham (Lord Grenville's) ministry, until he resigned in March 1807. Vansittart had established a reputation as an astute financier, so much so that in October 1809, Spencer Perceval offered the Chancellorship of the Exchequer to Vansittart. He decided however, to stay loyal to his chief, Henry Addington and was the first of five to turn down the offer to be Chancellor (Perceval eventually took the role simultaneously as Prime Minister). When Addington eventually joined the Perceval administration, Vansittart was at first suggested as Lord Treasurer and Chancellor of the Exchequer for Ireland, but the assassination of the Prime Minister, Spencer Perceval, on 11 May 1812, gave him a chance of higher office and he was appointed Chancellor of the Exchequer on 20 May 1812. Vansittart presented his first Budget on 17 June 1812, when he made new proposals for taxation, preferring additions to the existing taxes on male servants, carriages, horses, dogs, agricultural and trade horses, as opposed to Perceval's proposed tax on private brewing establishments. On 3 March 1813, he brought forward, a number of resolutions in the House of Commons, and a 'new plan of finance', dealing with the sinking fund (setting aside money for the gradual repayment of a debt). The main feature in his Budget of 1813, was a general twenty-five per cent increase of the customs to raise an extra £1,000,000 required by the 'new plan of finance'. In the Budget of 1814, Vansittart found himself obliged not only to maintain the war taxes, £20,500,000 in amount, but also to raise immense loans for the sinking fund, which he insisted on maintaining. The observation is that if smoking and the consumption of alcoholic beverages had not as been widespread in British society as it was, the government would have experienced far greater difficulty in finding the money and resources to defeat Napoleon's Revolutionary France. Following the end of the Napoleonic War in 1815, the public mood of compliance with income tax rapidly evaporated. The government wanted to retain income tax to help reduce the National Debt, which by now had swelled to over £700 million. However, strong public opposition to the tax was demonstrated by landowners, merchants, manufacturers, bankers, and tradesmen. By 1816 Vansittart presented his financial policy for a period of peace, his proposal, to reduce instead of abolish the tax, was treated as a breach of good faith with the contention being that it had been entirely set up as a war tax. Numerous petitions including ones from the Corporation of London against Income Tax, strengthened discontent existing in the Commons and the Vansittart's motion for the continuance of the tax was repealed on 18 March 1816, 'with a thundering peal of applause'. Vansittart therefore found himself deprived of a large amount of revenue on which he had already calculated. To make up for the loss of taxes, he made additions to the post dues and excise, and a considerable increase on the soap tax, soap was therefore regarded as a luxury item and wasn't in common use until the mid-1800's. The soap tax was a significant source of revenue for the government and raised the equivalent income of which the alcohol duty does today, it was abolished in 1853. Vansittart resigned as Chancellor in December 1822, and on his resignation Robert Jenkinson (Lord Liverpool) offered Vansittart the post of Chancellor of the Duchy of Lancaster, which he accepted in February 1823. He was raised to the peerage as Baron Bexley, of Bexley in the County of Kent, in March 1823, and granted a pension of £3000 a year. He resigned as Chancellor of the Duchy of Lancaster in January 1828. Vansittart died aged 84, on 8 February 1851, at Foot's Cray in Kent. Upon his death and childless, his peerage became extinct.

Interesting Nicholas Vansittart facts:

Vansittart was a high steward of Harwich, and a director of Greenwich Hospital.

Vansittart received the freedom of the city of Edinburgh on 2 March 1814.

Vansittart married the Hon. Catherine Isabella (1778–1810) the daughter of William Eden, 1st Baron Auckland, in July 1806. The marriage was childless.

Frederick John Robinson
1782 - 1859 (76 years old) Tory

Chancellor of the Exchequer:
31 January 1823 –
27 April 1827 (4 years 2 months and 28 days)
Born
1 November 1782, Skelton-on-Ure, Yorkshire
Died
28 January 1859, aged 76, Putney Heath, Surrey
Title: Viscount Goderich

Constituencies Represented as MP:
Carlow 1806 - 1807
Ripon 1807 - 1827

Other Official Offices held:
Paymaster of the Forces 1813 - 1817
President of the Board of Trade 1818 - 1823
Treasure of the Navy 1818 - 1823
Secretary of State for War and the Colonies 1827 and 1830-1833
Prime Minister 1827 - 1828
Leader of the House of Lords 1827 - 1828
Lord Privy Seal 1833 - 1834
President of the Board of Trade 1841 - 1843
President of the Board of Control 1843 - 1846

Prime Minister served with as Chancellor:
Robert Jenkinson (Lord Liverpool)

Education:
St John's College, Cambridge.

Frederick John Robinson, 1st Earl of Ripon, (1 November 1782 – 28 January 1859), **The Honourable F. J. Robinson** until 1827, he was Chancellor of the Exchequer for over four years between 1823 and 1827, and Prime Minister between August 1827 and January 1828. He was known as **Viscount Goderich,** between 1827 and 1833.

Robinson was born on 1 November 1782, at Newby Hall, Yorkshire, the second of three children of Thomas Robinson the second Baron Grantham, a diplomatist and MP and his wife, Lady Mary Jemima Grey Yorke. He was raised mainly by his mother after his father died when he was only three years old, his mother inherited Grantham House from her husband together with the income from a £100,000 trust fund (worth approx. £13 million in 2020) and later, in 1797, she inherited a half-share in her mother's properties. Robinson was educated at a preparatory school at Sunbury-on-Thames, then attended Harrow School from 1796 to 1799, followed by St John's College, Cambridge from 1799 to 1802 where he graduated MA in 1802. Robinson was admitted to Lincoln's Inn where he remained until 1809, but he did not pursue a legal career and was not called to the bar.

Robinson's political career was initially sponsored by his uncle, the 3rd Earl of Hardwicke, who as Lord Lieutenant of Ireland made him his private secretary in Dublin in 1804 and then secured him a parliamentary seat at Carlow in 1806 (in the 1807 General Election he was elected MP for Ripon thanks to another relative). By then Robinson had developed an association with Lord Castlereagh, with whom he served as under-secretary in the War Office from May 1809. In October 1809, Robinson resigned along with Castlereagh as they were unwilling to serve under the new Prime Minister (Spencer Perceval), although in June 1810, Robinson was subsequently persuaded to serve as a member of the Admiralty board in Perceval's government. After Perceval's assassination in 1812, Castlereagh was appointed in Robert

Jenkinson's Cabinet, and he appointed Robinson the Vice-Presidency of the Board of Trade with a privy councillorship and a seat at the Treasury (which he exchanged for one of the joint paymaster-generalships in 1813). Robinson served under Jenkinson as Vice-President of the Board of Trade between 1812 and 1818 and as joint-Paymaster of the Forces between 1813 and 1817. From this position he sponsored the Corn Laws of 1815, which made the price of wheat artificially high, to the benefit of the landed classes but to the detriment of the working classes.

ARMS OF ROBINSON - NEWBY

The controversial Corn Laws provoked attacks on Robinson's home on 7 March 1815 by protestors, in which a nineteen year old midshipman named Edward Vyse, was shot and killed instantly and Jane Watson was fatally wounded. Three soldiers and Robinson's butler James Ripley were charged with Wilful Murder on 8 April 1815, but found not guilty. As time went on Robinson emerged as a leading architect of 'Liberal Tory' economic policy, first as President of the Board of Trade from January 1818 and then Chancellor of the Exchequer from January 1823. The first three years as Chancellor were regarded as a success but this was overshadowed in the fourth year when a run on the banks in the last months of 1825 led to a commercial crisis, with the government responding in 1826 with a bill to restrict the issue of paper money below the value of £5. In Robinson's 1826 speeches, he refused to concede that the crisis was as serious as his critics alleged. In opening his fourth and last Budget statement 13 March 1826, he adopted the same optimistic tone that had been a feature of his statements in previous years. Taxation, he claimed, had been reduced by £8 million since 1823, during which time government revenue had remained static and consumption had grown. The country was prosperous, he stated, and that prosperity was not going to be undermined by 'untoward circumstances'. However, the severity of the crisis was such that others were not convinced, and as 1826 drew to a close Robinson himself began to feel the strain, and in December he asked the Prime Minister, Robert Jenkinson for a peerage and a less onerous post. In January 1827, Prime Minister Jenkinson gave Robinson the change he asked for with a peerage as Viscount Goderich, although Robinson found the upper house no less stressful than the Commons.

In February 1827, Jenkinson resigned due to ill health and George Canning took over the leadership, but when Canning died in August 1827, King George IV, who was said to favour the Tories over the Whigs, announced his intention of appointing Robinson to the Premiership. Robinson led a coalition of moderate Tories and Whigs which constituted his government from 31 August 1827. His fragmented ministry was at odds over the demands of the King and those of his Whig allies. The pressure of government and personal problems (his wife suffered from hypochondria and depression) became too much and on 11 December he wrote to the King stating that his own health and, more importantly, that of his wife, were so poor that he felt unfit for the duties of his post. George IV chose to construe this as a resignation and immediately set about finding an alternative Prime Minister, the King allegedly called Robinson "a damned, snivelling, blubbering blockhead." On 8 January 1828, Robinson's ministry came to an end, but despite the distress of his time in office, Robinson, remained a front-bench politician for a further twenty years. In April 1833, as the newly created Earl of Ripon, he joined Lord Grey's ministry as Lord Privy Seal, having already served the Whig premier as Colonial Secretary from 1830. In 1834, he resigned over the government's policies on the Irish Church and in 1836 he joined the Conservative Party. In 1841, he was back as Sir Robert Peel's President of the Board of Trade, and in May 1846, he took his final government post as President of the India Board. In a fitting finale to his political career he moved the abolition of the Corn Laws, a month before his resignation.

Robinson died at Putney Heath, London, in January 1859, aged 76. He was succeeded by his only son, George who became a noted Liberal statesman and Cabinet minister.

Interesting Frederick John Robinson facts:

"Prosperity" Robinson: The Life of Viscount Goderich, 1782-1859 was a biography published in 1967 by Wilbur Devereux Jones.

Robinson has the unique distinction of being the only Prime Minister in history to never face a session of Parliament.

Robinson was known as 'Goody Robinson' for his support of causes such as Catholic emancipation and the abolition of the slave trade.

Robinson was succeeded by his only son, George who became a noted Liberal statesman and Cabinet Minister and was created Marquess of Ripon. George was unique in being conceived at No 11 Downing Street, while Robinson was Chancellor of the Exchequer, and being born at No 10, when his father, now Viscount Goderich, was then Prime Minister.

As well as his political career, Robinson served as president of the Royal Geographical Society from 1830 to 1833, and of the Royal Society of Literature from 1834 to 1845.

Robinson is 'the man with the hat' in the painting "The Staircase of the London Residence of the Painter" by the Dutch painter Pieter Christoffel Wonder.

Robinson married Lady Sarah Albinia Louisa Hobart in 1814, they had three children but only one survived to adulthood.

George Canning
1770 - 1827 (57 years old) Tory

Chancellor of the Exchequer:
27 April 1827 -
8 August 1827 (104 days)
Born
11 April 1770, Marylebone, London
Died
8 August 1827, age 57, Chiswick House, Middlesex

Constituencies Represented as MP:

Newtown (Isle of Wight) 1793 - 1796, 1806 - 1807, 1826 - 1827
Wendover 1801 - 1802
Tralee 1802 - 1806
Hastings 1807 - 1812
Petersfield 1812
Liverpool 1812 - 1823
Harwich 1823 - 1826
Seaford 1827

Other Official Offices held:

Paymaster of the Forces 1800 - 1801
Treasurer of the Navy 1804 - 1806
Foreign Secretary 1807 - 1809 and 1822 - 1827
President of the Board of Control 1816 - 1821
Leader of the House of Commons 1822 - 1827
Prime Minister 1827

Prime Minister served with as Chancellor:

Himself

Education:

Christ Church, Oxford.

George Canning, (11 April 1770 – 8 August 1827) was a Tory statesman who became Chancellor of the Exchequer on the 27 April 1827 and concurrently as Prime Minister from 12 April to 8 August 1827. He occupied various senior Cabinet positions under numerous Prime Ministers, finally becoming Prime Minister for the last 119 days of his life which is still the record for the shortest period of time held by a Prime Minister.

Canning was born in Marylebone, Middlesex, on 11 April 1770, the son of George Canning and his wife, Mary Ann Costello. His parents were both Irish and he described himself as 'an Irishman born in London' identifying himself with the Irish demand for Catholic emancipation, although he only visited Ireland once, in 1824. Canning was the second of their three children and sadly the only one to reach adulthood. Further family tragedy struck, when on Cannings first birthday George senior died. Canning senior's death left his wife Mary with such little resources that she turned to acting to make a living and in doing so excluded herself from respectable society. Canning's early years were then spent touring provincial theatres with his mother until 1778, when the Canning family provided money to pay for his maintenance and education. His uncle, Stratford Canning, who was a well established merchant banker in the City, and the British Ambassador of the Ottoman Empire became his guardian and took him into his home in Clements Lane. Canning was sent to his first respectable school, Hyde Abbey, Winchester in 1778 and then to Eton College and Christ Church, Oxford, where he graduated in 1791 with a BA, before deciding on a political career.

In July 1792, Canning came under the influence of the Prime Minister, William Pitt the Younger, who undertook to find him a seat in Parliament. In July 1793, he was elected for the privately controlled borough of Newtown on the Isle of Wight. Canning was soon highly regarded and became Paymaster of the forces in 1800, but with Pitt's resignation in 1801, Canning who was still aligned closely with Pitt also left office. When Pitt formed his last ministry in 1804, Canning became the Treasurer of the Navy, and after Pitt's death in 1806, he again left office, although he returned to Cabinet as Foreign Secretary in 1807 under William Cavendish Bentinck. As Foreign Secretary, Canning's greatest success came when he outmanoeuvred Napoleon at Copenhagen by seizing the Danish navy, but a vicious argument ensued with the War Minister (Robert Stewart, Viscount Castlereagh), over the deployment of troops. When Castlereagh discovered in

September 1809 that Canning had made a deal with Cavendish-Bentinck to have him removed from office, he was furious. Demanding redress, Castlereagh challenged Canning to a duel, which was fought on 21 September 1809 on Putney Heath. Before the duel Canning made his will and wrote a touching farewell letter to his wife. At the duel, Canning who had never fired a pistol before completely missed, whilst Castlereagh wounded Canning in the thigh. There was much outrage that two Cabinet ministers had resorted to such a method, that they both felt compelled to resign from the government, and for the next three

STATUE OF CANNING IN
PARLIAMENT SQUARE

years Canning was in a political wilderness. After Perceval's assassination in 1812, the new Prime Minister, Robert Jenkinson offered Canning the position of Foreign Secretary but Canning refused as he was reluctant to serve in any government with Castlereagh.

However, after a spell as ambassador to Portugal, Canning returned to join Robert Jenkinson's government in 1816 as President of the Board of Control.

Canning resigned from office once more on 12 December 1820 in opposition to the treatment of Queen Caroline, the estranged wife of the new King George IV. Canning and Caroline were personal friends and Canning had infuriated King George by expressing sympathy for her in the Commons. In 1822, Castlereagh committed suicide and Canning replaced him as Foreign

GEORGE CANNING

Secretary, despite opposition from the King, who was opposed to Cannings appointment, and only gave way after all members of the Cabinet, including Peel, Wellington and the other opponents of Catholic emancipation, declared that Canning's appointment was necessary to sustain the government's position in the Commons. Canning succeeded Castlereagh as both Foreign Secretary and Leader of the House of Commons, and despite his previous personal issues with Castlereagh, he continued many of his foreign policies. During this period Canning was prominent in preventing South America from falling under the influence of France and his foreign policy from 1822 to 1827, was on which his reputation was forged.

In 1827, Robert Jenkinson was forced to stand down as Prime Minister after suffering a severe stroke and on April 10 1827, Canning, being Jenkinson's right hand man, was chosen by George IV to succeed him, and the Duke of Wellington (Arthur Wellesley) resigned from the Cabinet along with the command of the army, followed by Sir Robert Peel and three other 'Protestant' peers. Consequently the Tory party was heavily split between the 'High Tories' (supporters of a very traditionalist form of conservatism) and the moderates supporting Canning, often called 'Canningites'. As a result, Canning found it difficult to form a government and chose to invite a number of Whigs to join his Cabinet to create a coalition with his 'Canningites'. A month after

his mother's death and a week after Canning had taken office as Prime Minister in April 1827, Earl Grey who had always disliked him, declared in the Lords that he should be disqualified for the post because his mother had been an actress. From the early part of 1827, Canning's own health had been in decline, he was heavily overworked through being leader of

CANNING'S BLUE PLAQUE IN HINCKLEY   the Commons, Foreign Secretary

and Chancellor of the Exchequer and he finally succumbed to pneumonia on August 8, 1827, at the age of 57. Canning's death produced an outpouring of sympathy from the press and the public. It was emphasised that he was one of the people, who was untitled, without inherited wealth and connections, but still had made his way to the top by his own ability and exertions.

Canning was buried in Westminster Abbey in London.

Interesting George Canning facts:

Canning's total period in office as Prime Minister, remains the shortest of any Prime Minister, at 119 days.

Canning regarded Pitt the Younger as his leader and hero and promoted a birthday dinner for him on 28 May 1802, attended by 975 people, for which he wrote the song *'The Pilot that Weathered the Storm'*.

Canning Street in Belfast is named after George Canning.

Canning married Joan Scott (later 1st Viscountess Canning) on 8 July 1800, with John Hookham Frere and William Pitt the Younger as witnesses. George and Joan Canning had four children, three boys and a girl. Canning named his second child William Pitt Canning in 1802 after his mentor. His other children were named George (b. 1801), Harriet (b. 1804) and Charles (b. 1812).

'Canning Street' in Hinckley is named after Canning and a Blue Plaque is sited on the side of his home in Burbage.

A square in downtown Athens, Greece, is named after Canning (Πλατεία Κάνιγγος, *Plateía Kánningos*, Canning Square), in appreciation of his supportive stance toward the Greek War of Independence (1821–1830).

Canning Town in London is often thought of as being named after George Canning but it was in fact named after his son Charles Canning, 1st Earl Canning, who was Governor-General of India during the Indian Mutiny.

The village of Canning in the Annapolis Valley of Nova Scotia was adopted in honour of Prime Minister, George Canning.

The Canning Club is a gentlemen's club in central London. Founded in 1911 as the Argentine Club for expatriate businessmen, it was renamed in 1948, as the club extended its remit to the rest of Latin America in honour of Canning's strong ties to the region.

Canning Dock and Canning Half Tide Dock on the River Mersey are also named after Canning.

On Canning's death his wealth was estimated at 'under' £39,000 which would be approx. worth over £4 million in 2020.

John Charles Herries
1778 - 1855 (76 years old) Tory

Chancellor of the Exchequer:
3 September 1827 –
25 January 1828
(145 days)

Born
(c) November 1778, Marylebone,
London
Died
24 April 1855, age 76, St Julians,
Kent

Title: None

Constituencies Represented as MP:
Harwich 1823 - 1841
Stamford 1847 - 1853

Other Official Offices held:
Joint Secretary to the Treasury 1823 - 1827
Master of the Mint 1828 - 1830
President to the Board of Trade 1830 - 1830
Secretary at War 1834 - April 1835
Conservative Leader of the Commons   1849 - 1851
President of the Board of Control 1852.

Prime Minister served with as Chancellor:
Frederick John Robinson (1st Viscount Goderich)

Education:
University of Leipzig.

John Charles Herries, (November 1778 – 24 April 1855), known as **J. C. Herries**, was a British politician, who represented Harwich and Stamford as a Tory MP, and served in the Cabinet in the early to mid-19th century. Herries was Chancellor of the Exchequer in 1827 taking over from interim Chancellor Charles Abbott (1st Baron Tenderdon) who had held the post for twenty seven days.

John Charles Herries, was the eldest son of Charles Herries, a London merchant, and Colonel of the light horse volunteers and his wife Mary Ann Johnson. Herries was born in 1778 (sometime in November but date unknown) and was educated at Cheam and Leipzig University where he became proficient in French and German.

After leaving Leipzig in July 1798, Herries was appointed as a junior clerk in the treasury and was soon promoted in the revenue department. In 1800, Herries was actioned to produce counter-resolutions for William Pitt the Younger against George Tierney's financial proposals (Pitt and Tierney fought a duel in May 1798). Upon the formation of the Henry Addington ministry in 1801, Herries became private secretary to Nicholas Vansittart, a position he held while Vansittart was in office until March 1807. When William Grenville's government fell Vansittart refused to join William Cavendish-Bentinck's government and Herries found himself unemployed. His father wrote on his son's behalf to Spencer Perceval, the new Chancellor of the Exchequer resulting in Herries becoming Perceval's private secretary at £300 p.a. (approx. worth £28,000 in 2020). It was under Perceval's patronage that Herries began to attract wider notice for his administrative and financial skills. During the period 1807 to 1809 Herries produced two short-lived government newspapers, and in 1810 he did the spadework for the Budget presented by Spencer Perceval, who went on to appoint Herries as Secretary to the Chancellor of the Irish Exchequer, William

Wellesley Pole, in June 1811. Herries's time in Ireland, however, was brief as he refused Wellesley Pole's offer to become a Lord of the Irish Treasury. In October 1811, Herries returned to London to be appointed Commissary-in-Chief in the Treasury with a salary of £2700 (worth approx. £223,000 in 2020). Herries's work was an important and largely neglected aspect of the war effort against Napoleon, he successfully formed and carried out a plan for the collection of French specie (money in the form of coins rather than notes) for the use of Wellington's army, and in 1814, he went to Paris in order to negotiate financial treaties with the allies. With the continued dearth of specie, a large number of twenty-franc pieces, were at his suggestion, coined at the mint in the following year for the use of the army. In 1817 Vansittart, the then Chancellor of the Exchequer, claimed in the Commons that the great allied push of 1812 - 1813 had depended on Herries's efforts. Herries's reward came in the form of a pension of £1350 (approx. worth just over £134,000 in 2020) and the new post of Auditor of the Civil List in 1816.

Herries was later appointed Financial Secretary to the Treasury by Robert Jenkinson (Lord Liverpool) on 7 February 1823, and at a By-election in the same month he was returned for Harwich as a colleague of George Canning. Herries's first reported speech in the House of Commons was delivered on 18 March 1823, when he opposed the repeal of the window tax (the window tax, was a tax on the number of windows per dwelling house, first imposed in England in 1696 and repealed in 1851).

Herries played an important background role in the development of free-trade policies in Robert Jenkinson's government, with one of his achievements being the consolidation of the customs laws, and another was an engineered revival in the Lancashire silk industry in which he pursued advancement of free trade. Upon Canning's death in 1827, Herries was at the request of King George IV, appointed as Chancellor of the Exchequer in Frederick

Robinson's (Viscount Goderich) ministry on 3 September 1827. After disagreements in the Cabinet, Frederick Robinson resigned as Prime Minister on 21 January 1828 and Arthur Wellesley (Duke of Wellington) was appointed. Wellesley appointed Henry Goulburn as Chancellor and Herries became Master of the Mint

(the most senior person responsible for the operation of the Royal Mint) in February 1828. After two years in the post, on 2 February 1830, Herries succeeded Vesey Fitzgerald as President of the Board of Trade, while retaining the post of Master of the Mint. Herries was returned unopposed in the 1830 General Election for Harwich, which only had thirty-two registered electors at that time, Herries resigned both his offices upon the accession of Charles Earl Grey (Lord Grey) as Prime Minister on 22 November of that year. At the 1831 General Election, Herries was returned unopposed, and at the 1832 General Election, where the registered electors in Harwich had gone up to 214 (from 32), Herries was returned as a Tory MP with 97 votes against the Whig, Christopher Thomas Tower, who was also elected with 93 votes. The losing candidates were Nicholas Leader (Tory) with 90 votes and John Disney (Whig) with 89 votes.

JOHN CHARLES HERRIES

On the formation of Sir Robert Peel's first administration, Herries was appointed Secretary at War on 16 December 1834, a post which he held until the overthrow of the ministry in 1835. At the 1835 General Election, Herries was re-elected as a Conservative with 97 votes, alongside fellow Conservative Francis Robert Bonham who received 78 votes, although the registered electorate had gone down to 156 from 214. At the 1837 General Election, the registered electors was 162 and although there were two seats available, Herries just scraped though with 75 votes against two Whig opponents who received 75 and 74 votes respectively, with the other Conservative candidate, Francis Robert Bonham losing his seat with 66 votes.

At the dissolution of Parliament in June 1841, Herries retired from the representation of Harwich, and in the following month's General Election he unsuccessfully contested the borough of Ipswich, losing out to the Whigs in which he came fourth out of four candidates, the two Whigs received 659 and 657 votes

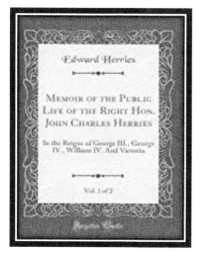

EDWARD HERRIES' BOOK

against the two Conservatives, Fitzroy Kelly 611 votes and Herries' 604 votes. For the next six years Herries remained both out of Parliament and office, but at the General Election in July 1847, he was again elected to Parliament in the two seat borough of Stamford which had 616 registered voters. Herries came second behind his fellow Conservative Charles Manners who received 349 votes to Herries's 288, with the third Conservative candidate, John Rolt coming third with 236 votes. In February 1852, Herries was appointed President of the Board of Control in Edward Smith-Stanley's (Lord Derby) first administration, and retained that post until the overthrow of the administration in December 1852. Herries was again returned for Stamford at the General Election in July 1852, this time unopposed as there was only two candidates, but he retired from parliamentary life at the end of the session making his last speech on 11 July 1853 on the *Government of India Bill*.

An assessment of Herries's political career is that he played a significant role in politics for more than fifty years, his most notable contributions being the reform of the commissariat in 1809 - 1812, the settlement on favourable terms of the huge subsidy payments to the allies in the fourth coalition, the advancing of free trade in the 1820s, the reorganisation of toryism during the reform period, and almost continuously (and well into his seventies) the giving of expert and pragmatic advice on the economy.

Herries died suddenly at St. Julians, near Sevenoaks, on 24 April 1855, aged 76.

Interesting John Charles Herries facts:

Herries's son, Charles Herries, was appointed Chairman of the Board of Inland Revenue by Benjamin Disraeli during Disraeli's second premiership in 1877.

Herries married Sarah, daughter of John Dorington clerk of the fees of the House of Commons, in 1814. They had three sons, one of whom, Sir Charles Herries, was a well-known financier. Sarah sadly died in her early thirties in February 1821.

Herries was one of few men of ministerial experience to side with the protectionist Tories after the repeal of the Corn Laws. (Protectionism is the economic policy of restricting imports from other countries through methods such as tariffs on imported goods, import quotas, and a variety of other government regulations).

Before becoming Chancellor, Herries was appointed as one of the commissioners for supervising the restoration of Windsor Castle.

Henry Goulburn
1784 - 1856 (71 years old) Tory

Chancellor of the Exchequer: (2 Stints)
26 January 1828 -
22 November 1830 (2 years, 9 months and 28 days)
3 September 1841 - 27 June 1846 (4 years, 9 months and 25 days)
Born:
19 March 1784, London
Died:
12 January 1856, age 71, Betchworth, Surrey

Constituencies Represented as MP:
Horsham 1808 - 1812
St Germans 1812 - 1818
West Looe 1818 - 1826
Armagh City 1826 - 1831
Cambridge University 1831 - 1856

Other Official Offices held:
Under Secretary of State for War and the Colonies 1812 - 1821
Under Secretary of State for the Home Department 1823 - 1827
Chief Secretary for Ireland 1821 - 1827
Home Secretary 1834 - 1835

Prime Minister served with as Chancellor:
Arthur Wellesley (Duke of Wellington) and Robert Peel

Education:
Trinity College, Cambridge.

Henry Goulburn, (19 March 1784 – 12 January 1856) was a British Conservative statesman and Chancellor of the Exchequer on two separate occasions, over ten years apart, 1828 to 1830 and 1841 to 1846.

Henry Goulburn was born in London on 19 March 1784, he was the eldest son of Munbee Goulburn and his wife Susannah. Goulburn was educated at Trinity College, Cambridge where he gained a B.A. in 1805 and an M.A. in 1808.

Following the premature death of his father, Goulburn came into possession of a Jamaican plantation, Amity Hall, on his coming of age in 1805. With the Amity Hall Estate, Goulburn inherited a whole host of problems. Amity Hall was one of the most problematic sugar plantations on the island of Jamaica, and Goulburn was forced into a difficult situation because although the estate's plantations brought essential income for him and his family, it jeopardised his parliamentary career at a time when there were many different solutions to the problem of slavery. Goulburn never visited Jamaica himself and although the trade in slavery from Africa to the British colonies was banned in 1807, it was not until 1833 that Parliament finally abolished slavery in the British Caribbean, Mauritius and the Cape. In 1819 the Office for the Registry of Colonial Slaves was established in London, and copies of the slave registers were kept by the colonies. When slavery ended in 1834, slave owners were granted £20 million in compensation (paid for by British taxpayers) for their loss of 'assets'. Goulburn 'owned' 277 slaves in Jamaica and received a £5,601 payment (equivalent to over £700,000 in 2020).

Upon leaving Cambridge in 1808, Goulburn became the second member for Horsham, taking over the seat from Love Jones-Parry who was unseated on petition (a petition/challenge can be applied to a UK Parliament election if either of the following apply: you had the right to vote in it or you were a candidate. Or you have to give a reason why you are challenging, for example you think the votes were counted incorrectly. If approved, a court in the constituency will hold a trial where the result can then be challenged). In 1810, Goulburn was appointed Under-Secretary of State for Home Affairs, and just over two years later in 1812, he was made Under-Secretary of State for War and the Colonies. At the 1812 General Election, Goulburn was returned as second Tory member for St Germans (a rotten borough in Cornwall), and then following on at the next General Election in 1818, he was returned as second member for West Looe in Cornwall. After

being Under-Secretary of State for War and the Colonies for over nine years, Goulburn had earned a reputation for diligence, efficiency and reliability. He was also closely acquainted with future Prime Minister Robert Peel. Goulburn became a Privy Counsellor in 1821, and shortly afterwards was appointed Chief Secretary for Ireland, a position which he held until April 1827. As Chief Secretary for Ireland

HENRY GOULBURN

he managed to pass the Composition for Tithes Act of 1823, also known as the Tithe Composition Act, it was an act of the British Parliament requiring all citizens of Ireland to pay monetary tithes (one-tenth part of something, paid as a contribution to a religious organisation or compulsory tax to government) to support the Anglican Church in Ireland. This led to the 'Tithe War' from 1830 to 1838, when Irish Catholics conducted a mass tax strike against the mandatory tax. At the June 1826 General Election, Goulburn was elected as MP for Armagh City in Ireland and on 26 January 1828. He was then appointed Chancellor of the Exchequer by Arthur Wellesley (Duke of Wellington) a position he was to hold until late November 1830. Goulburn brought in his first Budget on 11 July 1828, his second in 1829 and in his third Budget which he introduced on 15 March 1830, he was able to abolish the existing taxes on leather, cider, and beer. Goulburn's achievements were to reduce the interest rate on part of the national debt, and allowed anyone to sell beer upon payment of a small annual fee. The Alehouse Act 1828 (later the Beerhouse Act 1830) established a General Annual Licensing Meeting to be held in every city, town, division, county and riding, for the purposes of granting licences to inns, alehouses and victualling houses. The Act's supporters hoped that by increasing competition in the brewing and sale of beer, hopefully lowering its price, the population might be weaned off stronger alcoholic drinks such as  gin. But this proved to be controversial, removing as it did the monopoly of local magistrates to lucratively regulate local trade in alcohol, and did not apply retrospectively to those who already ran public houses, it was also denounced as promoting drunkenness. The passage of the Act during the reign of King William IV, led to many taverns and public houses being named in his honour; he remains 'the most popular monarch among pub names.' Upon the defeat of the ministry in November 1830, Goulburn resigned office and at the General Election in May 1831, he was returned at the head of the poll for Cambridge University with 805 votes out of 1,450. He went on to represent the Cambridge seat as MP until his death in January 1856. Throughout the 1830's Goulburn's political ambitions were focused on the speaker's chair, he had hoped he might succeed in 1830 but nothing came of his aspiration, and in 1838, he was confident of victory until the Whigs put up the popular Shaw Lefevre who narrowly defeated Goulburn by 317 votes to 299. Goulburn was appointed Home Secretary under his close friend Robert Peel from December 1834 to April 1835. When Peel returned as Prime Minister in his second ministry in August 1841, he appointed Goulburn for his second stint as Chancellor of the Exchequer. Goulburn came to office during an economic recession which had seen a slump in world trade and a Budget deficit of £7.5 million run up by the Whigs. Confidence in banks and businesses was low, and a trade deficit existed. To raise revenue Peel personally conducted the March 1842 Budget, which saw the re-introduction of the income tax, which had previously been removed at the end of the Napoleonic War. The rate was 7d in the pound, or just under 3 per cent. The money raised was more than expected and allowed for the removal and reduction of over 1,200 tariffs on imports including the controversial sugar duties. It was also in the 1842 Budget that the repeal of the Corn Laws was first proposed, but it was defeated in a Commons vote by a margin of four to one. The Budget of 1845 showed a marked advance in the direction of Free Trade, from which there had been some warning in the previous year. Export duties were to be abolished, as well as duties on the import of four hundred and thirty articles of raw material. The Budget wasn't satisfactory to the Protectionists in Peel's government but it was carried through with support from the opposition. The Irish potato famine of 1845 which eventually brought about the repeal of the Corn Laws, had enhanced the profits and political power associated with land ownership, split the Conservative party and in June 1846, it led to the end of the Peel ministry, with Goulburn's last Budget (as in 1842 delivered by Peel) being on 29 March 1846. Goulburn as Peel's faithful lieutenant, carried on as Conservative MP for Cambridge University, having been unopposed in four consecutive General Elections, but in the General Election of 1847 he won the second seat by a narrow majority of 42 (1,189 votes to fellow Conservative Rudolph Fielding's 1,147) and was unopposed in his last General Election on 10 July 1852. After Peel died falling from his horse in 1850, Goulburn acted as a pallbearer and executor but Peels' death caused him great anguish. Goulburn continued as a church commissioner until he died from pleurisy aged 71, in the village of Betchworth, in January 1856.

Interesting Henry Goulburn fact:

Goulburn married Jane Montagu on 20 December 1811, Jane was the 3rd daughter of Matthew Montagu MP. They had four children (3 sons and a daughter), Jane died a year after Henry in 1857.

John Charles Spencer
1782 - 1845 (63 years old) Whig

Chancellor of the Exchequer:

22 November 1830 –
14 November 1834
(3 years, 11 months and 24 days)

Born
30 May 1782, St James's, London

Died
1 October 1845, age 63,
Wiseton, Nottinghamshire

Title: None

Constituencies Represented as MP:
Okehampton 1804 - 1806
Northamptonshire 1806 - 1832
South Northamptonshire 1832 - 1834

Other Official Offices held:
Leader of the House of Commons 1830 - 1834

Prime Minister served with as Chancellor:
Charles Grey (Earl Grey) and William Lamb (2nd Viscount Melbourne

Education:
Trinity College, Cambridge.

John Charles Spencer, 3rd Earl Spencer, (30 May 1782 – 1 October 1845), was Chancellor of the Exchequer and leader of the House of Commons under Charles Grey (Lord Grey) and William Lamb (Lord Melbourne) from 1830 to 1834. He was known as **Viscount Althorp** from 1783 to 1834,

John Charles, was born at Spencer House, London, on 30 May 1782, his mother was Lady Lavinia Bingham daughter of the first Earl of Lucan and his father was George Spencer, 2nd Earl Spencer who had served in the ministries of Pitt the Younger, Charles James Fox and Lord Grenville and was First Lord of the Admiralty from 1794 to 1801. Spencer attended Harrow from the age of eight from 1790 to 1798, although his father withdrew him for private tutoring for two years to prepare him for Cambridge. Spencer went on to Trinity College Cambridge from 1800 to 1802, studying mathematics, but he spent most of his time on his passion for hunting and racing. Leaving Trinity College, thanks to the peace of Amiens, he embarked on a Grand Tour from 1802 to 1803.

After returning home from his travels, Spencer's father purchased the constituency of Okehampton for £60,000 (worth over £6m in 2020) and arranged for his son to become MP for the borough in 1804. Known under his courtesy title as Lord Althorp, he supported William Pitt, but didn't take part in any of the debates in his first five years in Parliament. In 1806, Spencer's father compelled him to stand as Pitt's successor for the parliamentary seat of Cambridge University, but he was soundly beaten by the future Chancellor of the Exchequer, Lord Henry Petty. Later in 1806 Spencer became MP for Northampton, another constituency under the control of his father, but he spent most of the next decade devoting his life to hunting and shooting, becoming the master of the Pytchley hunt at a time when the political and social élite were embracing fox-hunting as a core element of English culture. The idea was that the mastership would give Spencer more confidence and experience than serving as junior Lord of the Treasury in the 'Ministry of all the Talents' which he did from 1806 to 1807. When he did attend the House of Commons, Spencer came under the influence of Charles Fox, and as a result switched his support from the Tories to the Whigs. After the end of the war with Napoleon's France in 1815, Spencer began to argue in favour of parliamentary reform while also being very critical of the Corn Laws, he also supported Joseph Hume in his campaign for Catholic Emancipation. Spencer, at the age of 34,

married Esther Acklom on 13 April, 1814, but Esther died only four years later, on 11 June 1818 in childbirth at the age of 29, at Halkin Street, Belgravia, London. Spencer was devastated and his devout religious faith wavered, he withdrew into a period of black depression and social isolation and as a penance he gave up fox-hunting and vowed never to remarry. On his return to political life in 1819, Spencer pressed for establishing a more efficient bankruptcy court and of expediting

JOHN SPENCER
COAT OF ARMS

the recovery of small debts, with both of these reforms being accomplished before 1825. In March 1830, Spencer was chosen as leader of the Whigs in Parliament and when Arthur Wellesley (Duke of Wellington) resigned as Prime Minister on 16 November of that year, Spencer was expected to become Prime Minister, but he was reluctant to accept the responsibility and instead he persuaded Charles Grey (Earl Grey) the leader of the Whigs in the House of Lords to become Prime Minister instead. In Grey's government of 1830, Spencer was appointed Chancellor of the Exchequer and leader of the House of Commons. Spencer and Earl Grey had long been supporters of parliamentary reform and the two men were determined to use their power to increase the size of the electorate. Spencer's first Budget in 1831 was a disaster owing to constraints of time and Spencer's inexperience, but subsequent years saw more effective legislation that gradually came to fruition by reducing tariffs. As leader of the House of Commons, Spencer played an important role in persuading Parliament to pass the Reform Bill in 1832, which disenfranchised 56 boroughs in England and Wales and reduced another 31 to only one MP. The Act also created 67 new constituencies and brought about the formal exclusion of women from voting in Parliamentary elections, as a voter was defined in

the Act as a male person. On occasion before 1832, although rare, there had been instances of women voting. Spencer was also totally against the idea of a 'ten hour day' for children and as Chancellor of the Exchequer, he led the opposition to Michael Sadler (Sadler introduced legislation that proposed limiting the hours of all persons under the age of 18 to ten hours a day). In the debates that took place on this issue. Spencer argued "whether a measure which would prevent children from obtaining any employment in factories would not be more injurious than beneficial to the labouring classes?" Spencer did sponsor the Factory Act of 1833, called *Althorp's Act,* which gave mandatory provisions for the education of children and the founding of a factory inspectorate, while restricting the employment of children in textile mills.

Under Spencer's leadership in 1833, the reformed House of Commons enacted abolition of slavery in the British Empire. After the dissolution of Parliament later in 1833, the Whig government which had been slowly weakening, was weakened further when

Spencer was obliged to resign after his father's death on 10 November 1834, which elevated him to the House of Lords. William IV used the excuse of Prime Minister William Lamb's inability to compensate for the loss of Spencer from the Commons as an excuse to exercise for the last time, the royal prerogative of dismissing a ministry. The new Lord Spencer returned to the country life with great delight, and from then on, agriculture and not politics, was his main interest. He was the first President of the Royal Agricultural Society (founded in 1838) and a notable cattle-breeder. Occasionally he helped out political friends, but he preferred the peaceful country pleasures in life. Spencer died aged 63 of kidney failure at Wiseton in Nottinghamshire on 1 October 1845, and was succeeded by his brother Frederick.

Interesting John Charles Spencer facts:

Princess Diana (born Diana Frances Spencer) was a descendant of John Charles Spencer.

Spencer was highly respected and was given the nickname of 'Honest Jack' and was also at the forefront of scientific improvement in farming.

Spencer Street in Melbourne, is named in Spencer's honour.

On Spencer's death, his wealth was estimated at under £160,000 which would be approx. worth over £19 million in 2020.

Upon his death Queen Victoria noted: 'He will be a great loss, not only to his family, but to the country'.

Under Spencer's leadership in 1833 the reformed House of Commons enacted abolition of slavery in the British Empire.

Robert Peel
1788 - 1850 (62 years old) Conservative

Chancellor of the Exchequer:
15 December 1834 -
8 April 1835 (115 days)
3 September 1841 - 27 June 1846
(4 years, 9 months and 25 days)
Born:
15 February 1788, Bury, Lancashire

Died:
2 July 1850, age 62, Westminster,
London

Title: Sir Robert Peel

Constituencies Represented as MP:
Cashel 1809 - 1812
Chippenham 1812 - 1817
Oxford University 1817 - 1829
Westbury 1829 - 1830
Tamworth 1830 - 1850

Other Official Offices held:
Chief Secretary of Ireland 1812 - 1818
Home Secretary 1828 - 1830
Prime Minister (2 Terms) 1834 - 1835 and 1841 - 1846.

Prime Minister served with as Chancellor:
Himself

Education:
Christ Church, Oxford.

Sir Robert Peel, 2nd Baronet, (5 February 1788 – 2 July 1850) was a Conservative Member of Parliament, who was Chancellor, Home Secretary and twice British Prime Minister (1834–35 and 1841–46). His period in government saw landmark social reforms and the repeal of the Corn Laws. He is considered as one of the founders of the modern Conservative Party, and is regarded as the patriarch of modern British policing owing to his founding of the Metropolitan Police Service.

Peel was born on February 5, 1788, at Chamber Hall, Bury, Lancashire. He was the eldest son and the third of the eleven children of Sir Robert Peel, 1st Baronet and his first wife Ellen Yates. Peel senior was one of the early textile manufacturers of the Industrial Revolution and a Member of Parliament for Tamworth. Peel was firstly educated at Bury Grammar School, then Hipperholme Grammar School and in February 1800 Harrow School. While at Harrow he was a contemporary of the poet Lord Byron. In 1805, he attended Christ Church, Oxford where he excelled, gaining a double first in 1808 studying classics and mathematics. After Oxford, Peel studied law at Lincoln's Inn.

In 1809, at the age of 21, using his father's influence, Peel secured the vacant seat at Cashel (County Tipperary in Ireland) and entered the Commons immediately. His mentor in Parliament was Arthur Wellesley, the future 1st Duke of Wellington (Peel later named one of his sons after the Duke of Wellington). Peel quickly rose in power and in 1817 he gained the coveted honour of being elected unopposed as Member of Parliament for the University of Oxford. He served as Chief Secretary for Ireland (1812–1818), twice as Home Secretary (1822-1827 and 1828-1830), Chancellor of the Exchequer (1834–1835) and Leader of the Opposition when William Lamb was Prime Minister (1835–1841). When George Canning succeeded as Prime Minister in 1827, Peel, who opposed Catholic emancipation, resigned on the issue, although he returned to office again in

1828 under Arthur Wellesley. It was as Home Secretary In 1829 when Peel introduced the Metropolitan Police Act, which set up the first disciplined police force for the Greater London area. It was far-ranging criminal law and prison reform, and it established the Metropolitan Police Force which was based at Scotland Yard in London. The constables were nicknamed "Bobbies" or "Peelers" after Peel, and he became known as the father of modern policing, devising the 'Peelian Principles' which defined the ethical requirements police officers must follow. The 'Peelian Principles'

SIR ROBERT PEEL

have been used not only in the United Kingdom but also in Canada, Australia, New Zealand and the United States. The Wellesley government in which Peel had been Home Secretary fell in the General Election of 1830, and Peel was now in opposition to a new administration, headed by Earl Grey. Peel stood for the first time in Tamworth and was elected unopposed, as he was again in the General Elections of 1831, 1832 and 1835. Though he was not opposed to moderate parliamentary reform, Peel argued against Grey's sweeping measures, nonetheless, in 1832 the Reform Act was passed. The Whig Government of William Lamb was dismissed in November 1834 by William IV, who appointed Peel as the new Prime Minister. Peel's Tamworth Manifesto, issued in 1834, was in response to the sweeping parliamentary reform that had passed under Lord Grey's Whig government and was a statement of the new Conservative reform principles. It is widely considered to have laid the foundations for the modern British Conservative party. Although in power, Peel's Tories remained a minority in the House of Commons, a situation which Peel found increasingly intolerable, and in April 1835, defeated by a combination of Whigs, radicals, and Irish nationalists, he resigned his office. During the next six years, aided by his astute and cautious tactics, he signalled a significant shift from staunch, reactionary 'Tory' to progressive 'Conservative' politics. In the General Election of 1837, Peel faced his first public vote in an election, and from the 497 registered electors (of which 444 voted) Peel

PEEL STATUE IN LEEDS

was comfortably returned with 387 votes against fellow Conservative Edward Henry A'Court's 245 (elected in the second seat) and the Whigs vote of 185. In 1839, Peel was offered the chance to form a government by the young Queen Victoria, to succeed William Lamb (Lord Melbourne). Lamb had recently resigned following several parliamentary defeats and was well-known to be a favourite of the Queen. Before replacing Lamb, Peel requested that Victoria dismiss some of her existing household as he hoped to remove some of the ladies-in-waiting who were loyal to Lamb and the Whig party, with a number of them married or related to Whig ministers. The young Victoria held friendships with many of the ladies that Peel wanted to remove and so refused his request, this sparked the first constitutional crisis of her reign, which became known as 'The Bedchamber Crisis'. Although Victoria's refusal was widely condemned for not being politically partisan, Peel promptly resigned. The crisis was eventually resolved after Prince Albert intervened by encouraging some of the ladies to voluntarily resign their positions. The Queen went on to have a good working relationship with Peel, and after his death in 1850, Victoria fondly described him as her "worthy Peel, a man of unbounded loyalty, courage, patriotism and highmindedness". The crisis was dramatised in series one of ITV's drama *Victoria.* The Conservative Party under Peel steadily increased in numbers and confidence, in the General Election of June 1841, they gained a majority of more than 70 seats in the House of Commons. Peel was again returned in Tamworth with 365 votes to A'Court's 241 and the Whigs 147. Peel formed his second administration which turned out to be one of the most memorable of the century. Peel faced international problems with war in China and Afghanistan as well as strained relations with France and the United States. He also faced severe commercial distress at home with agitation by the workingmen's reform movement of the Chartists and the Anti-Corn Law League. There was also O'Connell's campaign for the repeal of the union of Ireland and Great Britain, and a five-year accumulation of budgetary deficits, but Peel still managed to pass some ground-breaking legislation, such as the Mines Act of 1842 that banned the employment of women and children underground, and The Factory Act 1844 that limited working hours for children and women in factories. In 1845, he faced the defining challenge of his career when failed harvests led to much of the population to call for the repeal of the 30-year-old Corn Laws, which banned the import of cheap foreign grain, a crisis triggered by the Irish potato famine. Unable to send sufficient food to Ireland to stem the famine, Peel eventually decided the Corn Laws must be repealed. Landowners saw the attempt as an attack on them, and fiercely protested in the House of Commons. Peel's Conservative Party which was very sensitive to the issue of Corn Laws, would not support him and the debate lasted for 5 months. Peel's ministry boldly reintroduced the income tax (originally instituted during the Napoleonic Wars) which put internal revenues onto a sound footing, enabling him to make sweeping reductions of duties on food and raw materials entering the country. Eventually, in June 1846, the Corn Laws were repealed, an undertaking which was to split the Conservative Party in two. In the unsavoury atmosphere that followed, the protectionists amongst the Conservatives combined with the Whigs to defeat the government's Irish Coercion Bill. Peel

promptly resigned on 29 June 1846 and was cheered by crowds as he left the Commons. On June 29, 1850, Peel went out for his usual evening ride on a new horse, the horse acted up throwing Peel off and landing on his prostrate body. Doctors found that Peel had broken his left collar-bone and probably several ribs. They also suspected severe internal bleeding. Peel's condition worsened and he died at his London home, Whitehall Gardens on July 2, 1850 aged 62.

Interesting Robert Peel facts:

Peel married Julia Floyd (daughter of General Sir John Floyd, 1st Baronet) on the 8 June 1820, they had seven children, five boys and two girls.

Peel's eldest son, Sir Robert Peel 3rd Baronet, followed in his father's footsteps and became MP for Tamworth from 1850 to 1880 and was the Chief Secretary for Ireland from 1861 to 1865.

Nigel Lindsay plays Sir Robert Peel in the ITV historical drama 'Victoria'.

Peel named his fifth and youngest son Arthur Wellesley Peel after the Duke of Wellington. Arthur went on to be a Liberal MP for Warwick from 1865 to 1895 and Speaker of the House of Commons from 1884 to 1895.

There are 14 statues of Robert Peel in British towns.

Peel was the first serving British Prime Minister to have his photograph taken.

Peel is featured on the cover of The Beatles' Sgt. Pepper's Lonely Hearts Club Band album.

Peel's Second son, Frederick Peel was a Liberal MP for Leominster and Bury from 1849 to 1865 and was Financial Secretary to the Treasury from 1860 to 1865.

There is a Sir Robert Peel Community Hospital in Tamworth.

'Peelites' was a breakaway faction of the Conservative Party which eventually joined with the Whigs and Radicals to form the Liberal Party.

Peel Park, in Bradford, West Yorkshire is named after Sir Robert Peel. It is one of the largest parks in the Yorkshire.

Peel is credited with breeding the first Tamworth pig, by crossing pigs local to Tamworth with pigs from Ireland.

In 1843, when Peel was Prime Minister, he was the target of a failed assassination attempt. A Scottish wood turner named Daniel M'Naghten stalked Peel for several days before killing Peel's personal secretary Edward Drummond on 20 January, thinking he was Peel. The killing led to the formation of the criminal defence of insanity and established the 'M'Naghten Rules', which remain the principal method of deciding insanity in English law.

There are at least thirteen public houses in the UK named after Sir Robert Peel.

On his death, Peel had an income of £40,000 p.a. which is approx. worth over £5.5 million in 2020.

Thomas Spring Rice
1790 - 1866 (76 years old) Whig

Chancellor of the Exchequer:
18 April 1835 –
26 August 1839 (4 years, 4 months and 9 days)

Born:
8 February 1790, Limerick, Republic of Ireland
Died:
17 February 1866, age 76, Mount Trenchard, near Limerick

Title: 1st Baron Monteagle of Brandon

Constituencies Represented as MP:
Limerick 1820 - 1832
Cambridge 1832 - 1839

Other Official Offices held:
Under Secretary of State for the Home Department 1827
Joint Secretary to the Treasury 1830 - 1834
Secretary of State for War and the Colonies 1834
Comptroller General of the Exchequer 1835 - 1866
Baron Monteagle of Brandon 1839 - 1866

Prime Minister served with as Chancellor:
William Lamb (2nd Viscount Melbourne)

Education:
Trinity College, Cambridge.

Thomas Spring Rice, 1st Baron Monteagle of Brandon, (8 February 1790 – 7 February 1866) was an MP for Limerick and Cambridge, who served as Chancellor of the Exchequer from 1835 to 1839.

Spring Rice was born into a well-connected Irish gentry family (his paternal grandmother was a daughter of the knight of Kerry) and he was a descendant of Sir Stephen Rice 'Lord Chief Baron Exchequer'. Matriculated at Trinity College, Cambridge, in 1809 his university career was terminated prematurely by his marriage on 11 July 1811, to Theodosia Pery (1787–1839), daughter of Edmond Henry Pery, the first Earl of Limerick. Thomas and Theodosia produced eight children while he studied law, although he was never called to the bar.

In 1820, Spring Rice won a seat in Parliament for Limerick, where he continued to sit until the *Reform Act* of 1832, which made his return there unlikely, so he transferred to Cambridge where he remained for the rest of his Commons career. Spring Rice joined Canning's coalition ministry as Under-Secretary for the Home Office in July 1827, even though this required accepting deferral of Catholic emancipation. He resigned in January 1828 following Canning's death. When the Whigs returned to power as a unified party in November 1830, Spring Rice was made Secretary of the Treasury where he worked closely with John Charles Spencer (Lord Althorp) on budgetary policy. He was offered but turned down the Irish Secretaryship in May 1833, instead he was appointed Colonial Secretary with a seat in the Cabinet after Stanley's resignation in 1834. In the position of Colonial Secretary he was able to progress the anti-slavery movement, helping to smooth the process of emancipation with the help of his friend Thomas Fowell Buxton (Buxton took over as leader of the abolition movement in the House of Commons after William Wilberforce retired in 1825). In April 1835 Spring Rice (with some reluctance) succeeded John Charles Spencer as Chancellor of the Exchequer, after Peel's abortive attempt to form a government collapsed. The post of Chancellor in this period was a difficult one, there was a small government majority and a succession of deficits in the Budget. Spring Rice himself admitted 'inadequacy' in the role, with his Church Rate Bill in 1837 being abandoned and his attempt to revise the charter of the Bank of

Ireland also being regarded as a debacle. Spring Rice also held the post of Comptroller of the Exchequer, which was a position in the Exchequer between 1834 and 1866. The Comptroller General had responsibility for authorising the issue of public monies from the Treasury to government departments. The holder of the position received a generous salary of £2,000 per year (approx. worth £265,000 in 2020) and the office became widely seen as an extravagant and unnecessary position and was abolished on Spring Rice's death in 1866. Spring Rice's

COAT OF ARMS
THOMAS SPRING RICE

Budgets as Chancellor were steady, but depression and crop failures, combined with rebellion in North America and the compensation charges owed to plantation owners in the West Indies, created large deficits, and he departed from office in 1839 in the face of scornful criticism. Spring Rice was raised to a peerage following his departure from the Commons as Baron Monteagle of Brandon, in the County of Kerry. He occasionally spoke in the House of Lords on matters generally relating to government finance and Ireland, but he mainly retired from public life. After the death of his first wife (Lady Theodosia Pery) in 1839, Spring Rice married Marianne, daughter of the Leeds industrialist John Marshall, in 1841. Spring Rice died aged 76 in Ireland at Mount Trenchard, co. Limerick, on 7 February 1866, and was buried at Shanagolden, co. Limerick.

Interesting Thomas Spring Rice facts:

Spring Rice was a trustee of the National Gallery, and a member of the senate of the University of London.

BUST OF THOMAS SPRING RICE

Mount Monteagle in Antarctica and Monteagle County in New South Wales were named in honour of Spring Rice.

Spring Rice had five sons and three daughters from his first marriage to Lady Theodosia Pery who he married aged 21. After Lady Thedosia died in 1839, Spring Rice married Marianne in 1841, the marriage lasted until his death in 1866.

Spring Rice loved poetry and contributed articles to the *Edinburgh Review*.

Lucy Knox (born as Lucy Spring Rice) who was Spring Rice's second daughter, was an Anglo-Irish poet of the Victorian era. Knox's first published work, a sonnet, appeared in an 1870 edition of *Macmillan's Magazine*, and her first collection of poetry, *Sonnets and Other Poems* was published privately in

London in 1870, it was largely concerned with social and political concerns, love, and marriage.

Spring Rice's great-granddaughter Mary Spring Rice was an Irish nationalist activist during the early 20th century who helped train local women as nurses to tend to wounded nationalists.

Spring Rice's second son, Hon. Charles William Thomas Rice, was the father of the diplomat Sir Cecil Spring Rice, British Ambassador to the United States from 1912 to 1918.

Spring Rice was succeeded in the barony by his grandson Thomas Spring Rice, the son of his eldest son Hon. Stephen Edmund Spring Rice.

Spring Rice's eldest son, Stephen Spring Rice, was an Anglo-Irish civil servant and philanthropist. He served as the Secretary of the British Relief Association between 1847 and 1848.

On probate, Spring Rice had £16,000 which is approx. worth just short of £2 million in 2020.

Spring Rice was a strong unionist and even went so far as to suggest in 1834, in a parliamentary speech which he later published, that Ireland be renamed 'West Britain'.

As a young man Spring Rice once escaped the Dublin police who were trying to prevent a duel, by disguising himself as a servant and hiding on a roof-top.

Spring Rice chaired the royal commission on decimal coinage from 1855 to 1859, but he resigned following parliamentary criticisms of the commissioners' slowness in producing a report.

Francis Baring
1796 - 1866 (70 years old) Liberal Whig (before 1859)

Chancellor of the Exchequer:
26 August 1839 –
30 August 1841
(2 years and 5 days)

Born:
20 April 1796, Calcutta, India

Died:
6 September 1866, age 70,
Micheldever, Hampshire

Title: 1st Baron Northbrook

Constituency Represented as MP:
Portsmouth 1826 - 1865

Other Official Offices held:
Lord of the Treasury 1834 and 1835 - 1839
Financial Secretary to the Treasury 1835 - 1839
First Lord of the Admiralty 1849 - 1852.

Prime Minister served with as Chancellor:
William Lamb (2nd Viscount Melbourne)

Education:
Christ Church, Oxford.

Francis Thornhill Baring, 1st Baron Northbrook, (20 April 1796 – 6 September 1866), was known as **Sir Francis Baring, 3rd Baronet** from 1848 to 1866. He was a Whig politician who represented Portsmouth and served in the governments of William Lamb (Lord Melbourne) and Lord John Russell.

Baring was born in Calcutta on 20 April 1796, the eldest son of Sir Thomas Baring, second baronet (1772–1848) and his wife Mary Ursula, daughter of Charles Sealy, barrister, of Calcutta. At the time of Francis's birth Baring senior was working in the East India Company's civil service in Calcutta. Francis Baring was educated at Winchester College and Christ Church, Oxford, graduating with a double first in classics and mathematics in 1817, before being called to the bar in 1823.

Baring married Jane Grey (1804–1838) on 7 April 1825, with whom he had five children. Jane was the niece of Earl Grey, a link that took Baring into the inner circle of Whig politics. Baring was elected to the House of Commons as a Whig MP, for the Portsmouth constituency in the General Election of 1826, alongside John Bonham Carter as they were the only two candidates for the two available seats. Portsmouth was the only constituency Baring would serve (continuously) until he retired in 1865. At the time of being elected which was pre-reform, the constituency consisted of around 100 eligible male voters. Baring was again elected unopposed in the General Elections of 1830 and 1831, but in the 1832 General Election he faced his first vote, and was returned with 707 votes just behind fellow Whig John Bonham-Carter who won with 826 votes and the Radical candidate Charles Napier who received 258 votes. Baring was made Lord of the Treasury in Earl Grey's government in 1830, until he was promoted to Financial Secretary to the Treasury from June 1834 until November 1834. At the General Election of 1836, Bonham-Carter and Baring were again re-elected with 643 and 571 votes respectively, the Conservative Charles Rowley came third with 557 votes and the Radical Charles Napier came fourth with 335 votes. Baring was again appointed Financial Secretary to the Treasury in April 1835 until September 1839. In the General Election in between in 1837, Baring topped the poll in Portsmouth with 635 votes to Bonham-Carters 630 votes, with two Conservatives George Cockburn and James Harris coming a close third and fourth with 518 and 438 votes respectively. In August

1839, with William Lamb's hold on power appearing to weaken, Baring was made Chancellor of the Exchequer. Barings finances were impaired though with his antipathy towards income tax, which meant he had to borrow while raising assessed and indirect taxes. By 1841 there was an economic recession which had seen a slump in world trade and a budget deficit of £7.5 million, Barings proposal to cut the discriminatory tariff on foreign sugar, produced by

BARING FAMILY CREST

slave labour, was defeated and led to Lamb's government falling on the resulting vote of confidence on 27 August 1841. At the General Election, Baring was returned in Portsmouth unopposed, but refused the offer of the Treasury under Lord John Russell in 1846, and he stayed out of the government, put off by the demands of his old post stating "figures worked the brain as no other work did". He was again returned unopposed in the 1847 General Election in Portsmouth, eventually going back into the Cabinet under Lord Russell from January 1849, as First Lord of the Admiralty. Baring took over the Admiralty at a time of growing concern, when the navy was at a critical stage in its transition from sail to steam. Baring and his Admiralty board were responsible for the domination of the fleet in the early 1850's, which was dominated by screw-assisted ships of the line and frigates, Baring's plans for a naval reserve to meet the acute problem of manning ships without reviving the press-gang, bore fruit by the end of the decade. After the fall of the Russell ministry in 1852, Baring was again returned unopposed in the General Election, but was squeezed out by the

STRATTON PARK

George Hamilton-Gordon's coalition and he kept up his aversion to income tax by voting against the increases in Gladstone's historic budget of 1853. Baring, who had inherited his father's baronetcy and estates in 1848, refused a peerage in 1852 and again in 1857. At the 1857 General Election, Baring took the second seat behind the Conservative James Dalrymple-Horn-Elphinstone with a 26 vote majority, 1,496 votes to Elphinstone's 1,522, with fellow Whig Charles Monck missing out with 1,466 votes. In his final General Election in 1859, Baring stood as a Liberal and took the second seat behind Elphinstone (1,640 votes) with 1,574 votes to the Conservative's Thomas Charles Bruce 1,447, and fellow Liberal Henry Keppel 1,386. Baring became Baron Northbrook on 4 January 1866, but died nine months later aged 70, at Stratton Park, Micheldever, on the 6 September 1866 and was buried at Micheldever parish church on 13 September. He was succeeded by his eldest son, Thomas George Baring MP, later the first earl of Northbrook.

Interesting Francis Baring facts:

Barings daughter, Mary Baring, married Liberal MP for Winchester, John Bonham-Carter, who was the son of Baring's fellow Portsmouth Whig MP John Bonham-Carter senior.

Baring Bay on the western Devon Island in the Canadian Arctic is named in Baring's honour.

Following the death of his first wife Jane in 1838 (with whom he had two children), Baring married again in 1841 to Lady Arabella Georgina Howard, the daughter of Kenneth Alexander Howard, first Earl of Effingham, and they had one son.

Baring's son from his first marriage, Thomas, was a Liberal MP for Penyryn and Falmouth and was Viceroy of India - 1872 to 1876.

On Baring's death his wealth was estimated at under £16,000 which would be approx. worth over £19 million in 2020.

Baring married twice and was the father of: Hon. Mary Baring (d. 1906), who married John Bonham-Carter, son of John Bonham-Carter.

Thomas George Baring (1826–1904), who married Elizabeth Sturt, daughter of Henry Charles Sturt and sister of Lord Alington.

Hon. Francis Henry Baring (1850–1915), who married Lady Grace Boyle, daughter of Richard Boyle, 9th Earl of Cork.

Baring was a member of the Canterbury Association which was formed in 1848 in England by members of parliament, peers, and Anglican church leaders, to establish a colony in New Zealand. The settlement was to be called Canterbury, with its capital to be known as Christchurch. Organised emigration started in 1850 and the colony was established in the South Island, with the First Four Ships bringing out settlers steeped in the region's history. The Association was not a financial success for the founding members and the organisation was wound up in 1855.

Charles Wood
1800 - 1885 (84 years old) Whig/Liberal

Chancellor of the Exchequer:
6 July 1846 – 21 February 1852
(5 years, 7 months and 16 days)
Born:
20 December 1800, Pontefract,
Yorkshire
Died:
8 August 1885, age 84, Hickleton Hall,
Doncaster

Title: 1st Viscount Halifax

Constituencies Represented as MP:
Great Grimsby 1826 - 1831
Wareham 1831 - 1832
Halifax 1832 - 1865
Ripon 1865 - 1866

Other Official Offices held:
Parliamentary Secretary to the Treasury 1832 - 1834
First Secretary of the Admiralty 1835 - 1839
President of the Board of Control 1852 - 1855
First Lord of the Admiralty 1855 - 1858
Secretary of State for India 1859 - 1866
Lord Keeper of the Privy Seal 1870 - 1874

Prime Minister served with as Chancellor:
John Russell (1st Earl Russell)

Education:
Oriel College, Oxford.

Charles Wood, 1st Viscount Halifax, (20 December 1800 – 8 August 1885), was an Anglo-Indian Whig politician who represented four different constituencies and served as Chancellor of the Exchequer from 1846 to 1852.

Wood was born on 20 December 1800, the eldest son of Sir Francis Lindley Wood, second baronet of Hickleton Hall, near Doncaster and his wife Anne, daughter of Samuel Buck, recorder of Leeds. Wood attended Eton College before moving on to Oriel College, Oxford, where he took firsts in classics and mathematics in 1821. He graduated B.A. on 17 December 1821 and M.A. on 17 June 1824. His tutor, Mr Hawkins, described him as the cleverest pupil he had ever had. At Oriel he formed a lasting friendship with fellow Whig and future Chancellor Francis Baring.

After leaving Oxford and travelling on the Grand Tour, Wood returned to England and entered Parliament as a Whig MP at a cost of £4,000, for Great Grimsby in June 1826. On 29 July 1829, Wood married Lady Mary Grey (1807–1884) who was the daughter of Prime Minister Charles Grey, second Earl Grey. In April 1830, Wood voted for Jewish emancipation and in May 1830 for the abolition of the death penalty for forgery. At the 1830 General Election, he was re-elected for Great Grimsby, though this time through the ballot box, winning the seat with 227 votes to George Harris (Tory) who was also elected with 215 votes. Also standing were George Heneage (Whig) 186 votes and Thomas-Chaloner Bisse-Challoner (Tory) 156 votes. On the formation of the Whig ministry in November 1830, Prime Minister Earl Grey (Wood's father-in-law) made him his private secretary, which made him one of six close relations with whom Grey immediately appointed to office. Wood was then returned unopposed as MP for the pocket borough of Wareham in Dorset, at the May 1831 General Election, where he was able to work on his preparation for the *Great Reform Bill*. Wood had great enthusiasm for the *Great Reform Bill* of 1832, and worked tirelessly on its build-up having a strong appreciation of its value. In a letter to his father he said the Bill had "substantial, anti-democratic, pro-property measure, but it sweeps away rotten boroughs...and of course disgusts their proprietors". In August 1832, Grey promoted Wood to joint Secretary to the Treasury as chief, and in December 1832, he was duly elected in the second seat for the newly created constituency of Halifax with 235 votes against fellow Whig, Rawdon Briggs 242 votes, Michael Stocks (Radical) 186 votes and James Stuart-Wortley (Tory) 174 votes. Wood went on to represent Halifax for a further thirty-three years until 1865. In the General Election of 1835, Wood was returned as MP with 336 votes to Stuart-Wortley's 308 and the Radical's Edward Protheroe's 307. In William Lamb's government he became Secretary to the Admiralty on 27 April 1835, and was re-elected in Halifax at the 1837 General Election with 496 votes. He resigned from government in September 1839, in sympathy with his brother-in-law, Lord Howick, when the latter fell out with the Premier and Lord John Russell. At the 1841 General Election, Wood took the second seat with 383 votes behind Radical Protheroe's 409 votes. Wood who was seen as a progressive liberal, was committed to trying to repeal the Corn Laws by 1844. He succeeded to his father's baronetcy on 31 December 1846 and had been appointed Chancellor of the Exchequer in Lord John Russell's ministry on 6 July 1846, during which time the Great Famine in Ireland (1845 to 1851) was ongoing. Wood opposed any further help or intervention in Ireland during the Great Famine in the hope that the famine would lead to a 'better economic situation'. In the 1847 General Election, Wood was returned in the second seat in Halifax with 507 votes to the Conservative Henry Edwards 511 votes, the Radical Edward Miall received 349 votes and Ernest Charles Jones the Chartist received 280 votes. In 1848, there was effectively three Budgets, and with the economy in good order, and the Treasury's overall control of public expenditure restrained, Wood was against any increase in income tax during his Chancellorship. His ethical aversion to deficit finance made him an unwilling borrower and he continued to limit the spending on famine relief in Ireland. In his 1851 Budget, Wood liberalised trade, reducing import duties and encouraged the sale of consumer goods. When Russell resigned as Premier in February 1852, Wood also left office but retained his seat in Halifax with 596 votes. In December 1852, he was appointed as President of the Board of Control responsible for overseeing the British East India Company, and generally served as the chief official in London responsible for Indian affairs. Wood laid the ground for the modern education system in India when he sent a despatch to Governor-General Lord Dalhousie in 1854, recommending that an education department should be set up in every province, and that universities be established in major cities. The Universities of Calcutta, Bombay and Madras were founded in 1857, Punjab in 1882 and Allahbad in 1887. As Secretary of State for India, Wood dealt with the aftermath of the 1857 Indian Rebellion against the rule of the East India Company. Wood also disappointed the Cotton Lobby with his insistence on protecting native interests, for which he was dubbed Maharaja Wood. In the 1857 General Election, Woods took the second seat in Halifa, with 714 votes behind the Radical Francis Crossley who received 830 votes, and in the 1859 General Election he was elected unopposed as a Liberal. In the July 1865 General Election, Wood decided to represent the less demanding seat at Ripon which ultimately became his last constituency, winning with 215 votes alongside fellow Liberal Robert Kearsley who received 189 votes, with the third Liberal candidate John Greenwood receiving 173 votes. In November 1865 Wood fell from his horse while hunting, suffering from heavy concussion he decided to resign from Russell's ministry the following February and was elevated to the peerage in the same year. He subsequently served in Gladstone's first ministry as Lord Privy Seal from July 1870 to February 1874 from the Lords. Wood died at Hickleton Hall on 8 August 1885, aged 84, passing his estate to his eldest son and successor in the peerage, Charles Lindley Wood (1839-1934), who was a leading Anglo-Catholic.

Interesting Charles Wood facts:

Wood spent half a century working to hold together the political broad church of old Whigs, Liberals, and Radicals gaining him his affectionate nickname of the 'Spider'.

Wood and his wife Mary (Viscountess Halifax) had seven children (four boys and three girls) Charles, Francis, Henry, Frederick, Emily, Alice and Blanche.

Woods eldest son Charles, along with his sister Emily, was invited to play with the royal children at Buckingham Palace, forming a lifelong friendship with the Prince of Wales, later Edward VII.

Woods father (Sir Francis Lindley Wood) had extensive business interests, from which Charles inherited 10,000 acres in the East and West Ridings of Yorkshire.

Wood's grandson (Charles's son); Edward Frederick Lindley Wood, 1st Earl of Halifax was a Viceroy of India from 1925 to 1931 and Conservative Foreign Secretary between 1938 and 1940.

Wood's left £55,478 in his will, approx. worth £7,290,313 in 2020.

Wood's tutor at Oriel College, Oxford, Edward Hawkins, described Wood as the cleverest pupil he had ever hadand Wood formed lasting friendships with future Whig cabinet colleagues George Grey and Francis Baring while at Oriel.

Benjamin Disraeli
1804 - 1881 (76 years old) Conservative

Chancellor of the Exchequer: (3 Stints)
27 February 1852 - 17 December 1852 (9 months and 21 days)
26 February 1858 - 11 June 1859 (1 year, 3 months and 17 days)
6 July 1866 - 29 February 1868 (1 year, 7 month and 24 days)
Born:
21 December 1804, Bloomsbury London
Died:
19 April 1881, age 76, London

Title: Earl of Beaconsfield

Constituencies Represented as MP:
Maidstone 1837 - 1841
Shrewsbury 1841 - 1847
Buckinghamshire 1847 - 1876

Other Official Offices held:
Leader of the Opposition 1868 - 1874 and 1880 - 1881
Prime Minister (2 terms) 1868 and 1874 - 1880
Leader of the House of Commons 1874 - 1876
Leader of the House of Lords 1876 - 1880
Lord Privy Seal 1876 - 1878

Prime Minister served with as Chancellor:
Edward Smith Stanley (Earl of Derby)

Education:
Did not attend University.

Benjamin Disraeli, 1st Earl of Beaconsfield, (21 December 1804 – 19 April 1881) was a novelist and British politician of the Conservative Party who served three times as Chancellor of the Exchequer and twice as Prime Minister. He played a major role in the creation of the modern Conservative Party and the first mention of the term "Prime Minister" in an official government document, occurred during the premiership of Benjamin Disraeli.

Disraeli was born at 6 King's Road, Bedford Row, London, the eldest son and second of five children to Isaac D'Israeli and Maria

Basevi. An important event in Disraeli's boyhood was when he was twelve, his father quarrelled with the synagogue of Bevis Marks, which led to the decision in 1817 to have his children baptised as Anglicans, Disraeli being twelve when he was baptised. Until 1858, Jews by religion were excluded from Parliament, so without his father's decision, Disraeli's political career may never have taken the form it did.

Disraeli was educated at small private schools, first to a Nonconformist, and later to a Unitarian school. In November 1821, shortly before his seventeenth birthday, Disraeli was articled at his father's arrangement to a solicitor's firm in the Old Jewry, spending three years there. Diraeli's name was entered at Lincoln's Inn, but he had already rejected the idea of a career at the bar and withdrew his name in November 1831. Disraeli was enamoured with the idea of Romanticism, and from the early 1820s he had adopted an appropriately eye-catching and narcissistic style of dress, with ruffled shirts, velvet trousers, coloured waistcoats, jewellery, and he wore his hair in cascades of ringlets. Also in 1824, he wrote his first novel, the crude and simplistic political satire *Aylmer Papillon.* Also in 1824, he speculated recklessly in South American mining shares, and, when he lost all a year later, he was left so badly in debt that he did not recover until well past middle age. Earlier he had persuaded the publisher John Murray, his father's friend, to launch a daily newspaper, the *Representative.* The newspaper was a complete failure. Disraeli, unable to pay his promised share of the capital, quarrelled with Murray and others. Moreover, in his novel *Vivian Grey* (1826–27) which was published anonymously

in four volumes, it lampooned Murray while telling the story of the failure. When Disraeli was unmasked as the author he was widely criticised. In later editions Disraeli made many changes, softening his satire, but the damage to his reputation proved long-lasting. Disraeli had always been sensitive and moody but the criticism had now made him seriously depressed. He was still living with his parents in London, and on advice from his doctor he went in search of 'a change of air'. Along with his sister's fiancé, William Meredith, Disraeli travelled

BENJAMIN DISRAELI
WESTMINSTER ABBEY

widely in southern Europe and beyond in 1830–31. The trip was financed partly by another high society novel, *The Young Duke*, written in 1829–30, but the tour was cut short suddenly by Meredith's death from smallpox in Cairo, in July 1831. Disraeli wrote two novels in the aftermath of the tour, *Contarini Fleming* (1832) was avowedly a self-portrait and the following year, *The Wondrous Tale of Alroy* which portrayed the problems of a medieval Jew. After the two novels were published, Disraeli turned his attention to politics. As an independent radical, he stood for and lost High Wycombe twice in 1832, firstly in a By-election on 26 June against the Whig, Charles Grey, by 23 votes to 12, and secondly later in the year, in a General Election he lost out again to Charles Grey (140 votes) and a second Whig Robert Smith, who received 179 votes, Disraeli received 119. In the 1835 General Election, Disraeli again lost out to the same two candidates (Smith 289 votes, Grey 147 votes and Disraeli 128 votes). Realising that he must attach himself to one of the main political parties, he unsuccessfully stood on 29 April 1835 at the Taunton By-election as the official Conservative candidate, losing

BENJAMIN DISRAELI

to the Whig candidate, Henry Labouchere by 452 votes to 282. After failing in four elections in five years, finally in 1837, he was successfully returned in the second seat as Conservative MP for Maidstone in Kent. Along with fellow Conservative candidate Wyndham Lewis (782 votes), Disraeli defeated two Radical candidates with his 668 votes against 559 and 25 respectively. In 1837, Disraeli also published the novels *Venetia* and *Henrietta Temple.* In 1839, he spoke on the Chartist petition and declared "the rights of labour" to be "as sacred as the rights of property" and in the same year he married Mrs. Mary Anne Wyndham Lewis, 12 years his senior and widow of his fellow Maidstone colleague, who's wealth helped with Disraeli's mounting debts. In 1841 the Conservatives won the General Election and Disraeli sought a cheaper constituency, taking the second seat in Shrewsbury with 785 votes along with fellow Conservative George Tomline (793 votes), the two Whig candidates received 605 and 578 votes respectively. After the election, Robert Peel became Prime Minister, Disraeli was not given office in Cabinet, which he considered a rebuff and so became the inspiration of a group of young Tories, nicknamed

'Young England', led by George Smythe (later Lord Strangford). Disraeli wrote a novel in 1844, *Coningsby; or, The New Generation* in which the hero is patterned on Smythe. The cool, pragmatic, humdrum, middle-class Conservatism that Peel represented is contrasted to 'Young England's' romantic, aristocratic, nostalgic, and escapist attitude. Disraeli wrote *Sybil* and *Tancred* in 1845 with Tancred being the last novel he wrote for 25 years. Also in 1845, when Peel repealed the Corn Laws, Disraeli found issue and 'Young England' rallied against Peel, with

FREDERICK'S PLACE, LONDON

not only their own members, but with the great mass of country squires who formed the backbone of the Conservative Party. Although Disraeli and his fellow protectionists could not stop the repeal of the Corn Laws (because the Whigs also backed the bill) the rebels put Peel in the minority, and on the issue of the Irish Coercion Bill forced him to resign in 1846. In the 1847 General Election, Disraeli stood for one of the three available seats in the Buckinghamshire constituency and was elected unopposed. The new House of Commons had more Conservative members than Whig, but the depth of the Tory schism enabled Russell to continue to govern. The Conservatives were led by Bentinck in the Commons and by Stanley in the Lords. In 1848, Disraeli became leader of the Tories (Conservatives) in the House of Commons and in February 1851, despite Disraeli's financial ignorance, Edward Smith Stanley offered him the position of Chancellor of the Exchequer, (a position he held within all of Stanley's ministries). The Cabinet was known as the "Who? Who?" a term gained from the deaf old Duke of Wellesley's repeated questions to Stanley. At the 1852 General Election, Disraeli was re-elected in the second seat in

Buckinghamshire with 1,973 votes against fellow Conservative Caledon Du Pre (2,000 votes) and the elected Whig candidate Charles Cavendish with 1,403 votes, the Radical John Lee received 656 votes. Disraeli lowered the tax on tea in his April 1852 Budget and extended the income tax for a year.

Disraeli's major test came in December, when he was forced (by Peelite pressure) to introduce another budget in the light of the abandonment of protection. Politically, he could not afford to give landowners rate relief, since this would open him to the charge of class favouritism. Instead, he offered them a halving of the malt tax, which would also please the urban beer drinker, and he coupled this with a staged reduction of the tea duty. In order to pay for this and what he hoped would be a popular reduction of the income tax, he extended the house tax (which had been reintroduced the previous year). Opposition MPs had no difficulty in finding enough criticisms of Disraeli's three hour Budget to justify a vote of no confidence,

"THERE IS NO EDUCATION LIKE ADVERSITY" BENJAMIN DISRAELI

which the Smith-Stanley-Disraeli government lost by 305 to 286 votes, as a result the government resigned the next day. With the fall of the government, Disraeli along with the rest of Conservatives returned to the opposition benches. Disraeli ended up spending three-quarters of his 44-year parliamentary career in opposition. His ten-month spell in office had been a very important step in his career, as his ability had been widely recognised and he had become a national figure. In 1853, Disraeli began publication of his weekly newspaper, The *Press,* which ran for five years. At the 1857 General Election, Disraeli was re-elected in Buckinghamshire unopposed and during this period he met Queen Victoria who was said to be fascinated by him, referring to him by his nickname of 'Dizzy'. In the second Smith-Stanley government, Disraeli was again appointed Chancellor with the government again being seen as moderately progressive. The Government of India Act 1858 ended the role of the East India Company in governing the subcontinent. It also passed the Thames Purification Bill, which funded the construction of much larger sewers for London. Disraeli had supported efforts to allow Jews to sit in Parliament—the oaths required of new members could be made in good faith only by a Christian. Disraeli had a bill passed through the Commons allowing each house of Parliament to determine what oaths its members should take. This was reluctantly agreed by the House of Lords, with a minority of Conservatives joining with the Opposition to pass it. In 1858, Baron Lionel de Rothschild became the first MP to profess the Jewish faith. The Tories pursued a Reform Bill in 1859 but was defeated in a vote of no confidence in June 1859, 323 votes to 310, at the General Election of 1859, Disraeli was returned unopposed and Henry John Temple (Lord Palmerston) was invited to form the first Liberal government. At the 1865 General Election, Disraeli was re-elected unopposed and after Gladstone introduced a Reform Bill in June 1866, which brought down the Russell-Gladstone government, Smith-Stanley formed his third government, with Disraeli again appointed Chancellor in July 1866. Disraeli as Chancellor helped to push through the 1867 Reform Act which added to the distrust of Disraeli felt by his critics in the party, however, it increased his reputation. After Edward Stanley's resignation in February 1868 due to ill health, Disraeli was returned unopposed in the General Election in Buckinghamshire and Queen Victoria invited him to become Prime Minister. On accepting the role, Disraeli famously remarked "I have reached the top of the greasy pole". Disraeli immediately struck up an excellent rapport with Queen Victoria, who approved of his imperialist ambitions and his belief that Britain should be the most powerful nation in the world. As Prime Minister, Disraeli was unable to implement tax reductions and income tax, which in 1866 was 4*d*. rising to 6*d*. by 1868. In May 1868, the Capital Punishment Act received Royal Assent, which required that all prisoners sentenced to death for murder, were to be executed within the walls of prison in which they were being held, bringing to an end the 'grotesque spectacle' of public executions. Disraeli's first term of 279 days, ended within the same year, as there was a General Election victory for Gladstone's Liberals in December 1868. The following 12-year period, marked a change in politics from the chaotic collection of ill-defined groups that had been common from the beginning of Disraeli's career, to an emergence of two parties with coherent policies. Disraeli became Prime Minister again at the 14 February 1874 General Election when he was 70 years of age, winning his own seat in Buckinghamshire with 2,999 votes to fellow Conservative Robert Harvey's 2,902, and Liberal Nathaniel Lambert 1,720, with the Independent Conservative William Talley receiving 151 votes. Disraeli's second ministry was notable for many social developments, including the Artisan Dwelling Act 1875 which provided houses for the poor, the Public Health Act 1875 which provided water to housing along with refuse collection and the Trade Union Act 1876 which allowed picketing. There was also the abolition of using children as chimney sweeps and the Education Act 1880 which made attendance at school compulsory for children between the ages of four and ten. Queen Victoria rewarded Disraeli with the title of the Earl of Beaconsfield in 1876. Disraeli notable success on foreign policy was the success of his negotiation of the Congress of Berlin in 1878, where he secured 'Peace with Honour' in Europe. In April 1880, the Conservatives were defeated in the General Election by Gladstone's Liberals, and Disraeli retired to the country. He died on 19 April 1881, aged 76, at his home in Curzon Street, London.

Interesting Benjamin Disraeli facts:

In 1870 Disraeli published his first novel for 25 years, *Lothair,* and in total he wrote 16 completed novels, his last one, Endymion was published the year before he died in 1880.

At the 1841 General Election election Disraeli's crest made its first appearance, with the motto *forti nihil difficile* ('nothing is difficult to the brave').

Both Disraeli's grandfathers were born in Italy.

'There are three kinds of lies: lies, damn lies and statistics' is a quote often attributed to Disraeli, although no version of this is in any of his published works.

George Arliss won an Academy Award for Best Actor in a Leading Role for his performance as British Prime Minister Benjamin Disraeli in the 1929 film 'Disraeli'. The film was adapted from the 1911 play *Disraeli* by Louis N. Parker.

Number 6 King's Road, Bloomsbury in London, where Disraeli was born was renamed around 1824 as Theobald's Road. A commemorative plaque marks the current 22 Theobald's Road as Disraeli's birthplace. Erected in 1904, the plaque was destroyed during the Second World War and was replaced with a replica in 1948.

A plaque was also erected in 1908 at 19 Curzon Street, in Mayfair London, where Disraeli died.

Disraeli left £84,019 in his will, approx. worth £10,447,265 in 2020.

William Ewart Gladstone
1809 - 1898 (88 years old) Tory/Liberal

Chancellor of the Exchequer: (4 Stints)
28 December 1852 - 28 February 1855
(2 years and 2 months)
18 June 1859 - 26 June 1866
(7 years and 9 days)
11 August 1873 - 17 February 1874
(6 months and 7 days)
28 April 1880 - 16 December 1882
(2 years, 7 months & 19 days)
Born
29 December 1809, Liverpool
Died
19 May 1898, age 88, Hawarden Castle, Flintshire

Constituencies Represented as MP:
Newark 1832 - 1845
Oxford University 1847 - 1865
South Lancashire 1865 - 1868
Greenwich 1868 - 1880
Midlothian 1880 - 1885

Other Official Offices held:
President of the Board of Trade 1843 - 1845
Secretary of State for War and the Colonies 1845 - 1846
Prime Minister 1868 - 1874, 1880 - 1885, 1886 & 1892 - 1894.

Prime Minister served with as Chancellor:
Edward Smith Stanley (Earl of Derby)

Education:
Christ Church, Oxford.

William Ewart Gladstone, (29 December 1809 – 19 May 1898) represented five different constituencies in a political career lasting over 60 years. He was of Scottish origin and served as Chancellor of the Exchequer four times (over a thirty year period). He also served for over 12 years as Prime Minister in four different ministries, beginning in 1868 and ending in 1894.

Gladstone was born in Liverpool to Scottish parents on 29 December 1809, he was the fifth child and youngest son of Sir John Gladstone MP (originally Gladstones), who was also a successful merchant, their fortune based on trading in corn with the United States and the West Indies sugar plantations. William Gladstone was educated from 1816–1821 at a preparatory school at the vicarage of St. Thomas' Church at Seaforth (Lancashire), close to his family's residence Seaforth House. In 1821, William followed in the footsteps of his elder brothers and attended Eton College, before enrolling at Christ Church, Oxford, in 1828, where he made a speech in 1831 against the Reform Bill, saying that electoral reform would result in revolution. He achieved a double first-class degree in December 1831 in Mathematics and Classics.

In the December/January General Election of 1832, the Duke of Newcastle, who was a Conservative party activist, encouraged Gladstone with the offer of one of the two seats in Newark (the Duke controlled about a fourth of the very small group of 1,221 registered electors), Gladstone was elected as the Tory MP with 887 votes (against fellow Tory William Farnworth Handley's 798 votes and the Whigs 726 votes). Initially a disciple of High Toryism, Gladstone's maiden speech as a young Tory, was a defence of the rights of West Indian sugar plantation magnates (slave-owners) of which his father was prominent, defending his father about the treatment of slaves on his plantation. He immediately came under attack from the anti-slavery movement who demanded the immediate abolition of slavery, but Gladstone opposed this and said in 1832, that emancipation should come through the adoption of an education among the slaves, and when this is achieved "with the utmost speed that prudence will permit, we shall arrive at that exceedingly desired consummation, the utter extinction of slavery". In June 1833, Gladstone

"NOTHING THAT IS MORALLY
WRONG CAN BE POLITICALLY
RIGHT"
WILLIAM E. GLADSTONE

concluded his speech on the 'slavery question' by declaring that though he had dwelt on 'the dark side' of the issue, he looked forward to "a safe and gradual emancipation". Parliament passed the Slavery Abolition Act in 1833, with the act giving all slaves in the British Empire their freedom. Gladstone was heavily involved with his father's claim for 2,508 slaves, and Gladstone senior eventually received £106,769 (modern equivalent £83m) in compensation. The British government paid out £20m to compensate some 3,000 families that owned slaves for the loss of their "property". This figure represented a staggering 40 per cent of the Treasury's annual spending budget and, in today's terms, calculated as wage values, equates to around £16.5bn. Two years after entering the House of Commons, Gladstone was appointed by the Prime Minister Robert Peel, as his junior Lord of the Treasury. In 1835, Gladstone was promoted to Under-Secretary for the Colonies but he lost office when Peel resigned later in the year (he was re-elected unopposed in the 1835 and 1837 General Elections) but then spent the next six years on the opposition benches. Around this time, Gladstone began his charitable work, (which at the time was open to a great deal of misinterpretation), with the 'rescue and rehabilitation' of London's prostitutes. In later years, even while serving as Prime Minister, he would walk the streets trying to convince prostitutes to change their ways, spending large amount of his own money on this project, and later in 1848, he founded the Church Penitentiary Association for the Reclamation of Fallen Women, which ran until 1951. When the Whigs were forced out of power in August 1841, Gladstone retained his seat in Newark as the Conservative candidate, winning with 633 votes against fellow Conservative John Manners 630 votes, and Whig Thomas Hobhouse's 394 votes. Gladstone returned to the government in Peel's second ministry, and although his early parliamentary performances were strongly Tory, over time the effects of Tory policy forced him to take a more liberal view. His conversion from conservatism to liberalism gradually happened over a generation. In 1843, he entered the Cabinet as President of the Board of Trade, and his Railway Act of 1844 set up minimum requirements for railroad companies (including limiting the cost to a penny a mile) and provided for eventual state purchase of railway lines, while also improving the working conditions for London dock workers. Early in 1845, when the Cabinet proposed to increase a state grant to the Irish Roman Catholic College at Maynooth, Gladstone resigned, not because he did not approve of the increase, but because it went against the views he had published seven years previous. Later in 1845, he re-joined the Cabinet as Secretary of State for the Colonies until the government fell in 1846. At the July/August 1847 General Election, Gladstone was elected as the 'Peelite' MP for Oxford University, taking the second seat with 997 votes with the Conservative Robert Inglis's receiving 1,700 votes, and the third placed Conservative Charles Gray Round receiving 824 votes. Although there were more Conservatives (325) than Whigs (292) in the house, the Tory schism enabled Lord Russell to continue to govern. After Peel's death in 1850, Gladstone emerged as the leader of the Peelites in the House of

Commons, and at the end of 1852, a brilliant attack on Disraeli's Budget brought the government down, with Gladstone duly rising in the public's estimation. At the July 1852 General Election, Gladstone again took the second seat at Oxford University as a 'Peelite' with 1,108 votes, behind Ingis's 1,369 votes, with the third placed Conservative candidate, Robert Bullock Marsham receiving 758 votes. With the appointment of George Hamilton Gordon (Earl of Aberdeen) as Prime Minister and the head of a coalition of Whigs and Peelites, Gladstone became Chancellor of

"SELFISHNESS IS THE GREATEST CURSE OF THE HUMAN RACE"
WILLIAM E. GLADSTONE

the Exchequer. Upon becoming Chancellor, he had to face a By-election on 20 January 1853, in which he won with a majority of 124 (1,022 to the Conservative candidate Dudley Montagu Perceval's 898 votes). Gladstone presented his first Budget in April 1853, and although he defended the Crimean War as necessary for the defence of the public law of Europe, its outbreak disrupted his financial plans. He was determined to pay for the war as far as possible by taxation, and between 1854 and 1856, income tax increased from 7d to 10.5d in the pound. Gladstone served as Chancellor until February 1855, but three weeks into Lord Palmerston's (Henry Temple) first premiership, he resigned along with the rest of the Peelites after a motion was passed to appoint a committee of inquiry into the conduct of the war. At the General Elections of 27 March 1857, and 29 April 1859, Gladstone was re-elected unopposed in Oxford, although he had to stand in a By-election (the first time as a Liberal) on 1 July 1859, as he was again appointed Chancellor. Gladstone won the By-election with a majority of 191 (1,050 votes to the conservative's 859). After the General Election in 1859, Lord Palmerston formed a new mixed government including Radicals, with Gladstone as Chancellor of the Exchequer, and along with most of the other remaining Peelites he became part of the new Liberal Party. In his second Budget, Gladstone reduced considerably the number of articles subject to customs duty, and the Budget helped to reduce the cost of living. Gladstone's reputation as a financier was growing, and in 1861, the Post Office Savings Bank was established, enabling people with small savings to open a bank account. Gladstone also committed himself to supporting a Bill to lower the franchise qualification, which pleased the Radicals but horrified both Queen Victoria and Henry Temple. Because of his support of an extension of the franchise, Gladstone lost his Oxford University seat, in the 18 July 1865 General Election, coming third behind the two Conservative candidates (3,236 votes to 1,904 votes against Gladstone's 1,724 votes). Gladstone wasn't to miss out though as he was returned as MP for South Lancashire at a later poll in the same election. Gladstone took the third available seat in South Lancashire in a close contest with 8,786 votes (Con 9,171, Con 8,806, Gladstone Lib 8,786, Con 8,476, Lib 7,703 and Lib 7,653). When Lord Russell retired in 1867, Gladstone became leader of the Liberal Party, and in the 1868 General Election, Gladstone was elected as MP for Greenwich in the second seat with 6,386 votes (Lib 6,684, Gladstone Lib 6,386, Con 4,704 and Con 4,732).

More than a million votes were cast in the 1868 General Election, which was nearly three times the number of people who voted in the previous election. The Liberals won 387 seats against the Conservatives 271, and Gladstone became Prime Minister for the first time, announcing that his "mission was to pacify Ireland". In 1869, the Irish Church Act was passed which meant the Church of Ireland was no longer entitled to collect tithes from the people of Ireland. In 1871, Gladstone passed the Universities Test Act in the United Kingdom, abolishing religious 'Tests' and allowing Roman Catholics, non-conformists and non-Christians to take up professorships, fellowships, studentships and other lay offices

at the Universities of Oxford, Cambridge and Durham. It also forbade religious tests for 'any degree (other than a degree in divinity)' and also in 1871, the purchasing of commissions in the Army was abolished. When an Irish University Bill failed to pass the Commons in March 1873, Gladstone resigned, but was forced back into office by Disraeli's refusal to form a government.
In August, he reshuffled his Cabinet and again took on the Chancellorship of the Exchequer himself. He dissolved Parliament in January 1874, but his party was heavily defeated and his

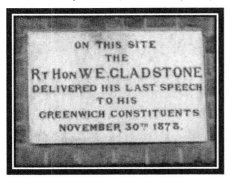

government resigned, with Gladstone giving up the party leadership, though he remained MP for Greenwich in which he was returned again in the second seat at the 1874 General Election, with 5,968 votes (Con 6,193, Gladstone Lib 5,968, Con 5,561 and Lib 5,255). In March 1880, Gladstone gave up his Greenwich seat and was elected in Midlothian with a majority of 211 (1,579 votes to Conservative 1,368), and upon his return to Parliament, he overthrew a Conservative government, securing a large Liberal majority. Gladstone again combined the duties of Prime Minister and Chancellor of the Exchequer for the next two and a half years. When troubles arose in Ireland in 1881, he established the Irish Coercion Act, which permitted the Lord Lieutenant of Ireland to detain people for as "long as was thought necessary", also in 1881, the Irish Land Act which was largely Gladstone's own work, was intended to promote the prosperity of the Irish peasant, but it still didn't stop the violent crime continuing. In 1882, Lord Frederick Cavendish (the Chief Secretary for Ireland) and T.H. Burke (the Undersecretary) were murdered in Phoenix Park, Dublin. Which led to an even more severe Coercion Bill being introduced as a result of the murders. Gladstone resigned as

Chancellor of the Exchequer, and in 1885 the government was defeated on the Budget by an alliance of Conservatives and Irish Nationalists. Gladstone resigned as Prime Minister and Robert Gascoyne-Cecil (Lord Salisbury) was appointed. Gladstone was re-elected in the Midlothian seat with a majority of 4,631 (7,879 votes to Conservative's 3,248).

STATUE OF WILLIAM GLADSTONE IN WESTMINSTER ABBEY

Queen Victoria offered Gladstone an Earldom, which he declined as he preferred to remain in office. The Conservatives vowed to maintain the union of Great Britain and Ireland, but in late January 1886, Gladstone and the Irish Nationalists led by Charles Parnell, joined forces to defeat the government. Lord Salisbury resigned and Gladstone became Prime Minister for the third time, combining the office with that of Lord Privy Seal. In July 1886, Gladstone introduced a Home Rule Bill for Ireland which split the Liberal party and was defeated on the second reading. Gladstone again resigned after only 170 days into his third ministry. The Liberals were in opposition until 1892, when they won a minority administration at the General Election and Gladstone became Prime Minister for the fourth time. He retained his seat in his last General Election in 1892, with a majority of 690 (5,845 votes to Conservative's 5,155). Gladstone again combined the office of Prime Minister with that of Lord Privy Seal. The Second Home Rule Bill for Ireland was introduced in 1893, and unlike the first attempt, which was defeated in the House of Commons, the second Bill was passed by the Commons, only to be vetoed by the House of Lords, causing Gladstone to resign for the final time from the premiership on 2 March 1894. He died of cancer on 19

May 1898 at Hawarden Castle, Hawarden, aged 88, and his funeral was held at Westminster Abbey.

Interesting William Gladstone facts:

Two of Gladstone's sons and a grandson, followed him into parliament as MP's.

A statue of Gladstone erected in 1905, stands at Aldwych, London, near the Royal Courts of Justice.

Gladstone married Catherine Glynne in July 1839 at the Gladstone family home of Hawarden, they had eight children.

In 1848, Gladstone enrolled as a Special Constable and was called into action during the Chartist rallies.

Gladstone's burial in 1898 was commemorated in a poem by William McGonagall.

Ralph Richardson played Gladstone in the 1966 film *Khartoum*.

In 1876 Gladstone's book *The Bulgarian Horrors and the Question of the East* was published. In it, Gladstone attacked Disraeli's foreign policy and when Disraeli died in 1881 Gladstone didn't attend his funeral.

Gladstone left £59,506 in his will, approx. worth £7,909,510 in 2020.

A Gladstone bag (a small portmanteau suitcase) is a light travelling bag, which is named after William Gladstone.

George Cornewall Lewis
1806 - 1863 (56 years old) Whig/Liberal

Chancellor of the Exchequer:
28 February 1855 - 21 February 1858 (2 years, 11 months and 25 days)

Born
21 April 1806, London

Died
13 April 1863, age 56, Harpton Court, Radnorshire

Title: Baronet of Harpton Court

Constituencies Represented as MP:
Hertfordshire 1847 - 1852
Radnor 1855 - 1863

Other Official Offices held:
Joint Secretary to the board of Control 1847 - 1848
Under Secretary of State for the Home Department 1848 - 1850
Financial Secretary to the Treasury 1850 - 1852
Home Secretary 1859 - 1861
Secretary of State for War 1861 - 1863

Prime Minister served with as Chancellor:
Henry John Temple (Viscount Palmerston)

Education:
Christ Church, Oxford.

Sir George Cornewall Lewis, 2nd Baronet, (21 April 1806 – 13 April 1863) was a Whig/Liberal politician who represented the constituencies of Hertfordshire and Radnor. He served as Chancellor of the Exchequer from 1855 to 1858, and is best known for preserving peace in 1862 when the British cabinet debated intervention into the American Civil War.

Lewis was born in London on 21 April 1806. He was the elder son of Sir Thomas Frankland Lewis, first baronet and politician, of Harpton Court, Old Radnor and his first wife, Harriet. Lewis was educated first at Monsieur Clement's school in Chelsea, before moving to Eton in 1819 where he distinguished himself as a writer of Latin verse. After leaving school in December 1823, Lewis matriculated at Oxford on 10 February 1824, and after travelling abroad for a few months he commenced his residence at Christ Church in the Michaelmas term of that year. In the Easter term of 1828, he gained a first class honours degree in classics and second class honours in mathematics, in June of the same year he was elected a student of Christ Church, Oxford from where he graduated B.A. in 1829 and M.A. in 1832.

Lewis shared his father's strong interest in political economy, and in August 1833, he undertook his first public work as one of the commissioners to inquire into the condition of poor Irish residents in Britain and Ireland. Lewis submitted his report for the inquiry in December 1834, and the knowledge he gained enabled him to become an authority of the highest order on the Irish problem in the 1830s. Lewis's knowledge led him to have his work published in 1836, entitled '*On Local Disturbances in Ireland; and on the Irish Church Question'*. The first part of the book offered a detailed analysis of the widespread violence in rural Ireland, and the second part offered a remedy for Ireland's ecclesiastical problems. In suggesting a 'remedy' to the problem of rural violence, Lewis called for 'a legal provision for the poor' and the introduction in Ireland of the principles of the 1834 English poor law. When the Irish poor law was enacted, it was Lewis's and not the Irish commissioners' remedy which the law prescribed. Along with theorist John Austin, Lewis left Britain on 20 September 1836, for the troubled state of Malta, where they reviewed the running of the government making recommendations for improvements. They recommended reforms of the fiscal system, the elimination of some offices, reduced expenditure on pensions, the police force and education. All their recommendations were

GEORGE CORNEWALL LEWIS

accepted an acted upon. On returning to Britain from Malta in January 1839, Lewis took his father's seat on the permanent poor law commission serving as chairman until its dissolution in 1847. The dissolution of the commission came about after adverse publicity from the Andover Workhouse Scandal of 1845, which involved allegations of mistreatment of inmates, the appointment of an inhumane and unqualified master, and a bungled investigation thereof by the commission, leading to Lewis's resignation from office in July 1847. Lewis served on numerous further commissions, while continuing to publish works on a wide range of political and literary topics. At the General Election in August 1847, Lewis was elected unopposed to the House of Commons for Herefordshire as a Whig candidate, and the following November, he was appointed one of the Secretaries to the Board of Control in Lord John Russell's first administration. On 15 May 1848, Lewis became Under-Secretary for the Home Department, introducing two important bills, one for the abolition of turnpike trusts (road tolls), and the management of highways by a mixed county board, and the other for the purpose of defining and regulating the law of parochial assessment. In 1849, Lewis's book, *An Essay on the Influence of Authority in Matters of Opinion* was published, and in July 1850, he became Financial Secretary to the Treasury. On the dissolution of Parliament following the resignation of Lord John Russell's ministry in 1852, Lewis sought re-election in the 1852 General Election, but he was defeated for Herefordshire, coming fourth with 2,836 votes behind three Conservative candidates (3,167, 3,143 and 3,030 votes). Lewis was then defeated in a By-election in Peterborough, on 6 December 1852, by the Radical George Hammond Whalley, by 233 votes to 218 (majority 15). From 1853 to 1854, he sat on Royal Commission on the City of London, but unable to gain a seat in Parliament, Lewis accepted the editorship of the *Edinburgh Review,* remaining its editor until 1855. During the break in his parliamentary career, Lewis wrote a book 'Inquiry into the Credibility of the Early Roman History', and on the death of his father in January 1855, Lewis succeeded to the baronetcy. The following month he was elected to his father's seat for the Radnor boroughs, for which he was returned without opposition, a seat he continued to represent unopposed until his death in 1863. Shortly after returning as an MP, Lewis resigned as the editor of the Edinburgh Review and was appointed by Henry Temple (Lord Palmerston) as Chancellor of the Exchequer in February 1855. Following on as Chancellor from the impressive Gladstone, Lewis had to produce a War Budget with large additional taxation in just a few weeks. He soon faced a severe crisis with the nation's finances, brought on by the Crimean war (1853 – 1856) which was more prolonged and expensive than anyone had expected. His first Budget, on 20 April 1855, had to meet a deficit of £23 million. Lewis raised £16 million by a loan, £3 million by exchequer bills (later increased to £7 million), and the remaining £4 million by raising income tax from the already high 14*d.* to 16*d.* in the pound, while also raising indirect taxes. The £68 million thus raised was easily the largest sum raised up to this time by a British government. To help sustain Temple's government, in 1855, Lewis carried through the Commons the *Newspaper Stamp Duties Bill*, an inheritance from Gladstone and an important step in repealing the 'taxes on knowledge' (as the duties on newspapers and paper were called). Lewis's policy of loans meant excellent commissions and profits for the City of London, who much preferred him to Gladstone. The expenditure for the year 1855–1856 was; £88,428,345, the revenue derived from taxation for the same year being £65,704,491, leaving an excess of expenditure over

GEORGE CORNEWALL LEWIS
STATUE

revenue of £22,723,854. In his second Budget on 19 July 1856, Lewis again resorted to financing by loans and stated that "At the beginning of the war we found ourselves to a certain extent, unprepared for the contest. During the last two years we have devoted large sums to extending and improving our naval and military establishments. Our military arsenals are now much fuller, our stores are greater, our guns more perfect, our troops armed with much more efficient weapons than was the case at the commencement of the war". In the financial crisis of 1857, Lewis found it necessary to recommend that Peel's

Bank Charter Act of 1844 be suspended. He then proposed in his third (and last) Budget, on 13 February 1857, (his first in peacetime) to reduce income tax from 16*d*. to 7*d*. and only slightly to reduce the war duties. Lewis's Budget was attacked in the Commons by both Gladstone and Disraeli, who demanding reduced taxation and a sharp reduction in 'extravagant' public spending, Gladstone was particularly angry, leading to Lewis demanding, and receiving, an apology from Gladstone for language 'reflecting upon his personal honour'. Lewis made one of his most successful speeches in the House of Commons on 12 February 1858, in support of Henry Temple's motion for leave to bring in a bill for the better government of India. Also in 1858,

Temple introduced a Conspiracy to Murder bill which made it a felony to plot in Britain to murder someone abroad. At the first reading, the Conservatives voted for it, but at second reading they voted against it. Temple lost by nineteen votes and along with Lewis resigned from office. After the fall of Edward Smith-

MONUMENT IN NEW RADNOR
IN MEMORY OF CORNEWALL LEWIS

Stanley's government in June 1859, Temple, in his new government wanted Lewis to be Chancellor again, but Gladstone, who disagreed with Lewis on finance, claimed the post and Lewis was instead appointed as Home Secretary. He stayed as Home Secretary until 1861, after which, against his wishes, he was made Secretary of War.

As Secretary of War, Lewis was effective in his Cabinet opposition to Russell and Gladstone's pressure for British intervention in the American Civil War. He contested the issue with Gladstone, arguing that the Confederacy had not vindicated its claim to be an independent state and that the time had not arrived for either British mediation or British recognition of the Confederacy. On 7 November 1862, Lewis laid his case against intervention before the Cabinet, with arguments grounded in law, precedent, and expediency. Earl Russell could not match his arguments, and so, Temple moved toward a policy of watchful waiting for a more decisive result on the battlefield, and eventually the crisis of intervention passed, with Lewis achieving a notable victory among his colleagues. He had out-debated Gladstone and had liberated himself from the tutelage of both Temple and Russell. This was unfortunately to be Lewis's last victory, as the stresses had taken a toll on his health, and after a short illness he died at Harpton Court on 13 April 1863, aged 56, with the House of

Commons being adjourned on the following day out of respect to his memory.

Interesting George Cornewall Lewis facts:

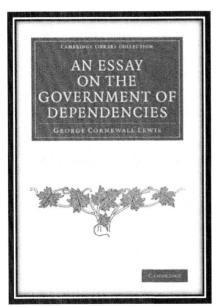

In 1859 Lewis published the *Essay on Foreign Jurisdiction and the Extradition of Criminals*, the subject being the attempt on Napoleon III's life.

Lewis wrote '*Treatise on the Methods of Observation and Reasoning in Politics*', in 1852. His final works were the *Survey of the Astronomy of the Ancients* and the *Dialogue on the Best Form of Government* in 1863.

Letters of the Right Hon. Sir George Cornewall Lewis, bart, to various friends (1870).

In October 1844 Lewis married Lady Theresa Lister (1803–1865), a widow with three young children from her first marriage to novelist Thomas Henry Lister. Lady Theresa was exceedingly well connected, with two of her brothers, the Earl of Clarendon and Charles Villiers, being prominent Liberal politicians, and the third brother, Montague Villiers, was an eminent London clergyman and later the Bishop of Durham.

George Ward Hunt
1825 - 1877 (51 years old) Conservative

Chancellor of the Exchequer:
29 February 1868 - 1 December 1868
(9 months and 3 days)

Born
30 July 1825, Buckhurst, Berkshire

Died
29 July 1877, age 51, Bad Homberg, Germany

Title: None

Constituency Represented as MP:
North Northamptonshire 1857 - 1877

Other Official Offices held:
Joint Secretary to the board of Control 1847 - 1848
Under Secretary of State for the Home Department 1848 - 1850
Financial Secretary to the Treasury 1866 - 1868
First Lord of the Admiralty 1874 - 1877.

Prime Minister served with as Chancellor:
Benjamin Disraeli

Education:
Christ Church, Oxford.

George Ward Hunt, (30 July 1825 – 29 July 1877) was
a Conservative Member of Parliament who represented North
Northamptonshire from 1857 to 1877. He was Chancellor of the
Exchequer and First Lord of the Admiralty in the first and second
ministries of Benjamin Disraeli.

*Hunt was born at Buckhurst, Berkshire, on 30 July 1825 and was
the eldest son of the Revd George Hunt and Emma, the youngest
daughter of Samuel Gardiner of Coombe Lodge, Oxfordshire. Hunt
was educated at Eton College from 1841 to 1844 and on 31 May
1844 matriculated to Christ Church, Oxford, where he was a
student from 1846 to 1851, graduating with a B.A in 1848 and a
M.A in 1851. He was called to the bar at the Inner Temple on 21
November 1851, and went on the Oxford circuit but he preferred
politics to the legal profession.*

Hunt stood unsuccessfully as a Conservative candidate in the two
seat constituency of Northampton in the General Election of 1852,
coming third with 745 votes behind Robert Vernon the Whig
candidate (855 votes) and Raikes Currie the Radical (825 votes).
In the General Election of 1855, Hunt again came third in
Northampton with 815 votes to Vernon's 1,079 votes and Charles
Gilpin, the Radical 1,011 votes. Hunt did finally gain a seat in
Parliament as one of the members for the northern division of
Northamptonshire, in a By-election on 16 December 1857, with
1,849 votes against the Whig candidate Fitzpatrick Vernon's
1,119 votes, for a majority of 487. Hunt went on to represent
North Northamptonshire for twenty years, until his death in 1877.
Hunt was re-elected in the General Election of 1859, with 1,831
votes, in the second seat, against William Cecil, Con 1,849 and
Liberal Fitzpatrick Vernon 1,344 votes. At the General Election of
1865, he was re-elected unopposed. In early 1866, Hunt began to
get noticed as a back-bencher, when he carried a motion
defeating the government over regulations controlling foot-and-
mouth disease. He campaigned against the Liberal government

over its inactivity over a rinderpest outbreak during the latter months of 1865, which had infected almost 75,000 cattle by the start of the 1866 session. Hunt's dogged campaigning confirmed his worthiness for office, and he was appointed Financial Secretary to the Treasury in Edward Smith-Stanley's (Lord Derby) third administration, from July 1866 to February 1868. Hunt's correspondence with Disraeli, the then Chancellor of the Exchequer, also showed him to be quite an active financial expert. It still came as a surprise though when Disraeli became Prime Minister for the first time in February 1868, that he appointed Hunt as Chancellor of the Exchequer. Disraeli referenced Hunt (who was 6' 4" tall and weighed between 21 and 25 stone) to Queen Victoria saying about him *"he has the sagacity of the elephant, as well as the form … simple, straightforward & truthful … & of a very pleasing & amiable expression of countenance"*. Queen Victoria on accepting Hunt's appointment, is said to have remarked that it was a 'strange description' and allegedly joked that Hunt would 'add weight to our counsels'. Hunt's one and only Budget was on 23 April 1868, and is best remembered for him performing the annual custom of the Chancellor of the Exchequer, of holding up a red box to the press in Downing Street, to then keeping the House waiting while his speech was retrieved as has he had forgot to put it in the red box. The actual reading of the Budget was a low-key affair, it levied additional indirect taxation to meet rising expenditure and to pay for the military expedition to Abyssinia. After the Conservatives defeat in the December 1868 General Election, Hunt was once again re-elected in North Northamptonshire unopposed, but resigned as Chancellor. On the return of the Conservatives to power in 1874 (in which Hunt was again re-elected in the General Election unopposed), he was appointed first Lord of the Admiralty, and in his speech on 20 April 1875, which effectively accused his Liberal predecessor of creating 'a mere paper navy' which produced a 'navy scare'. He had to explain his comment, and apologising he said "it may be that my own niggardly ideas misled the House". As the first Lord, he was intent on naval expansion and conducted with some success a campaign for increased naval estimates from 1874 to 1877. Hunt had suffered through his life from gout due to his weight, and went to Homburg on 23 June 1877 for treatment, but he died there from the effects of gout on 29 July 1877 aged 51.

Interesting George Ward Hunt facts:

GEORGE WARD HUNT BLAZON

Hunt's residence was Wadenhoe House in Northamptonshire.

Wadenhoe House was built in 1617, by the Earl of Westmoreland and Prime Minister Disraeli and the great and good of the day were frequent visitors there. Wadenhoe was the first village to have a telegraph office outside of London so that contact with Westminster was possible.

In 1857, Hunt married Alice, daughter of the Right Reverend Robert Eden, Bishop of Moray, Ross and Caithness. They had ten children together (five sons and five daughters).

Canada's Ward Hunt Island just off Ellesmere Island, was named after Hunt.

Hunt who was a very heavy-set person, is said to have been responsible for the semicircle that is cut out from the end of the table in the Admiralty Board Room.

After Hunt forgot his Budget speech, it is said to be the start of the tradition that, when a Chancellor leaves for the House of Commons on Budget Day, he shows the assembled crowd the ministerial 'red box' by holding it aloft.

Robert Lowe
1811 - 1892 (80 years old) Liberal

Chancellor of the Exchequer:
9 December 1868 - 11 August 1873 (4 years, 8 months and 3 days)

Born
4 December 1811, Bingham, Nottinghamshire

Died
27 July 1892, age 80, Surrey

Title: 1st Viscount Sherbrooke

Constituencies Represented as MP:
Kidderminster 1852 - 1859
Calne 1859 - 1868
London University 1868 - 1880

Other Official Offices held:
Joint Secretary to the board of Control 1852 - 1855
Vice President of the Board of Trade 1855 - 1858
Vice President of the Committee of the Council on Education 1859 - 1864
Home Secretary 1873 - 1874.

Prime Minister served with as Chancellor:
William Ewart Gladstone

Education:
University College, Oxford.

Robert Lowe, 1st Viscount Sherbrooke, (4 December 1811 – 27 July 1892), was a Liberal politician who represented three different constituencies. Lowe held office under William Ewart Gladstone as Chancellor of the Exchequer between 1868 and 1873, and as Home Secretary between 1873 and 1874.

Lowe was born at Bingham, Nottinghamshire, on 4 December 1811, the second son of Robert Lowe and Ellen Lowe. His father was rector of the parish and prebendary of Southwell. Lowe was an albino, and his eyes extremely sensitive to light with imperfect vision in both eyes, and was able to read with only one of his eyes. Lowe entered Winchester College in 1825 as a commoner and was said to be bullied, but unfortunately due to his poor eyesight he was unable to recognise people, especially in groups. As time progressed, he became more self-reliant and grew in confidence, with a high level of intellect and great powers of memory. Lowe matriculated at University College, Oxford, on 16 June 1829, where he often spoke at the union adopting unpopularly radical opinions and relishing the controversy and notoriety that this brought him. He took a first class degree in classics in 1833, but much to his disappointment he only achieved a second in mathematics. Lowe decided to read for the bar and remained in Oxford as a private tutor, until a lay fellowship at Magdalen College became vacant in 1835. Lowe resigned this position after his impulsive marriage to Georgiana Orred, on 29 March 1836.

To earn a living, Lowe returned to private tutoring, but having failed to be appointed as professor of Greek at Glasgow University in 1838, he gave up hope of an academic career, and in 1840 he went to London to resume his law studies and was called to the bar at Lincoln's Inn on 28 January 1842. Shortly afterwards, Lowe decided to emigrate to Australia, to work in law in Sydney, where he stayed for eight years. In November 1843, he was nominated by Sir George Gipps, the Governor of New South Wales, to a seat in the New South Wales Legislative Council, but after a difference of opinion with Gipps, Lowe resigned from the Council on 9 September 1844. He was elected for the Counties of St Vincent and Auckland in April 1845, a seat he held until 20 June 1848. From July 1848, Lowe was elected for the City of Sydney, a seat he held until November 1849. Having made his mark in the political world, especially on finance and education, he also built up a large legal practice. During his time in Australia, Lowe was also involved with the founding and was a principal writer for the

COAT OF ARMS
ROBERT LOWE

Atlas newspaper. Lowe and his wife had adopted two orphaned children (Bobby and Polly) after their father (who Lowe defended) was hanged for murder, and they returned back to England in early 1850, where they purchased a small country house at Warlingham in Surrey as well as a town residence. On returning to England with a big reputation, Lowe was employed as a lead-writer at the *Times,* his ambition though was for a political career in Britain, and with his connections at the *Times,* Lowe was returned as MP for Kidderminster at the General Election of 1852, presenting himself as a Whig to Lord Ward, whose influence carried the seat and was beholden to neither Lord John Russell nor Lord Palmerston. Lowe won the Kidderminster seat at the General Election of 1852, with 246 votes against the Conservative candidate, John Best, who received 152 votes (majority 94). Lowe was then appointed as joint Secretary to the Board of Control in the Liberal–Peelite coalition government formed by George Hamilton-Gordon (Lord Aberdeen) in December 1852. In this post, Lowe was largely responsible for the *India Act* of 1853, but he quickly became bored by the routine of subordinate office, and when, on the break-up of the Hamilton-Gordon ministry in early 1855, he was offered the same post by the new premier, Henry John Temple (Lord Palmerston) but he declined it. Later in August 1855, Lowe accepted the Vice-Presidency of the Board of Trade, and was sworn of the Privy Council. During his time in the Trade Department, he saw the Joint Stock Companies Act 1856 passed, which was the first nationwide codification of company law in the world, leading Lowe to be referred to as 'the father of modern company law'. He was re-elected for Kidderminster in the 1857 General Election, with a majority of 88 (234 votes to the Conservative William Boycott's 146 votes). In the 1859 General Election, Lowe stood as the Liberal candidate in Calne in Wiltshire, winning the seat with 103 votes, against the Conservative Thomas Large Henry's 35 votes (Calne only had 174 registered electors, of which 138 voted).

> THE CHANCELLOR OF THE EXCHEQUER IS A MAN WHOSE DUTIES MAKE HIM MORE OR LESS OF A TAXING MACHINE. HE IS INTRUSTED WITH A CERTAIN AMOUNT OF MISERY WHICH IT IS HIS DUTY TO DISTRIBUTE AS FAIRLY AS HE CAN.
>
> - ROBERT LOWE -

With Temple back in power in June 1859, Lowe was given the non-Cabinet post as the Vice President of the Committee of the Council on Education. Although not in Cabinet, Lowe was determined to use his powers to the utmost to improve efficiency and attack complacency. He presented a robust policy, and insisted on payment by results, bringing in a revised code in 1862, which incorporated this concept and made an examination in 'the three R's' the test for grants of public money. The code was greeted with great hostility by schoolteachers, inspectors and dissenting opponents of state activity, who thought the code depicted Lowe in a philistine and anti-clerical light. In April 1864, the Commons censured the committee of council for heavily editing inspectors' reports before publishing them, Lowe resigned his post immediately on the censure and stayed out of office until 1868. In 1868, he was elected unopposed at the November/ December General Election for the new London University seat, which had been created by the Reform Act of 1867 (an Act that Lowe had opposed). The new Prime Minister, William Gladstone had been impressed with Lowe's expenditure reductions as

Education Minister and his capacity for resisting pressure, and made him Chancellor of the Exchequer on December 9, 1868. Lowe was famously quoted as saying about the role; *"The Chancellor of the Exchequer is a man whose duties make him more or less of a taxing machine. He is entrusted with a certain amount of misery which it is his duty to distribute as fairly as he can."* Lowe had early successes as Chancellor, and during his tenure over £12 million was cut from taxes, and over £26 million cut from the national debt. Income tax was reduced from 6d. to 3d, sugar tax was halved in both 1870 and

STATUE OF LOWE STANDING ON A BOX OF MATCHES **1873** CARLO PELLEGRINI

1873, and he removed the shilling registration duty on corn in 1869. But the working classes, who were already wary of Lowe due to his opposition to reform debates, were further distanced when Lowe tried to sell Crown owned land in Epping Forest which deprived working class voters of access to it. But Lowe's worst mistake came in 1871, when he needed to raise taxes in order to fund the extra defence spending. He planned to distribute the burden between the classes by increasing the succession duties and the income tax, and by putting a small stamp tax on each box of matches sold, which were known as 'lucifer' matches

(Lucifer matches were invented in 1829 by Liberal MP for Knaresborough Sir Issac Holden who adopted sulphur as the medium between the explosive material and the wood). Matches were big business and Lowe's stamp tax created fears of unemployment among match girls, many of whom marched on the Commons in protest. To avoid the protest and to get in the Palace of Westminster, Lowe had to be snuck in through the passage from the underground station. Lowe had introduced the tax with a Latin tag, *Ex luce lucellum* ('Out of light, a little gain') which he thought funny, but his reputation was damaged, and in August 1873 he was forced to withdraw his Budget, with Gladstone deciding to move him from Chancellor to Home Secretary. His tenure as Home Secretary was to be the last office

LOWE'S GRAVE IN
BROOKWOOD CEMETARY

Lowe would hold, as the Liberals lost the next General Election in January/February 1874, although Lowe was re-elected unopposed for London University.

Lowe continued on the opposition benches and was re-elected in his last General Election in 1885 for London University, winning with 1,014 votes against the Conservative Arthur Charles's 535 votes, for a majority 479.

Lowe was then raised to the peerage as Viscount Sherbrooke, of Sherbrooke in the County of Surrey (a peerage that became extinct on his death) and was further honoured by being created Knight Grand Cross of the Order of the Bath in 1885. Lowe became a supporter of the Liberal Unionist party in 1886 but he suffered ill health for the last few years of his life and died in 1892 aged 80. Lowe was buried in Brookwood cemetery in Surrey.

Interesting Robert Lowe facts:

Lowe was a trustee of the British Museum and a fellow of the Royal Society.

Lowe was a keen sportsman and he enjoyed various athletic sports such as; rowing, horse-riding, skating.

The Division of Lowe, a now abolished Australian electoral division located in Sydney, was named after Lowe.

Lowe married Georgiana Orred in 1836, but tried unsuccessfully to separate from her in the late 1860s. Georgiana suffered a stroke in 1882 which left her partially paralysed, and Lowe tended her until she died on 3 October 1884 after another seizure. On 3 February 1885 Lowe married Caroline Anne Sneyd, daughter of Thomas Sneyd of Ashcombe Park, Staffordshire. He had no children in either marriage, and although he adopted two children in his first marriage, his viscountcy became extinct upon his death.

Lowe left £15,768 in his will, which is worth approx. £2,037,083 in 2020.

In 1844, Lowe defended a Royal Navy captain, John Knatchbull, on a charge of murdering a widowed shopkeeper in Sydney, Australia, named Ellen Jamieson with a tomahawk while stealing money for his upcoming marriage. Lowe was one of the earliest to raise the plea of moral insanity (unsuccessfully). Knatchbull was hanged on 13 February 1844 in Taylor Square, Sydney, in front of a crowd of 10,000 people. Lowe and his wife adopted Mrs. Jamieson's two orphaned children, Bobby and Polly Jamieson.

Stafford Henry Northcote
1818 - 1887 (68 years old) Conservative

Chancellor of the Exchequer:
21 February 1874 - 21 April 1880
(6 years 2 months and 1 day)

Born
27 October 1818, London
Died
12 January 1887, age 68
10 Downing Street
Title
(1st Earl of Iddesleigh)

Constituencies Represented as MP:
Dudley 1855 - 1857
Stamford 1858 - 1866
North Devon 1866 - 1885

Other Official Offices held:
Financial Secretary to the Treasury 1859
President of the Board of Trade 1866 - 1867
Secretary of State for India 1867 - 1868
Leader of the House of Commons 1876 - 1880
First Lord of the Treasury 1885 - 1886
Foreign Secretary 1886 - 1887.

Prime Minister served with as Chancellor:
Benjamin Disraeli

Education:
Balliol College, Oxford University.

Stafford Henry Northcote, 1st Earl of Iddesleigh, (27 October 1818 – 12 January 1887), was a Conservative politician who represented three different constituencies as an MP. He served as Chancellor of the Exchequer between 1874 and 1880 and as Foreign Secretary between 1885 and 1886.

Northcote was born in London on October 27 1818, and was the eldest son (he had two brothers and two sisters) of Sir Stafford Northcote and his wife Agnes Cockburn. Northcote was initially educated in Brighton before moving on to Eton in 1831, after which in October 1836 he went into residence at Balliol College, Oxford University. Northcote graduated from Oxford BA in 1839 with a first class in Classics (he excelled in poetry) and a third in Mathematics. After leaving Oxford Northcote studied Law at Lincoln's Inn Fields and entered the Inner Temple in 1840.

After the death of his mother in 1840, Northcote's religious views increased and he began to speak on the behalf of the Society for Promoting Christian Knowledge. While engaged in a career in law Northcote's career took a turn, when William Gladstone, who at the time was Vice-President of the Board of Trade, asked Edward Coleridge an Eton housemaster to recommend one of his former pupils to be his personal secretary. Coleridge suggested three former pupils, of which Gladstone chose Northcote. Gladstone at that time was involved in reducing tariffs for Robert Peel, and Northcote was tasked with dealing with Gladstone's mail and accompanying him throughout the country. When Gladstone resigned in 1845, Northcote continued in his role as Gladstone's private secretary, while also holding the position of legal assistant at the Board of Trade from 1845 to 1850, (although he was not called to the bar until November 1847).

In early 1850, Northcote was appointed as one of the secretaries of the Great Exhibition, which was the first in a series of World Fairs showcasing exhibitions of culture and industry. The Exhibition attracted over six million people (one third of the population) when it ran from 1 May through to 15 October 1851. In the position of secretary, Northcote came into frequent contact with Prince Albert, with whom he had a great rapport, and resulted in Prince Albert dissuading Northcote from resigning when he succeeded his grandfather's Baronetcy in March 1851. Northcote was ultimately awarded a CB (Companion) in 1851 for service of the highest calibre, for his work on behalf of the Great Exhibition. After the Great Exhibition, Northcote, along with Sir Charles Trevelyan, served on eight commissions in regards to Civil Service reform. The Northcote-Trevelyan report in November 1853, was a famous mid-Victorian reform which recommended the removal of 'old corruption' and patronage, for a more diverse use of examination and recruitment in the Civil Service. Northcote followed this up with a published paper entitled 'Suggestions under which university education may be available for clerks in government offices, for barristers and solicitor'. As time progressed, Northcote began to move away from 'Peelism' to 'stiff Conservatism', and was elected in a By-election in March 1855 as Conservative Member of Parliament for Dudley, with the support of the influential local landowner Lord Ward. As the MP for Dudley, Northcote became involved in the establishment of reformatory schools and the welfare of reformatory students, drafting a bill in 1855 which was enacted in 1856, which provided industrial schools where truant and vagrant children could be

NORTHCOTE FAMILY CREST

sent. Northcote and Lord Ward had a disagreement over a vote regarding conflict with China, which resulted in Northcote not contesting Dudley again, instead he stood unsuccessfully in North Devon in the General Election of 1857, coming third in a two member seat behind the Whigs and a fellow Conservative. Due to the large expenses incurred while fighting the election in Devon, Northcote and his family moved to France until mid-1858. On Northcote's return to England, Benjamin Disraeli suggested that Northcote stand as Conservative candidate at Stamford (a seat in Lincolnshire) in a July 1858 By-election. Although Northcote thought the move would be 'disagreeable' with his old mentor Gladstone, he was elected unopposed at Stamford. Northcote formed a close working relationship with Disraeli, and over the next twenty three years they worked alongside each other on financial matters, with Disraeli referring to Northcote as his 'right hand'. At the General Election of 1859, Northcote was again returned unopposed for Stamford, along with future Prime Minister Robert Gascoyne-Cecil in the two member seat. Northcote was appointed by the then Chancellor, Disraeli, as Financial Secretary to the Treasury. With the Conservatives in opposition for the next seven years, gradually, Northcote became a leading spokesman for the party, and after a number of impressive speeches in Parliament his growing reputation was enhanced further. He produced a book in 1862, entitled 'Twenty Years of Financial Policy' in which he warned of excessive reliance on taxation and increased government expenditure. Northcote, who was strongly opposed to slavery, kept the Conservative party on a neutral stance by not supporting the South in the American Civil War. In the General Election of 1865, he was again returned unopposed alongside Gascoyne-Cecil at Stamford, but then stood for his local constituency of North Devon in a May 1866 By-election, where he was returned unopposed. When Edward Smith-Stanley (Earl of Derby) formed his third government the following month, Northcote was appointed in his first Cabinet position as President of the Board of Trade, and at the same time he was sworn of the Privy Council. Northcote's tenure as President of the Board of Trade was short-lived, as he was appointed Secretary of State for India on 6 March 1867, a position in which he introduced the 'Government of India Amendment Bill' and an Indian Budget, while advocating non-intervention in Afghanistan.

Upon Disraeli's resignation on 1 December 1868, Northcote left office as Indian Secretary, and upon leaving he donated £1,000 (approx. worth £115,640 in 2020) of his own money to hospitals in India. He was then appointed as Chairman of the Hudson Bay Company and travelled around Canada and the United States in a business capacity. While on his travels, he attended the opening of the Suez Canal in November 1869, as a guest on board Sir George Stucley's yacht. In the

NORTHCOTE'S STATUE IN EXETER

following years, Northcote sat on several commissions, before being appointed as Chancellor of the Exchequer in Disraeli's second ministry. The period of 1874 to 1880 was considered as the time when the Conservative Party's 'One Nation' toryism was embraced. Northcote himself was not a radical reformer, and stated that he wanted the working classes 'to get them to work out their own improvement for themselves'. On 16 April 1874, Northcote delivered his first Budget, taking a penny off income tax, he abolished taxes on horses as well as the sugar taxes (worth £2 million) and reduced further local taxes to the tune of £500,000. Northcote acknowledged and congratulated Gladstone's previous government's finances for allowing him to be able to make such reductions, due to a £5.5 million surplus. Northcote's second Budget on 15 April 1875, introduced a new 'Sinking Fund' (the setting aside of revenue to fund future capital expenses) in which he fixed the annual charge for the debt in order to make regular payments from the capital, although his surplus was now down to only £497,000. In his third Budget on 3 April 1876, Northcote faced a more difficult proposition than in his

first two Budgets, as there was a proposed deficit of £774,000. To alleviate this, Northcote placed an extra penny on income tax as well as tweaking other taxes, therefore estimating a surplus of £368,000. Worst was to come for Northcote as Chancellor, when he faced a dire financial position with his 1868 Budget, due to a £6 million supplement for military preparations against Russia. To combat the cost, Northcote issued exchequer bonds (a type of short term government bond) and raised income tax to 5d. in the pound. By the time of Northcote's last Budget in March 1880, he left a £2 million deficit, which was mainly due to the £5 million cost of the 1879 Anglo-Zulu war. In the April 1880 General Election, Northcote was again

NORTHCOTE STATUE IN PARLIAMENT

returned unopposed in North Devon but the Conservative government was defeated. When Parliament reassembled in May 1880, the Conservatives numbered only 243 MP's against 349 Liberals and 60 home-rulers. Northcote became the Conservative leader in the House of Commons, but as opposition leader his position was described as 'invidious and unenviable'. The Liberal front bench contained at least six men of the highest parliamentary talent, while the Conservatives were dispirited and disorientated. From April 1881, Northcote was joined as joint leader in the House of Commons alongside his previous Stamford colleague, Robert Gascoyne-Cecil (Lord Salisbury) and in May 1881, speaking on the Irish question, Northcote described the Irish land Bill as 'the three 'f's', a force, fraud and folly. Upon the fall of Gladstone's government in June 1855, Gascoyne-Cecil

NORTHCOTE'S STATUE IN NORTHERNHAY

formed his first administration and appointed Northcote as First Lord of the Treasury, with a peerage to the House of Lords as Earl of Iddesleigh and Viscount St Cyres. As First Lord of the Treasury Northcote was made President of the Royal Commission to inquire into trade depression, in which he recommended free-trade practice. A quick turnaround of events occurred in 1886, when Gascoyne-Cecil's government fell at the end of January and was replaced by Gladstone's short lived third term in office (which only ran until July) which in turn led to Gascoyne-Cecil's second term as Prime Minister. In Gascoyne-Cecil's new administration, Northcote was appointed as Foreign Secretary on 3 August 1886, a position in which he had to deal with the kidnapping and abdication of Prince Alexander of Bulgaria, along with trouble in the Balkans. Northcote had already decided on resigning as Foreign Secretary, but on the 12 January 1887, while visiting Gascoyne-Cecil at 10 Downing Street, Northcote suffered a heart attack and died. Gascoyne-Cecil was present at his death, and Northcote's passing at 68 caused national mourning. Northcote was buried at Upton Pyne, Exeter, with memorial service's simultaneously held at Westminster Abbey, Exeter Cathedral, and St Giles's Cathedral, Edinburgh. Statues of him by Sir Joseph Edgar Boehm were placed after his death in the vestibule of the House of Commons and at Northernhay, Exeter.

Interesting Stafford Henry Northcote facts:

Northcote lived at No. 10 Downing Street, normally the prestigious address of the sitting Prime Minister. But because Northcote had ten children and Disraeli was a childless widower, the two men agreed to swap residences. One of Northcote's grandchildren, Dame Flora MacLeod, was born in number 10 on February 3, 1878. It wasn't until another 122 years had passed before another child would be born at 10 Downing Street - Leo Blair, the son of Prime Minister Tony Blair and his wife Cherie.

Northcote was regarded as one of Britain's kindest politicians, owing much to his deep religious faith.

Northcote was rector of Edinburgh University from 1863 to 1887.

Northcote married Cecilia Frances on 5 August 1843 and they had ten children together (seven sons and three daughters).

Northcote's second son, Henry 1st Baron Northcote became an MP for Exeter, Governer of Bombay and 3rd Governer-General of Australia.

Northcote's youngest child and seventh son, Amyas Northcote, was a Justice of Peace and writer of ghost stories. Amyas had a book published in 1921 titled 'In Ghostly Company'.

Andrew Lang published a biography of Northcote in 1890, title 'Life, Letters and Diaries of Sir Stafford Northcote, First Earl of Iddesleigh'.

Northcote built up a small collection of Ethiopian artefacts that are now housed in the British Museum.

Hugh Childers
1827 - 1896 (68 years old) Liberal

Chancellor of the Exchequer:
21 December 1882 - 9 June 1885
(2 years, 5 months and 25 days)

Born
25 June 1827, London
Died
29 January 1896, age 68
London

Title:
None

Constituencies Represented as MP:
Pontefract 1860 - 1885
Edinburgh South 1886 - 1892

Other Official Offices held:
Civil Lord of the Admiralty 1864 - 1866
Financial Secretary to the Treasury 1865 - 1866
First Lord of the Admiralty 1868 - 1871
Chancellor of the Duchy of Lancaster 1872 - 1873
Paymaster General 1872 - 1873
Secretary of State for War 1880 - 1882
Home Secretary 1886

Prime Minister served with as Chancellor:
William Ewart Gladstone

Education:
Wadham College, Oxford and Trinity College, Cambridge.

Hugh Culling Eardley Childers, (25 June 1827 – 29 January 1896) was a Liberal Member of Parliament for Pontefract and Edinburgh South from 1860 to 1892. He Chancellor of the Exchequer for over two years in the early 1880's. He is perhaps best known for his reform efforts while at the Admiralty and the War Office.

Childers was born at his uncle (Sir Culling Eardley Eardley's) house in Brook Street, London on 25 June 1827, to his parents, Reverend Eardley Childers and his wife Maria Charlotte. He was educated at Cheam School in Headley, Hampshire before moving to Wadham College, Oxford in April 1845. In May 1847 he moved on to Trinity College, Cambridge where he achieved a Senior Optime (a student who has achieved a second class in mathematical tripos) and graduated in February 1850.

Three months after graduating from Cambridge, Childers married Emily Walker in May 1850, and then set sail for a career in the colonies in Australia. They set off on 10 July, before finally arriving in Melbourne on 26 October 1850. Once settled in Australia, Childers started work as an inspector of schools in January 1851, and in September of the same year he became Secretary to the Education Department and an Immigration agent. Childers progressed quickly and was given the office of Auditor General in October 1852, producing his first Budget on 4 November 1852, in which he provided £10,000 to set up the University of Melbourne, becoming its first Vice-Chancellor when it founded on 17 May 1853, a position he held until 12 March 1857. After Victoria became a self-governing colony in 1855, Childers was elected to represent Portland on 23 September 1856 in the new Parliament, serving on the first Cabinet as Commissioner of Trades and Customs. He remained on the Victorian Legislative Assembly until resigning in February 1857, when he decided to return to England. Childers by now had decided to devote himself to politics, and on his return to

England, stood as Liberal candidate for Pontefract in West Yorkshire at the 1859 General Election. Childers came third in a two member seat, but after a petition was presented and then withdrawn, the Conservative candidate (William Overend) resigned, causing a By-election which was held in January 1860. Childers won the resulting By-election with a majority of 63 (320 votes against 257) out of 689 registered voters, and would go on to represent Pontefract for the next twenty-five years. Once installed in Parliament, Childers rose in the political world, chairing a select committee on transportation in the colonies in 1863, and became Civil Lord of the Admiralty in 1864. In August 1865, he was appointed Financial Secretary to the Treasury where he struck up a strong rapport with the then Chancellor William Gladstone. As Financial Secretary, Childers played a large part in the Audit Act of 1865, which established a

CARICATURE OF CHILDERS
PUNCH MAGAZINE **1882**

cycle of accountability for public funds. On the fall of the Liberal government in June 1866, Childers left office and acted on a royal commission to investigate the condition of the law courts. When Gladstone formed his first government in December 1868, Childers was appointed First Lord of the Admiralty and was sworn of the Privy Council. Childers set about the reform of the Admiralty with great zeal, improving throughout the efficiency and economics of the Admiralty, while introducing a new policy for shipbuilding; producing new iron-clad ships, improving productivity and reducing expenditure. But some of Childers re-organisation of the Admiralty was unpopular and his strengthening of his own position, by reducing the role of the Board of the Admiralty, was to ultimately lead to his downfall. Childers new policies had brought about the construction of HMS Captain, a warship built for the Royal Navy, but designed by a private contractor against the advice of the Controllers Department. HMS Captain was commissioned in April 1870, but capsized in the Bay of Biscay on 7 September 1870, with the loss of 469 people, including Childers 18 year old second son midshipman Leonard Childers. There were major recriminations

after the sinking of HMS Captain, with Childers being accused of sending to sea an insufficiently stable ship. Although Childers produced a large document to clear his name, the death of his son and the following disputes led to Childers having a nervous breakdown, causing him to resign in 1871. He then embarked on a period of international travel and reflection before returning to England in 1872. On his return, he took office again as Chancellor of the Duchy of Lancaster which triggered a By-election in Pontefract on 17 August 1872, in which Childers was returned with

PAINTING OF CHILDERS BY
MILLY CHILDERS

a majority of 80 (658 votes to 578). The By-election was most notable for it being the first election to be held after the Ballot Act of 1872, which introduced the requirement for local and parliamentary elections to be held by a secret ballot. Childers was again returned as MP for Pontefract in the January/February 1874 General Election, receiving 934 votes of the 2,038 voters registered (37.3%), but the Liberals lost to Disraeli's Conservatives, even though they won the majority of votes

(1,281,159 against 1,091,078). It wasn't until April 1880 before the Liberals would gain power again. Gladstone formed his second administration and appointed Childers as Secretary of War. It turned out to be a challenging position, having to balance cuts in arms expenditure, and then having to provide for the Boer War in South Africa in 1880, followed the invasion of Egypt in 1882. In 1881, Childers Reforms were introduced, which re-organised the infantry regiments of the British Army, a reform that was not universally liked, and made Childers unpopular in some sections. Following on from being Secretary of War, Childers was appointed by Gladstone as Chancellor of the Exchequer in December 1882. In his first Budget in 1883, Childers didn't propose any significant changes as he had "only held only held office for a short space of time", but his Budget contained three main divisions: An interesting explanation of his plans to reduce the National Debt; an elaborate dissection of the complex problem of the annual expenditure, and the proposal for the financial year of 1883– 1884. Childers Budget for the following year was delivered with much more confidence, with him stating that the National Debt had been reduced in the past year by £8,000,000, and that estimated revenue for 1884–1885 was £85,550,000, with expenditure at £85,290,000 leaving a surplus of £260,000. But there was trouble ahead, his 1885-1886 Budget brought the government's financial philosophy into question, with the root problem being the bankruptcy of Egypt (Britain had occupied Egypt in 1882). The total expenditure for 1884-1885 was £89,093,000 of which the charge for the Army was £18,955,000 which was £3,801,000 over estimated budget. In an attempt to resolve the shortfall Childers tried to introduce new taxation, including increasing income tax, as well as increasing the taxes on beer and spirits, altering death duties by 30% and suspending the Sinking Fund. His Budget was rejected by Parliament, which was already under enormous pressure after Queen Victoria had rebuked Gladstone over the death of Major-General Charles Gordon in Khartoum. In the chaos that ensued both Gladstone and Childers resigned from office on 9 June 1885. In the following General Election of November/December 1885, Childers lost his Pontefract seat to the Conservatives by a majority of 36 (1,111 votes to 1,075). He wasn't without a seat for long though, as the death of Independent Liberal, George Harrison, in Edinburgh South, opened the way for Childers to return in a January 1886 By-election. Childers took the Edinburgh South seat with 70% of

CHILDERS GRAVE
BROMPTON CEMETERY

the vote (4,029) for a 2,299 majority. In the following month of February 1886 he was appointed Home Secretary in Gladstone's short-lived third ministry, which was brought down by a defeat on the Home Rule Bill (341 votes against 311) at the end of June, and a General Election was called for July 1886. In the General Election, Childers was again returned for Edinburgh South with a slightly reduced majority of 1,587 (63.3% - 3,778 votes). This was to be the last election Childers would stand in as he retired from Parliament in 1892. His last act of politics was as Chairman of the Irish Financial Relations Commission (known as the Childers Commission) which came to the conclusion that Ireland had been overtaxed, giving the Irish Nationalists ammunition that some form of fiscal freedom was needed to end over-taxation. Over the following years the Irish Nationalists often quoted the Childers Commission report, stating it evidenced the prolonging of Irish poverty.

Childers died in retirement from the effects of influenza in London on 29 January 1896, aged 68, and was buried in Brompton Cemetery, London.

Interesting Hugh Childers facts:

Childers had six sons and two daughters with his first wife Emily Walker and when Emily died in 1875, Childers married for a second time, four years later in 1879 to Katherine Anne Gilbert.

One of Childers daughters; Emily Maria Eardley Childers (1866–1922), known as Milly Childers, was an English painter of the late Victorian era and the early twentieth century. Emily exhibited her work at the Palace of Fine Arts at the 1893 World's Columbian Exposition in Chicago, Illinois.

MILLY CHILDERS SELF PORTRAIT

Childers's cousin, Erskine Childers, was an English-born Irish writer, whose works included the influential novel *The Riddle of the Sands*. Erskine became a supporter of Irish Republicanism, smuggling guns into Ireland in his sailing yacht *Asgard*. He was executed by the authorities of the Irish Free State during the Irish Civil War.

Childers is a rural town and locality in the Bundaberg Region of Queensland, Australia which was established in 1885 and named after Hugh Childers.

A bust of Childers was cast in England and sent to the University of Melbourne in 1893, and a portrait of him painted by his daughter Milly is also displayed in the university.

Michael Edward Hicks Beach
1837 - 1916 (78 years old) Conservative

Chancellor of the Exchequer:
(2 Stints)
25 June 1885 - 28 January 1886
(1 year and 6 days)
29 June 1895 - 11 August 1902 (7 years, 1 month and 14 days)
Born
23 October 1837, London
Died
30 April 1916, age 78
Gloucestershire
Title: 1st Earl St Aldwyn

Constituencies Represented as MP:
Gloucestershire East 1864 - 1885
Bristol West 1885 - 1906

Other Official Offices held:
Parliament Secretary to the Poor Law Board 1868
Under-Secretary of State for the Home Department 1868
Chief Secretary for Ireland 1874 - 1878 and 1886 - 1887
Secretary of State for the Colonies 1878 - 1880
Leader of the House of Commons 1885 - 1886
Minister without Portfolio 1887 - 1888
President of the Board of Trade 1888 - 1892

Prime Minister served with as Chancellor:
Robert Gascoyne-Cecil

Education:
Christ Church, Oxford University.

Michael Edward Hicks Beach, 1st Earl St Aldwyn, (23 October 1837 – 30 April 1916), **The Viscount St Aldwyn**, was a Conservative Member of Parliament for Gloucestershire East and Bristol West. He served as Chancellor of the Exchequer from 1885 to 1886, and again from 1895 to 1902. He also led the Conservative Party in the House of Commons from 1885 to 1886.

Hicks Beach was born on 23 October 1837 in Portugal Street, Grosvenor Square, London, being the eldest son of the eighth baronet Sir Michael Hicks Beach and his wife Harriet Vittiria. Hicks Beach was first educated at Eton College, before moving on to Christ Church, Oxford, where he gained a first class honours in law and modern history, graduating in 1858.

After leaving Oxford, Hicks Beach travelled around the Middle East, before returning to England in the role of country squire and Justice of the Peace (a role created for him after the death of his father in 1854). Hicks Beach from a young age, appeared aloof and shy and had no ambitions of a career in politics, until he agreed to contest a By-election as a Conservative candidate in East Gloucestershire, in July 1864, in which he was returned unopposed (a seat his father had once briefly represented in 1854). Also in 1864 Hicks Beach married Caroline Susan, but the marriage ended in tragedy when Caroline died in the August of 1865 during pregnancy, and to cope with the loss of his wife, he immersed himself in public work. Hicks Beach was seen as an implacable Tory squire who disapproved of compulsory education and was opposed to the 1867 Reform Bill. In Parliament in 1868, Hicks Beach was appointed to two positions; Parliamentary Secretary to the Poor Law Board and then Under Secretary of State for Home Affairs. He was again returned unopposed in both the 1868 and 1872 General Elections. When Benjamin Disraeli took his second term in office in 1874, he appointed Hicks Beach as the Chief Secretary for Ireland, and although the post didn't hold Cabinet rank it was still a major post nonetheless. During the agricultural depression in the 1880's, Hicks Beach was forced to adopt extraordinary measures of retrenchment, his personal circumstances only improved when the War Office purchased his Netheravon estate from him as part of the new artillery range on Salisbury Plain in 1898, in the transaction Hicks Beach as Chancellor negotiated on behalf of the government, with the landowner…Hicks Beach. Despite this, he continued to rise in government and Disraeli's next move was to give him the role of Secretary of State for the Colonies, which was a difficult role considering the problems with the Zulu's and the Boers in the South African territories. Disraeli's defeat in the April 1880 General Election didn't stop Hicks Beach's influence on government, with his opposition amendment to the Budget on 8 June 1885 leading to Gladstone's resignation as Prime Minister. At this time there was also wrangling's within the Conservative party between Lord Randolph Churchill and other leading parliamentary leaders. Churchill wanted progressive Conservatism, which was known as 'Tory Democracy' (also known as 'One-nation conservatism') stating that Conservatives ought to adopt, rather than oppose popular reforms, unlike traditional parliamentarians who didn't want change. The two sides reached a compromise by appointing Hicks Beach as the Chairman of the National Union's Council as he could placate the traditional parliamentarians, and he was also good friends with Churchill, which appeased the rebels. With a compromise reached, the Conservatives came back into power under Robert Gascoyne-Cecil in June 1885, and Hicks Beach was appointed as Chancellor of the Exchequer and Leader of the House of Commons. Up to this point in his political career, Hicks Beach had been elected in seven elections in East Gloucestershire but had never had to face a vote, having been elected unopposed on each occasion. He faced his first voted election due to the Redistribution of Seats Act of 1885, in which the East Gloucestershire seat was abolished. Standing in the 1885 General Election as Conservative candidate in Bristol West, Hicks Beach was returned as MP with a majority of 1,413, after receiving 3,786 votes (61.1%) from a turnout of 6,339. The Liberals won the General Election but with no overall majority, and with the failure of the first Home Rule Bill, the Conservatives came back into office in August 1886, Hicks Beach did not return as Chancellor though as he made way for the more flamboyant Lord Randolph Churchill. He was also overlooked as the Leader of the House after his handling of the Maamtrasna murders (five members of one family killed as they slept in their own home in Maamtrasna, Ireland after which three people were found guilty and executed), Hicks Beach had changed his decision to allow a judicial review, causing dismay in the Conservative party. He was instead appointed as Chief Secretary for Ireland again, but decided to resign in March 1887, giving failing eyesight as the reason, as he suffered from cataracts in both eyes. After receiving treatment in Germany, and with his eyesight much improved, Gascoyne-Cecil offered Hicks Beach a Cabinet position in early 1888, as President of the Board of Trade, a position he held until the Conservatives lost office in 1892. But when Gascoyne-Cecil gained power for a third time in June 1895, Hicks Beach was again appointed as the Chancellor of the Exchequer, in what became a crucial period in Conservative financial policies. While trying to relieve taxation for the party's traditional supporters, he also had to balance the strengthening of the Royal Navy, while spending more on Social Reforms. Hicks Beach who by now had a reputation for friction with colleagues was commented on in a letter from Gascoyne-Cecil saying "It is rare to get letter from Hicks Beach without a 'No, I will not' on the first page", and future Prime Minister Arthur Balfour describing Hicks Beach as 'dropping little grains of sand into the wheels of every department'. But even with underlying conflict he managed to keep the economy flowing, with revived trade which boosted revenue and managed to keep a budget surplus. In doing so he was able to reduce the National Debt, relieve half the burden of rates on agricultural land and keep income tax at 8d. in the pound. But towards the end of the 1890's events took a turn for the worse, with pressure still on expanding the Navy, and the outbreak of the South African War in the Autumn of 1899, He faced mounting problems. He had to borrow £8 million towards the cost of the war and reduce fixed debt charges, but his preferred option of extra taxation was met with reluctance from colleague's unwilling to face alienating their supporters. With the cost of the South African war continuing to spiral, the Budget for 1899-1900 was £111 million but the expenditure for 1900-1901 was £154 million, creating a massive deficit. Therefore Hicks Beach had to introduce a number of unwelcome manoeuvres to counteract the deficit, including increasing income tax from 8d. to 1 shilling in the pound, imposing extra duties on beer, spirits, tea and tobacco, while suspending the Sinking Fund, as well as raising short-term loans. There was still a shortfall, and so in 1901, Hicks Beach put a further 2d. on income tax and introduced 1 shilling per ton duty on coal. The 1902 Budget saw him impose another penny on income tax and he re-imposed the registration duty on corn which had been abolished in1869, which pleased the protectionists but angered free traders in both parties. By nature Hicks Beach believed in low taxation, but events had conspired against his principles, and so when Gascoyne-Cecil resigned as Prime Minister in July 1902, he followed his lead and resigned as Chancellor on 11 August 1902. After deciding to give up his seat in the House of Commons, Hicks Beach was raised to the peerage in 1906 as Viscount St Aldwyn and from the Lords he opposed many of the Social Reforms of the Liberal government. With the outbreak of the First World War in August 1914, he served both as Chairman on the committee on clearing banks and on the Treasury committee on new issues, with his work being recognised by being honoured as Viscount Quenington in the County of Gloucestershire.

Hicks Beach died of heart failure on 30 April 1916, aged 78, only one week after his son, Michael, was killed in action from wounds received in Egypt.

Interesting Michael Hicks Beach facts:

Hicks Beach along with David Lloyd George and Nigel Lawson, remains the only Chancellor to have introduced seven consecutive Budgets. Hicks Beach delivered his between 1895 and 1902 (only Gladstone managed more).

'Black Michael' was a Westminster nickname given to Hicks Beach due to his gloomy outlook, which soon found its way into the pages of Punch magazine. With the Conservative leader Robert Gascoyne-Cecil (Lord Salisbury) quipping 'He would make a very good Home Secretary… and would hang everybody.'

Beachport, which is a small coastal town in the Australian state of South Australia, was named in the honour of the then British Secretary of State for the Colonies, Michael Hicks Beach, on 23 May 1878.

Hicks Beach's grandson, Michael John Hicks Beach, 2nd Earl St Aldwyn (9 October 1912 – 29 January 1992) followed in his grandfather's footsteps in becoming a Conservative politician, achieving the distinction of serving in the governments of five different Prime Ministers (Winston Churchill, Anthony Eden, Harold Macmillan, Alec Douglas-Home and Edward Heath).

Hicks Beach was the Father of the House (The Father of the House is a title that is bestowed on the senior member of the House of Commons who has the longest continuous service) from 1901 until he took his peerage in 1906.

Due to the length of his service, Hicks Beach was Father of the House from 1901 to 1906, after which he took a peerage.

William Vernon Harcourt
1827 - 1904 (76 years old) Liberal

Chancellor of the Exchequer:
(2 Stints)
6 February 1886 - 20 July 1886
(5 months and 15 days)
18 August 1892 - 21 June 1895
(2 years, 10 months and 4 days)
Born
14 October 1827, Yorkshire
Died
1 October 1916, age 76
Title: Sir William Vernon Harcourt
(1873)

Constituencies Represented as MP:
Oxford 1868 - 1880
Derby 1880 - 1895
West Monmouthshire 1895 - 1904

Other Official Offices held:
Solicitor General for England and Wales 1873 - 1874
Home Secretary 1880 - 1885
Leader of the House of Commons 1894 - 1895
Leader of the Opposition 1896 - 1898

Prime Ministers served with as Chancellor:
William Ewart Gladstone
Archibald Primrose

Education:
Trinity College, Cambridge University.

Sir William George Granville Venables Vernon Harcourt, (14 October 1827 – 1 October 1904) was a lawyer, journalist and Liberal statesman. He served as MP for Oxford, Derby and West Monmouthshire from 1868 to 1904. He held the offices of Home Secretary and Chancellor of the Exchequer under William Ewart Gladstone before becoming Leader of the Opposition.

Harcourt was born in Yorkshire on 14 October 1827, into an ecclesiastical family, his father was William Venables Vernon Harcourt (1789–1871), a clergyman of the Church of England and his grandfather, Edward Venables Vernon Harcourt, was Archbishop from 1807 until he died in 1847. Harcourt was initially home schooled by a Swiss governess before being sent aged eight, to a private school in Southwell, Nottinghamshire. Harcourt was then enrolled in a small group of pupils to be educated by John Owen Parr, the Vicar of Durnford who was based in Preston. After leaving Preston, Harcourt was then home schooled again for a further two years before he entered Trinity College, Cambridge, in 1846 to study mathematics. While at Cambridge he moved away from the family tradition of toryism moving towards liberalism instead. His move away from toryism would cause future friction with his elder brother Edward, who was tory MP for Oxfordshire from 1878 to 1886. Although he didn't enjoy mathematics, Harcourt was still named senior optime (second class in mathematic tripos) and he also received a first class in classics.

While still at Cambridge, Harcourt was given a choice of a fellowship at Cambridge or a career in politics, at the time he decided on neither option. After writing articles for the Morning Chronicle (a paper Charles Dickens also wrote for) he decided instead to pursue his interest in law and journalism. Harcourt enrolled at Lincoln's Inn in 1852, and on 1 May 1854 he was called to the bar at the Inner Temple, practicing railway law and commenting on international law. He continued with his writing and wrote articles for the newly established London weekly newspaper, the Saturday Review, from 1855 to 1859 (other notable contributors to the Review were; H.G. Wells, George Bernard Shaw, Oscar Wilde and Robert Gascoyne-Cecil). Harcourts first foray into politics came in the 1859 April/May General Election, when he stood as a Conservative candidate (described as a Peelite Liberal Conservative) in the Kirkcaldy

WILLIAM HARCOURT

Burghs constituency, losing out by only 18 votes to the Liberal, Robert Ferguson by 312 votes to 294. Later on 5 November 1859, Harcourt married Lady Maria Theresa Lewis who was the step-daughter of Liberal MP Sir George Cornewall Lewis. The marriage was tragically cut short when Lady Maria died on 31 January 1863 after giving birth to their second child (their first son Julian, had also tragically died the year before at only 15 months old). Harcourt's second son (Lewis) survived, and later became a Cabinet minister in both H.H.Asquith and Sir Henry Campbell-Bannerman's governments. Throughout the following years Harcourt focused again on his legal practice but he was still undecided on his true political allegiance. In 1866, he was offered a safe Conservative seat in Wales by Benjamin Disraeli but declined. He eventually entered Parliament at the age of 40, by standing and winning in the November/December 1868 General Election as a Liberal. Harcourt was elected along with fellow Liberal Edward Cardwell in a two member seat in Oxford, with Cardwell receiving 41.7% of the vote (2,765) and Harcourt receiving 39.9% (2,636). Upon entering Parliament, Harcourt soon became a leading figure with his excellent debating skills. He was regarded as being strongly opinionated when favouring reform in the judiciary and also in land law. Harcourt was opposed to the secret ballot in 1872, and was openly critical of Gladstone's government, but Gladstone recognised Harcourt's high standing as a debater on behalf of the Liberal party, and in November 1873 offered him the post of

Solicitor-General for England and Wales, and as customary with the position, he was also knighted. Harcourt's stint as Solicitor-General was short-lived though, as the Liberals lost the February 1874 General Election to Benjamin Disraeli's Conservatives. He was again returned as MP for Oxford with 34.2% of the vote (2,332 votes). Harcourt was a dynamic figure on the opposition benches for the following six years, criticising much of Disraeli's government, but he was also frustrated with Gladstone's position of officially being retired, (his first retirement was in January 1875) but still politically active. With the

SERMONS BOOK BY
WILLIAM VERNON HARCOURT
1873

Liberals defeating Disraeli and the Conservatives in the General Election of March/April 1880, (again under Gladstone), Harcourt was re-elected for Oxford, along with fellow Liberal Joseph Chitty, in a closely fought election with the two Liberals only having a majority of 10. Harcourt was then appointed by Gladstone as Home Secretary, which at the time caused a mandatory By-election as appointed ministers had to be re-elected to Parliament. The By-election was held in May 1880, in which Harcourt lost to his Conservative rival Alexander William Hall by 2,735 votes to 2,681 (majority 54). Hall's election was declared void though on account of bribery, but by then Harcourt had moved to a vacant seat in Derby, and was elected unopposed on

26 May 1880, (Oxford was then left without an MP from 1881 to 1885 after Chitty was appointed a judge and resigned the seat in 1881). As Home Secretary from 1880 to 1885, Harcourt played a crucial role in the problems in Ireland, with the Fenian Dynamite Campaign against the British Empire from 1881 to 1885, and the murders of Lord Frederick Cavendish (Chief Secretary for Ireland) and Thomas Henry Burke (Permanent Undersecretary) in Phoenix Park in May 1882. The response to the murders was to form the Special Irish Branch in March 1883, (later becoming the Special Branch as the unit's remit widened to include more than just Irish Republican-related counterespionage). Also the Explosive Substances Act of 1883 was introduced, which made it illegal 'to use (or conspire to use) any explosive substance likely to endanger life or cause serious injury to property, whether or not any explosion takes place', an act which carried a term of life imprisonment. After the Liberal government was defeated in June 1885, by an alliance of Irish and Tory members due to Hicks Beach's opposition amendment to the Budget, Harcourt resigned with the government. At the following November to December 1885 General Election, (the first General Election after the redistribution of seats), Harcourt retained his seat in Derby receiving 35.3% of the vote (7,630 votes with a 2,687 majority). The Liberals won most seats but with no overall majority (336 seats were needed for a majority; the Liberals won 319, Conservatives 247 and Irish Nationalists 63). Gladstone formed a minority government and appointed Harcourt as Chancellor of the Exchequer on 6 February 1886, again triggering a By-election in which Harcourt was returned unopposed on 9 Feb 1886. At this time, Home Rule was dominating the agenda, with Harcourt speaking in favour when it was debated in May 1886. His first Budget on 15 April 1886, was a straightforward affair with existing taxes covering a deficit of £2.5 million. Harcourt's first stint as Chancellor was short lived though, when the Liberal government was defeated in the summer of 1886 on the Home Rule, and subsequently lost the July 1886 General Election, with

Harcourt resigning as Chancellor. Harcourt retained his Derby seat at the election with 6,431 votes (37.1% of the vote) but spent the next six years in opposition. On the return of the Liberals to power in 1892, Gladstone, in his fourth and final ministry commented that "the addition of another Harcourt would have gone far to make my task impossible" but he still re-instated Harcourt as Chancellor of the Exchequer for the second time. With Gladstone now in his eighties, a lot of responsibility was

HARCOURT FAMILY CREST

placed on Harcourt, putting him in a prime position to eventually take over from Gladstone. As Chancellor, Harcourt in his Budget on 24 April 1893, raised income tax from 6d. to 7d. but it was his Budget in 1894 which was the most memorable, when he introduced death duties in opposition to Gladstone and Archibald Primrose who thought that easily increased taxes would encourage frivolous government spending . Although estates had paid inheritance tax before, the new death duties brought a new attitude towards inheritance. The Budget took three months to pass but was seen as a triumph for Harcourt. After losing the support of his Cabinet, Gladstone did eventually retire in March 1894, and Harcourt had a claim for the post of Prime Minister, but Queen Victoria did not ask for any recommendations and instead chose the more popular figure of Archibald Primrose (Earl of Rosebery). Harcourt remained as Chancellor of the Exchequer, and became leader of the Liberal party in the House of Commons, although Primrose and Harcourt had different ideas of Liberalism and Liberal party policies. At the July/August 1895 General Election,

Harcourt lost his seat in Derby, finishing third behind the two Conservative candidates by a majority of 291, but he was successful in the same election in the safe seat of West Monmouthshire where he received 78.7% of the vote (7,019

NUNEHAM HOUSE OXFORDSHIRE

votes). Harcourt eventually resigned as Leader of the opposition in December 1898, but continued as MP until standing down in 1904, Harcourt had declined a peerage in 1902, in order to stay in the House of Commons enabling him to mentor his son, Lewis's (Loulou) blossoming political career.

Harcourt died unexpectedly on 1 October 1904, aged 76, survived by his wife.

He was buried in the family vault in the church in the grounds of Nuneham Park.

Interesting William Vernon Harcourt facts:

Harcourt's only surviving son, Lewis, was his private secretary while he was Home Secretary, and later went on to serve as Secretary of State for the Colonies in H.H. Asquith's government.

Harcourt was the subject of several parody novels based on Alice in Wonderland, such as Caroline Lewis's *Clara in Blunderland* (1902) and *Lost in Blunderland* (1903).

The author A.G. Gardener wrote a biography on Harcourt in 1923, titled *'The Life of Sir William Harcourt'*

Harcourt left £190,264 19s 3d. approx. £23,286,745 in 2020.

Randolph Henry Spencer Churchill
1849 - 1895 (45 years old) Conservative

Chancellor of the Exchequer:
3 August 1886 - 22 December 1886
(4 months and 20 days)

Born
13 February 1849, London

Died
24 January 1895, age 45 London

Title: Lord Randolph Churchill Courtesy title

Constituencies Represented as MP:
Woodstock 1874 - 1885
Paddington South 1885 - 1895

Other Official Offices held:
Chairman of the National Union of Conservative and Constitutional Associations 1884
Secretary of State for India 1885 - 1886
Leader of the House of Commons 1886

Prime Ministers served with as Chancellor:
Robert Gascoyne-Cecil

Education:
Merton College, Oxford University.

Lord Randolph Henry Spencer-Churchill, (13 February 1849 – 24 January 1895) was a Tory radical and father of Winston Churchill. He coined the term 'Tory democracy' inspiring a generation of party managers, and created the National Union of the Conservative Party.

Churchill was born at 3 Wilton Terrace, Belgravia, London on 13 February 1849, the third son of John Winston Spencer Churchill, the seventh Duke of Marlborough and his wife, Lady Frances Anne Emily. Churchill was educated firstly at Tabor's Preparatory School in Cheam before moving on to Eton College in 1863, where he made lifelong friendships with future Prime Ministers; Arthur Balfour and Archibald Primrose (Lord Rosebery). Churchill moved on to Merton College in Oxford University in 1867 where he read jurisprudence and modern history, as well as having a fondness for partying and hunting. Churchill left Oxford in 1870 with a second class degree in jurisprudence and modern history, and spent the next three years hunting on the Churchill estate in Blenheim, Oxfordshire. In 1873 Churchill met a young American, Jeanette (Jennie) Jerome who was the daughter of a wealthy New York financier and fell in love. Randolph and Jennie were eventually married at the British Embassy in Paris on 15 April 1874, and their first child, Winston Churchill was born prematurely at Blenheim Palace on 30 November 1874.

Churchill followed his parent's Conservative views, and in return for his father's consent to marry (at the time it was highly unusual for an aristocrat to marry an American) Churchill stood as Conservative candidate for Woodstock, where his father was a principal landowner. At the January/February 1874 General Election, Churchill was elected as MP for Woodstock with 58.5% of the votes (569 votes against 404) from 1,071 registered voters, for a majority of 165. Although he had the courtesy title of Lord, Churchill was able to sit in the House of Commons as a commoner. From 1874 up to 1880, Churchill was a proponent of independent Conservatism and constantly criticised members of the 'old gang'. During Gladstone's Liberal ministry of 1880-1885, Churchill joined three other leading Conservatives; Sir Henry Drummond Wolff, John Eldon Gorst and Arthur James Balfour to form what became known as 'the 'Fourth Party', setting out it's ideals as 'Tory Democracy'. Churchill was attempting to create a new Conservatism, and strengthened the party's central organisation with more 'rank and file' members. Churchill's

appointment as Chairman of the National Union of Conservative and Constitutional Associations in 1884, split the Conservative party, but after concessions were made by both Robert Gascoyne Cecil and Churchill, the party was re-united, and t the June 1885 General Election, Gascoyne-Cecil was elected as Prime Minister. At the election, Churchill had to move constituencies as the Woodstock seat had been abolished in boundary changes, and therefore stood, and won, in Paddington South, being elected with 67.5% of the vote (2,731 votes) with a majority of 1,706. Churchill was then appointed by Gascoyne Cecil as Secretary of State for India, where he ordered the Third Anglo Burmese War in November 1885, leading to the takeover of all of Burma (Myanmar). A fall out occurred between the Conservatives and the Irish Nationalists in February 1886, which led to Gascoyne-Cecil and Churchill resigning from office. When the Conservatives returned to power again at the General Election on 25 July 1886, Gascoyne-Cecil appointed Churchill (who had been returned again in Paddington South with a majority of 1,706) as the Chancellor of the Exchequer, and as Leader of the House of Commons. Churchill had ambitions to be head of government but had alienated most of his colleagues. In his first Budget, he wanted to reduce the defence estimates below those of the last Liberal government, a move which was opposed by the Secretary for War, W. H. Smith. When Gascoyne-Cecil backed Smith, Churchill wrote a letter to Gascoyne-Cecil, on 20 December 1886, stating his wish to resign from the government.

Churchill had misjudged the mood, and when Gascoyne-Cecil

accepted his resignation with 'profound regret' he replaced him with George Goschen. Churchill was left in political wilderness. Although Churchill remained in the House of Commons until his death, he lost interest in politics and devoted much of his time to his passion for horse racing. Churchill's health declined in the 1890's and he spent time travelling in search of both health and relaxation, but after a visit to Cairo in December 1894, he arrived back in London in early 1895, and died aged only 45, on 24 January 1895.

CHURCHILL BUST

Interesting Randolph Churchill facts:

Churchill had a great passion for horse racing and his Thoroughbred racehorse *L'Abbesse de Jouarre* won the 1889 Epsom Oaks.

Churchill's son, Winston, who became Prime Minister twice, wrote a two-part biography between 1903 and 1905 about his father, titled *'His Father's Son the Life of Lord Randolph Churchill'* the book was published in 1906.

Derek Fowlds plays Randolph Churchill in the historical television series *Edward the Seventh*.

George Spencer-Churchill the Duke of Marlborough was Randolph Churchill's elder brother.

"I COULD NEVER MAKE OUT WHAT THOSE DAMNED DOTS MEANT"
RANDOLPH CHURCHILL ON DECIMAL POINTS

Robert Shaw played Randolph Churchill in the film 'Young Winston'.

Randolph Churchill died age 45 on 24 January 1895 and Winston Churchill died on the exact same day in 1965, exactly twice his father's age (90).

In 2002 Randolph Churchill was portrayed by actor Tom Hiddleston in *The Gathering Storm*, the BBC – HBO co-produced television biographical film about Winston Churchill in the years just prior to World War II.

George Joachim Goschen
1831 - 1907 (75 years old) Liberal - Liberal Unionist - Conservative

Chancellor of the Exchequer:
14 January 1887 - 11 August 1892
(4 years, 11 months and 29 days)
Born
10 August 1831, London

Died
7 February 1907, age 75 London

Title: 1st Viscount Goschen

Constituencies Represented as MP:
City of London 1863 - 1880
Ripon 1880 - 1885
Edinburgh East 1885 - 1886
St George, Hanover Square 1887 - 1900

Other Official Offices held:
Paymaster General 1865 - 1866
Chancellor of the Duchy of Lancaster 1866
President of the Poor Law Board 1868 - 1871
First Lord of the Admiralty 1871 - 1874 and 1895 - 1900

Prime Minister served with as Chancellor:
Robert Gascoyne-Cecil

Education:
Oriel College, Oxford University.

George Joachim Goschen, 1st Viscount Goschen, (10 August 1831 – 7 February 1907) was a Member of Parliament for four different constituencies. He was businessman born in London with a German heritage. He is best remembered for being "forgotten" by Lord Randolph Churchill from whom he took over as Chancellor. He was initially a Liberal, then a Liberal Unionist before crossing the floor to the Conservative Party in 1893.

Goschen was born in Stoke Newington, London, on 10 August 1831. The eldest son and second child in a family of ten (five boys and five girls) to William Henry Goschen and his wife

A YOUNG GOSCHEN

Henrietta. Goschen senior was a prominent merchant banker in the City of London who had emigrated from Leipzig, Germany, to London in 1814. George Goschen was home schooled by a German relative until he was nine, and then attended Blackheath Proprietary School, before being sent to Dr Bernhards School in Saxe-Meiningen in Germany in 1842, close to his German family. On returning to England, Goschen then attended Rugby School in 1845, where he became absorbed with the notion of free markets and free trade. At first he struggled to settle in at Rugby, by the time he left in 1850, he had become head of the school and gained awards in English and Latin. Goschen moved to Oriel College, Oxford, in 1850, from where he graduated with firsts in classical moderations and litarae humaniores (focusing on classics of Ancient Rome, Ancient Greece, latin and philosophy) while also becoming Michaelmas President of the Oxford Union in 1853-54.

After leaving Oxford, Goschen was prepared for working in the family firm of merchant bankers; Fruhling and Goschen, and planning on marrying his sweetheart Lucy Dalley. But before his father would allow the marriage to go ahead, he insisted that Goschen supervise the firms business in New Granada (now Columbia), to which Goschen reluctantly agreed. After two years spent successfully in New Granada, Goschen returned to London wiser and more experienced, and in return got his wish of marrying Lucy on 22 September 1857. A happy marriage ensued, producing two sons and four daughters. Goschen had accrued a shrewd business sense at Fruhling and Goschen, and in 1858, age 27, he became Director of the Bank of England. He wrote *The Theory of Foreign Exchange* in 1861, which became famous within banking circles, and he retained the post of Director until 1865. Goschen had followed his father as an exponent of free trade and liberalism, and with these views he was encouraged by colleagues to contest a By-election for the City of London on 2 June 1863. Standing as a Liberal, Goschen was elected unopposed, and on entering Parliament, he advocated support for the secret ballot, an ending to all religious disabilities and the abolition of church rates. At the July 1865 General Election, Goschen was returned with three other Liberals, in the four seat constituency, in the City of London, finishing with the most votes (7,102) 19.9% of the vote on a turnout of 10,529. The 1865 General Election was noted for a large degree of corruption, with fifty election petitions being lodged, thirty-five of them going to trial, leading to thirteen MP's being unseated and ultimately led to the Ballot Act of 1872. Goschen became the Vice President of the Board of Trade and Paymaster General in November 1865, before being given the role of Chancellor of the Duchy of Lancaster, with a seat in the Cabinet in January 1866. Goschen's first Cabinet position didn't last long though, with the Liberal's disunited over reform, Lord John Russell resigned on 26 June 1866, and Goschen spent the following two years on the opposition front bench. In 1868, Goschen became a Cabinet minister again in Gladstone's first government, as President of the Poor Law Board. Goschen had again polled most votes (6,520) in the four seat City of London (this time two other Liberals and a Conservative were also elected). Goschen then spent three years as President of the Poor Law Board implementing some useful reform, before it was abolished in 1871, to be replaced by the Local Government Board. In March 1871, Goschen gained promotion when he was

 appointed First Lord of the Admiralty, a position in which he offered naval support to Sir Garnet Wolseley in the Third Anglo Ashanti War (now Ghana) which was fought from 1873 into 1874. Goschen stayed at the Admiralty until the 1874 General Election, which Benjamin Disraeli's Conservative's won decisively (their first General Election win since 1841) and Goschen had to step down from the Admiralty. He was again elected in the City of London at the General Election, but only after finishing fourth behind three Conservatives, scraping through by 133 votes (6,787 against 6,654). In 1876, Goschen was sent to Cairo in Egypt to negotiate with the Khedive (honourific title for the Viceroy of Egypt), who had suspended payments on foreign loans. The Khedive accepted most of Goschen's proposals which became known as 'Goschen's Decree'. He then found himself at odds with his party over reform, and with the City of London becoming more Conservative, he decided to stand in the March/April General Election of 1880, in the safe seat of Ripon in Yorkshire. He was elected with 62% of the vote (591 against 362) for a 229 majority. Goschen excluded himself from Gladstone's new government in 1880 due to his opposition to household suffrage (the right of voting in elections, consequent of being a householder) and also turned down Gladstone's offer of Viceroy of India. In 1884, when the Representation of the People Bill was introduced, Goschen turned down the offer of Speaker of

the House of Commons, and was still at odds with his own party. When Gladstone adopted Home Rule for Ireland, Goschen followed Lord Hartingdon (whose younger brother, Lord Frederick Hartingdon had been murdered at Phoenix Park in Ireland) in becoming a Liberal Unionist (a breakaway faction of the Liberal party). Goschen decided to leave Ripon and contend the Edinburgh East seat at the November/December 1885 General Election, polling 69.2% of the vote, with 4,337 votes against the Liberal candidates 1,929, for a majority of 2,408. But following

the defeat of the governments Ireland Bill in 1886, another General Election was called for July 1886, in which Goschen was defeated by the new Liberal candidate (Robert Wallace) after only receiving 37.9% of the vote and losing by a majority of 1,441 (3,694 to 2,253). After Conservative leader Robert Gascoyne-Cecil had unexpectedly accepted Lord Randolph Churchill's resignation as Chancellor (removing a rival colleague in the process), Gascoyne-Cecil turned to Goschen, and although the Liberal Unionists had rejected a proposal for a coalition government, Goschen accepted the post of Chancellor of the Exchequer on 14 January 1887, with Churchill famously saying he had "forgotten Goschen". After the defeat in Edinburgh South, Goschen stood as a Liberal Unionist in a By-election in Liverpool Exchange on 26 January 1887, against Ralph Neville the Liberal candidate, but was distraught when he was beaten by just 7 votes, 3,217 to 3,210. Still looking for a new seat, he stood in a By-election when the Conservative Algernon Percy agreed to resign in St George's Hanover Square, Goschen won the seat on 9 February 1887, with 5,702 votes against the Liberal candidates 1,545. Goschen then concentrated on the Treasury, and gained a notable achievement in 1888 with the considerable saving he made for the nation, when he reduced the core of the National Debt from 3 per cent to 2.5 per cent. He is also remembered for introducing the first vehicle tax (leading up to the first car tax in 1888). Goschen at this time was worried that income tax was being used excessively and in his 1889 Budget, he decided to put a one per cent estate duty on all real and personal estates worth more than £10,000. The following year in his 1890 Budget, Goschen acted decisively when one of the largest merchant banks, Baring Brothers, was on the verge of collapse, by setting up a guarantee fund, in which he as Chancellor, would agree to share all losses with the bank for twenty four hours. The banking and financial community responded with their own fund and Barings soon repaid its debts. At the July 1892 General Election, Goschen was elected unopposed again as a Liberal Unionist in St George's, Hanover Square. He was then appointed as the First Lord of the Admiralty for the second time in 1895, in Gascoyne-Cecil's third term as Prime Minister. His appointment triggered a By-election on 29 June 1895, in which Goschen was returned unopposed, but this time he had stood as a Conservative. He was returned again unopposed in the General Election the following month, which turned out to be the last election he would contest. In his last political position as First Lord of the Admiralty, which he held from 1895 – 1900, he supervised a large expanse of the fleet in preparation for the Second Boer War in October 1899. He had indicated that he intended to retire at the September/October 1900 General Election, and was raised to the peerage as Viscount Goschen of Hawkhurst, Kent. Although retired, Goschen kept a keen interest in public affairs until his death aged 75, on 7 February 1907.

Interesting George Goschen facts:

Goschen's eldest son George (1866–1952), was a Conservative M.P. for East Grinstead from 1895 to 1906.

Goschen wrote a two-volume biography of his grandfather, '*The Life and Times of George Joachim Goschen, publisher and printer of Leipzig'* which was published in 1903.

Goschen appears as a minor character in the historical-mystery novel *Stone's Fall*, by Iain Pears.

Following Robert Gascoyne-Cecil's death in 1903, Goschen was elected unopposed as Chancellor of Oxford University, a position he held until his death in 1907.

While Chancellor of the Exchequer, in 1888 he introduced the Goschen formula to allocate funding for Scotland and Ireland.

As well as The Theory of the Foreign Exchanges, Goschen published several financial and political pamphlets and addresses on educational and social subjects, among them were *Cultivation of the Imagination,* Liverpool, 1877, and that on *Intellectual Interest,* Aberdeen, 1888.

At Oxford in 1849, Goschen won the Queen's medal for the English historical essay, and in 1850, the prize for the Latin essay, "Marcus Tullius Cicero."

Goschen left £141,568 1s. 5d. in his will, which is worth approx. £17,415,876 in 2020.

Goschen had always been interested in reading and intellectual activity, he enthusiastically endorsed the university extension movement, saying "everyone's mind should be cultivated, for there is far more to life than just earning a livelihood". He took great delight from being appointed Chancellor of Oxford University in 1903, after the death of Robert Gascoyne-Cecil (Lord Salisbury).

Charles Ritchie
1838 - 1906 (67 years old) Conservative

Chancellor of the Exchequer:
11 August 1902 - 9 October 1903
(1 year, 1 month and 29 days)
Born
19 November 1838, Dundee, Scotland
Died
9 January 1906, age 67, London

Title: 1st Baron Ritchie of Dundee

Constituencies Represented as MP:
Tower Hamlets 1874 - 1885
Tower Hamlets, St George 1885 - 1892
Croydon 1895 - 1905

Other Official Offices held:
Parliamentary Secretary to the Admiralty 1885 - 1886
President of the Local Government Board 1886 - 1892
President of the Board of Trade 1895 - 1900
Home Secretary 1900 - 1902

Prime Minister served with as Chancellor:
Arthur Balfour

Education:
City of London School

Charles Thomson Ritchie, 1st Baron Ritchie of Dundee, (19 November 1838 – 9 January 1906) was born in Scotland, he was a Conservative politician in three London constituencies. He sat in the House of Commons from 1874 until 1905, when he was raised to the peerage. He served as Home Secretary from 1900 to 1902 and as Chancellor of the Exchequer from 1902 to 1903.

Ritchie was born on 19 November 1838 at Hawkhill, Dundee, the third of three sons to William and Elizabeth Ritchie. Ritchie's father William was the head of the firm William Ritchie and Son of London and Dundee; jute spinners, East India merchants and manufacturers. Ritchie was educated at the City of London School from 1849 to 1853, from where he joined the London office of his father's firm continuing to work there for the next twenty-one years, until 1874.

Ritchie first stood at the 1874 General Election, which was the only election after secret ballots were introduced, that a party, the Liberals, who had an absolute majority was defeated. This was mainly due to over one hundred Conservatives being elected unopposed. Ritchie stood as the only Conservative against four Liberal candidates in the two seat constituency of Tower Hamlets, in London, topping the poll with 29.7% of the vote (7,228) out of a turnout of 15,786 (32,937 were registered). His election in Tower Hamlets as a Tory was remarkable, in what was seen as a strong working class constituency. His success being partly attributed to him having no aristocratic connections. Ritchie immediately increased his popularity by extending the Bank Holiday Act to include dockyard and custom workers in 1875. He was a strong advocate of the free-trade movement and with his constituency containing several large sugar refineries, he proposed several motions proposing countervailing duties on sugar. On the strength of his local support, Ritchie was again elected for Tower Hamlets in the March/April 1880 General Election, this time taking the second seat but with a larger vote

(11,720), with a similar percentage (29.9%) which was due to the turnout almost doubling to 28,025. From 1880 to 1885, Ritchie became a vociferous critic of the Gladstone government, gaining him a solid reputation, and in 1885 he was appointed as Parliamentary Secretary to the Admiralty. He chaired a committee which investigated the management of dockyards and the slow production of ironclad warships, and succeeding in reducing the cost and the time of construction from seven to three years. When the Tower Hamlets constituency was split due to redistribution, Ritchie then stood in the newly created Tower Hamlets, St George constituency, in the November/December 1885 General Election. He won the seat with 59% of the vote (1,744) for a 564 majority, and followed this up by winning the seat in July 1886 General Election with 1,561 votes, 59.2%, for a majority of 485. And when Ritchie was appointed as President of the Local Government Board in Gascoyne-Cecil's second ministry, it triggered Ritchie's third election in less than a year, which he won on 12 August 1886 with 1,546 votes (65%) for a 657 majority. As President of the Local Government Board, Ritchie passed the Local Government Act 1888, which established County Councils, as well as introducing several other Acts; Acts on Allotments (1887, 1890) Infectious Diseases Notification (1889), Housing of the Working Classes (1890) and Public Health for London (1891) bringing in significant reform. At the July 1892 General Election, Ritchie lost his St George seat to the Liberal John Benn to a majority of 398 (1,661 to 1,263 votes), and so contested the Walsall seat in a By-election on 9 February 1893, in which he again lost to a Liberal, by a majority of 79 (5,235 to 5,156 votes). It wasn't until a safe seat in Croydon became vacant, due to Sidney Herbert's elevation to a peerage, that Ritchie returned to the House of Commons, when he was returned unopposed in a May 1895 By-election. Back in Parliament, Ritchie was appointed as President of the Board of Trade, where he produced the Conciliation Act (1896), the Light Railways Act (1896) and the Railway Employment (Preventions of Accidents)

Act of 1900. After the September/October General Election when he was returned unopposed, Ritchie was promoted to Home Secretary, amending the Factories Workshop Act (1901), so instead of young offenders being sent to the workhouse or prison, they were accountable to a responsible person, thanks to the Youthful Offenders Act. Ritchie's last act as Home Secretary, was a licensing Bill to deal with suppression of drunkenness in 1902. In the July of 1902, Arthur Balfour replaced Gascoyne-Cecil as Prime Minister and appointed 64 year old Ritchie as the Chancellor of the Exchequer. He only produced one Budget as Chancellor, on 23 April 1903, in which he cut 4d. from income tax and abolished corn duty. He was still seen as a fair trader, strongly opposing Colonial Secretary Joseph Chamberlain's movement for a preferential tariff, leading to a Cabinet fallout, and on principle, he resigned in October 1903. Ritchie was then created a peer as Baron Ritchie of Dundee in December 1905, but at the time he was in ill health and died on 9 January 1906, aged 67, in Biaritz, France.

Interesting Charles Ritchie facts:

Ritchie's elder brother, James, was the Lord Mayor of London in 1903-1904.

A few days after his twentieth birthday on 7 December 1858, Ritchie married Margaret Ower, they went on to have ten children together (three sons and seven daughters).

Ritchie left £116,245 8s.10d in probate on his death in 1906 (worth over £14 million in 2020).

Ritchie was succeeded in the title of Baron Ritchie of Dundee by his second but only surviving son, Charles.

Joseph Austen Chamberlain
1863 - 1937 (73 years old) Liberal
Unionist - Conservative

Chancellor of the Exchequer: (2 Stints)
9 October 1903 - 4 December 1905
(2 years, 1 month and 26 days)
10 January 1919 - 1 April 1921
(2 years, 2 months and 23 days)
Born
16 October 1863, Birmingham
Died
16 March 1937, age 73 London
Title: Sir Austen Chamberlain

Constituencies Represented as MP:
East Worcestershire 1892 - 1914
Birmingham West 1914 - 1937

Other Official Offices held:
Civil Lord of the Admiralty 1895 - 1900
Financial Secretary to the Treasury 1900 - 1902
Postmaster General 1902 - 1903
Secretary of State for India 1915 - 1917
Lord Privy Seal 1921 - 1922
Conservative Leader in the Commons 1921 - 1922
Foreign Secretary 1924 - 1929
First Lord of the Admiralty 1931

Prime Ministers served with as Chancellor:
Arthur Balfour and David Lloyd George

Education: Trinity College, Cambridge.

Sir Joseph Austen Chamberlain, (16 October 1863 – 16 March 1937) served as Chancellor of the Exchequer (twice) and was briefly Conservative Party leader before serving as Foreign Secretary. He was the son of Joseph Chamberlain who was Secretary of State for the Colonies, and the older half-brother of Prime Minister Neville Chamberlain.

Chamberlain was born on 16 October 1863, in Harbone Road Edgbaston, Birmingham, the second child of Joseph Chamberlain and his first wife, Harriet. Just three days after Chamberlains birth, Harriet died, leaving Chamberlain senior to bring up Austen

and his older sister, Beatrice, with the help of his in-laws. Chamberlain senior eventually remarried in 1868 to Harriet's cousin, Florence, with who he had another four children, the eldest being Austen's half-brother and future Prime Minister Neville. Chamberlain was educated from a young age with politics in mind, his father who had been a notable Mayor of Birmingham, was also known for holding high office in both Liberal and Conservative governments. Austen Chamberlain first went to Preparatory School in Birmingham, before moving on to Rugby School at the age of fourteen, and then on to Trinity College, Cambridge, where he read history, graduating in 1885. His father had ambitions for him to be a statesman, and so Chamberlain was sent for further education to Paris, where he spent nine months at the Ecole des Sciences Politiques (Paris Institute of Political Studies). He embraced the Paris culture warmly before moving on to Berlin in 1887 to continue his European education, and although spending twelve months in Germany, he didn't warm to it as he had France. One positive Chamberlain did gain was dining with the 'Iron Chancellor', Otto Von Bismark, which he said left a lasting impression on him.

As soon as he was back in England, Chamberlain was set on course for a political career, and was adopted as the Liberal Unionist candidate for the Hawick district in the Scottish borders. From early in 1888, he was in preparation for the 1892 General Election. However, when the opportunity of election to the House of Commons arose through a By-election in East Worcestershire, Chamberlain took it. The sitting Liberal Unionist MP, George

Hastings was expelled from the House of Commons for fraudulent conversion (stealing as a trustee from a will) in early 1892, to which Chamberlain was elected unopposed at the resulting By-election on 30 March 1892. At the General Election four months later in July 1892, he was returned again, this time beating a Liberal candidate by 5,111 votes to 2,517, for a 2,594 majority. In Parliament Chamberlain was appointed a junior Whip for the Liberal Unionists, shadowing his

AUSTEN AND HIS FATHER JOSEPH

father in matters of policy. Chamberlain's maiden speech in April 1893, on the second reading of the Liberal governments Home Rule Bill, earned rave reviews, including from the Prime Minister, William Gladstone. With victory for the Conservatives/Liberal Unionists at the July/August 1895 General Election, Chamberlain was appointed Civil Lord of the Admiralty, holding the post until 1900, when he became Financial Secretary to the Treasury. But with his father holding the more powerful position of Secretary of State for the Colonies, Chamberlain still remained in his shadow. At the 1900 General Election, which was held during the South African war, Chamberlain was again returned unopposed in East

Worcestershire, after having to refute allegations that he and his father had profited from the war through their armaments firm with government contracts. In November 1900, at the age of 37, Chamberlain was promoted to the position of Financial Secretary to the Treasury, a sign of his promise and potential future progression. Another promotion was forthcoming in August 1902, after Arthur Balfour had succeeded Gascoyne-Cecil as Prime Minister in the July, appointing Chamberlain as Postmaster General, enabling him to sit alongside his father in the Cabinet. Although it wasn't to last long, as relations became strained between Chamberlain senior and Balfour over the thorny issue of tariff reform, Chamberlain senior took it on himself to resign from

AUSTEN CHAMBERLAIN

Cabinet in September 1903, to fight the issue from the freedom of the back benches. The decision didn't negatively impact the younger Chamberlain, in fact in an attempt for balance, Balfour promoted him to the high office of Chancellor of the Exchequer on 9 October 1903. As Chancellor, Chamberlain enhanced his own growing reputation, although the government itself was drifting towards a disastrous demise. Chamberlain presented two Budgets as Chancellor in this period, in 1904 and 1905, both which were described as 'mainly orthodox', but the tariff reform controversy created a split in the government, which led to a crushing defeat in the January 1906 General Election. Chamberlain was re-elected for East Worcestershire as a Liberal Unionist with 63.7% of the vote (10,129 against the Liberal's 5,763) for a majority of 4,366, but the Conservative and Liberal Unionist lost 246 seats in a Liberal landslide. In the July of 1906, Chamberlain senior suffered a severe stroke from which he never fully recovered. He withdrew from the political scene, leaving his son to take over the mantle of the tariff reform campaign, and as possible future leader of the Liberal Unionists. With the Parliament Bill causing a crisis for Balfour in the summer of 1911, and following three successive General Election defeats, Balfour decided to step down as leader in November 1911. Chamberlain was a front runner for the leadership, but he withdrew along with Walter Hume Long to avoid splitting the party, leaving the way open for Andrew Bonar Law to become the new unexpected leader. Bonar Law's promotion led to the formal merger between the Liberal Unionist and the Conservative parties, which was agreed to in May 1912. The following years before the outbreak of the First World War, were dominated by the issue of Ireland, with Chamberlain opposing the dissolution of the Union with Ireland. The Ireland 'problem' was soon overshadowed by the outbreak of the First World War in July 1914, the same month in which Chamberlain senior sadly died. Chamberlain junior resigned his seat in East Worcestershire and stood at the resulting By-election in Birmingham West on 14 July 1914, and was returned unopposed as a Unionist in the seat his father had held for over twenty eight years. With the formation of a coalition wartime government led by H.H Asquith, Chamberlain joined the Cabinet as Secretary of State for India, and when Asquith stepped down as Prime Minister in late 1916, David Lloyd George succeeded him and set up an inquiry into the handling of the Mesopotamia campaign, which had resulted in the Seige of Kut. The lack of provision provided for the sick and wounded in the Mesopotamia conflict had resulted in many deaths from sickness. As Secretary of State for India, Chamberlain took ultimate responsibility and resigned his post in 1917, although he didn't stay out of the Cabinet for long, as Lloyd George appointed him as a Minister without Portfolio on 18 April 1918. After the Armistice with Germany which ended the First World War on 11 November 1918, a General Election was immediately called and was held on 14 December 1918, it was the first General Election (called the 'Coupon Election' due to the number of seats not contested) to be held in a single day, and the first election where all men over twenty one, and women over thirty could vote. The outcome was a landslide victory for the coalition government of Lloyd George. Chamberlain was once again re-elected unopposed in Birmingham West, and on 10 January 1919, Lloyd George appointed him in his second stint as Chancellor of the Exchequer.

Chamberlain faced the massive task of restoring Britain's finances after the expense of the First World War. The National Debt had increased from £754 million in 1913 to a record £6,142 million in 1919, Chamberlain announced in his first Budget a substantial reduction in planned public expenditure, while reducing the rate of the excess profits duty, with a Royal Commission appointed in 1919 to consider the problems of

AUSTEN CHAMBERLAIN

income tax. Chamberlains Budget of April 1920, increased both direct and indirect taxes, while at the same time he sought ever greater economies in the government's spending programmes. On 17 March 1921, Andrew Bonar Law was forced to resign from the government on the grounds of ill health, and Chamberlain faced no serious challenge for the succession to the leadership of the Conservative Party, and he took over office of Lord Privy Seal on 1 April 1921, with Sir Robert Horne taking on the role of Chancellor. Although seen as a possible future Prime Minister, events turned against Chamberlain, the Conservative party were becoming restless with the coalition government and at a famous Carlton Club meeting on 19 October 1922, a motion was passed to fight the next election as an independent party. Chamberlain who was an advocate of maintaining a coalition, resigned. Bonar Law, who had spent six months in the South of France recuperating, re-emerged and was again elected Conservative leader. With the collapse of the coalition, Lloyd George resigned and the King asked Bonar Law to form a government. A General Election was called for 15 November 1922, in which Chamberlain was re-elected in Birmingham West with 61.6% of the vote (15,405 to 9,599) for a majority of 5,806, with the Conservatives gaining an overall majority, winning 344 seats (308 was needed for a majority). Chamberlain was not offered a post in government, and when Bonar Law resigned through ill health after only seven months as Prime Minister, he was succeeded by Stanley Baldwin in 1923. After two more General Elections (there were three General Elections held in less than two years), Baldwin formed his second ministry (after a brief Labour government) and appointed Chamberlain as Foreign Secretary on 3 November 1924. As Foreign Secretary, Chamberlain faced a difficult period in international relations with Europe still very unsettled, France regarded Germany as a potential enemy and Germany felt wronged by the Treaty of Versailles, particularly the 'war guilt' clause. In 1924, the League of Nations was promoting the Geneva Protocol, aimed at strengthening the League and penalising countries going to war, Chamberlain agreed to meet with German Foreign Minister Gustav Stresemann, and the soon to be French Prime Minister Aristide Briand at Locarno, Switzerland. The meetings took place from 5 to 16 October 1925, with negotiations on post war territorial settlements, and the normalising of relations with the defeated German Reich. Seven agreements were reached in Locarno, and they were signed in London on 1 December 1925, becoming known as the 'Locarno Treaties'. They were looked upon as a great success, with all sides agreeing to settle all differences between nations by arbitration, not war. Chamberlain was awarded the Nobel Peace Prize 'for his crucial role in bringing about the Locarno Treaty' and was made a Knight of the order of the Garter for his services to peace. Chamberlain continued as Foreign Secretary until the 1929 General Election, in which time he had to deal with problems in Egypt, China, Soviet Union and the United States, but ill health in 1928 made him take a back seat. He continued as an MP, and at the 1929 General

Election he was re-elected for Birmingham West by the slimmest of margins, when he received 50.1% of the vote, with only a 43 majority (16,862 to 16,819), beating Labour into second place. Chamberlain briefly returned to government in 1931, as First Lord of the Admiralty in Ramsay MacDonald's first National Government, but stepped down later in the same year. Chamberlain stayed on the backbenches and stood in two further General Elections, 1931 and 1935, winning both of them comfortably with 68.1% and 64.35% respectively. From 1934 to 1937 Chamberlain along with Winston Churchill, called for British rearmament to face the growing threat from Hitler's Nazi Germany. Chamberlain was 73 when he died in his London home on 16 March 1937, sadly ten weeks before his half-brother Neville became Prime Minister.

Interesting Austen Chamberlain facts:

Chamberlain was one of the last MPs to maintain the old tradition of wearing a top hat inside the chamber.

Austen and Neville Chamberlain along with Iain Duncan Smith are the only three Conservative leaders not to lead the party into a General Election.

Austen and his father, Joseph, represented Birmingham West continuously between them for over 52 years, from 1885 to 1937.

Chamberlain held honorary degrees from the universities of Oxford, Cambridge, London, Birmingham, Glasgow, Toronto, and Lyons.

Chamberlain left £45,044 18s. 1d. in his will, which is worth approx. £3,137,884 in 2020.

Herbert Henry Asquith (H.H. Asquith) 1852 - 1928 (75 years old) Liberal

Chancellor of the Exchequer:
10 December 1905 - 12 April 1908 (2 years, 4 months and 3 days)
Born
12 September 1852, Morley, West Yorkshire
Died
15 February 1928, age 75, The Wharf, Sutton Courtenay, Oxfordshire

Title: 1st Earl of Oxford and Asquith

Constituencies Represented as MP:
East Fife 1886 - 1918
Paisley 1920 - 1924

Other Official Offices held:
Home Secretary 1892 - 1895
Prime Minister 1908 - 1916
Leader of the House of Commons 1908 - 1916
Secretary of State for War 1914

Prime Minister served with as Chancellor:
Sir Henry Campbell-Bannerman

Education:
Balliol College, Oxford University.

Herbert Henry Asquith, 1st Earl of Oxford and Asquith, (12 September 1852 – 15 February 1928), known as H. H. Asquith, was a Liberal politician who was born in Leeds and represented East Fife and Paisley in Scotland. He introduced significant domestic reform and served as Chancellor from 1905 to 1908. He was the Prime Minister at the time of the First World War and the last Prime Minister to lead a majority Liberal government.

Asquith was born in Morley, in the West Riding of Yorkshire, the younger son of Joseph Dixon Asquith (1825–1860) and his wife Emily, née Willans (1828–1888), in his younger days he was

called Herbert ("Bertie" as a child). After the death of his father, a wool merchant, in 1860, Asquith and his family moved to Huddersfield, where Herbert and his brother, went to day school, later they attended a Moravian boarding school in Fulneck near Leeds. In 1863, at the age of 11, Herbert was sent to London with his brother to live with relatives and to attend the City of London School. In 1870, Asquith won a scholarship to attend Balliol College, Oxford, where he studied the classics and served as President of the Oxford Union. While still at Oxford, Asquith entered Lincoln's Inn to train as a barrister and was admitted to the bar in June 1876.

ASQUITH (LEFT) WITH HIS BROTHER, WILLIAM AND SISTER EMILY

After his graduation, Asquith set up a legal practice with two other junior barristers, but business was lean. Between 1876 and 1884, Asquith supplemented his income by writing regularly for *The Spectator*, which at that time had a broadly Liberal outlook. Asquith's career as a barrister took a turn for the better when in 1883, R. S. Wright invited him to join his chambers at the Inner Temple, with work involving giving legal advice to ministers and government departments. In the July 1886 General Election, Asquith stood as a Liberal candidate in East Fife, where he defeated the previous Liberal candidate (who stood as a

Liberal Unionist) by 2,863 votes to 2,489, a majority of 374.   In September 1891, Asquith's wife of 14 years (Helen Kelsall Melland), died of typhoid fever, following a few days' illness while on a family holiday in Scotland, leaving Asquith widowed with five young children (he remarried three years later). When William Gladstone and the Liberals returned to power in the July 1892 General Election, Asquith again succeeded in East Fife with more votes (3,743 to 3,449), but with a slightly reduced majority of 294. Gladstone offered Asquith a Cabinet office as Home Secretary, but in a government which was sharply divided over fundamental issues. Asquith himself was a strong believer in free trade, Home Rule for Ireland, and social reform, all of which were the vital issues of the day. He remained at the Home Office until the government fell to the Conservatives in the July/August 1895 General Election, in which Asquith was returned in East Fife with an increased majority of 716 (4,332 to 3,616). But with no government post, Asquith divided his time between politics and the bar. He remained in opposition from 1895 until 1906, winning a General Election seat in East Fife in 1900, and doubling his majority to 1,431 (4,141 to 2,710).

After the Liberal landslide at the General Election of 1906, (Asquith won his seat 4,723 to 3,279 a majority of 1,444), Henry Campbell-Bannerman appointed Asquith as Chancellor of the Exchequer, a post he held for over two years and in which he produced three Budgets. Although the first Budget was restrained by what he had inherited, Asquith was able, in his second and third Budgets, to lay the foundations for limited redistribution of wealth and welfare provisions for the poor. Through taxation, he used the increased revenues to fund old-age pensions, which was the first time a British government had provided them.

In June 1906, three suffragettes, Annie Kenney, Adelaide Knight, and Mrs Sparborough were arrested when they tried to obtain an audience with the then Chancellor Asquith, who refused them a delegation. Asquith at that point was a known advocate of denying woman the vote, although in later years he came around to supporting woman's suffrage. When the suffragettes were offered the choice of six weeks in prison or giving up campaigning for one year, they chose prison. In April 1908, Campbell-Bannerman became seriously ill and

Herbert Henry
Asquith

"YOUTH WOULD BE AN IDEAL STATE IF IT CAME A LITTLE LATER IN LIFE"

resigned as Prime Minister, and Asquith was appointed by King Edward VII as the new Prime Minister.

In his first Cabinet reshuffle he promoted David Lloyd George to be his replacement as Chancellor, and Winston Churchill succeeded Lloyd George as President of the Board of Trade. Churchill entered the Cabinet despite being only 33, and despite the fact that he had crossed the floor to become a Liberal only four years previously. Asquith had decided to take on the House of Lords, which often blocked reforming Liberal bills and preventing them from becoming law. The Lords had unwisely rejected Chancellor Lloyd George's 'People's Budget' of 1909, leading to a General Election in December 1910, in which Asquith was once again returned in East Fife, with 5,242 votes against the

Conservative's 3,183 for a majority of 2,059. The 1910 General Election was billed as a referendum on a Lords versus Commons issue. The General Election resulted in a hung Parliament, with the Conservative and Liberal Unionists receiving the largest number of votes, but the Liberals the largest number of seats (274 against 272). Asquith formed a government with the support of the Irish Parliamentary Party who had 71 seats, and although Asquith had no overall majority, he was convinced that he had the public support he needed.

He therefore introduced the Parliament Bill which became law in 1911, forcing the Lords into passing the Bill with the threat that hundreds of new Liberal peers would be created if they did not. The Parliament Act of 1911 drastically changed the way the British government operated. The act prevented the Lords from vetoing any financial legislation, and also reduced the duration of any Parliament term from seven years to five years. In addition, the act provided for MP's to be paid, to enable 'ordinary' people who were not in possession of an independent income to enter into politics. The 1911 act ultimately reduced the power that the House of Lords wielded over Britain.

Although it was successful in implementing significant reforms, Asquith's government faced additional challenges in the years between 1911 and 1914. Most pressing was the growing crisis in Ireland. In 1912, Asquith renewed attempts to introduce Home Rule in Ireland, but Unionists, comprised largely of Conservatives and the military, wanted Ireland to remain as part of the British Union. The situation deteriorated to such an extent that in 1914, it appeared civil war would result. Asquith was successful in getting the Home Rule Law passed, but it was delayed by the outbreak of World War I, postponed further and then never enacted. The assassination of Archduke Franz Ferdinand of Austria (and his wife) in Sarajevo on 28 June 1914, initiated a month of unsuccessful diplomatic attempts to avoid war. The First World War broke out in July 1914, but a dearth of munitions in 1915 resulted in Asquith having to form a new coalition government (elections were suspended for the duration of the war). The pressure continued on Asquith with the ongoing

stalemate on the Western Front. In 1916, the Easter Rising in Dublin and the Battle of the Somme, with its massive casualties, led to Asquith being blamed in the press for the military failures. The long-awaited introduction of conscription was insufficient to quell dissent, and he resigned on 5 December 1916, replaced by David Lloyd George. After resigning, Asquith continued in his post as Liberal leader, even after losing his seat in East Fife in the December 1918 General Election, to the Unionist, Alexander Sprot, by 8,996 to 6,996 votes (a majority of 2,002). He eventually

ASQUITH'S STATUE IN PARLIAMENT

regained a seat by standing in, and winning, a By-election in Paisley in 1920, with 14,736 votes against the Labour Co-op's 11,902 for a majority of 2,834. Asquith also stood in his final election in the November 1922 General Election, when he was

again elected for Paisley with 15,005 votes against 14,689, for a majority of 316. In 1925, Asquith was granted the title of Earl of Oxford and elevated to the House of Lords, and in October 1926, he finally resigned as Liberal leader. He filled his retirement with reading, writing and developed an interest in painting and sculpture.

Asquith died, aged 75, after having two strokes in two years, at The Wharf on the morning of 15 February 1928.

Interesting H.H Asquith facts:

Asquith's fondness for fine wines and spirits, earned him the nickname "Squiffy".

The award winning actress Helena Bonham-Carter (1966) is Asquith's great-granddaughter.

Asquith's will was proven on 9 June 1928, with his estate amounting to £9345 9s. 2d. equivalent to approx £590,940 in 2020.

Asquith's eldest son Raymond, was killed at the Somme in 1916.

Asquith is the only Prime Minister to have taken office on foreign soil. King Edward VII was in Biarritz so Asquith travelled there for the official 'kissing hands' with the monarch.

Asquith had five children by his first wife, Helen, and two surviving children (three others died at birth or in infancy) by his second wife, Margot.

In the last years of his life he wrote a number of novels, the best known being *The Genesis of the War* (1923), *Fifty Years of Parliament* (1926), and *Memories and Reflections* (1928).

A Blue commemorative plaque is on display at 20 Cavendish Square, London, showing that Asquith lived there.

Asquith's second son, Herbert (1881-1947) was a soldier, writer and poet, who wrote poems including "The Volunteer" and "The Fallen Subaltern", the latter being a tribute to fallen soldiers.

David Lloyd George
1863 - 1945 (82 years old) Liberal

Chancellor of the Exchequer:
12 April 1908 - 25 May 1915
(7 years, 1 month and 14 days)

Born
17 January 1863, Chorlton-on-Medlock, Lancashire
Died
26 March 1945, age 82, Ty Newydd, Caernarfonshire
Title: 1st Earl Lloyd George of Dwyfor

Constituency Represented as MP:
Caernarfon Boroughs 1890 - 1945

Other Official Offices held:
President of the Board of Trade 1905 - 1908
Minister of Munitions 1915 - 1916
Secretary of State for War 1916
Prime Minister 1916 - 1922
Father of the House of Commons 1929 - 1945

Prime Minister served with as Chancellor:
H.H Asquith

Education:
Llanystumdwy National School.

David Lloyd George, 1st Earl Lloyd-George of Dwyfor, (17 January 1863 – 26 March 1945) was a Welsh Member of Parliament for Caerarfon Boroughs from 1890 to 1945. He served as Chancellor for over seven years leading into the First World War. He was also the Prime Minister of the United Kingdom from 1916 to 1922, and was the last Liberal to hold the post of Prime Minister.

Lloyd George was born on 17 January 1863 in Chorlton-on-Medlock, Manchester to Welsh parents, and was brought up as a Welsh-speaker. His father, William George, had been a teacher in both London and Liverpool. On his father's death in Pembrokeshire in 1864 his mother moved with her children to Llanystumdwy, to live with her brother, Richard Lloyd (1834 - 1917). Lloyd George was educated at the Llanystumdwy National School and passed the Preliminary Law Examination in 1877, taking his final with honours in 1884. In 1885 he began to practice as a solicitor in Cricieth and gained a reputation as a fearless advocate and eloquent speaker.

On 10 April 1890, Lloyd George was elected Liberal MP at a By-election for Caernarfon, aged only 27, winning the seat with a very small majority of 18 (1,963 votes against the Conservative's 1,945). Caernarfon was a closely fought seat that Lloyd George would go on to represent for the following 55 years. At the July 1892 General Election, he increased his majority slightly to 196 (2,154 to 1,958 votes). At the time backbench members of the House of Commons were not paid, so Lloyd George supported himself and his growing family by continuing to practise as a solicitor. During the 10 years of Liberal opposition that followed the election of 1895, he became a leading figure in the radical wing of the party, and was elected again in the September/October General Election with 2,412 votes against the Conservatives 2,116, a majority of 296. Lloyd George bitterly and courageously opposed the Boer war (1899-1902), but while attempting to address a Liberal meeting in Birmingham in December 1901, his life was threatened during an anti-war speech by an angry mob, but he managed to escape from the building dressed as a policeman. In 1905, he entered the new Liberal Cabinet after being appointed President of the Board of Trade by Sir Henry Campbell-Bannerman.

The first priority of the Liberal government on taking office was the repeal of the 1902 Education Act. Lloyd George took the lead, and the bill was introduced in the Commons on 9 April 1906, the

bill passed the House of Commons greatly amended, but was then completely mangled by the House of Lords. For the rest of the year, Lloyd George made numerous public speeches attacking the House of Lords for mutilating the bill with wrecking amendments, but was rebuked by King Edward VII for his speeches. At the January/February 1906 General Election, Lloyd George's popularity was starting to shine through, and reflected with his first majority over one thousand (1,224) winning the seat with 3,221 votes against 1,997.

When H.H Asquith became Prime Minister on 8 April 1908, Lloyd George succeeded him Chancellor of the Exchequer, with his first task as Chancellor being the 1908 Budget. The Budget had already been prepared by Asquith, it introduced the first old-age pensions for over seventies, which paid five shillings a week or 7s 6d for married couples. By 1909, when his own first Budget was due, the Liberal government was in trouble. Much of its reforming legislation had been blocked by the House of Lords and Lloyd George feared that the fledgling Labour Party might steal its thunder. At the same time, the need for more battleships to counter the looming threat from Germany, made it harder to find the money for further reforms. Lloyd George's response was what became known as the 'People's Budget', which was supported in Cabinet by both Asquith and Winston Churchill, and was introduced with a four hour speech in the House of Commons by

"DIPLOMATS WERE INVENTED SIMPLY TO WASTE TIME"
LLOYD GEORGE

Lloyd George, on April 29 1909. Income tax and death duties were both raised, and a new supertax at sixpence in the pound was levied on the amount of incomes above £5,000 a year (equivalent to more than £350,000 today). Lloyd Georges' most controversial proposals, however, were for a Capital Gains tax on 'unearned increment', in the value of land created. Not by the landowner, but by the community at large, and a duty placed on the capital value of undeveloped land. The Budget raised fierce opposition from rich landowners in the City, and in the House of Lords. The Budget finally passed the Commons on November 3rd and was passed to the Lords. In the first instance the Budget was thrown out by the Lords, after having endured 549 divisions which occupied 90 hours of voting time, and was decisively voted down on 30 November by 350 votes to 75. The inevitable result was a General Election, which was held in January 1910. Lloyd George was comfortably returned in Caernarfon again with a majority of 1,078 (3,183 to 2,105), and the Liberals remained in power, but only with the support of the Irish Parliamentary Party and Labour. The Budget eventually passed through the Commons again, and this time was accepted by the Upper House, becoming law in April 1910. Another General Election was held in December 1910 to try to break the deadlock achieved in the January election, Lloyd

George was again elected, with a majority of 1,208 (3,112 to 1,904) and the Liberals, together with the Irish Nationalists and Labour, retained their Commons majority. The key consequence, was the Parliament Act of 1911, which severely reduced the powers of the House of Lords. Lloyd George's next major reform was the 1911 National Insurance Act. This provided British workers with insurance against illness and unemployment. All wage-earners had to join his health scheme, in which each worker made a weekly contribution, with both the employer and the State adding an amount. In return for these payments, free medical attention and medicines were made available, as well as a guaranteed 7-shillings per week unemployment benefit. Towards the end of July 1914, it became clear that the country was on the verge of war with Germany. Despite his initial reluctance to sanction Britain's entry into the First World War, Lloyd George served in Asquith's coalition war cabinet as Minister for Munitions and as Secretary for War. In December 1916, unhappy with Asquith's conduct of the war, and with ambitions of his own, he conspired with the Conservative's to oust Asquith and succeed him as the Prime Minister. The effective overthrow of Asquith caused a split in the party from which it never entirely recovered, with Asquith and several other prominent Liberals resigning from the government. Throughout the war, although Lloyd George argued constantly with military leaders on how to conduct the battles, his leadership was a huge reason the war was won. One of Lloyd George's great contributions to the war, was formulating the need for convoys that travelled the ocean as a possible antidote to the U-boat attacks. In late April 1917,

DAVID LLOYD GEORGE
STATUE IN PARLIAMENT
SQUARE

the War Cabinet discussed the 'convoy controversy', and although not a popular avenue with certain members of the Admiralty, his idea became the standard for shipping. Just weeks before the end of the conflict, on 11 September 1918, Lloyd George was cheered by crowds that lined the streets to greet his arrival in Manchester. But within hours, he was confined to bed having collapsed with a fever (the 'Spanish Flu' pandemic of 1918-1920). He spent the next 10 days immobile with a respirator to aid his breathing. His plight was hushed up for fear that the news would sap public morale and hand the German enemy a propaganda coup. The war finally ended when Germany was forced to seek an armistice (truce) on November 11, 1918. Lloyd George, as Prime Minister, was acclaimed as the man who had won the war, and in the December 1918 General Election, the coalition won a huge majority. It was also notable for being the first election in which women were allowed to vote. The Representation of the People Act was passed, which allowed women over the age of 30 who met a property qualification to vote. Although 8.5 million women met this criteria, it was only about two-thirds of the total population of women in the UK. The same Act abolished property and other restrictions for men, and extended the vote to virtually all men over the age of 21. Additionally, men in the armed forces could vote from the age of 19. The electorate increased from eight to 21 million, but although it was a start there was still huge inequality between women and men.

The 1918 Education Act was drawn up by Lloyd George's President of the Board of Education, Herbert Fisher, which raised the school leaving age to fourteen and included the provision of ancillary services (medical inspection, nursery schools, special needs provision, etc). In 1919, Lloyd George signed the Treaty of Versailles, which established the League of Nations and the war reparations settlement. He was troubled by domestic problems at home though, his agreement to the independence of the South of Ireland (Irish Treaty) had stalled after prolonged negotiations (it was finally signed on 6 December 1921). But he had to preside over a period of depression, unemployment, strikes and serious allegations that he had sold honours, resulting in a fading of his popularity. After a famous meeting at the Carlton Club, the Conservative Party sealed Lloyd George's fate on 19 October 1922, by voting in favour of the motion to end the coalition and fight the election 'as an independent party with its own leader and its own programme'. Lloyd George submitted his resignation to the King that afternoon and although he remained politically

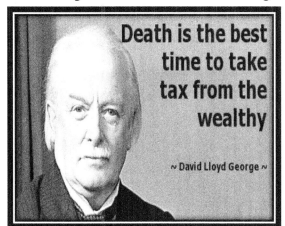

active for some years, he never again held office. In 1926, he set in train the Liberal Industrial Enquiry, and from 1933 to 1936, he wrote his War Memoirs and 'The truth about the peace treaties' which was published in 1938. In August 1936, he visited Germany and met Hitler saying "Chancellor Adolf Hitler is one of the greatest of the many great men I have ever met". When war came in 1939, he took no part in its direction but remained a member of the House of Commons until January 1945, when he resigned his seat and was granted an earldom, taking as his titles Earl Lloyd-George of Dwyfor and Viscount Gwynedd. Lloyd George died aged 82, on 26 March 1945. He was buried according to his own wishes in the wooded slope above the river Dwyfor near his home.

Interesting David Lloyd George facts:

Lloyd George was the last Liberal leader to hold the post of Prime Minister.

In the Marconi scandal of 1913, Lloyd George was accused of insider trading regarding government contracts with the British Marconi company, Lloyd George told the House of Commons that he had not speculated in the shares of "that company", he had in fact bought shares in the American Marconi Company.

The Lloyd George Museum Trust was founded in 1948, three years after his death. The main exhibition was opened in 1960, and it is run by Gwynedd Council.

Lloyd George is the only Prime Minister to speak Welsh as his first language.

BLUE PLAQUE IN WANDSWORTH

Although Wales has been part of the United Kingdom since the Middle Ages, Lloyd George is the only Welshman (to date) to be the country's Prime Minister.

The "Lloyd George's Crown" is a coin representing the first old age pension to be paid in Wales.

The Canadian historian Margaret MacMillan, who detailed Lloyd George's role at the 1919 Peace Conference in her book, *Peacemakers* is Lloyd George's great-granddaughter.

It was announced in the 1945 New Year Honours that Lloyd George would be made an Earl (Earl Lloyd-George of Dwyfor), on 12 February 1945, however, he did not live long enough to take his seat in the House of Lords.

Lloyd George left £139,855 8s. 2d. in his will, which is worth approx. £6,172,836 in 2020.

Reginald McKenna
1863 - 1943 (80 years old) Liberal

Chancellor of the Exchequer:
27 May 1915 - 10 December 1916
(1 year, 6 months and 14 days)

Born
6 July 1863, Kensington, London
Died
6 September 1943, age 80, London

Title: None

Constituency Represented as MP:
North Monmouthshire 1895 - 1918
Other Official Offices held:
Financial Secretary to the Treasury 1905 - 1907
President of the Board of Education 1907 - 1908
First Lord of the Admiralty 1908 - 1911
Home Secretary 1911 - 1915
Prime Minister served with as Chancellor:
H.H Asquith
Education:
Trinity Hall, Cambridge University.

Reginald McKenna, (6 July 1863 – 6 September 1943) was a Liberal politician who represented North Monmouthshire from 1895 to 1918. His served in Cabinet under Henry Campbell-Bannerman as President of the Board of Education, and also served as First Lord of the Admiralty. His most significant roles were as Home Secretary and Chancellor of the Exchequer during the premiership of H. H. Asquith.

McKenna was born in Kensington, London, the fifth son and youngest child of William Columban McKenna and his wife Emma. McKenna's father was a civil servant with the Inland Revenue but due to financial difficulties, McKenna senior and the two eldest sons stayed and worked in London, while Reginald, along with his other brothers and sisters moved to France with their mother where the cost of living was a lot cheaper. McKenna was educated firstly in St Malo, France until 1874, where he became fluent in French before moving to Ebersdorf, Germany until 1877, where he became fluent in German. On returning to England McKenna attended King's College School, London, where he won a scholarship to Trinity Hall, Cambridge, studying mathematics and ranking among the senior optimes in 1885.

After leaving Cambridge, McKenna was called to the bar by the Inner Temple in 1887, building a successful law practice in the process. McKenna's first foray into politics came when he stood in the July 1892 General Election as a Liberal, but losing to Conservative candidate Percy Thornton by 5,710 to 4,526 for a majority of 644. McKenna had to wait until the next General Election in July/August 1895 for his next opportunity, when he stood successfully in North Monmouthshire, being elected with 54.2% of the vote, 4,965 to 4,203 a majority of 762. McKenna soon became active in the House of Commons, representing his Wales constituency and working closely with David Lloyd George. He attacked the Conservative governments Education Bill of

1897, and the South African War (1899-1902). When the South African War concluded, McKenna fought against Joseph Chamberlain's protectionist crusade, helping to found the Free Trade Union in 1903. McKenna furthered his reputation by opposing the government's anti-temperance Licensing Bill of

REGINALD MCKENNA

1904, alongside Lloyd George and the new Liberal recruit Winston Churchill. When Campbell-Bannerman formed a Liberal government in December 1905, McKenna was appointed Financial Secretary of the Treasury, and at the January/February 1906 General Election, McKenna was re-elected in North Monmouthshire with 71% of the vote (7,730 to the Conservative's 3,155). He worked closely with the Chancellor, H.H Asquith, until January 1907, when he was appointed President of the Board of Education, ahead of Churchill. As President of the Board of Education (his first Cabinet post), McKenna introduced a school medical service which was set up to carry out compulsory physical examination of schoolchildren, and implemented free places in secondary schools. When Asquith became Prime Minister in April 1908, he appointed McKenna as First Lord of the Admiralty, in which position McKenna urged that with the Anglo-German relationship taking a turn for the worse, a yearly program of building six new dreadnoughts per year should be enacted. McKenna's plan was opposed by both Lloyd George and Churchill, who wanted to build fewer ships and spend more on social reform programs instead. McKenna got his wish and eighteen new dreadnoughts were built by 1911, which ultimately gave Britain a big advantage over Germany at the start of the First World War. McKenna, who by this time, had distanced himself from Lloyd George and Churchill over the naval and 'People's Budget' which had forced Prime Minister Asquith into change in November 1911. McKenna swapped offices with Churchill, with McKenna becoming Home Secretary and Churchill First Lord of the Admiralty. As Home Secretary, McKenna brought about the Mental Deficiency Act (1913) which made provisions for treatment for people deemed 'feeble minded' and 'moral

UNIONIST ELECTION SLOGAN

defectives', and introduced the Criminal Justice Administration Act (1914) which was brought in to diminish the number of cases committed to prison. When the Marconi affair happened in 1913 (accusations of insider trading by the Liberal government in regards to a lucrative contract with the British Marconi company), McKenna who was not involved, was of the opinion that Lloyd George and other ministers accused, should resign. Also in 1913, he voted against compulsory military training, and at the start of the First World War in 1924, McKenna as the person in charge of State Security, investigated over six thousand espionage cases, of which none produced any traitors. When Asquith formed a wartime coalition government in May 1915, McKenna who wasn't in favour of a coalition, became Chancellor of the Exchequer, with his endeavour to pay for the war without debilitating Britain's economic future. His wartime Budgets of September 1915 and April 1916, included unprecedented excess profit tax, large increases in income tax and what became known as 'McKenna's duties', which was custom duties imposed on 'luxury' items such as cars, cinematographic film, musical instruments and clocks. All the duties were intended to be temporary war initiatives, but were fated to become permanent. McKenna had to negotiate new loans from American banks due to the enormous cost of the war, and strongly fought against military conscription, contending that it would ruin the economy and hamper the war effort, by stripping industry of its manpower. McKenna continued to have big differences with his predecessor Lloyd George, and tried in vain to get Asquith to dismiss him, but after a decisive meeting on 4 December 1916, Asquith resigned

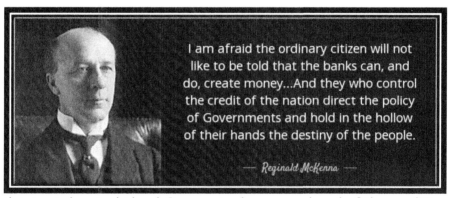

I am afraid the ordinary citizen will not like to be told that the banks can, and do, create money...And they who control the credit of the nation direct the policy of Governments and hold in the hollow of their hands the destiny of the people.

— Reginald McKenna —

the next day and Lloyd George took over as head of the coalition government. With the fall of Asquith, McKenna also resigned himself to the opposition benches, and a split had occurred in the Liberal party, which resulted in Lloyd George becoming the last Liberal Prime Minister to date. The December 1918 General Election was called on the conclusion of the First World War, McKenna's North Monmouthshire constituency had been abolished, so he stood in Pontypool, but came third behind Labour and the Unionist, receiving 28.5% of the vote (6,160, Labour 8,438 and Unionist 7,021). With the defeat, McKenna left politics and became a director of the Midland Bank, a position he would keep for the rest of his life. Two future Prime Minister's (Andrew Bonar Law and Stanley Baldwin) did try to tempt him out of his political retirement with the offer of the Chancellorship again, but

McKenna declined on both occasions. In general, McKenna enjoyed good health and kept physically fit until the time of his death on 6 September 1943, aged 80. He died in his London residence above the Midland Banks Pall Mall branch, and was buried at St Andrew's Church in Mells, Somerset.

Interesting Reginald McKenna facts:

McKenna's nephew, Stephen McKenna, was a popular novelist who published a biography of his uncle in 1948, titled *Reginald McKenna, 1863-1943: A Memoir*.

While McKenna was studying at Cambridge University he was a notable rower. In 1886, he was a member of the Trinity Hall Boat Club eight that won the Grand Challenge Cup at Henley Royal Regatta. He rowed bow in the winning Cambridge boat in the 1887 Boat Race. Also in 1887 he was a member of the Trinity Hall coxless four that won the Stewards' Challenge Cup at Henley.

McKenna featured on the cover of Time magazine on 3 March, 1924, the article inside discussed reparation and stated 'No. 2 Committee of Experts is led by the strong, silent English financier-statesman, Reginald McKenna'.

McKenna married when he was forty-five to Pamela Jekyll who was twenty six years his junior, they had two sons, Michael and David.

McKenna's wife, Pamela died two months after he passed away in November 1943.

Mckenna left £89,948 1s. 4d. in his will, which is worth approx. £3,970,071 in 2020.

Andrew Bonar Law
1858 - 1923 (65 years old) Conservative

Chancellor of the Exchequer:
10 December 1916 – 10 January 1919
(2 years, 1 month and 1 day)

Born
16 September 1858, Kingston, Colony of New Brunswick, Canada
Died
30 October 1923, age 65, Kensington, London

Title: None

Constituencies Represented as MP:
Glasgow Blackfriars 1900 - 1906
Dulwich 1906 - 1910
Bootle 1911 - 1918
Glasgow Central 1918 - 1923

Other Official Offices held:
Parliamentary Secretary of the Board of Trade 1902 - 1905
Secretary of State for the Colonies 1915 - 1916
Prime Minister 1922 - 1923
Leader of the House of Commons 1922 - 1923

Prime Minister served with as Chancellor:
David Lloyd George

Education:
High School of Glasgow.

Andrew Bonar Law, (16 September 1858 – 30 October 1923) was a Conservative politician who served Chancellor of the Exchequer for over two years, and as Prime Minister and Leader of the House of Commons for just over six months.

Andrew Bonar Law (he disliked the name Andrew and never used it) so his family and close friends called him Bonar (rhyming with honour) was born in Rexton, on the east coast of Canada. The son of the Rev. James Law (1822 - 1882), who was pastor of St.

BONAR LAW'S HOUSE IN REXTON

Andrew's Presbyterian Church for 32 years from 1845 to 1877. James Law had five children, four boys and a girl. Only one of the family, Robert, remained in Rexton until his death. Bonar Law's first three years of public schooling were spent in Rexton, but after the death of his mother, at the age of twelve, an aunt took him to Scotland to live with her, and he completed his high school in Glasgow. It was the only formal education he ever received as he finished school aged sixteen. His first job was that of a bookkeeper for an iron firm and when he retired in business to enter politics, he was head of the largest iron company in Scotland.

Although leaving school at sixteen, Bonar Law became a member of the Glasgow Parliamentary Debating Association, where he gained the kind of training that the Oxford and Cambridge unions provided for many of his future colleagues. Early in 1898, Bonar Law was named the prospective Conservative candidate for the Glasgow Blackfriars and Hutchesontown division of Glasgow, historically a safe Liberal seat. At the 'Khaki' General Election of 1900 (named khaki due to it being heavily influenced by post-Boar war sentiment) Bonar Law was elected to the House of

Commons as a Conservative for Glasgow Blackfriars and Hutchesontown with 56.8% of the vote, a majority of 990 (4,130 to 3,140 votes). On 11 August 1902, with his proven experience in business matters, and his skill as an economic spokesman for the government, Arthur Balfour offered him the position of

Parliamentary Secretary to the Board of Trade, which he accepted. At the January/February 1906 General Election, Bonar Law again stood in Blackfriars and Hutchesontown but was defeated by the Labour candidate George Barnes by 3,284 votes against 2,974, a majority of 310, with his percentage of votes dropping by over 20% (35.8%). Bonar Law wasn't out of Parliament for long though, as he stood in a By-election on 15 May 1906 in Dulwich, winning the seat with 6,709 votes to 5,430 a majority of 1,279.

Bonar Law married Annie Pitcairn Robley on 24 March 1891, and they had six children, four boys and two

ANDREW BONAR LAW

girls. Sadly Annie died on 31 October 1909, and although devastated, he continued his political career, deciding to work even harder as a strategy to cope with his grief. At the December 1910 General Election, Bonar Law was re-elected in Dulwich with an increased majority of 2,418 (8,472 to 6,054) and then stood for, and unexpectedly won the Conservative party leadership in 1911, after Austen Chamberlain and Walter Long stepped down to avoid splitting the party. The Conservative party had bitter divisions over tariffs at this time, and as a result Bonar Law encouraged his own extremists to pursue their attack on Irish Home Rule, in the belief that this was a calculated way to restore party unity. The outbreak of First World War in July 1914 resolved the Irish dilemma, but it created a new one. Bonar Law found himself under pressure, both to maintain the party truce and to follow his backbenchers and the press in attacking the Liberals' conduct of the war. In May 1915, he made a private agreement with H.H Asquith to join a coalition, and in December 1916, in collaboration with David Lloyd George, they presented Asquith with proposals for the reorganisation of the machinery of war which led to Asquith's resignation. Bonar Law then served under Lloyd George as Chancellor, Leader of the House of Commons and effectively the deputy premier. He was also a member of the War Cabinet trying to placate a smooth period of joint co-operation. Bonar Law, as Chancellor, had to find the funds to finance the war effort, and so in 1917, he raised the enormous sum of £600 million via a War Loan campaign, overruling his officials and the Governor of the Bank of England by setting interest rates at 5, rather than 6 per cent, thus securing a significant saving to the nation. He borrowed huge sums, but in total he found 26 per cent of wartime expenditure from taxation, and he astutely managed war-loan and war-bond programs. When the war ended on 11 November 1918, Bonar Law judged that the Conservatives' best interests lay in keeping the coalition and fighting the election under Lloyd George's leadership. At the 'Coupon Election' on December 14, 1918 - the 'Coupon Election' which was so-called, as candidates for the Liberal Party, who had supported the coalition government of Lloyd George during World War One, were issued with a letter of support signed by both Lloyd George and Bonar Law. Asquith, the official leader of the Liberals, referred to the letter as a 'Coupon'. Where a 'Coupon' Liberal stood for election, no Conservative challenged him. Where a Conservative stood, no 'Coupon' Liberal challenged him. Therefore there was no chance of a coalition candidate competing against another. The coalition was re-elected by a landslide, with the 1918 General Election also being remembered as the first election when everyone in the UK voted on the same day (14

December 1918), however, the count did not begin until December 28. 10,786,818 people voted which was over double the voters of December 1910, when 5,235,238 voted. Bonar Law stood in the General Election for Glasgow Central, winning with a large 78.8% of the vote (17,653 to 4,736 a majority of 12,917). Lloyd George and Bonar Law then formed an unlikely, but highly successful partnership, but Bonar Law's resignation from the government, (but not from the Commons) on 17 March 1921, due

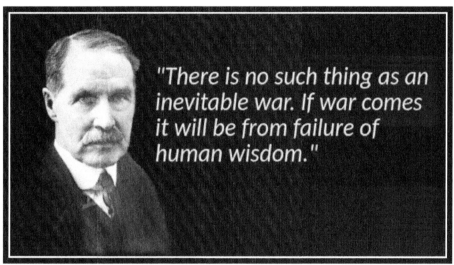

"There is no such thing as an inevitable war. If war comes it will be from failure of human wisdom."

to dangerously high blood pressure, signalled the beginning of the end of the coalition government. Bonar Law's health improved after six months in the South of France, and on his return he became critical of the policies of the government. At the Carlton Club on 19 October 1922, Bonar Law along with Stanley Baldwin, was instrumental in the Tories voting by 187 against 88 to fight the next election on their own. The Conservative withdrawal from the coalition forced Lloyd George to resign. King George V then invited Bonar Law to form a new administration on 23 October 1922, and for the first time since 1910, a single party with a parliamentary majority governed Britain. The wartime coalition government had ended, and so on the 15 November 1922, a General Election was held. Bonar Law was re-elected in Glasgow Central with 49.9% of the vote (15,437 to Labour's 12,923 a majority of 2,514) and the Conservative Party won 344 seats, and formed the next government. The Labour Party rose from 57 to 142 seats after promising to nationalise the mines and railways, along with a massive house building programme and revising the peace treaties. The Liberal Party increased their vote and went from 36 to 62 seats. Sadly, Bonar Law had just seven short months (209 days) as Prime Minister, before throat cancer forced his retirement in May 1923.

He died six months later on 30 October 1923, aged 65.

Interesting Andrew Bonar Law facts:

Bonar Law's two eldest sons were both killed whilst fighting in the First World War.

ONSLOW GARDENS LONDON

Bonar Law was a keen amateur chess player and would challenge fellow commuters to matches on his many train journeys.

In the 1981 TV series 'The Life and Times of David Lloyd George' Bonar Law appears in two episodes and is played by Fulton Mackay.

Bonar Law was the shortest-serving Prime Minister of the 20th century, serving for 209 days.

He was the first British Prime Minister to be born outside the British Isles.

Bonar Law left £35,736 in his will (approx. £2,209,898 in 2020).

Sir Robert Horne
1871 - 1940 (69 years old) Conservative

Chancellor of the Exchequer:
1 April 1921 – 19 October 1922
(1 year, 6 months and 9 days)

Born
28 February 1871, Slamannan, Stirlingshire
Died
3 September 1940, age 69

Title: Viscount Horne of Slamannan

Constituency Represented as MP:
Glasgow Hillhead 1918 - 1906

Other Official Offices held:
Minister of Labour 1919 - 1920
President of the Board of Trade 1920 - 1921

Prime Minister served with as Chancellor:
David Lloyd George

Education:
University of Glasgow.

Robert Stevenson Horne, 1st Viscount Horne of Slamannan, (28 February 1871 – 3 September 1940) was an academic, legal, administrative businessman who was a board member of several companies including directorships of the Suez Canal Company, Chairman of the Great Western Railway Company and director of several other companies. He served under David Lloyd George as a Unionist politician and as Minister of Labour between 1919 and 1920, as President of the Board of Trade between 1920 and 1921 and as Chancellor of the Exchequer between 1921 and 1922.

Horne was born on 25 February 1871, the youngest son to the Church of Scotland Minister, Robert Stevenson Horne and his wife Mary. Horne was educated at George Watson's College in Edinburgh and then the University of Glasgow, where he obtained a first-class degree in mental philosophy in 1893 and a university fellowship in 1894. While in university, Horne took a strong interest in politics and became President of the University Conservative Club. He then spent a year as a philosophy lecturer at the University College of North Wales in Bangor, spending the next four years between 1896 and 1900 as an examiner at the University of Aberdeen, but he was keen to follow a legal career.

Horne joined the Scottish bar in 1896, specialising in commercial and shipping cases, and he was made a King's Council in 1910. Horne's first taste of political electioneering came in the January 1910 General Election, when he stood as the Conservative candidate in Stirlingshire, but was beaten into second place by the Liberal, William Chapple by 10,122 votes to 6,417 (3,705 majority). The same two candidates also contested the December 1910 General Election in Stirlingshire, with the same outcome, Chapple beating Horne 9,183 votes to 6,487 for a reduced majority of 2,696. With the commencement of the First World War in 1914, Horne served briefly as the secretary to the agricultural section of the national service department, before joining the Royal Engineers, with an honorary rank of Lieutenant-Colonel, he worked on the railways on the Western Front. In 1917, Horne joined the Admiralty as Assistant Inspector-General of Transportation and then became Director of Materials and Priority. Finally before the end of the war in 1918, Horne became Director of Labour and Third Civil Lord. At the conclusion of the First World War, a General Election was held on 14 December 1918, in which Horne stood in the new seat of Glasgow Hillhead as a Unionist, and was elected to Parliament with a majority of 8,617 (12,803 votes to 4,186). Horne's organisational work and contributions to the war effort were rewarded with a KBE (Knight Commander of the Most Excellent Order of the British Empire) and the offer of rapid ministerial advancement. He then had the unusual distinction upon entering Parliament, of his first political office being in Cabinet, with a seat on the front benches. During the period of reconstruction after the war, Horne was made Minister of Labour in 1919, where he had to deal with a wave of industrial unrest, negotiating with Union leaders in railways, coal and road transport disputes, and was responsible for the Unemployment Insurance Act of 1920. In March 1920, he was appointed President of the Board of Trade, where he had to address the issue of trade policy and negotiate a trade agreement with Soviet Russia, while resisting calls for the nationalisation of the coal industry. In April 1921, Horne was appointed by Lloyd George as Chancellor of the Exchequer, but as he was still dealing with the threat of a national coal strike, his predecessor Austen Chamberlain gave the following Budget speech. In his 1922 Budget, Horne faced a severe economic downturn, but he did manage to cut expenditure on housing while imposing education and civil service cuts, enabling him to reduce the standard rate of income tax from 6s. to 5s. He was in favour of prolonging the coalition government, but after the Conservative Party's insistence of fighting the next General Election as an independent party, after the famous meeting at the Carlton Club in October 1922, Horne joined other 'Chamberlainite' former ministers in refusing to join Bonar Law's Conservative government. Horne stood in the Glasgow Hillhead seat on 15 November 1922, winning with a 4,959 majority (12,272 votes to 7,313). When Stanley Baldwin became Prime Minister, Horne was offered other Cabinet positions, but he turned them down in favour of more lucrative roles in the City and in commerce. He retained his parliamentary seat until 1937, winning in seven consecutive General Elections (1923 - 4,698 majority, 1924 – 7,615 majority, 1929 – 7,330 majority, 1931 – 13,740 majority and 1935 – 9,801 majority) but he preferred his place among the business elite to Parliament. He chaired numerous high paying companies and was a noted member of the 'high society' and regular party goer. Baldwin took a dim view of Horne's lifestyle, with his frequent switching of directorships in search of higher fees and his preference for private income before public service. Baldwin said of Horne that he was "that rare thing, a Scots cad" a term that stuck with Horne. Baldwin therefore never considered him for high office again. Horne gave up his seat in the House of Commons in May 1937, and was enobled as Viscount Horne of Slamannan. He died on 3 September 1940, aged 69, after an operation for appendicitis.

Interesting Robert Horne facts:

Horne never married and his peerage became extinct upon his death.

Horne was the Rector of the University of Aberdeen from 1921 – 1924.

Horne's wealth at his death was £64,923 8s 6d, worth approx. £3,658,325 in 2020.

Horne was a renowned and often 'risque' after dinner speaker.

Stanley Baldwin
1867 – 1947 (80 years old) Conservative

Chancellor of the Exchequer:
27 October 1922 – 27 August 1923
(10 months and 1 day)

Born
3 August 1867, Bewdley, Worcestershire
Died
14 December 1947, age 80, Stourport-on-Severn, Worcestershire

Title: 1st Earl Baldwin of Bewdley

Constituency Represented as MP:
Bewdley 1908 - 1937

Other Official Offices held:
Financial Secretary to the Treasury 1917 - 1921
President of the Board of Trade 1921 - 1922
Prime Minister 1923 - 1924, 1924 - 1929 and 1935 - 1937
Lord President of the Council 1931 - 1935

Prime Minister served with as Chancellor:
Andrew Bonar Law and Himself

Education:
Trinity College, Cambridge University.

Stanley Baldwin, 1st Earl Baldwin of Bewdley, (3 August 1867 – 14 December 1947) was a Conservative Member of Parliament for Bewdley from 1908 to 1937. He influenced the government of the United Kingdom between the two World Wars, serving as Chancellor in 1922 – 1923 and Prime Minister on three occasions between 1923 and 1937.

Baldwin was the only son of Alfred Baldwin, chairman of the Great Western Railway and head of a large concern that included iron and steel manufactories and collieries. Born in 1867 at Lower Park House (Lower Park, Bewdley) in Worcestershire, Baldwin went to St Michael's School, at the time located in Slough, Berkshire, followed by Harrow School. He then went on to the University of Cambridge, where he studied history at Trinity College. Baldwin studies deteriorated by year, he got a First at the end of his first year, a Second at the end of his second, and a Third at the end of his third, and so graduated from Cambridge University with a third class degree.

After leaving Cambridge Baldwin worked for his father's business, and in 1898 he oversaw the company's flotation on the Stock Market. In 1902, he saw the rationalisation of the various parts of the business amalgamated into Baldwins Ltd, together with other steelworks and collieries in South Wales. In 1904, he was selected as the candidate for what was considered the safe Conservative seat of Kidderminster. However, in the 1906 General Election, the Liberal Party achieved a landslide victory and Baldwin lost out to Edmund Broughton Barnard by 2,354 votes to 2,083 (majority 271). In 1908, Baldwin's father died and he inherited nearly £200,000 (worth over £20 million in 2020) and was also offered his father's parliamentary seat of Bewdley. After an unopposed return in a By-election, he was introduced into the House of Commons on 3rd March 1908. At the January/February 1910 General Election, he faced opposition from the Liberals in Bewdley, but he was returned with a comfortable 4,248 majority (6,618 votes to 2,370). On the outbreak of the First World War in 1914, Baldwin was forty-seven, and too old for military service, but he encouraged his own workers to join the armed forces by paying out of his own pocket, the Friendly Society subscriptions. Bonar Law, appointed Baldwin as his Parliamentary Private Secretary, and by late 1916, he gave his support to David Lloyd George in his plot to overthrow H. H. Asquith, the Prime Minister. Baldwin became Secretary of the

Treasury in 1917, in Lloyd George's wartime coalition government, and after the war he was re-elected unopposed in Bewdley at the December 1918 General Election. He also won the By-Election which was called when he was appointed to the Cabinet as President of the Board of Trade in April 1921, (14,537 votes to 1,680, a majority of 12,857 - 89.6%). In the following October of 1922, at a meeting for Conservative backbenchers at the Carlton Club in London,

A YOUNG STANLEY BALDWIN

Baldwin made a key speech saying he could no longer support the coalition government, which ultimately brought about Lloyd George's resignation. In Bonar Law's Conservative government that followed, Baldwin had at first rejected the idea of being Chancellor of the Exchequer, and suggested former Liberal Chancellor Reginald McKenna, but when McKenna turned down the offer, Baldwin gave way and accepted the post. In January 1923, Baldwin visited the United States and negotiated terms for the repayment of Britain's war debt, which were not ideal, but in his view the best available. Bonar Law opposed the terms and relations between Baldwin and Bonar Law became strained. When ill health forced Bonar Law to retire as

Prime Minister on 20 May 1923, King George V asked Baldwin to form a government. And after the forming of the government, Baldwin called a General Election on 6 December 1923, to seek approval for the government's plans to introduce protective tariffs. At the election he failed to gain a majority, resulting in a first Labour government under Ramsay MacDonald, with support from the Liberal's. Baldwin won his seat at the election with a

BALDWIN WITH HIS WIFE AND DAUGHTER

slightly larger majority of 6,369 (12,395 votes to 6,026). Labour's first government was short-lived though, and by November 1924, the Conservatives were back in power with a landslide majority, and Baldwin as Prime Minister. In the General Strike of 1926, from 4th to 12th May, Baldwin proclaimed a state of emergency and refused to negotiate further until the strike was over. The following year he passed the Trade Disputes Act, which declared general strikes to be revolutionary and illegal. Baldwin wanted to change the image of the Conservative Party to make it appear a less right-wing organisation, and so in March 1927, he suggested to his Cabinet that the government should propose legislation for the enfranchisement of nearly five million women between the ages of twenty-one and thirty. This measure meant that women would constitute almost 53% of the British electorate. There was little opposition in Parliament to the bill, and it became law on 2nd July 1928, and as a result, all women over the age of 21 could vote in elections, but the Conservatives lost the following General Election of May 1929, when Labour came back to power. Baldwin retained his Bewdley seat with another increased majority of 9,407 (16,593 to 7,186), but considered leaving politics, and spent much of the next two years fighting elements within his own party. With the Great Depression, the world financial crisis began to overwhelm Britain in 1931, Baldwin returned to government as Lord President of the Council in the

National Coalition. The Labour Party was virtually destroyed, which left MacDonald as Prime Minister for a largely Conservative coalition. In February 1934, the Defence Requirements Committee (DRC), reported to Cabinet, that upon Adolf Hitler's rise to power in Germany in 1933, Nazism had become recognised as an international threat, and Germany was now

STATUE OF BALDWIN IN WORCESTERSHIRE

Britain's 'ultimate potential enemy'. It was decided that Neville Chamberlain should be put in charge of the defence expenditure. In June 1935, Baldwin became Prime Minister for the third time when MacDonald resigned. He called for a General Election on 14th November, which resulted in a large, albeit reduced, majority for the National Government, with the greatest number of members being Conservatives (Baldwin was returned unopposed). In December 1936, with King Edward VIII's proposed marriage to the twice-divorced Mrs Wallis Simpson, and his consequent abdication, Baldwin took the lead in making it plain that if the King persisted he should give up the throne. His management of the abdication crisis was highly praised.

Baldwin was acutely aware of most opposition MPs having difficulty living on their pay of £200 a year, and so in one of his final acts as Prime Minister, he doubled their pay and introduced a salary for the Leader of the Opposition. In doing so he felt that they would not need to indulge in potentially corrupting work outside of Parliament. Baldwin resigned from office on 28th May, 1937, following the successful coronation celebrations of George VI, and was ennobled as Earl Baldwin of Bewdley. Baldwin's wife, Lucy, died in June 1945 and he died two years later, in his sleep at Astley Hall, near Stourport-on-Severn, Worcestershire, on 14 December 1947, aged 80.

Interesting Stanley Baldwin facts:

From an early age Baldwin had a love of reading and walking.

Baldwin was the Chancellor of the University of Cambridge from 1930 until his death in 1947

Baldwin was (through his Scottish mother) a first cousin of the writer and poet Rudyard Kipling.

In 1956, Baldwin's son, A. W. Baldwin published a biography entitled *My Father: The True Story.*

In his time in politics, Baldwin served under three monarchs.

There is a blue plaque put up by Greater London Council, at 93 Easton Square, Belgravia to commemorate that Prime Minister Stanley Baldwin lived there.

Baldwin's wealth at his death was £280,971 3s 1d, worth approx. £11,242,728 in 2020

Neville Chamberlain
1869 - 1940 (71 years old) Conservative

Chancellor of the Exchequer:
(2 stints)
27 August 1923 - 22 January 1924
(4 months and 27 days)
5 November 1931 - 28 May 1937
(5 years, 6 months and 24 days)

Born
18 March 1869, Edgbaston
Died
9 November 1940, age 71,
Heckfield, Hampshire

Title: None

Constituencies Represented as MP:
Birmingham Ladywood 1918 - 1929
Birmingham Edgbaston 1929 - 1940

Other Official Offices held:
Postmaster General 1922 - 1923
Minister of Health 1923, 1924 - 1929 and 1931
Prime Minister 1937 - 1940
Lord President of the Council 1940

Prime Minister served with as Chancellor:
Ramsay MacDonald
Stanley Baldwin

Education:
Mason College (now the University of Birmingham).

Arthur Neville Chamberlain, 18 March 1869 – 9 November 1940) was a Conservative MP for Birmingham, who served as Chancellor of the Exchequer on two separate occasions in the 1920's and 1930's, he was also the Conservative Prime Minister of the United Kingdom from May 28, 1937 to May 10 1940, and was the Prime Minister who led Britain into World War II.

Arthur Neville Chamberlain was born into a political family at Southbourne House in the Edgbaston district of Birmingham, on 18 March 1869. His father, Joseph, was an influential politician of the late 19th century and Neville's older half-brother Austen held many Conservative Cabinet positions (including Chancellor of the Exchequer) in the early 20th century and won the Nobel Peace Prize. His mother was Florence Kenrick, cousin to William Kenrick MP, she died in childbirth when he was only six. Chamberlain was educated at home by his elder sister Beatrice, and he later went to school at Rugby where he was said to have hated school, but still did well academically. Chamberlain left Rugby in 1886, but didn't follow his elder brother Austen to Cambridge, instead he attended Mason College in Birmingham, where he studied science and engineering design.

Chamberlain was working in an accounting firm until 1890, when his father announced that the family was going to start a business growing and processing sisal (a plant with strong fibres that can be used to make rope and other products) in the Bahamas. Neville and his brother Austen were put in charge of the operation and moved to the Bahamas, establishing the Andros Fibre Company. Austen soon returned to England, while Neville became the company's managing director. Although the 20,000 acre plantation seemed promising at first, it eventually failed. Chamberlain returned to England extremely disappointed, but he had gained valuable experience and a reputation for being a hands-on manager, who took a strong interest in the day-to-day running of affairs. On his return to England, Chamberlain was much more self-reliant and he became a leading manufacturer in Birmingham, where he was also elected as a councillor in 1911. Chamberlain was in his early forties, when he met and fell in love with Anne Cole, and the two were married in January 1911. Their daughter, Dorothy, was born that December, and son Frank two years later. Chamberlain served as Lord Mayor of Birmingham for a year in 1915, and in December 1916, the new Prime Minister

David Lloyd George, on the suggestion of Neville's elder brother Austen, offered him the newly created post of Director-General of National Service, which he accepted and resigned as Lord Mayor. His brief was to recruit volunteers for essential war work, but despite three interviews with Lloyd George, he had no detailed instructions or terms of appointment. In eight months only a few thousand volunteers were

NEVILLE CHAMBERLAIN   placed in employment essential for war work, but the underlying problem, was that Lloyd George had taken a dislike to Chamberlain, dismissing him as a 'pin-headed incompetent'. Chamberlain returned the disdain, later referring to Lloyd George as a 'dirty little Welsh Attorney'. With such a fraught relationship, Chamberlain resigned within the year. In 1918, he was elected as the Conservative MP for a new seat, Birmingham Ladywood, which he won with a majority of 6,833 (9,405 votes against Labour's 2,572 and the Liberal's 1,552), but he refused to serve under Lloyd George in the coalition government. At the November 1922 General Election, Chamberlain was again returned to Parliament in Ladywood with a 2,443 majority (13,032 to Labour's 10,589) and was appointed Postmaster General, before being made Minister of Health within months. In August 1923, he was appointed Chancellor of the Exchequer in the Stanley Baldwin government, a position he only held for five months due to the 1923 General Election defeat to

Labour. Chamberlain was re-elected in the 1923 election in Ladywood, but with a smaller majority of 1,554 (12,884 to 10,589).

When the Labour government was defeated on a motion of no confidence, a third General Election in less than two years was held in October 1924, Chamberlain narrowly defeated the Labour candidate, Oswald Mosley (who later led the British Union of

Fascists), by only 77 votes (13,374 to 13,297 with the Liberal's 539). Chamberlain served as Minister of Health again, a position he held until June 1929. His Local Government Act of 1929 reformed the Poor Law, effectively laying the foundations of the welfare state, and he reorganised local government finance. Labour won the 1929 election, where Chamberlain stood in Birmingham Edgbaston, winning with a majority of 14,760 against W.H.D Caple of Labour (8,590) and P.R.C Young, Liberal (4,720). At the 1931 General Election, Chamberlain almost doubled his

NEVILLE CHAMBERLAIN

majority to 27,928 (33,243 to 5,157) and Ramsay MacDonald made him Chancellor of the Exchequer in his National government. Chamberlain presented his first Budget in April 1932, maintaining the severe budget cuts that had been agreed at the inception of the National Government, and reduced the annual interest rate on most of Britain's war debt from 5% to 3.5%. Between 1932 and 1938, Chamberlain halved the percentage of the Budget devoted to interest on the war debt. Chamberlain proved to be a powerful Chancellor in the five and a half years he spent at the Treasury. He reduced the standard rate of income tax by 6*d*. (2.5 per cent), restored the cut in unemployment benefit, and began restoring the cuts in the pay of state and local government employees. In his time in office, Chamberlain confidently asserted that the nation had recovered 80 per cent of its prosperity. He had aimed his financial policy at both deflation sufficient to restore confidence, and by maintaining purchasing power in the economy. He had done so with considerable courage and success, making his record as Chancellor an impressive one. After the abdication of the King, Stanley Baldwin announced that he would remain as Prime Minister until shortly after the coronation of King George VI and Queen Elizabeth. On 28 May 1937, two weeks after the Coronation, Baldwin resigned, advising the King to send for

CHAMBERLAIN GREETS HITLER

Chamberlain. Unfortunately Neville's brother, Austen, did not live to see him become Prime Minister having died two months earlier. Some of Chamberlain's early efforts as Prime Minister focused on improving the lives of workers. The Factories Act of 1937, restricted the number of hours that children and women worked. The following year, Chamberlain supported the Holiday with Pay Act, which gave workers a week off with pay. However, his work on the domestic front was quickly overshadowed by growing foreign relations issues. Rather than challenge acts of aggression by Nazi Germany, Chamberlain sought ways to pacify Hitler. In an attempt to sway Fascist Italy away from German influence, he agreed on April 16, 1938, to recognise Italian supremacy in Ethiopia and kept Great Britain out of the Spanish Civil War (1936–39). On three occasions in September 1938, Chamberlain went to Germany in an effort to prevent the outbreak of a general European war over

Hitler's demand that Czechoslovakia cede the Sudetenland to Germany. Hitler agreed to meet in Munich with Chamberlain, the Italian leader Benito Mussolini, and French Premier Edouard Daladier to discuss a diplomatic resolution to the crisis. The four leaders, without any input from Czechoslovakia in the negotiation, agreed to cede Sudetenland to Hitler. Chamberlain also drafted separately a non-aggression pact between Britain and Germany that Hitler signed. On Chamberlain's return to London's Heston Aerodrome, a large thankful crowd cheered wildly as the door to his airplane opened. As the rain fell, Chamberlain stepped onto the tarmac, holding aloft the non-aggression pact that had been signed by him and Hitler only hours before. The Prime Minister read to the nation the brief agreement and reaffirmed "the desire

"PEACE IN OUR TIME"

of our two peoples never to go to war with one another again". After a royal audience, Chamberlain returned to his official residence at 10 Downing Street and from a second floor window, he addressed the crowd and invoked Benjamin Disraeli's famous statement upon returning home from the Berlin Congress of 1878, "My good friends, this is the second time in our history that there has come back from Germany to Downing Street peace with honour. I believe it is peace in our time". Nonetheless, he immediately ordered the acceleration of the British rearmament program. Chamberlain seemed to have underestimated Hitler's ambitions, because in March 1939, Hitler violated the Munich Pact by invading Czechoslovakia. Britain and France agreed to protect Poland later that month, but after Hitler's forces entered Poland that September, Chamberlain officially declared war on Germany. The declaration came shortly after the invasion, but his attempted appeasement of Hitler, and the delay in making the announcement, had negatively impacted on Chamberlain's popularity. Plans for limited conscription which applied to single men aged between 20 and 22, was given parliamentary approval in the Military Training Act in May 1939, and on the day Britain declared war on Germany, 3 September 1939, Parliament immediately passed far more reaching measure. The National Service (Armed Forces) Act imposed conscription on all males aged between 18 and 41 who had to register for service. Those medically unfit were exempted, as were others in key industries and jobs such as baking, farming, medicine and engineering. Chamberlain remained Prime Minister during a period of sporadic military action, and added Winston Churchill into his War Cabinet, as first Lord of the Admiralty. After the failure of a British expedition to Norway in April 1940,

Chamberlain lost the support of many Conservatives in the House of Commons. He resigned on May 10 1940, the day of the German invasion of the Low Countries. In Churchill's coalition government he served loyally as Lord President of the Council until September 30, 1940, when ill health forced him to resign, along with the Conservative Party leadership. Chamberlain died of bowel cancer on 9 November 1940, at the age of 71, and a funeral service took place at Westminster Abbey (but due to wartime security concerns, the date and time were not widely publicised).

Interesting Neville Chamberlain facts:

Chamberlain's cousins, Wilfred Byng Kenrick and Sir Wilfrid Martineau, like Chamberlain, were Lord Mayors of Birmingham.

Chamberlain grew up to be a man of broad interests and avocations. In his youth a keen entomologist, he later developed an even keener interest in flowers, eventually becoming a fellow of the Royal Horticultural Society. Ornithology was another of his passions, which he improved on by rising at five in the morning to learn to distinguish the songs of the various species.

Chamberlain said he inherited a deep love of music from his mother's side of the family.

Chamberlain was given the Honorary Freedom of Birmingham and the City of London in 1940, but he died before acceptance, the scroll was presented to his widow in 1941.

A commemorative blue plaque for Chamberlain is on display in Edgbaston by the Birmingham Civic Society.

Chamberlain left £84,013 6s in his will, approx. worth £4,734.021 in 2020.

Chamberlain was an avid reader and an aficionado on Shakespeare, when leaving Heston Airport for Germany in 1938, Chamberlain quoted Hotspur from Henry IV saying he hoped to 'pluck from this nettle danger, this flower, safety'.

On resigning as wartime Prime Minister Chamberlain broadcast to the nation saying; 'And you and I, must rally behind our new leader, and with our united strength, and with unshakeable courage, fight and work until this wild beast, that has sprung out of his lair upon us, has been finally disarmed and overthrown'.

Philip Snowden
1864 - 1937 (72 years old) Labour

Chancellor of the Exchequer:
(2 stints)
22 January 1924 -
3 November 1924
(9 months and 13 days)
7 June 1929 - 5 November 1931
(2 years, 4 months and 30 days)
Born
18 July 1864, Cowley, Yorkshire
Died
15 May 1937, age 72, Tilford,
Surrey

Title: 1st Viscount Snowden

Constituencies Represented as MP:
Blackburn 1906 - 1918
Colne Valley 1922 - 1931
Other Official Offices held:
Chairman of the Independent Labour Party
1903 - 1906 and 1917 - 1920
Lord Privy Seal 1931 - 1932
Prime Minister served with as Chancellor:
Ramsay MacDonald
Education:
Left school at fifteen year old.

Philip Snowden, 1st Viscount Snowden, 18 July 1864 – 15 May 1937) was a Labour politician who was popular in trade union circles for his denouncement of capitalism as unprincipled, and for his for socialist views. He was the first Labour Chancellor of the Exchequer, a position he held twice, once in 1924 and again between 1929 and 1931. He broke with Labour policy in 1931 and was expelled from the party. He was denounced as a turncoat, when the party was overwhelmingly crushed that year by the National Government coalition that Snowden had supported.

Snowden was born on 18 July 1864 in Ickornshaw, Cowling, near Keighley in West Yorkshire. Born into a family of weavers he was the only son and third child of John Snowden and his wife Martha. Snowden started his education in Sunday school when he was five, and at ten he moved to the local Board School and not the mill as expected where his mother, father and two sisters worked. At thirteen he was a pupil teacher and took advanced lessons in French and Latin from the schoolmaster, with the expectation of him becoming a schoolteacher.

Things took an unexpected turn in 1879 though, when the mill the family worked in closed, forcing the family to move to Nelson in Lancashire to find work. At the age of fifteen, Snowden obtained a job as an insurance clerk in Burnley, and for the next six years while working as a clerk, he studied for the entrance exam for the Civil Service, eventually passing the exam in 1885. Twelve months later in 1886, Snowden was offered the position of Assistant Revenue Officer in Liverpool, which he accepted. Over the next few years he moved around as Revenue Officer, from Liverpool he went to Aberdeen before being seconded to the Orkneys and finally finishing up in Redruth, Cornwall. Whilst in Redruth, Snowden purchased a bicycle for work and pleasure, but he began to suffer from back pain, and on occasion had difficulty in walking. In August 1891, he became paralysed from the waist down, which he said resulted in a fall from his bike. It was thought however, that he was suffering from 'Potts Disease' (tuberculosis spondylitis) which is a rare infectious disease of the spine. Although Snowden never fully recovered, with help, support and nursing from his mother, within two years he was able to walk with the aid of walking sticks. He was still discharged from the Civil Service in November 1893, with a £30 16s gratuity (approx. £4,000 in 2020). Snowden had spent his time recuperating, by reading political books and writing for local

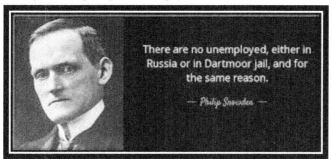

There are no unemployed, either in Russia or in Dartmoor jail, and for the same reason.

— Philip Snowden —

newspapers, also making a small income from accounting for small businesses and neighbouring farmers. With improved mobility

Snowden began giving political lectures, and with the formation of the Independent Labour Party (ILP) in Bradford in 1893, under the chairmanship of Keir Hardie, Snowden, who up until then had been of Liberal persuasion, was drawn to the idea of socialism. Upon joining the Cowling Parish council in 1894 as its first secretary, he then won a seat on the Cowling School Board in 1895, and was due to stand for the ILP in Keighley at the 1895 General Election, but there was no funds available for the deposit so they withdrew. Snowden continued writing for local newspapers, becoming editor of the Keighley Labour journal in 1898, and was elected to the Keighley Town Council and School Board the following year. Although intending to stand for the ILP in Keighley, he agreed to stand as the 'Labour Representation Party' (LRC) candidate in Blackburn, Lancashire, in the General Election of 1900. Snowden who was unknown in Blackburn, and faced a solid Conservative vote (the Conservatives had comfortably won the two available seats in Blackburn at the previous four General Elections). He had little cash and few helpers, but made a big impression in the constituency. Although finishing third behind the two Conservative candidates, Snowden received a very respectable 7,096 votes and laid a solid foundation for future representation. The level of response in Blackburn gave a boost to the working class movement, and enabled the opening up of its own political and social club in Blackburn. Snowden went on to stand in a By-election in Wakefield, West Yorkshire in 1902, and again gave a good representation in defeat, losing to the Conservative Edward Brotherton who had a majority of 981 (2,960 votes to Snowden's 1,979, which was an impressive 40.1% of the vote). In 1903 Snowden replaced the original chairman of the ILP, Keir Hardie, and set about increasing the party membership and advancing the level of the party's publicity. Snowden produced party political pamphlets which sold up to forty thousand copies at 1d each. He decided to stand in Blackburn again in the January/February 1906 General Election, this time facing two Conservatives and a Liberal. Snowden relished the prospect of taking on the Tory elite and called out the old Conservative regime as 'complacent' (Sir Harry Hornby one of the Conservative candidates spent twenty-three years in the House of Commons and never made a speech). Snowden campaigned tirelessly in the month prior to the election, speaking at two meetings every evening, and on Election Day there was great interest with over a 95% turnout. Snowden defied all predictions and took the second seat in a tight vote with 10,282 votes (26.7%) to Harry Hornby's 10,291 (only 9 vote difference) with the two other candidates finishing with 8,932 (Conservative) and 8,892 (Liberal). Snowden therefore became the very first Labour Member of Parliament Blackburn had ever had, and one of twenty-nine Labour MP's elected. Snowden's achievement was even more remarkable when considered that he was a forty-one year old working class man with a disability. The Liberals won a landslide victory in the 1906 General Election, and on the completion of the election, the Labour Representation

Committee took the official title of the Labour Party. Snowden focused heavily on financial policy and produced a 'Socialist Budget' in 1909 to rival the Liberals 'People's Budget'.

At the January/February General Election in 1910, Snowden was again elected for Blackburn in the second seat, increasing his vote to 11,916 (28.1%) against the newly elected Liberal candidate (Henry Norman) who received 12,064 (the first time in 57 years that Blackburn didn't have a Conservative MP). Snowden campaigned for minimum wages in 1912 and 1913, but by July 1914 and the build up to the First World War, Snowden had become disillusioned with politics and left England to go on a worldwide lecturing tour. He returned to England in 1915, and with the war ongoing he took an anti-war stance, refusing to back a recruitment campaign stating "I refuse to ask any young man to sacrifice his life before me". When conscription was introduced in 1916, he spoke strongly against it, and his anti-war stance was to work against him when the war finished, and a General Election was called for December 1918. Snowden stood in Blackburn against two coalition candidates, a Liberal and a Unionist (Percy Dean) who had been awarded the Victoria Cross for heroism in battle. Snowden came third with 15,274 votes (19.7%) against Liberal 32,078 and Unionist (Dean) 30,158. Snowden carried on as the Chairman of the ILP until 1920, when he became Treasurer for twelve months, while continuing to write for newspapers and lecturing. At the November 1922 General Election, Snowden decided to stand as a Labour candidate in Colne Valley, West Yorkshire, where he was elected with 12,614 votes, 39.5% of the vote, a majority of 1,282, taking what had been up to then a safe Liberal seat. In the December of 1923, another General Election was held, Snowden again won the Colne Valley seat with a slightly increased majority of 1,921 (40.4%) beating the Unionist candidate by 13,136 to 11,215 votes. The election resulted in a hung Parliament but Labour, led by Ramsay MacDonald, with the support of H.H Asquith's Liberals, formed the first ever Labour government. Snowden was appointed Labour's first ever

Chancellor of the Exchequer and produced what was called the 'Housewives Budget', when he reduced duty on some staple foods, while increasing unemployment benefits and doubling children's allowance's to 2s. He also cut expenditure on armaments and he expanded subsidies for the building of council houses. Snowden's Budget was widely welcomed, but the Labour government fell within the year over its alleged communist influence in the party, causing another General Election to be called on 29 October 1924. At the election, Labour lost forty seats and the Conservatives gained a landslide victory. Snowden however, increased his majority in Colne Valley, taking 43.3% of

PHILIP SNOWDEN

the vote (14,215 to 10,972) a majority 3,243. He resigned from the ILP over criticisms over his economic policy, but Labour won the most seats in the House of Commons in 1929 for the first time in its history (287 to the Conservatives 260 and Liberals 59 seats). Snowden, again increased his own majority in Colne Valley, taking 48.3% of the vote (21,667) for a majority of 9,135 (an increase of 5,892 votes), and was appointed as the Chancellor of the Exchequer. His second stint as Chancellor was beset with economic and unemployment problems, forcing him to raise direct taxes while proposing a cut in unemployment benefit, and he was also responsible for taking Britain off the Gold Standard in 1931. But he refused to consider deficit spending on tariffs, which led to the collapse of the second Labour government. After the collapse, a National government was formed, headed by Ramsay MacDonald, and Snowden remained as Chancellor, this was seen as him being a 'turncoat' by Labour, and both he and MacDonald were expelled from the party.

Snowden did not stand for Parliament in the October 1931 General Election, instead he went to the House of Lords in November 1931, as Viscount Snowden and became Lord Privy Seal. When the government introduced a variety of protective tariffs in August 1932, Snowden stated 'I cannot be dragged any further along this road without a loss of all honour and self-respect' and he resigned on 28 September 1932. He launched a bitter attack on the Labour Party, and the National Government. In his resignation letter in 1932, he launched a stinging assault on MacDonald's alleged compliance with the abandonment of free trade. He said of MacDonald; "everytime he speaks he exposes his ignorance or incapacity". In the 1935 General Election, Snowden supported the Keynesian (John Maynard Keynes) economic programme proposed by Lloyd George ("Lloyd George's New Deal"), despite it being a complete reversal of Snowden's own liberal fiscal policies. Snowden claimed that he was returning to his original economic views, but that these had been ill-advised during the crisis of 1931, when it was essential in the national interest to demand a cutting in public expenditure. Snowden died of a heart attack at his home, Eden Lodge, Tilford, Surrey on 15 May 1937, aged 72. After cremation at Woking Crematorium his ashes were scattered on Cowling Moor near Ickornshaw.

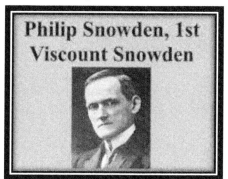

Interesting Philip Snowden facts:

Snowden's vast collection of books and pamphlets were donated to Keighley Public Library, where they still remain.

Snowden published a two volume autobiography in 1934.

Snowden had a love of music and detective novels.

I hope you have read the election programme of the Labour Party...this is not socialism. It is Bolshevism run mad.

(Philip Snowden, 1st Viscount Snowden)

Snowden moved to Leeds in 1902, where his met his future wife (Ethel) at a Fabian meeting. They married in 1905.

Snowden's wife Ethel, was a socialist, human rights activist and woman's suffragette. She wrote four books *The Woman Socialist* 1907, *Women and the State* 1907, *British Standards and Welfare* 1926 and *Welfare as Tested by The Declaration of Geneva* 1926.

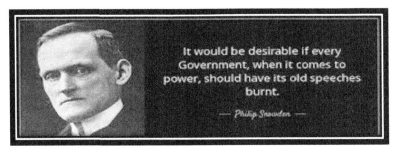

It would be desirable if every Government, when it comes to power, should have its old speeches burnt.

— Philip Snowden —

Snowden's viscountcy died with him, and his wife Ethel (Lady Snowden) died in February 1951, aged 69.

Snowden left £3366 13s 11d, in his will, worth approx. £230,802 in 2020.

Winston Churchill
1874 - 1965 (90 years old)
Liberal/Conservative

Chancellor of the Exchequer:
6 November 1924 –
4 June 1929
(4 years, 6 months and 30 days)
Born
30 November 1874, Blenheim Palace, Oxfordshire
Died
24 January 1965, age 90, London
Title: Sir Winston Churchill

Constituencies Represented as MP:
Oldham 1900 - 1906 Conservative
Manchester North West 1906 - 1908 Liberal
Dundee 1908 - 1922 Liberal
Epping 1924 – 1945 Constitutionalist/Unionist/Conservative
Woodford 1945 – 1960 Conservative

Academic Offices:
Rector of the University of Aberdeen 1914 - 1918
Rector of the University of Edinburgh 1929 - 1932
Chancellor of the University of Bristol 1929 - 1965

Honorary Titles:
Lord Warden of the Cinque Ports 1941 - 1965
Senior Privy Counsellor 1949 - 1965
Laureate of the Nobel Prize in Literature 1953

Other Official Offices held:

Undersecretary of State for the Colonies 1905 - 1908
President of the Board of Trade 1908 - 1910
Home Secretary 1910 - 1911
First Lord of the Admiralty 1911 - 1915
Chancellor of the Duchy of Lancaster 1915
Minister of Munitions 1917 - 1919
Secretary of State for Air 1919 - 1921
Secretary of State for the Colonies 1921 - 1922
First Lord of the Admiralty 1939 - 1940
Leader of the House of Commons 1940 - 1942
Prime Minister 1940 - 1945
Minister of Defence - 1940 - 1945
Leader of the Opposition 1945 - 1951
Prime Minister 1951 - 1955
Minister of Defence 1951 - 1952

Other Distinctions:

Honarary Bencher, Gray's Inn 1942
Albert Gold Medal, Royal Society of Arts 1945
Grotius Medal, Netherlands 1949
Nobel Prize in Literature 1953
Grand Seigneur of the Hudson Bay Company 1955
The Williamsburg Award 1955
Franklin Medal, City of Philadelphia 1956
Karlspresis (Charlemagne Prize) 1956
Honoraray Member, Lloyds of London
President of the Victoria Cross and George Cross Association 1959 - 1965

Prime Minister served with as Chancellor:

Stanley Baldwin

Education:

Sandhurst (Officer Cadet).

Sir Winston Leonard Spencer Churchill, (30 November 1874 – 24 January 1965) was an extraordinary person throughout a long and eventful life. Churchill was the Chancellor of the Exchequer in Stanley Baldwin's government from 1924 to 1929. He was Prime Minister of the United Kingdom on two occasions, from 1940 to 1945, when he led the country to victory in the Second World War, and again from 1951 to 1955. Apart from two years between 1922 and 1924, Churchill was a Member of Parliament from 1900 to 1964 and represented a total of five constituencies. Ideologically an economic liberal and imperialist, he was for the largest part of his career a member of the Conservative Party, leading the party from 1940 to 1955. He was a member of the Liberal Party from 1904 to 1924.

Churchill was born at Blenheim Palace, Oxfordshire, and from an early age, young Churchill displayed the traits of his father, Lord Randolph Churchill, a British statesman from an established English family and his mother, Jeanette "Jennie" Jerome, an independent-minded New York socialite. Churchill spent three of

CHURCHILL 1895

his early years (1877 – 1880) in Dublin, Ireland, where his father was employed by his grandfather, the 7th Duke of Marlborough, John Spencer-Churchill. Back in London, Churchill attended a boarding school in Ascot and at 13 he scraped into the lowest class at Harrow. His father believing that he was academically unsuited for politics or law, had him placed in the army class. Churchill enrolled at Sandhurst as an officer cadet in September 1893, though it took him three attempts to pass the entrance exam. He took to Sandhurst well, but the death of his father aged 45, on 24 January 1895, had a profound impact on him, convincing him of the need to make his mark early in life.

Churchill obtained his commission as a cavalry officer in the 4th (Queen's Own) Hussars in February 1895, and was also employed as a war reporter, spending his 21st birthday in Cuba, where he acquired two lifelong habits – siestas and Havana cigars. The following year Churchill sailed with his regiment for India, and in 1898 fought in Sudan. While in the Army, he wrote military

A YOUNG CHURCHILL 1900

reports for the *Pioneer Mail* and the *Daily Telegraph*, and two books on his experiences, *The Story of the Malakand Field Force* (1898) and *The River War* (1899). On 6 July 1899, Churchill stood for the Conservatives at the Oldham By-election but narrowly lost to the Liberals. Two Liberals were elected with 12,976 and 12,770 votes to Churchill's 11,477, with his fellow Conservative candidate receiving 11,449 votes. When the Boer Republic declared war on Britain on 11 October 1899, Churchill travelled to South Africa to cover the conflict as a war correspondent. On 15 November, he was on an armoured train in Natal when it was ambushed. The legend has it, that after a heroic defence in which he helped most of the train to escape, Churchill was captured and taken to a makeshift prison. Not to be held long, he soon took his opportunity to escape and clambered over a prison wall into the night, jumping on a passing train and hiding among sacks. The Boer authorities issued a reward for his capture and Churchill was alone and on the run in Africa. While on the run he met two mining engineers from England, John Howard and Dan Dewsnap, who hid him in a coal mine for three days. Churchill's escape made him a national hero, and although he stayed in South Africa until the following summer, the incident was enough to ensure him celebrity status. Upon his return to Britain, he wrote about his experiences in the book *London to Ladysmith via Pretoria* (1900). Churchill stood for the Conservative Party in

Oldham in the October General Election in 1900, and this time he was successfully returned as MP, along with Alfred Emmott the Liberal candidate. The votes were close as Emmott received 12,947 votes to Churchill's 12,931, the other Liberal candidate (Walter Runciman) was a further 222 votes behind on 12,709. At this time, a wing of the Conservative Party had wanted to introduce tariffs (or taxes) on imported foods and goods, while others like Churchill defended the Victorian policy of Free Trade. This led to the Oldham Conservative Party formally passing a motion of no-confidence in Churchill. The decision was ratified by

CHURCHILL **1904**

the Executive Committee in January 1904, and Churchill ceased to be the official Conservative candidate. On 31 May 1904, he completed his break with the Conservative Party, crossing the floor of the House of Commons to take up a seat on the Liberal opposition benches alongside Lloyd George. Churchill still remained as MP for the borough until the General Election of 1906. In the General Election of 1906, Churchill stood as a Liberal candidate for North-West Manchester, where he was victorious with a 1,241 majority (5,639 to the Conservative's 4,398) and became a junior minister in the Liberal Government. He then rose rapidly within the Liberal government, and in 1908, he entered the Cabinet as President of the Board of Trade (aged 33, he was the youngest Cabinet member since 1866). He was obliged to submit to re-election after his appointment, as the Ministers of the Crown Act required newly appointed Cabinet ministers to re-contest their seats. He lost the North-West Manchester seat in a By-election to the Conservative William Joynson Hicks, by 429 votes (5,417 votes to 4.988), but on 9 May 1908, the Liberals stood him in the By-election for Dundee where he won comfortably with a majority of 2,709 (7,079 to 4,370). In the January 1910 General Election, Churchill was again re-elected as a Liberal in the two seat constituency, along with Alexander Wilkie the Labour candidate, (10,747 votes to Wilkie's 10,365 with the Conservatives third with 4,552), Churchill was then promoted to Home Secretary in February 1910, giving him control over the police and prison services where he implemented a prison reform programme. Another General Election was called in December 1910, by the Liberal government to try to get it's 'People's Budget' passed, and to get a mandate for the Parliament Act of 1911. Churchill was returned in Dundee with a slightly reduced majority of 3,555 (9,240 votes to Wilkie's 8,957 and the Liberal Unionist 4,914). In March 1911, Churchill introduced the second reading of the Coal Mines Bill in Parliament, which imposed stricter safety standards in coal mines. In October 1911, Asquith appointed Churchill as First Lord of the Admiralty, and he took up official residence at Admiralty House. Over the next two and a half years he focused on naval preparation, visiting naval stations and dockyards, seeking to improve morale, and scrutinising German naval developments. He oversaw the naval effort when World War I started in 1914. On 18 March 1915,

1916

Churchill planned to sail through the Dardanelles and force Germany's ally, Turkey, out of the war. An attack was launched and troops landed on Gallipoli on 25 April. It was a disaster, they were pinned down and losses were heavy. Churchill was held by many MPs, particularly Conservatives, to be personally responsible. In May 1915, Asquith agreed under parliamentary pressure, to form an all-party coalition government, but the Conservatives' one condition of entry was that Churchill must be removed from the Admiralty, Churchill had to accept demotion and instead became Chancellor of the Duchy of Lancaster. On 25 November 1915, Churchill resigned from the government (although he remained an MP) and joined the Army, stating that he wanted to take an active part in the war and fight on the Western Front. When his battalion was amalgamated with another, rendering his command redundant, he returned to London, and was able give his colleagues in the House of Commons a soldier's view of the conflict. Churchill made a comeback when he was appointed Minister of Munitions in 1917, resulting in a By-election in Dundee, in which he was returned with a majority of 5,266 (7,302 to 2,036). By the end of the First World War, Churchill won again in Dundee in the 14 December post-war General Election, with a much improved majority of 15,365 (25,788 against 24,822 and 10,423 votes). In the following years he held a number of positions including: Secretary of State for War and Air 1919–1921 and the Secretary of State for the Colonies 1921–1922. In October 1922, he underwent an operation for appendicitis, and while he was in hospital the Conservatives withdrew from Lloyd George's coalition government. This precipitated the 15 November 1922 General Election, in which Churchill lost his Dundee seat, coming fourth with 20,466 votes but behind the Scottish Prohibition candidate's 32,578, the Labour candidate's 30,292, and another National Liberal's 22,224. He then spent much of the next six months in France, where he devoted himself to painting and writing his memoirs. He wrote an autobiographical history of the war, '*The World Crisis*' and had the first volume published in April 1923, with the rest being published over the next ten years. At the 1923 General Election, Churchill stood as the Liberal candidate at Leicester West, but lost to Labour by 4,398 votes (13,634 to 9,236). In a By-election on 19 March 1924, he stood as an independent candidate in the Westminster Abbey constituency, standing under the label of 'Constitutionalist', but he was narrowly defeated by the Conservatives by 43 votes (8,187 to 8,144), it was his third election defeat in less than two years, and his political affinities now lay increasingly to the right of his Liberal colleagues. When his chief detractor, Andrew Bonar Law, was replaced by Stanley Baldwin as Conservative leader, Churchill seized the opportunity, and in the 1924 General Election he again stood as a 'Constitutionalist' independent candidate, this time in Epping. The Conservative's didn't stand a candidate, and gave him their backing, he was elected with a majority of 9,763 (19,843 to 10,080). He formally re-joined the Conservative Party, and under Stanley Baldwin in November 1924, he was made Chancellor of the Exchequer. It was during this time that he made one of his worst political decisions (an opinion which he reflected on himself) when in his first Budget, he brought about Britain's restoration to the Gold Standard. The Gold Standard was a widely used monetary system in the 19th and early part of the 20th

BUDGET DAY 1929

century, and the consequences of its return were many. Although initially welcomed by the Bank of England, it damaged Britain's exports and resulted in high unemployment, deflation and the General Strike of 1926. Churchill, in total presented five Budgets as Chancellor, among his measures was the reduction of the state pension age from 70 to 65, immediate provision of widow's pensions, reduction of military expenditure, income tax reductions and the imposition of taxes on luxury items. In the 1929 General Election, Churchill retained his Epping seat with a majority of 4,967 (23,972 to 19,005), but the Conservatives were defeated and Ramsay MacDonald formed his second Labour government. For the next eleven years Churchill was mainly writing and making speeches, and he was prone to 'dark moods' for which he famously used the phrase 'Black Dog'. At the 27 October 1931 General Election, he was returned in Epping with a much increased majority of 20,286 (35,956 votes to 15,670). Throughout the 1930's Churchill wrote *Marlborough: His Life and Times* a biography about John Churchill, 1st Duke of Marlborough, who was a lineal descendant of his. The book comprises of four volumes, the first of which appeared in October 1933 (557 pages, 200,000 words) with subsequent volumes in 1934, 1936 and 1938. Churchill had continued writing as well as being and MP, and was returned in Epping for the last time at the 14 November 1935 General Election, with a majority of 20,419 (34,849 votes to 14,1430). On

CHURCHILL AND CHAMBERLAIN

3 September 1939, the day Britain declared war on Germany, Chamberlain re-appointed Churchill as First Lord of the Admiralty and he joined Chamberlain's War Cabinet. As First Lord, Churchill was one of the highest-profile ministers during the so-called 'Phoney War', when the only significant action by British forces was at sea. After the Allies failed to prevent the German occupation of Norway, the Commons held an open debate from 7 to 9 May 1940 on the government's conduct of the war. This has come to be known as the Norway Debate, and is renowned as one of the most significant events in parliamentary history. In the early hours of 10 May, German forces invaded Belgium, Luxembourg and the Netherlands, as a prelude to their assault on France. After a division vote, which was in effect a vote of no confidence in Chamberlain's government, Labour declared that they would not serve under his leadership, although they would accept another Conservative. Chamberlain advised the King to send for Churchill, who became Prime Minister of an all-party war-time coalition government on 10 May 1940. At sixty-five, Churchill belied his age with evocative speeches that boosted morale and included the iconic phrase 'we shall fight on the beaches'. When the Germans were over-running territory and forcing the evacuation from Dunkirk, Churchill showed that Britain was prepared to stand strong. In his 'finest hour' speech he told Parliament that he expected the Battle of Britain to occur very soon, refusing the armistice and uniting the British behind the resistance movement, while strengthening unity and resolve

across the British Empire. The 8th May 1945 was Victory in Europe Day (VE Day), when Churchill broadcast to the nation that Germany had surrendered, and that a final ceasefire on all fronts in Europe would come into effect at one minute past midnight that night (on the 9th). In the evening, Churchill made another broadcast to the nation, asserting that the defeat of Japan would follow in the coming months (the Japanese surrendered on 15 August 1945). Churchill resigned as Prime Minister on 23 May 1945, and later that day, he accepted the King's invitation to form a new government. The new government was known officially as the National Government, which stayed in place until

the General Election in July 1945. Polling day was 5 July, but the results of the election did not become known until 26 July. Churchill stood for the first time in Woodford (Essex) and was returned as the Conservative MP with a majority of 17,200 (27,688 votes to 10,488). Labour won the election with a landslide victory, gaining 239 seats. Having lost the election, Churchill, despite enjoying much personal support amongst the British population, resigned as Prime Minister. He was succeeded by Clement Attlee, who formed the first majority Labour government. Churchill continued to lead the Conservative Party, and for six years served as Leader of the Opposition. He made his famous 'Iron Curtain' speech in America alongside American President Harry S. Truman, in which he warned against the expansionistic policies of the Soviet Union. In addition to the 'iron curtain' that had descended across Eastern Europe, Churchill's 'iron curtain' phrase immediately entered the official vocabulary of the Cold War. At the 23 February 1950 General Election, Churchill retained his seat in Woodford with an increased majority of 18,499 (37,239 votes to 18,740) but Labour won the election, albeit with a much reduced majority, from 146 seats to just 5. Twenty months later, the Labour government called a snap election for Thursday 25 October 1951, in the hope of increasing their slender parliamentary majority. And although Labour got the most votes (13,948,883 against 13,717,850) Churchill at the age of 76, was returned as Conservative Prime Minister once again, with a 17 seat majority (26 above Labour). Churchill himself retained his seat with a similar result to the 1950 election, with a majority of 18,579 (40,938 votes to 22,359). Churchill's second ministry was concerned with the mass construction of new housing, the end of food rationing in 1954, the Mining and Quarries Act 1954 and the housing repairs and rent act 1955. Churchill suffered a serious stroke on the evening of 23 June 1953, and became partially paralysed down one side. Although he recovered and carried on through 1954, his declining health forced him to retire as Prime Minister on 5 April 1955, and he was succeeded by Anthony Eden. Churchill stood in two more General Elections winning them both in Woodford, in 1955 with a 15,808 majority (25,069 to 9,261) and in 1959 with a 14,797 majority (24,815 to 10,018). In June 1962, when he was 87, Churchill had a fall in Monte Carlo and broke his hip. He was flown home to a London hospital where he remained for three weeks. He suffered his final stroke on 12 January 1965, and he died nearly two weeks later on the 24th aged 90. He was given a state funeral six days later on 30 January 1965.

Interesting Winston Churchill facts:

Time Magazine named Churchill its Person of the Year for 1940.

Churchill was a prolific writer, writing forty-three books that filled seventy-two volumes, he was awarded the Nobel Prize in Literature in 1953 for his many published works.

Churchill excelled at polo and rifle shooting, winning the public schools fencing championship in 1892.

In his lifetime, Churchill received a worldwide total of 42 Freedoms of cities and towns, a record for a lifelong British citizen.

Churchill was declared the greatest Briton of all time in the BBC poll and television series Great Britons, A statue was erected in his honour and now stands at the BBC television studios.

Churchill was married to Clementine Hozier for 57 years, they married in September 1908 and had five children.

On 9 April 1963, United States President John F. Kennedy, acting under authorisation granted by an Act of Congress, proclaimed Churchill the first honorary citizen of the United States.

Churchill had the luxury of having a fully-equipped cinema in his home at Chartwell and he visited Charlie Chaplin in Hollywood in 1929.

CHURCHILL AND CHAPLIN   Churchill appeared on the 1965 crown coin, the first commoner to be placed on a British coin. He made another appearance on a crown issued in 2010 to honour the 70th anniversary of his Premiership.

Churchill was awarded 37 other orders and medals between 1895 and 1964. Of the orders, decorations and medals Churchill received, 20 were awarded by the United Kingdom.

Ten schools in Canada are named in his honour: one each in Vancouver, Winnipeg, Thunder Bay, Hamilton, Kingston, St. Catharines, Lethbridge, Calgary, Toronto (Scarborough) and Ottawa.

John Allsebrook Simon
1873 - 1954 (80 years old) Liberal

Chancellor of the Exchequer:
28 May 1937 - 10 May 1940
(2 years, 11 months and 13 days)

Born
28 February 1873, Moss Side,
Manchester

Died
11 January 1954, age 80,
Westminster, London

Title: 1st Viscount Simon

Constituencies Represented as MP:
Walthamstow 1906 - 1918
Spen Valley 1922 - 1940

Other Official Offices held:
Solicitor General for England and Wales 1910 - 1913
Attorney General for England and Wales 1913 - 1915
Home Secretary 1915 - 1916
Foreign Secretary 1931 - 1935
Lord High Chancellor of Great Britain 1940 - 1945

Prime Minister served with as Chancellor:
Neville Chamberlain

Education:
Wadham College, Oxford University.

John Allsebrook Simon, 1st Viscount Simon, (28 February 1873 – 11 January 1954), was a Member of Parliament for Walthamstow and Spen Valley from 1906 to 1940. He held senior Cabinet posts from the beginning of the First World War to the end of the Second World War. Along with Rab Butler and James Callaghan, he is one of only three people to have served as Home Secretary, Foreign Secretary and Chancellor of the Exchequer.

Simon was born on 28 February 1873, at 16 Yarburgh Street, a terraced house in Moss Side, Manchester. He was the only son and elder child of the Reverend Edwin Simon and his wife Fanny Allsebrook. Simon started his education in Manchester before moving to King's Edward School in Bath, winning a scholarship to Fettes College in Edinburgh. In 1891, Simon secured an open scholarship to Wadham College, Oxford, celebrating his distinguished undergraduate career, in which he gained a first in Greats (Literae Humaniores) and was Oxford Union President in 1895 – 1896.

Simon left Oxford at the end of 1898, and was called to the Bar at the Inner Temple in 1899. Although his career as a barrister got off to a slow start, he worked extremely hard to make it a success, and in 1903, he acted on behalf of the British government over a land dispute in Canada. While practicing law Simon had a great desire for a career in politics, and stood in his first candidacy in the January/February 1906 General Election, as a Liberal in Walthamstow, winning the seat with a 3,937 majority (15,011 votes to the Conservative's 11,074). With the Liberal landslide at the 1906 election, Simon joined the packed Liberal benches in Parliament, but he still managed to stand out in the crowd. At the January 1910 General Election, he was re-elected for Walthamstow with a majority of 2,195 (17,726 votes to 13,907) and was appointed Solicitor-General on 7 October 1910. Due to his promotion, a By-election was held in Walthamstow and Simon was again returned with a slightly increased majority of 2,766 (16,673 votes to 13,907). At the young age of 37, he received a customary knighthood with the position of Solicitor-General, and was the youngest appointee in the position since Sir William Webb Follett in 1834. Simon was seen as a rising star, and was unusually given a seat in the Cabinet on 19 October 1913, with his appointment as Attorney-General. With the outbreak of the First World War, Simon became Home Secretary at the formation of the wartime coalition government, on 25 May 1915, but with his reluctance to accept involvement in the conflict and his opposition to conscription on the grounds of every man's right to decide for themselves, he resigned as Home Secretary in January 1916. Although Simon's patriotism was questioned, he answered his critic's by serving as an officer in the Royal Flying Corps in the summer of 1917, serving until the end of the war with distinction in General Trenchard's staff. When the war ended in 1918, a General Election was called on 14 December, and with the Walthamstow constituency abolished, Simon stood in the Walthamstow East constituency, but unsurprisingly lost to the Unionist coalition 'coupon' candidate, Stanley Johnson, by a majority of 4,211 (9,992 votes to 5,781). Simon then stood in a By-election a year later on 20 December 1919, in Spen Valley (West Riding of Yorkshire), but Lloyd George put up a coalition Liberal candidate to split the vote to try and keep Simon out. The result, after a closely fought campaign, was a Labour victory for Tom Myers with 11,962 votes, for a majority of 1,718. Simon came second with 10,244 votes and Bryan Charles Fairfax the coalition Liberal received 8,134 votes to finish third. The Labour victory was seen as the beginning of a major threat to the older political party's grip on power. After his defeat, Simon continued practicing law before standing again in Spen Valley at the 15 November 1922 General Election, the By-election result was reversed with Simon beating Tom Myers into second place with a 787 majority (13,306 votes to 12,519 with the Conservative vote at 8,104). Simon served as the Deputy Leader of the Liberal party under H.H Asquith, and with ambitions of succeeding him as the future Liberal leader, he retired from the Bar. At the 6 December

1923 General Election, Simon fought a close battle with Tom Myers again, just managing to come out on top with a slightly improved majority of 1,075 (13,672 to 12,597, with the Conservatives third on 7,390 votes). In October 1924, Simon moved an amendment calling a motion of no confidence, that ultimately brought down the first Labour government. Simon's amended motion passed by 364 votes to 198, after which, Ramsay MacDonald requested a dissolution of his government the following day. At the resulting General Election, which was held on 29 October 1924, Simon had his final election battle with Tom Myers, winning in a two horse race by 18,474 votes to 13,999 (majority 4,475). But when Lloyd George was voted as Chairman of the Liberal MP's by 29 votes to 9, the fractious relationship the pair still had, led to Simon stepping down as Deputy Leader and returning to the Bar. Simon had always had a low opinion of socialism, and famously declared in the House of Commons on 6 May 1926, that the General Strike was illegal and that Union bosses should be held liable for any damage done to businesses. He was one of the highest paid barristers of his generation, but he retired permanently from the Bar while in his pomp, to concentrate fully on politics. In 1927, Simon accepted the governments invitation to be the Chairman of the Indian Constitutional Development Committee, what became known as the 'Simon Commission', the commission was set up to examine the effects and operations of constitutional reform and the future of India, with Clement Attlee the future Prime Minister, also a member of the commission. Simon was again re-elected for Spen Valley in the May 1929 General Election, with a reduced majority of 1,739 (22,039 votes to Labours 20,300), but frustrated by Lloyd George's refusal to put the minority Labour government out of office, Simon and around thirty supporters broke away and formed the Liberal Nationals (later named the National Liberal Party). On 5 November 1931, he was appointed by Ramsay MacDonald as the Foreign Secretary in the National Government, but his tenure at the Foreign office was at one of the most difficult times in history, and his time there was seen as somewhat of a failure, receiving criticism from all sides of the political divide. As Foreign Secretary, Simon had to deal with the Japanese invasion of Manchuria in 1931, the rise of Adolf Hitler to power in Nazi Germany in 1933 and the collapse of the World Disarmament Conference 1932 – 1934. He left the Foreign office in 1935 disappointed, but on 7 June 1935, he was appointed by Stanley Baldwin to a role he was much more suited, that of Home Secretary, where his legal skills enabled him to play an important part in the abdication of King Edward VIII. At the General Election on 14 November 1935, which was to be the last election Simon stood in, he was returned in a very closely fought campaign with Labour's Ivor Thomas, winning with a slender majority of 642 (21,671 vote to 21,029), and continued as Home Secretary. At the Home office, Simon oversaw the introduction of the Public Order Act 1936, which was specifically passed to control extremist political movements, especially the activities of Oswald Mosley's Blackshirts. Simon's time as Home Secretary restored his standing in political circles, to such an extent that when Neville Chamberlain was appointed as Prime Minister, Simon took over Chamberlain's vacated role and was promoted to be Chancellor of the Exchequer. As Chancellor, Simon continued on the same fiscal path as his predecessor, believing that a strong economy would best serve the nation as a 'fourth arm of defence' in any future war. In 1938, public expenditure passed the £1,000 million mark for the first time, and Simon increased income tax from 5s to 5s 6d. (27.5%) while also increasing duties on petrol and tea. In his Spring Budget of 1939, before war was declared, Simon increased indirect taxes on cars, sugar and tobacco. On the outbreak of World War Two, an emergency Budget was called in September 1939, when Simon further increased income tax from 5s 6d. to 7s 6d. as well as increasing postal charges, tax on tobacco, matches and alcohol. In his last Budget in April 1940, the purchase tax was introduced on 21 October 1940, aimed at reducing the wastage of raw materials during the war, and was set at 33.3%, the purchase tax was eventually abolished in April 1973 and replaced with Value Added Tax (VAT) which was initially set at 10%. When Churchill formed his wartime government in May 1940, Simon was relieved as Chancellor of the Exchequer and was appointed as Lord Chancellor, but without a place in the War Cabinet, and on 14 May 1940, he was created Viscount Simon of Stackpole Elidor in the county of Pembroke.

As Lord Chancellor, Simon was responsible for interrogating Hitler's deputy, Rudolph Hess, after Hess's bizarre solo flight to Scotland in May 1941. Simon stayed as Lord Chancellor until Churchill's defeat in the 1945 General Election, remaining active in the House of Lords, and campaigning against socialism across the country, in the General Elections of 1945, 1950 and 1951. Simon suffered a stroke during the Christmas recess of 1953, and died in the Westminster Hospital, London, on 11 January 1954. Despite his upbringing as a son of the manse he lacked religious faith, and following his own instructions, he was cremated in his Oxford robes without religious ceremony.

Interesting John Simon facts:

Simon published his memoirs *'Retrospect' in 1952, and his* personal papers are preserved in Bodleian Library, Oxford.

Simon married Ethel Mary Venables, on 24 May 1899. They had three children; Margaret (born 1900), Joan (born 1901) and John Gilbert, 2nd Viscount Simon (born 1902). Ethel died shortly after giving birth to their son in 1902. Simon married again in 1917 to Kathleen Manning.

Simon left £93,006 12s 0d. Approx. £2,563,279 in 2020.

Simon was appointed KCVO (Knight Commander of the Royal Victorian Order) in 1911 for his defence of George V in a libel case.

Kingsley Wood
1881 - 1943 (62 years old) Conservative

Chancellor of the Exchequer:
12 May 1940 - 12 September 1943
(3 years, 4 months and 1 day)

Born
19 August 1881, West Sculcoates, Hull

Died
21 September 1943, age 62, Westminster, London

Title: Sir Kingsley Wood

Constituency Represented as MP:
Woolwich West 1918 - 1943

Other Official Offices held:
Postmaster General 1931 - 1935
Minister of Health 1935 - 1938
Secretary of State for Air 1938 - 1940
Lord Privy Seal 1940

Prime Minister served with as Chancellor:
Winston Churchill

Education:
Central Foundation Boys School.

Sir Howard Kingsley Wood, (19 August 1881 – 21 September 1943) was a solicitor and Conservative politician who represented Woolwich West from 1918 until his death in 1943. He served as wartime Chancellor of the Exchequer in Winston Churchill's government.

Wood was born in West Sculcoates, Hull on 19 August 1881, the eldest of three children to the Reverend Arthur Wood and his wife Harriet. After his father was appointed minister of Wesley's Chapel in London, Wood attended the nearby Central Foundation Boy's School and was articled to a solicitor.

Wood qualified in 1903 with honours in his law examinations, winning the prestigious John Mackrell prize, and setting up his own City practice, specialising in industrial insurance law. He continued practicing law and was elected to the London County

Council in 1911, as a Municipal Reform member for Woolwich, where his importance in the field of insurance grew, chairing the London Old Age Pension Authority in 1915, and the London Insurance Committee from 1917 to 1918. Wood made his mark though in 1918, when he proposed a statement of facts proposing the establishment of a ministry for health, which in time, David Lloyd George adopted. Wood stood in his first election in Woolwich West, as a Unionist (Conservative) in the 'Khaki election' on 14 December 1918, where he was comfortably returned as an MP with 60.1% share of the vote (12,348 votes to 7,088). After the election, he was appointed Parliamentary Private Secretary to the first Minister of Health, Christopher Addison and then to his successor Sir Alfred Mond. Wood voted against the break-up of the coalition government but was re-elected at the subsequent General Election on 15 November 1922, in Woolwich West, with a reduced majority of 4,903 (14,453 votes to 9,550), although he was not offered a post in Bonar Law's Conservative government. Wood followed up his 1922 victory in the General Elections of 1923 (12,380 votes to 11,357 a 1,023 majority) and 1924 (16,504 votes to 12,304 a majority of 4,200). When Stanley Baldwin succeeded Bonar Law in 1924, Wood was appointed Parliamentary Secretary to the Minister of Health, Neville Chamberlain. Wood and Chamberlain

worked closely together from November 1924 to June 1929 on local government reform, becoming friends as well as close political allies. Wood's reputation in Parliament was on the increase and was reflected by his appointment as Civil Commissioner during the General Strike of 1926, and then as a Privy Councillor in 1928. At the General Election on 30 May 1929, Woods retained his seat in Woolwich West with a 4,140 majority (26,441 votes to 14,520) after which he sat on the opposition benches until the

(HOWARD) KINGSLEY WOOD

collapse of the Labour government over the Budget crisis in August 1931. The resulting General Election on 27 October 1931, resulted in a landslide victory for the National Government headed by Ramsay MacDonald, and a victory in Woolwich West for Wood with a 7,276 majority (24,649 votes to 17,373). MacDonald appointed Wood as Postmaster General in November 1931, putting Wood in charge of the Post Office (GPO) which at that time was still government owned. The Post Office was seen as in need of updating and modernising to meet the demand of ever changing and growing businesses. Wood looked to introduce new measures, such as reply paid arrangements for businesses, improved efficiency of the telephone service, lowering charges, and increasing subscribers with clever use of publicity. Wood also negotiated a deal with the Treasury, whereby instead of the Treasury taking all the revenue for the year, a fixed annual fee was agreed and any surplus profit was re-invested to improve Post Office services. Wood's commitment and advancement of the GPO resulted in Chamberlain recommending Wood for a place in the Cabinet in December 1933. His organisation and planning skills were a big factor in him being appointed as Minister of Health in Stanley Baldwin's third ministry in June 1935, a position which at that time was responsible for housing as well as health

WOOD AS CHANCELLOR **1940**

services in England and Wales. As Minister of Health, Wood vigorously pursued a slum clearance programme which greatly reduced overcrowding. The first commercially available antibiotics in the 1930's, came under Wood's tenure and the Midwives Act of 1936 (the fourth such Act) greatly improved maternal mortality, with the Act laying a foundation for a significant change to the working lives of midwives. For the first time, midwives supporting women in their homes received a regular income, planned annual leave, and financial security although still on a relatively low income. Wood's standing in the Conservative party was such that he succeeded Stanley Baldwin (unanimously elected) as Grand Master of the Primrose League, which had been set up in 1883 to spread Conservative principles. In May 1937, Neville Chamberlain became Prime Minister and in a re-shuffle on 16 May 1938, Chamberlain moved Wood to be Secretary of State for Air, giving him the commission to bridge the gap between British and German aircraft production, with the looming prospect of war. By the outbreak of the Second World War, under Wood's leadership, the large gulf in production between Britain and Germany had been eradicated. Wood had worked diligently as Secretary of State for Air, but due to his efforts, by early 1940 he was exhausted, and swapped places with Sir Samuel Hoare, becoming Lord Privy Seal for a brief period. With the British defeats in Norway in 1940, Wood, as a close friend and colleague, advised Chamberlain that his resignation was inevitable, and at the same time, he advised

CIVIC CENTRE DAGENHAM

Winston Churchill to ignore calls for Lord Halifax to be Prime Minister and to put himself forward instead. Churchill became Prime Minister on 10 May 1940, and appointed Wood as the Chancellor of the Exchequer on 12 May 1940. Churchill tasked Wood with the wartime role of financing the war with as little inflation as possible. In total, Wood presented four wartime Budgets to Parliament, his first in July 1940 was mainly following on from his predecessor and produced little change, but his second Budget was described by eminent economist, John Maynard Keynes as 'a revolution in public finance'. The standard rate of income tax was raised to 10s. in the pound, giving a top marginal rate of 19s 6. in the pound, while income and personal allowances were reduced, meaning for the first time in British history the majority of the population was liable to income tax. With public expenditure increased due to the war, Wood sought to head off inflationary wage claims by subsidising essential rationed goods, while imposing heavy taxes on goods classed as non-essential. Wood's last act as Chancellor was the system of Pay As You Earn (PAYE), which was the compulsory deduction of income tax directly from current pay as opposed to being paid retrospectively from the previous year's earnings. Unfortunately,

Wood did not live to see the new system come into effect, as he died unexpectedly of heart failure on 21 September 1943. He died aged 62, at his flat at 12 Buckingham Palace Mansions, Westminster, on the morning he was due to announce the new PAYE scheme. Churchill said in the House of Commons the following day "We shall not easily fill the gap, I feel more for the loss of a genial, sincere and faithful friend, with whom I and my colleagues have stood shoulder to shoulder during a period altogether without precedent in our long history".

Interesting Kingsley Wood facts:

Wood was knighted in 1918 at the young age of 36.

Wood served under four Prime Ministers; Ramsay MacDonald, Stanley Baldwin, Neville Chamberlain and Winston Churchill.

Wood was just over five foot tall.

On his death, Wood left £63,981 9s 3d. in his will, approx. worth £2,936,530 in 2020.

Wood married Agnes Lilian in 1905, they adopted one daughter.

Wood stood in seven consecutive General Elections in Woolwich West, winning them all, dating from 1918 to his death in 1943.

Wood was referred to in the book *Guilty Men* by Michael Foot, Frank Owen and Peter Howard, published in 1940 as an attack on public figures for their failure to re-arm and their appeasement of Nazi Germany.

John Anderson
1882 - 1958 (75 years old) National Independent

Chancellor of the Exchequer:
24 September 1943 - 26 July 1945
(1 year, 10 months and 3 days)

Born
8 July 1882, Eskbank, Midlothian, Scotland
Died
4 January 1958, age 75, Lambeth, London

Title: 1st Viscount Waverley

Constituency Represented as MP:
Combined Scottish Universities 1938 - 1950

Other Official Offices held:
Joint Permanent Under-Secretary to the Lord Lieutenant of Ireland 1920 - 1922
Permanent Under-Secretary for the Home Dept 1922 - 1932
Lord Privy Seal 1938 - 1939
Home Secretary 1939 - 1940
Minister of Home Security 1939 - 1940
Lord President of the Council 1940 - 1943

Prime Minister served with as Chancellor:
Winston Churchill

Education:
Edinburgh University.

John Anderson, 1st Viscount Waverley, (8 July 1882 – 4 January 1958) was a Scottish politician who represented the Combined Scottish Universities from 1938 to 1950. He is best known for his service in the Cabinet during the Second World War, and his involvement in the production of the 'Anderson Air Raid Shelter'. He served as Home Secretary, Lord President of the Council and as Winston Churchill's wartime Chancellor of the Exchequer.

Anderson was born in Eskbank, a part of Dalkeith in Midlothian, Scotland, the only son of David Anderson and his wife Janet. He was educated first at George Watson's College for Boys, before moving on to Edinburgh University. He graduated BSc from Edinburgh University in 1903 with special distinction in mathematics, natural philosophy and chemistry. Later he received an MA with first class honours in mathematics and Natural philosophy.

After leaving Edinburgh, Anderson spent a year (1903–1904) at Leipzig University in Saxony, Germany, with the intentions of becoming a scientist, studying specifically the properties of uranium. However, Anderson wanted to marry his childhood sweetheart, Christina (Chrissie) Mackenzie, and so on the advice of his father he chose a more financially rewarding career in the Civil Service. He returned to Edinburgh in 1904 and studied for the Civil Service examination, in the exam he took first place with one of the highest scores ever recorded. Anderson then entered the Colonial Office serving as secretary to committee's in the Nigeria and West Indies Departments, and got his wish of marrying Christina on 2 April 1907, they went on to have two children; David (1911) and Mary (1916). The Colonial Office, although prominent in repute, did not offer much opportunity for quickened advancement. In 1912, Anderson left the Colonial Office and was appointed to the National Health Insurance Commission, where a group of the most gifted Civil Servants from all Departments were gathered to launch the National Health

Insurance Scheme. At the outbreak of the First World War, Anderson was government representative on an advisory committee set up by the Royal Society to organise chemical research for wartime needs. In January 1917, he was appointed Secretary to the new Ministry of Shipping, at a time when Britain's food supplies were being threatened by a German 'U' boat campaign. Although Anderson had no knowledge of shipping, his organisational skills soon won the confidence of the shipowners and it marked him out for future advancement. After

VISCOUNT WAVERLEY

the war, in April 1919, Anderson was made an additional Secretary to the old Local Government Board, and later in 1919, when the Local Government Board and the Insurance Commission were merged into the new Ministry of Health, he became Second Secretary of that Ministry. In October 1919, he was appointed Chairman of the Board of Inland Revenue, but on 9 May 1920, he suffered personal tragedy when his wife (Christina) died aged only thirty-four, during an operation for cancer,

Christina's sister, Nellie took charge of the household and children. A distraught Anderson was offered the post of Under-Secretary for Ireland, not only for his excellent work ability but that also a change of role and scene would help him personally. After accepting the position, Anderson spent two years living and working in Dublin until 1922, two years in which his responsibility grew in a country beset by civil war, and where he was constantly exposed to physical dangers, the experiences of which created a toughening of his character. When he returned from Ireland, he was appointed Permanent-Under Secretary of State at the Home Office from 1922 until 1932, his longest spell in any official post. In February 1932, Anderson was appointed the Governor of Bengal, a province of India troubled by terrorism directed at

British authorities. Shortly before his arrival in Bengal, there had been an attempt to assassinate his predecessor (Sir Stanley Jackson) and morale was fragile, but Anderson with his calmness and composure improved security measures, and confidence was eventually restored. Anderson's remit had been to suppress terrorism which he did, but not just merely with prevention. He also saw the benefit of remedial action and the removal of underlying causes. Anderson arranged for suspected terrorists

GOVERNER OF BENGAL

who had been detained, to be trained in agriculture and manufacturing before they were released. His programme of rehabilitation, welfare, and the re-education of suspects gradually brought terrorism under control. One of the major turning points in the fight, came after an attempted assassination on Anderson at Lebong racecourse in 1934. He was shot at by a young man at short range and had a remarkable escape, the attempt at assassination proved to be something of a defining moment in the campaign against terrorism, with popular opinion in Bengal deeply shocked by the attempt on his life, the anti-terrorist movement gained considerably in strength. As a result of Anderson's personal intervention, the youth who shot at him was released from detention and sent to the United Kingdom for training, an act that gained Anderson great admiration from the people of Bengal. Anderson also addressed the economic and social problems in Bengal, bringing in legislation to scale down debts to farmers and introducing compulsory primary education. Anderson's five year term was extended by six months to allow him to implement the Government of India Act of 1935, whereby self-government within provinces was applied from 1937. Anderson returned to England in November 1937, and while travelling home by sea he was invited to be a candidate for the Combined Scottish Universities seat in Parliament, which had become vacant through the death of Ramsay MacDonald. The By-election was held from 21 to 25 February 1938, Anderson stood as a National Candidate with no party label and was elected with a larger majority than MacDonald had, winning with 14,042 votes to 5,618 and 5,246, a majority of 8,424. Anderson also became a Director of the Imperial Chemical Industries and of the Midland Bank, but within a year of his return to England he was once more in the public service. In May 1938, in preparation for a potential war, Anderson was appointed by the Home Secretary

A TYPICAL ANDERSON WW2 SHELTER

(Sir Samuel Hoare) to research problems with evacuating civilians from cities, and was responsible for air raid precautions in London and the Home Counties. Anderson was also appointed to the Civil Defence Research Committee, researching the physics of explosions and the effect of explosions on buildings, later proving to be of value for offensive as well as defensive purposes. Anderson had initiated the development of an air raid shelter that could be placed in domestic gardens, a design was presented by William Paterson and Oscar Kerrison, which incorporated a pre-fabricated shelter involving a modular of corrugated steel panels which were dug into the ground, the shelters were named the 'Anderson shelter' in his honour. Any household with an income of less than £5 per week, could have a shelter provided for free, while households earning over £5 had to pay £7 for their shelter. Between February 1939 and the declaration of war in September 1939, 1.5 million shelters had been distributed, and by the end of the war over 3.6 million had been produced and installed. When war broke out in September 1939, Anderson was appointed Home Secretary and Minister for Civil Defence, returning to the Department in which he had been the Permanent Secretary for ten years. At the outset of the war Anderson was not made a member of the War Cabinet, but he was one of the Ministers who was in 'constant attendance'. In

October 1940, when Neville Chamberlain resigned from the Government on the grounds of ill-health, Anderson was appointed to succeed him as Lord President with a seat in the War Cabinet. The work Anderson did in this post over the ensuing three years was of supreme importance for the war effort, with the Prime Minister pre-occupied with strategic and military problems, Anderson dealt with other major 'home front' issues such as prices, wages, rationing the concentration of industry

ANDERSON COAT OF ARMS

and the use of manpower (hence the nickname of the 'Home Front Prime Minister'). Anderson's handling of these issues was seen as a big success, so much so that with the tragic and unexpected death of Chancellor Sir Kingsley Wood on 21 September 1943, Anderson was given the role of Chancellor of the Exchequer three days later. His first task as Chancellor was to introduce the Wage Earners Income Tax Bill, which established the Pay As You Earn (PAYE) scheme, which he needed to quickly come up to speed with so he could guide it through the House of Commons. He also brought in the Finance Act of 1944, and the Income Tax Act of 1945, while giving tax relief to expenditure on scientific research. Anderson's standing in Parliament was such, that in January 1945, with Churchill and the Foreign Secretary

Anthony Eden attending the same conference, Churchill advised the King that if they were to die before the end of the war then he should invite Anderson to form a coalition government. At the end of the war, Churchill continued as Prime Minister until the General Election in July 1945, which Labour won, resulting in Anderson stepping down as Chancellor. Even though he sat on the opposition benches, he was still appointed to chair the UK advisory committee on atomic energy in 1945. After the abolition of University representation in 1950, Anderson had offers to be Conservative candidate for a safe Conservative seat, but he did not feel that it would be right for him to sit in Parliament as a member of either party. In 1952, he was raised to the Peerage as Viscount Waverley of Westdean in the County of Sussex. Anderson died on 4 January 1956, aged 75, in St Thomas' Hospital, Lambeth, London.

Interesting John Anderson facts:

Anderson married for a second time, in 1941 to Ava Wigram.

Anderson was the Chairman of the Port of London Authority in 1946 and Chairman of the Royal Opera House in the same year.

Anderson left £25,020 16s 8d. in his will approx. worth £628,672 in 2020.

Anderson received The Order of Merit a few weeks before he died.

Anderson's son, David, took the title of 2nd Viscount Waverley in 1958 having served in the Royal Air Force in the Second World War. He trained as a physician, specialising as a cardiologist and spoke on matters of health in the House of Lords.

Anderson's daughter, Mary, served with the Women Auxiliary Territorial Service, the forerunner of the Women's Royal Army Corps during World War 2. By 1946 she was ATS Group Commander Highland District based in Perth, making a career out of service life.

Hugh Dalton
1887 - 1962 (74 years old) Labour

Chancellor of the Exchequer:
27 July 1945 - 13 November 1947
(2 years, 3 months and 18 days)

Born
26 August 1887, Neath, Wales

Died
13 February 1962, age 74, St
Pancras, London

Title: Baron Dalton

Constituencies Represented as MP:
Peckham 1924 - 1929
Bishop Auckland 1929 - 1931 & 1935 - 1959

Other Official Offices held:
Under-Secretary of State for Foreign Affairs 1929 - 1931
Minister for Economic Welfare 1940 - 1942
President of the Board of Trade 1942 - 1945
Chancellor of the Duchy of Lancaster 1948 - 1950

Prime Minister served with as Chancellor:
Clement Attlee

Education:
Kings College, Cambridge University.

Edward Hugh John Neale Dalton, Baron Dalton, (26 August 1887 – 13 February 1962) was a Labour Party economist and politician who served as a Member of Parliament for Peckham and Bishop Auckland between 1924 and 1959. He was Chancellor of the Exchequer from 1945 to 1947. He also served in Winston Churchill's wartime coalition Cabinet.

Dalton was born at The Gnoll, near Neath, Glamorgan, on 26 August 1887, the eldest child of Canon John Neale Dalton and his wife, Catherine. Dalton entered St George's Choir School in Windsor (which his father had helped to set up) in 1895. In 1898, he was sent to Summer Fields, a boarding preparatory school in Oxford, and in 1901, he went to Luxmoore's House at Eton College. In 1906, he entered King's College, Cambridge, with a closed exhibition to read mathematics, and at the end of his first term, he joined the Cambridge University Fabian Society. While at Cambridge, Dalton abandoned mathematics, and in 1910 he was awarded an upper second-class degree in the new discipline of economics. He moved to London the same autumn to read for the bar at the Middle Temple, but he had little interest in law, and the following year he began work on a doctorate at the London School of Economics (LSE) on the inequality of incomes. In May 1914 he was called to the Bar.

ARMY SERVICE CORPS

On 28 May 1914, Dalton married Ruth Fox, a fellow Fabian and former student at the LSE, they had one daughter, Helen, born in December 1917. But she sadly died aged only four of kidney disease in December 1922, Dalton said the impact of which never left him. At the outbreak of the First World War, he joined the Army Service Corps, and was sent to France, where he witnessed the battle of the Somme. At his own request he transferred to the Royal Artillery, and in 1917, he was sent to the Italian front where he commanded a 6 inch howitzer, and was decorated by the Italian government (medaglio al valore militare) for his part in the retreat, following the battle of Caporetto. When the war ended, Dalton built a career as an academic economist, and after a brief experience of working at the Ministry of Labour, and as a teaching assistant, he was appointed a reader in economics at the LSE in 1920. Later in 1920, Dalton published '*Some Aspects of the Inequality of Incomes in Modern Communities'* which offered an intellectual justification for economic socialism.

HUGH DALTON

He still had ambitions of becoming a Labour MP, but found it difficult to get a seat. He stood unsuccessfully for Parliament four times in the early 1920's; at the 1922 Cambridge By-election (losing by 3,943 votes), in Maidstone at the 1922 General Election (coming a close third behind the Unionist 8,928, Liberal 8,895 and Dalton 8,004), in Cardiff East at the 1923 General Election (coming second in a close three horse race - Liberal 8,536, Dalton 7,812 and Unionist 7,513) and the 1924 By-election in Holland with Boston (coming a close second - Conservative 12,907 Dalton 12,101 and Liberal 7,596). He was finally successful at the 29 October 1924 General Election, in yet another closely fought campaign in Peckham, but this time he was triumphant, winning with a 947 majority (13,361 votes to the Unionist's 12,414 and the Liberal's 3,194). However, Dalton only lasted one parliamentary term in Peckham, as a dispute with the local party led him to switch seats. It was at this time, Dalton received the most unusual support from his wife, Ruth, who worked for the London County Council (LCC). In 1929, Dalton was still MP for Peckham, but due to the fall-out he had decided to fight a different seat at the General Election. He was selected for

Bishop Auckland, but in December 1928, a few months before the General Election was due to be called, the sitting MP, Benjamin Spoor, died. If Dalton had resigned his seat in Peckham it would have created three By- elections (in Bishop Auckland, Peckham, and Gateshead - the seat held by John Beckett, who was

RUTH DALTON

intending to contest Peckham). A solution was found in which Ruth stood in the By-election for Bishop Auckland, on the understanding that she would step aside in her husband's favour when the General Election was called. Ruth won the By-election held in February 1929 (with a majority of 7,072) she took her seat in Parliament, asked her first question, and made her maiden speech (which was well received) on 13 March 1929, it concerned the appalling poverty created by unemployment in her constituency. She was then asked by Ramsay MacDonald to consider continuing her political career, but she told him that she had never wished to become an MP, and preferred her work on the LCC: *"there we do things, here it all seems to be talk"* was her reply. In May 1929, when the General Election was called, Ruth stood aside and Hugh was elected with a majority of 8,203 (17,838 votes to 9,635 and 4,503). The election of the Labour Government in 1929 coincided with an economic depression, and Ramsay MacDonald was faced with the problem of growing unemployment. Dalton was rising fast in the Labour party ranks though, and gained ministerial experience when he was appointed as Under-Secretary at the Foreign Office by MacDonald. But trouble lay ahead, a report by Sir George May in July 1931, suggested that the government should reduce its expenditure by £96,500,000, of which £66,500,000 was unemployment insurance. MacDonald, and his Chancellor of the Exchequer, Philip Snowden, accepted the report but when the matter was discussed by the Cabinet, a consensus could not be reached on whether to cut unemployment benefits to ensure a balanced Budget. MacDonald was angry that most of his Cabinet had voted against him and decided to resign. When MacDonald saw King George V that night, he was persuaded to head a new coalition government that would include Conservative and Liberal leaders as well as Labour ministers. Most of the Labour Cabinet totally rejected the idea, and only three, Philip Snowden, Jimmy Thomas and John Sankey agreed to join the new government. MacDonald was determined to continue, and that his new National Government introduce the measures that had been rejected by the previous Labour Cabinet. Dalton voted to expel Ramsay MacDonald from the Labour Party, and only fifteen other MPs disagreed with Dalton. MacDonald who had expected a split in the party, soon found out that not a single local Labour Party decided to support him. The result was that the 1931 General Election on 27 October, was an unmitigated disaster for the Labour Party, with only 46 members winning their seats. Dalton was one of those who lost his seat in Bishop Auckland, in a close two horse race he was beaten by Aaron Curry the Liberal National by 17,551 votes to 16,796 (majority 955). After the defeat Dalton returned to teaching at the London School of Economics and released a book *Practical Socialism for Britain* in 1935, which is said to have had a big influence on the new Labour leader Clement Attlee. At the General Election on 14 November 1935, Dalton stood in Bishop Auckland again, reversing the 1931 defeat to Curry, winning with a comfortable 8,086 majority (20,481 votes to 12,395). After returning to Parliament, he was appointed Labour Foreign Affairs Spokesman, and set about changing the party's international policy, and in 1936 to 1937 he served as Chairman of the Labour NEC, moving the party from semi-pacifism to a policy of armed deterrence and rejection of appeasement. This change had an important effect in the months before the declaration of war in September 1939, by making it possible for the National Government in its post-Munich resolve to stand up to Hitler. It also bolstered the cross-party alliance that succeeded in bringing down Neville Chamberlain in May 1940.

When Winston Churchill became Prime Minister at the head of a wide-ranging war coalition, Dalton was appointed Minister of Economic Warfare, with responsibility for depriving the enemy of supplies. Churchill also placed Dalton in command of the Special Operations Executive (SOE), also known as 'Churchill's Secret Army', an unknown organisation with the purpose of conducting espionage, sabotage and reconnaissance in occupied Europe. In February 1942, in a Churchill reshuffle, Dalton was moved from the Ministry of Economic Warfare to the Board of Trade, where he was placed in charge of a wide domain that included consumer

DALTON AS CHANCELLOR

rationing and other wartime controls. As the end of the war approached, Dalton began working on organisation for post-war planning and reconstruction. A major legislative landmark was Dalton's 1945 *Distribution of Industry Act,* inspired by his own experience of poverty in his North-East constituency. This particular measure set the pattern for subsequent post-war regional policies, which was aimed at clearing up pockets of unemployment. With the conclusion of the war, Dalton again won the Bishop Auckland seat in the July 1945 General Election, with a slightly increased majority of 8,860 (20,100 votes to 11,240) and was appointed by Clement Attlee as Chancellor of the Exchequer in what had been a surprise landslide victory for the Labour party (393 seats to the Conservative's 197). Dalton's period at the Treasury endorsed his own background as an expert in economics and public finance, bringing his own socialist commitment with enthusiasm and expert knowledge, at a much needed time when post-war planning was essential. Over the next couple of years Dalton was able to play a vital role as one of the government's 'big five', together with Clement Attlee, Ernest Bevin, Herbert Morrison (Lord President) and Sir Stafford Cripps (Board of Trade), they provided the driving force to the Labour administration during its most energetic and radical phase. On his commencement as Chancellor, Dalton identified a list of urgent problems he had to face: the re-conversion of industry manpower and expenditure to peaceful purposes; reducing unemployment with a smooth transition from war to peace, tackling industrial unrest and inflation; honouring Labour's pledge to extend social services; altering taxation, while reducing the gap between rich and poor; carrying out the nationalisation pledges and finally, finding a way to pay for the imports needed to maintain employment and prevent poverty. In total Dalton introduced four Budgets - in October 1945, April 1946, April 1947, and November 1947, in all of which he followed his socialist principles in trying to level up the difference between rich and poor, with his tax cuts weighing heavily in favour of the worst off in society. Dalton introduced policies such as increased food subsidies, heavily subsidised rents to council house tenants, the lifting of restrictions on housebuilding, the financing of national assistance and family allowances, while offering extensive assistance to rural communities and development areas. He was also responsible for funding the introduction of Britain's universal family allowances scheme, doing so using the phrase "with a song in my heart" which became his famous trademark expression. Dalton also significantly increased spending on education (which included £4 million for universities and the provision of free school milk), and his period as Chancellor gave an unprecedented emphasis by central government on the redistribution of income. On 12 November 1947, Dalton was in Parliament to present his fourth Budget, and while walking through the lobby on his way to deliver his Budget speech, he was approached by a reporter from the London Evening Star who stopped him and asked a question. Dalton gave the reporter details of the main tax changes he was about to announce. The reporter immediately telephoned his editor, and copies of the Star containing the information in the stop-press section were on sale before Dalton had reached the relevant part of his speech. As the Stock Market was still open, this was seen as an unforgiveable error and Dalton offered his

DALTON (RIGHT) WAS 6' 3" TALL

resignation, which was accepted. Dalton's career as a major front-line minister came to an end on 13 November 1947, with the big five becoming the big four. Although Dalton did return to the Cabinet in June 1948, when Attlee appointed him as Chancellor of the Duchy of Lancaster, making him a minister without portfolio. In November 1948, he became head of the British delegation to the Committee of Western European Powers, a new body charged with looking at ways of increasing European unity. Negotiations eventually led to the *Statute of the Council of Europe* in May 1949. At the General Election on 23 February 1950, (the first to be televised), Dalton again improved his majority in Bishop Auckland from 8,860 to 11,370 (25,039 votes to Conservative 13,669 and Liberal 4,527), and he was appointed Minister of Town and Country Planning. In February 1951, his responsibilities were extended to include housing, with him becoming Minister of Local Government and Planning. But with Labour's defeat in the 25 October 1951 General Election, after only twenty months in power, Dalton's ministerial career came to an end. He was returned again as MP in Bishop Auckland, winning by 25,881 votes to 16,895 (majority of 8,896) although he lost his seat on Labour's national executive in 1952. After the 26 May 1955 General Election, in which Dalton's majority was reduced to 5,845 (21,804 votes to 15,959), he retired from the shadow cabinet, and in 1959 he stood down as an MP. He accepted a life peerage as Baron Dalton, *of Forest and Frith in the County Palatine of Durham* on 28 January 1960. He died aged 74, on 13 February 1962, at St Pancras hospital in London.

Interesting Hugh Dalton facts:

He was an imposing six foot three inches tall.

The publication of the first two volumes of Dalton's autobiography, *Call Back Yesterday* (1953) and *The Fateful Years* (1957), based on private diaries, caused a stir which set a new fashion for 'confessional' memoirs. A third volume, *High Tide and After*, was published early in February 1962, just a week before his death.

Dalton's papers, including his diaries, are held at the LSE Library.

The Pigou–Dalton principle (PDP) is a principle in welfare economics, named after Arthur Cecil Pigou and Hugh Dalton, it is a condition on social welfare functions, it states that all things being equal, a transfer of some defined variable (for example utility or income) from the rich to the poor is desirable, as long as it does not bring the rich to a poorer situation than the poor.

Dalton was president of the Ramblers' Association from 1948 to 1950.

Dalton left in his will, £26,966 approx. £579,129 in 2020.

Stafford Cripps
1889 - 1952 (62 years old) Labour

Chancellor of the Exchequer:
13 November 1947 –
19 October 1950
(3 years and 7 days)

Born
24 April 1889, Chelsea, London
Died
21 April 1952, age 62, Zurich, Switzerland

Title: Sir Stafford Cripps

Constituencies Represented as MP:
Bristol East 1931 - 1950
Bristol South East - 1950

Other Official Offices held:
Solicitor General for England and Wales 1931
Leader of the House of Commons 1942
Lord Privy Seal 1942
Minister for Aircraft Production 1942 - 1945
President of the Board of Trade 1945 - 1947
Minister for Economic Affairs 1947

Prime Minister served with as Chancellor:
Clement Attlee
Education:
University College, London.

Sir Richard Stafford Cripps, (24 April 1889 – 21 April 1952) was a Labour Party politician who served the constituency of Bristol from 1931 to 1950. He was a barrister, diplomat and Chancellor of the Exchequer from 1947 to 1950.

Cripps was born at Elm Park Gardens, London, on 24 April 1889. He was the fifth and youngest child of Charles Alfred Cripps and his wife, Theresa (née Potter) who died when he was only four. His father was a successful barrister, who became a Conservative MP and later (as first Baron Parmoor) a Labour Cabinet Minister and Leader of the House of Lords from 1929 to 1931. Cripps attended preparatory schools at Reigate and Rottingdean, before moving on to Winchester College. In 1907, he won a scholarship to New College, Oxford, the first ever offered in chemistry. He decided to decline the offer and studied for an MSc degree at University College, London, but after changing his mind again, he left science for a career in law and was called to the bar by the Middle Temple in 1913.

Cripps law career was interrupted by the outbreak of the First World War in August 1914, and in October he crossed to France on a freelance mission to deliver winter comforts to the troops. In France, Cripps was determined on joining the Red Cross, and soon became driver of the ambulance service, evacuating wounded men through Boulogne. He offered his expertise as a chemist to the newly created Ministry of Munitions and was posted to Queensferry near Chester. Cripps then took on full responsibility for one of the biggest munitions factories in Great Britain working very long hours, consequently suffering a physical breakdown, which was eventually diagnosed as colitis (inflammation of the colon), and he spent the rest of the war as an invalid. After the war Cripps returned to the Bar and concentrated on religious work, especially for the World Alliance for Promoting International Friendship through the Churches, of which he became treasurer. Throughout the 1920's, Cripps law career took off and in 1927, aged thirty-eight, he became

Britain's youngest King's Counsel. His work had brought him to the attention of Herbert Morrison, the Labour leader in London, and with Morrison's encouragement, Cripps joined the Labour Party in 1929. In 1930, Cripps accepted an invitation to join Ramsay MacDonald's Labour government as Solicitor-General, receiving the customary knighthood in the process. On 16 January 1931, he won a By-election in the safe Labour seat of Bristol East, with a large 11,324 majority (19,261 votes to Conservative 7,937 and Liberal 4,010). In the 27 October General Election, nine months later, Cripps won again, but in a much tighter two horse race, scraping through with a majority of 429 (19,435 votes to Conservative's 19,006), Ramsay MacDonald as the leader of the National Government, invited Cripps to continue as Solicitor-General, but Cripps politely declined. In 1932, Cripps helped found the Socialist League, becoming its Chairman in 1933. The Socialist League put forward the case for an austere form of democratic socialism, Cripps argued that on taking power the Labour Party should immediately enact an Emergency Powers Act, allowing it to rule by decree and thus "forestall any sabotage by financial interests". They also wanted to immediately abolish the House of Lords. At the 14 November 1935 General Election, Cripps had a much healthier majority (6,833) than in the previous election, receiving 22,009 votes to the National Labour candidates 15,126 (the Conservatives didn't stand a candidate). Cripps opposed an appeasement policy towards Nazi Germany, and in 1936, he was the moving force behind a Unity Campaign, involving the Socialist League, the Independent Labour Party and the Communist Party of Great Britain. The Unity Campaign was designed to forge electoral unity against the right, but opposed by the Labour leadership, the Unity Campaign failed in its intentions, and Cripps was expelled from the Labour Party. After the outbreak of World War Two, Cripps became ambassador in Moscow from May 1940 until January 1942. In 1942, Cripps returned to Britain and made a broadcast about the Soviet war effort which received a great response, with Cripps being hailed as the man who brought Russia into the war. He then joined the British War Cabinet, on behalf of which he conducted a negotiation between Great Britain and India that was an important milestone on the road to Indian independence. The meetings, known as the Cripps Mission, took place in Delhi from

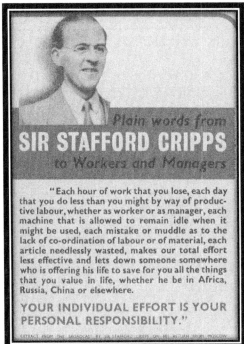

March 22 to April 12, 1942, and marked an attempt to rally Indian support through the rival Indian National Congress and Muslim League for the defence of the country against Japanese invasion. Consequently, despite having no party backing, he rapidly became one of the most popular politicians in the country. He was then appointed by Churchill as a member of the War Cabinet, along with the jobs of Lord Privy Seal and Leader of the House of Commons. Cripps tenure as Leader of the Commons was short-lived however, and he was appointed Minister of Aircraft Production in November 1942, a position he held with considerable success until the end of the war. After the war, Cripps was re-admitted to the Labour party and won a large majority in the 5 July 1945 General Election, beating the Conservative candidate by 27,975 votes to 10,073 (majority 12,550). He was appointed by the newly elected Prime Minister, Clement Attlee, as the President of the Board of Trade, the second most important economic post in the government. Although still a strong socialist, Cripps had modified his views sufficiently enough to be able to work alongside other mainstream Labour ministers. As President of the Board of Trade, Cripps initiated the post-war export drive while playing a pivotal role in working for Indian independence. In 1947, amid a growing economic and political crisis, Cripps tried to persuade Attlee to retire in favour of Ernest Bevin, however, Bevin was against the move and was in favour of Attlee remaining. Cripps was instead

STAFFORD CRIPPS

appointed to the new post of Minister for Economic Affairs. Six weeks later, Hugh Dalton resigned as Chancellor of the Exchequer and Cripps succeeded him on 13 November 1947, with the position of Minister for Economic Affairs merged into the Chancellorship, which created a potent mix of authority in determining economic policy. Cripps increased taxes, and continued strategic rationing to stifle consumption, in order to boost the balance of trade and stabilise the Pound. He wanted Britain to trade its way out of the risk of fiscal and economic gloom. He was among those who brought about the nationalisation of strategic industries such as coal and steel. As Chancellor, Cripps maintained a high level of social spending on housing, health, and other welfare services, and in his last Budget as Chancellor in 1950, the housebuilding programme was restored to a high level, income tax was reduced for low-income earners as an overtime incentive, as well as increasing spending on health, national insurance, and education. Cripps had suffered for many years from colitis, and his illness finally forced him to resign as both Chancellor and as an MP on 20 October 1950. Not only was he suffering from tubercular spondylitis, a spinal infection, but he also developed stomach tumours and was later diagnosed as having a form of bone marrow cancer. The illness ultimately proved fatal as he died at the Bircher Benner clinic,

Keltenstrasse 48, Zürich, Switzerland, on 21 April 1952 aged 62, and was cremated in Zürich three days later.

Interesting Stafford Cripps facts:

Cripps was a vegetarian.

Cripp's name once induced an infamous Spoonerism when the BBC announcer McDonald Hobley, introduced him as 'Sir Stifford Crapps'.

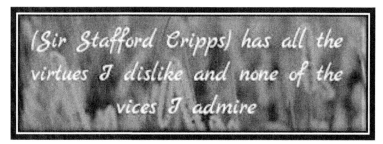

(Sir Stafford Cripps) has all the virtues I dislike and none of the vices I admire

WINSTON CHURCHILL

Cripps, together with other individuals, was instrumental in the foundation of the original College of Aeronautics, now Cranfield University, in 1946. The Stafford Cripps Learning and Teaching Centre on Cranfield's campus is named after him.

Cripps left in his will £15,190 17s 11d. approx. £439,946 in 2020.

A Blue Plaque was unveiled at 32 Elm Park Gardens, Chelsea to mark the site of Cripps' birth.

Hugh Gaitskell
1906 - 1963 (56 years old) Labour

Chancellor of the Exchequer:
19 October 1950 –
26 October 1951
(1 year and 8 days)
Born
9 April 1906, Kensington, London
Died
18 January 1963, age 56,
Marylebone, London

Title: None

Constituency Represented as MP:
Leeds South - 1945 - 1963

Other Official Offices held:
Parliamentary Secretary to the Minister of Fuel and Power 1946 - 1947
Minister of Fuel and Power 1947 - 1950
Minister for Economic Affairs 1950
Treasurer of the Labour Party 1954 - 1956
Leader of the Labour Party 1955 - 1963
Leader of the Opposition 1955 - 1963

Prime Minister served with as Chancellor:
Clement Attlee

Education:
New College, Oxford.

Hugh Todd Naylor Gaitskell, (9 April 1906 – 18 January 1963) was a Labour politician who served as MP for Leeds South from 1945 until his death in 1963. He was Leader of the Labour Party from 1955. Gaitskell was a leading component in Clement Attlee's governments, notably as Minister of Fuel and Power after the bitter winter of 1946–47, and eventually joining the Cabinet as Chancellor of the Exchequer in 1950.

Gaitskell was born at 3 Airlie Gardens, Kensington, London, on 9 April 1906, the youngest of the three children of Arthur Gaitskell and his wife, Adelaide. Gaitskell attended preparatory lessons at Dragon School in Oxford from 1912 to 1919, before moving to Winchester College (1919 to 1924) and finally on to New College, Oxford, from where he graduated in 1927 with a first-class degree in Philosophy, Politics and Economics.

After graduating, Gaitskell lectured in economics for the Workers Educational Association (adult learning) to miners in the Nottingham coalfields for a year, while at the same time publishing a booklet on the working-class Chartism movement. In the booklet Gaitskell argued that a successful working-class movement needed middle-class leadership. In 1928, Gaitskell was appointed as a lecturer in political economy at University College, London, and in 1931 he joined with G. D. H. Cole in forming the New Fabian Research Bureau. Their main objective was to persuade a future Labour government to implement socialist policies, while promoting the economic ideas of the esteemed economist John Maynard Keynes within the Labour Party. Gaitskell remained lecturing along with his political activities and remained at University College, until 1939, becoming head of the department of political economy, and university reader in 1938. While lecturing Gaitskell was adopted as prospective Labour Party candidate for Chatham in Kent in the autumn of 1932, but he was defeated in the 14 November 1935 General Election, losing to the Conservative candidate and radio entrepreneur, Leonard Plugge, by 19,212 votes to 13,135 (majority 5,897). Gaitskell married Dora Frost, on 9th April 1937 (Gaitskell's thirty-first birthday), and they went on to have two daughters, Julia (1939) and Cressida (1942). Gaitskell's best man at his wedding was Evan Durbin, who along with Gaitskell and another future Chancellor, Hugh Dalton, were members of the XYZ club, a select dining club of Labour's financial experts, who would meet to discuss fiscal and monetary planning. Gaitskell published his book *Money and*

HUGH GAITSKELL

Everyday Life in 1939, and with the outbreak of the Second World War, Gaitskell, who had been a strong opponent of appeasement, was recruited into Whitehall in May 1940, working for Hugh Dalton as a temporary civil servant in the Ministry of Economic Warfare. He moved to the Board of Trade in

February 1942, which gave him his first experience of government. After the war ended, Gaitskell had the opportunity to return to teaching but preferred to pursue a career in politics, and stood as a Labour candidate in the constituency of South Leeds. At the post-war General Election on 5 July, Labour won a landslide victory and Gaitskell was returned as a Labour MP with a resounding majority of 10,402 (17,899 votes to Conservative 7,497 and Liberal 3,933). A short illness prevented his immediate inclusion in the government, but Clement Attlee considered Gaitskell as one of the most talented new members of the House of Commons, and after recovering from his illness he was appointed Parliamentary Secretary to Emanuel Shinwell at the Ministry of Fuel and Power in May 1946. His main task was to help the passage of the Coal Nationalisation Bill through Parliament. Gaitskell believed in nationalisation on grounds of efficiency, economies of scale and rationalisation of production, while he also considered it to be morally right. Gaitskell had hoped that the move would result in the improved relationship between workers and employers, something that was never fully achieved.

In October 1947, Gaitskell replaced Shinwell as Minister of Fuel and Power, though remaining outside the Cabinet, it was a particularly difficult time to hold the position post-war, and he was heavily criticised for removing the basic petrol ration for private motorists. But he was praised for encouraging the building of oil refineries, a move which would have important repercussions in the future. Gaitskell stayed as Minister of Fuel and Power until the General Election on 23 February 1950, when he was again returned in Leeds South with a healthy majority of 15,359 (29,795 votes to Conservative 14,436 and Liberal 4,525). In February 1950, Attlee appointed Gaitskell as Minister for Economic Affairs, which was effectively the Deputy Chancellor but still outside the Cabinet, although he was made a full member of the Economic Policy Committee. Nine months later, on 19 October 1950, Gaitskell replaced Stafford Cripps, who had resigned as Chancellor, and he commenced with his commitment to the redistribution of wealth. In doing so, Gaitskell had to try to balance the Budget, the National Insurance Act had created the structure of the Welfare State and there was the passing of the National Health Service Act in 1948. The Act afforded people in Britain with free diagnosis and treatment of illness, at home or in hospital, as well as dental and ophthalmic services. On the afternoon of 10th April 1951, Gaitskell presented his Budget, including the proposal to save between £13 and £30 million in a full year by imposing charges on spectacles and dentures supplied under the Health Service. In addition, purchase tax was increased from 33% to 66% on certain luxury items such as cars, television sets and domestic appliances, while entertainment tax was increased on cinema tickets. At the same time, however, taxation on profits was raised and pensions increased to compensate retirees for a rise in the cost of living. The allowances for dependent children payable to widows, the unemployed and the sick, together with marriage and child allowances, were also increased, while the amount of earnings allowed without affecting the pension was increased from 20 shillings (£1) to 40 shillings (£2) a week. Besides taxing the better off and protecting pensions, Gaitskell increased NHS spending. The Budget increased defence spending by £500m to

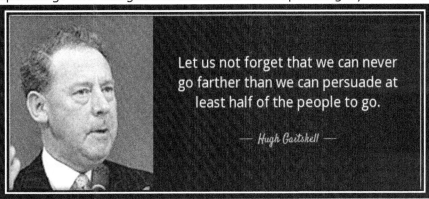

Let us not forget that we can never go farther than we can persuade at least half of the people to go.

— Hugh Gaitskell —

1.5bn for 1951–1952, helped by a surplus inherited from Cripps and optimistic growth forecasts. The Budget was not universally well received within the Cabinet and the following day, three members of the government, Harold Wilson, Aneurin Bevan (a long-time opponent of Gaitskell) and John Freeman resigned. Attlee called a snap General Election on 25 October 1951 in the hope of increasing his small parliamentary majority, however, despite winning the popular vote and achieving the highest-ever total vote up to date, Labour won fewer seats than the Conservative Party. It marked the return of Winston Churchill as Prime Minister and the beginning of Labour's thirteen-year spell in opposition. Gaitskell was returned in the General Election in Leeds South with a 14,219 majority in a two-horse race (30,712 votes to the Conservatives 16,493). In opposition, this period in Labour's history was characterised by infighting between the 'Bevanite' left of the Labour party led by Aneurin Bevan, whose strength lay mainly in the constituency Labour Parties ("CLP"s) and the 'Gaitskellite' right, who had the upper hand in the Parliamentary Party. Bevan stood against Gaitskell for Labour Party Treasurer, with Gaitskell winning comfortably by 4.3 million votes to 2 million. Anthony Eden replaced Winston Churchill as Prime Minister in April 1955, and called a snap General Election for 26 May 1955 in order to gain a mandate for his government, which he won with a 60 seat majority. Gaitskell was once again returned in Leeds South with a 12,016 majority (25,833 votes to 13,817). Clement Attlee finally decided to retire after twenty years as Labour Party leader after losing the General Election and in the ensuing leadership election, held in December 1955, Gaitskell won an emphatic victory (at the time, the Labour Party leader was elected solely by MPs). He received 157 votes against 70 for Bevan and 40 for Herbert Morrison. Gaitskell offered Bevan a public olive branch at the party meeting after the result, promising that he would "not be outdone in generosity" if Bevan accepted the vote. Bevan did accept the result of the vote, and in an attempt to unite the party, Gaitskell appointed Bevan as Shadow Foreign Secretary in 1956. The first major challenge which Gaitskell faced as leader was the Suez crisis, in his first speech on the crisis in the House of Commons on 2 August 1956, he clearly stated his view that he would only support armed intervention if it was endorsed by the United Nations. But on 31 October, he attacked the military intervention by Britain, France, and Israel, calling it 'an act of disastrous folly' which compromised the three principles of bipartisan foreign policy: solidarity with the Commonwealth, the Anglo-American alliance and the adherence to the charter of the United Nations. After the Suez Crisis in 1956, Anthony Eden, the Conservative Prime Minister, had become unpopular and resigned early in 1957, he was succeeded by Harold Macmillan. At that point, the Labour Party enjoyed large leads in the opinion polls over the Conservative Party, and it looked as if Labour would win. Leading up to the 8 October 1959 General Election, Gaitskell pledged that Labour's spending plans would not require him to raise income tax. But a third consecutive victory

GAITSKELL IN FULL FLOW

for the Conservative Party ensued, and for the second time in a row the Conservatives increased their overall majority in Parliament. This time to 100 seats having gained a further 20 seats, for a return of 365. The election defeat led to questions being asked about Gaitskell's leadership, but he remained as leader, winning his own seat for his fifth consecutive General Election victory in Leeds South, with an 11,486 majority (24,442 votes to the Conservative 12,956 and Liberal 4,340). Gaitskell felt very strongly about the party policy of unilateral nuclear disarmament. At the party conference in Scarborough in October 1960, two unilateralist resolutions from the transport workers and the engineers were carried, and the official policy document on defence was rejected. Gaitskell thought these were disastrous decisions and made a passionate speech where he stressed that he would "fight and fight and fight again to save the party we love". Harold Wilson challenged Gaitskell for the leadership in November 1960, but Gaitskell won comfortably by 166 votes to 81. In July 1961, Prime Minister Harold Macmillan applied for entry to the European Economic Community (EEC), Gaitskell had previously been in favour of joining the EEC but he now changed his position, stating "The end of Britain as an independent

European state. I make no apology for repeating it. It means the end of a thousand years of history". Gaitskell was taken ill in December 1962, and was taken to Middlesex Hospital, London. It was not until several weeks later that the doctors became aware, that initially he was suffering from the rare disease systemic lupus erythematosus in both his heart and lungs, but then the disease attacked every critical organ, and he died on 18th January 1963 aged 62.

Interesting Hugh Gaitskell facts:

Hugh Gaitskell Primary School is situated in Beeston, part of his former Leeds South constituency.

A memorial plaque in his name is prominently placed in the cloisters of New College, Oxford and a blue plaque is in place on his old house in Frognal Gardens, London.

Gaitskell had a stern public image, but in private he was fun loving and enjoyed ballroom dancing.

Gaitskell left in his will £80,013 10s approx. worth £1,686,560 in 2020.

Gaitskell married Dora on 9 April 1937. They had two daughters.

On his death a popular conspiracy theory involved a Soviet KGB plot to assassinate Gaitskell by poisoning, ensuring Harold Wilson would become Prime Minister.

Richard Austen (Rab) Butler
1902 - 1982 (79 years old) Conservative

Chancellor of the Exchequer:
28 October 1951 -
20 December 1955
(4 years, 1 month and 23 days)
Born
9 December 1902, Attock Serai, India
Died
8 March 1982, age 79, Great Yeldham,
Essex
Title: Baron Butler of Saffron Walden

Constituency Represented as MP:
Saffron Walden 1929 - 1965

Other Official Offices held:
Minister of Education 1941 - 1944
Minister of Labour and National Service 1945
Lord Privy Seal 1955 - 1959
Leader of the House of Commons 1955 - 1961
Home Secretary 1957 - 1962
First Secretary of State 1962 - 1963
Deputy Prime Minister 1962 - 1963
Secretary of State for Foreign Affairs 1963 - 1964
Father of the House of Commons 1964 - 1965

Prime Minister served with as Chancellor:
Winston Churchill and Anthony Eden

Education:
Pembroke College and Corpus Christie, Cambridge.

Richard Austen Butler, Baron Butler of Saffron Walden, (9 December 1902 – 8 March 1982), was more familiarly known from his initials as Rab. He was a prominent Conservative MP for Saffron Walden from 1929 to 1965 and he served as Chancellor of the Exchequer from 1951 to 1955.

Butler was born at Attock Serai, Punjab, India, on 9 December 1902, the eldest of a family of two sons and two daughters of Sir Montagu Sherard Dawes Butler and his wife, Anne. Butler attended the Wick preparatory school at Hove, and although he had a place reserved at Harrow School, he refused to go, preferring the option of Eton College instead. But after failing the scholarship exam for Eton, Butler settled on attending Marlborough College, where he studied until December 1920, before spending five months in France improving his French. After returning from France, Butler won an exhibition to Pembroke College, Cambridge, at first studying modern and Medieval languages in 1923, but he suffered a nervous breakdown that summer and had to postpone his plans to study History into a fourth year, he took a less strenuous course in German in the meantime. He spent part of the summer of 1923 abroad learning German, and on his return became President of the Union in 1924. In his fourth year, he gained a first in history (1925) and a fellowship at Corpus Christi College, Cambridge. After graduating, Butler spent a brief period as a don at Corpus Christi College from 1925, giving lectures on the politics of the French Third Republic.

While an undergraduate, Butler had met Sydney Elizabeth Courtauld with whom he married on 20 April 1926. Sydney's father, Samuel Courtauld, a wealthy industrialist, settled £5000 a year on Butler for life tax-free (equivalent to £305,797 in 2020). In the summer of 1926, Butler resigned his residential Cambridge fellowship to go on a honeymoon tour of the world, and with his guaranteed private income behind him, he decided on a political career. Whilst in Vancouver in June 1927, Butler had learned of a vacancy for the fairly safe Conservative seat of Saffron Walden in Essex, he returned from Quebec by sea on 31 August 1927. Courtauld's connections arranged for Butler to be selected unopposed as the Conservative candidate for Saffron Walden on 26 November 1927. At the 30 May 1929 General Election, Butler was returned as the Unionist MP with a 4,919 majority (13,561 votes to Labour's 8,642 and the Liberal 8,307). At the following General Election, on 27 October 1931, Butler was again returned in Saffron Walden, this time in a two horse race winning with a much increased 16,033 majority (22,501 votes to Labour's 6,468). Before the election, Butler had become Private Secretary to Sir Samuel Hoare, in the National Government, and in 1931, Hoare became India Secretary with Butler as his

A YOUNG RAB BUTLER

Parliamentary Private Secretary. After a tour of India, Butler became Hoare's Under-Secretary in September 1932, with his support for constitutional reform and knowledge of the Indian scene it had made Butler a natural choice, even though he had been in Parliament for only three and a half years and was the youngest member of the government. At the 14 November 1935 General Election, Butler was re-elected in Saffron Walden with a majority of 10,036 (19,669 votes to Labour's 9,663) and he continued as Under-Secretary for India in Stanley Baldwin's government, which ran from 1935 to 1937. When Neville Chamberlain became Prime Minister in May 1937, Butler became Parliamentary Secretary at the Ministry of Labour in the new government, until February 1938, when he was appointed Under-

Secretary of State for Foreign Affairs. Chamberlain's policy of appeasement cut across the Conservative Party and Butler who was an enthusiastic Chamberlainite, and like Chamberlain, he regarded the Munich agreement not as a means of buying time, but as a way of settling differences with Adolf Hitler, a view which was later held against him. Despite his support of appeasement, Butler survived Churchill's reconstruction of the government and was reappointed to his Foreign Office job on 15 May 1940. In July 1941, after nine years as an Under-Secretary, Butler became President of the Board of Education which had seen no major reform since 1902. Butler decided to go for comprehensive reform, and although in the end he had to exclude the public schools, every child was given the right to free secondary education. To make it a reality for the poor, provision was made for the expansion of both nursery and further education, as well as the raising of the school-leaving age.
All Butler's formidable diplomatic and political skills were needed to secure the agreement of the churches, as well as the consent of Churchill and Conservative back-benchers. The 1944 *Education Act*, which Butler believed would "have the effect of welding us into one nation—instead of two nations as Disraeli talked about" was Butler's greatest legislative achievement and was justifiably named after him. After World War Two ended in May 1945, Butler became Minister of Labour in Churchill's 'caretaker' government, and after the General Election defeat on 5 July 1945, in which Butler's own majority in Saffron Walden fell to just 1,158 (16,950 votes to Labour's 15,792 and Liberal's 3,395), Churchill made him the Chairman of the Conservative Research Department, and Butler emerging as the most prominent figure in the rebuilding of the Conservative party. In 1947, the Industrial Charter was produced, advocating full employment and acceptance of the welfare state, and in 1950, Butler welcomed the "One Nation" pamphlet produced by new MPs including Edward Heath, Iain Macleod, Angus Maude, and Enoch Powell. At the General Election on 23 February 1950, Butler once again retained his Saffron

Walden seat with a 4,889 majority (19,797 votes to Labour's 14,908 and Liberal's 4,963) but Labour were returned with a much reduced majority of only five seats. A snap General Election was called twenty months later on 25 October 1951, in which the Conservatives under Winston Churchill was returned with a twenty seat majority. Butler won the seat in Saffron Walden with

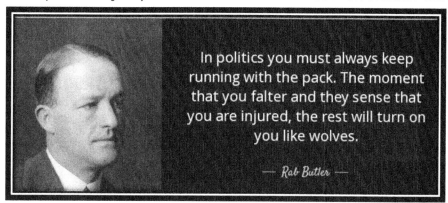

In politics you must always keep running with the pack. The moment that you falter and they sense that you are injured, the rest will turn on you like wolves.

— Rab Butler —

a slightly increased majority of 5,319 (20,564 votes to Labour's 15,245 and Liberal's 3,774) and was appointed by Churchill as Chancellor of the Exchequer on 28 October 1951. Butler inherited a balance of payments crisis which he attempted to tackle with import controls by raising interest rates from 2 to 2.5 per cent. Butler had wanted more drastic measures, having accepted a plan thought up in the Bank of England, under this plan, known as Robot (an acronym of the originators), the pound was to be allowed to float rather than be at a pegged rate and was to be made convertible into dollars, with most of the sterling balances held in London. But this idea would have alienated the American government and was blocked by Cabinet. In his Budget in March 1952, Butler raised the bank rate to 4 per cent and cut food subsidies by 40 per cent, but also cut income tax. He increased pensions and welfare benefits to help the worst off, and the reserves began to increase. By the end of the year the reserves were much higher than anybody in the Treasury had dared to think possible, and by 1953 Butler had more scope to promote expansion. In his second Budget, he was able to cut income tax and purchase tax and promised the abolition of the excess profits levy. While Churchill recovered from a stroke and the Deputy Prime Minister, Anthony Eden also ill, Butler took charge of the government, with many seeing it as a precursor to him becoming Prime Minister. Butler had been broadly following the economic policies of his Labour predecessor, Hugh Gaitskell, pursuing a mixed economy and Keynesian economics as part of the post-war political consensus. This led to *The Economist* introducing 'Mr Butskell' The name 'Butskellism', referring to the generally similar economic policies pursued by both the Conservative and Labour

BUTLER TIME MAGAZINE **1954**

governments, which was concocted partly in response to Butler's extension of Gaitskell's NHS charges in 1952. The Conservatives pledge to build 300,000 houses in a year, meaning that a lot of the nation's resources went into the housing drive, and so in 1954, Butler's third Budget was, as he said, a 'carry-on affair' with few changes, but later in the year he predicted the doubling of the country's standard of living within twenty-five years by 1970. Butler's wife, Sydney, died after a long illness in February 1955, which is said to have affected his political judgement. In his 1955 Budget he cut 6d off income tax, immediately before Anthony Eden succeeded Churchill as Prime Minister in April 1955. After the Conservatives won the May 1955 General Election, in which Butler was returned with a 6,418 majority (20,671 votes to Labour's 14,253 and Liberals 3,209), Butler declined Eden's request to move from the Treasury. But with the economy showing signs of 'overheating', inflation and balance of payment deficit sharply rising, and the Cabinet refusing to agree a cut in bread subsidies, there was a run on the pound. In Butler's final Budget on 26 October 1955, he had to reverse several of the measures from the spring Budget, this led to charges of electoral opportunism, with Gaitskell accusing him of deliberately misleading the electorate. The introduction of purchase tax on kitchen utensils led the Budget to be labelled the "Pots and Pans" Budget. In December 1955, Eden decided to replace Butler with Harold Macmillan, with Butler becoming Lord Privy Seal and Leader of the House, which effectively promoted Macmillan above Butler in the hierarchy for the position of Prime Minister. When Eden resigned as Prime Minister on Wednesday 9 January 1957, the Conservative Party had no formal mechanism for determining a new leader, but the Queen received overwhelming advice to appoint Macmillan as Prime Minister instead of Butler, rather than wait for a Party meeting to decide. Churchill had reservations about both candidates, but later admitted that he had advised the Queen to appoint "the older man", Macmillan. Butler took his defeat well, and Macmillan offered him the role of Home Secretary while he also remained Leader of the House, and as he had done under Churchill and Eden, he ran the government from time to time. In 1958, Macmillan went on his Commonwealth tour after settling his 'little local difficulties' over the resignation of his entire Treasury team, leaving Butler, as he said, 'to hold the baby'. At the 8 October 1959 General Election, Butler was returned in Saffron Walden with a majority of 6,782 (20,995 votes to Labour's 14,173 and the Liberal's 4,245) and became chairman of the Conservative Party, in addition to being Home Secretary and Leader of the House. He was Home Secretary for five years, but his liberal views on hanging and flogging did little to attach him to rank-and-file Conservative members, and he had come to favour the abolition of hanging, but still signed off on the execution of James Hanratty, known as the A6 murderer, who was one of the final eight people in the UK to be executed. Butler declined to reintroduce corporal punishment, with his refusal annoying the new MP for Finchley, Margaret Thatcher who had voted to bring back the birch or the cane for violent young offenders. It was the only time in her Commons career that Thatcher voted against the party line. In October 1961, Butler lost two of his offices, but retained the position of Home Secretary, and in March 1962, Macmillan formed a new central Africa department and persuaded Butler to take charge. In the 'Cabinet massacre' of July 1962, Butler left the Home Office and was left with his central African responsibilities, with the honorific title of 'First Secretary of State'. He was again overlooked as Prime Minister when Macmillan resigned in October 1963, in favour of Alec Douglas-Home who appointed Butler as Foreign Secretary, a position he had always coveted, although he lost the position of Deputy Prime Minister. At the 15 October 1964 General Election, Butler stood for the last time in Saffron Walden, winning with a majority of 4,955 (20,610 votes to Labour's 15,655 and the Liberal's 6,189). After the election Butler lost his chairmanship of the Conservative Research Department which he had held for twenty years. He refused an earldom which Home had offered him, and between the 1964 election and his retirement from the House of Commons, Butler was the Father of the House (longest serving member). In 1965, the new Prime Minister, Harold Wilson, offered him the Mastership of Trinity College, Cambridge, which he accepted. He then accepted a life peerage in 1965 as Baron Butler of Saffron Walden, and took his seat on the cross-benches, Butler was the first non-Trinity man to become master for 250 years. He earned respect for his chairing of College Council Meetings and by 1971, the fellows had warmed to him enough to vote recommending that he be given a second six-year term, despite the normal retirement age for masters being seventy. Butler was appointed to the Order of the Garter on 23 April 1971, which was seen as a gesture of recognition for his guidance of the young Prince of Wales who had studied at Cambridge. From 1972 to 1975, he chaired the high-profile Committee on 'Mentally Abnormal Offenders', widely referred to as the 'Butler Committee', which proposed major reforms to the law and psychiatric services. By the early 1970s, Butler's health began to decline, and his last public appearance, was on 13 January 1982, at the unveiling of his portrait at the National Portrait Gallery. He died of colon cancer in March 1982, aged 79, in Great Yeldham, Essex.

Interesting Rab Butler facts:

Butler's son, Adam Butler, was a Member of Parliament from 1970 to 1987 and a junior minister under Margaret Thatcher.

Butler's memoirs, *The Art of the Possible*, were published in 1971 and a further volume of memoirs, *The Art of Memory*, appeared posthumously in 1982.

Butler had an exceptionally long ministerial career and was one of only two British politicians (the other being John Simon, 1st Viscount Simon) to have served in three of the four Great Offices of State, but never to have been Prime Minister.

Butler's younger brother Jock, a Home Office civil servant and Pilot Officer, was killed in a plane crash at the end of 1942.

Butler won in nine consecutive General Elections in Saffron Waldon from 1929 to 1964.

In his 1953 Budget, Butler announced that the sugar ration would be increased from 10oz to 12oz a week to help the nation make celebratory cakes for the Queen's Coronation that year.

Butler left in his will £748,789 approx. worth £2,660,125 in 2020.

Harold Macmillan
1894 - 1986 (92 years old) Conservative

Chancellor of the Exchequer:
20 December 1955 -
13 January 1957
(1 year and 25 days)
Born
12 February 1894, London

Died
29 December 1986, age 92,
Chelwood Gate, Sussex

Title: 1st Earl of Stockton

Constituencies Represented as MP:
Stockton on Tees 1924 - 1929 and 1931 - 1945
Bromley 1945 - 1964

Other Official Offices held:
Parliamentary Secretary to the Ministry of Supply 1940 - 1942
Under-Secretary of State for the Colonies 1942
Secretary of State for Air 1945
Minister of Housing and Local Government 1951 - 1954
Minister of Defence 1954 - 1955
Foreign Secretary 1955
Prime Minister 1957 - 1963

Prime Minister served with as Chancellor:
Anthony Eden

Education:
Balliol College, Oxford.

Maurice Harold Macmillan, 1st Earl of Stockton (10 February 1894 – 29 December 1986) was an MP from 1924 to 1964 and was one of the outstanding Conservative leaders of the 20th century, serving as Foreign Secretary, Chancellor of the Exchequer and Prime Minister.

Macmillan was born at 52 Cadogan Place in Chelsea, London, to Maurice Crawford Macmillan, a publisher, and his wife, American-born Helen (Nellie) Artie Tarleton Belles. He was the youngest of three boys and grandson of a founder of the London publishing house of Macmillan & Co. Macmillan received an intensive early education, learning French at home every morning, and from an early age he received introductory lessons in classical Latin and Greek. Macmillan attended Summer Fields School, Oxford, from 1903, and in 1906 he won a scholarship to Eton. However, over the next three years he suffered poor health after contracting pneumonia, from which he only just survived. Once recovered he won a place at Balliol College in 1912, where his personal tutor was Ronald Knox, a Catholic priest, theologian, radio broadcaster and author of detective stories, Knox became a major influence on Macmillan's intellectual development. While at university Macmillan became involved in politics, where he joined the Canning Club (Conservative), the Russell Club (Liberal) and the Fabian Society (Socialist). He took a first class in classical moderations in Trinity term (third and final term) in 1914, but his war service prevented him taking Greats.

On the outbreak of the First World War, Macmillan was suffering from appendicitis, but as soon as he recovered he joined the Grenadier Guards. He was commissioned as a second lieutenant and was sent to a training battalion at Southend-on-Sea, leaving for France on 15th August, 1915. His battalion arrived to fight on the Western Front, where on 27th September 1915, Macmillan took part in the offensive at Loos, when towards the end of the battle he was shot through his right hand. He was evacuated to hospital and although it was not a serious wound, he never fully recovered the strength in that hand. The wound consequently affected the standard of his handwriting and was also responsible for what became known as the 'limp handshake'. After receiving treatment in London, Macmillan was sent back to the Western Front, where in April 1916 he took part in the offensive at the Somme. In July 1916, he was wounded again while leading a patrol in No Man's Land, and after being hit by a bomb on the back and face, he was hospitalised for a couple of days, but by the end of the month he moved with his battalion

A YOUNG HAROLD MACMILLAN

to Beaumont-Hamel. On 15th September 1916, Macmillan was wounded again during an attack on the German trenches, after being shot in the leg, he took refuge in a shell-hole until he was found by members of the Sherwood Foresters regiment. He had received serious wounds and the surgeons decided it would be too risky to attempt to remove the bullet fragments from his pelvis. He was returned to England where for a while his life was in danger, so his mother arranged for him to be transferred to a private hospital in Belgrave Square, where he spent the final two years of the war undergoing a long series of operations. He was still on crutches on Armistice Day on 11 November 1918, with the hip wound eventually taking four years to completely heal, and still leaving him with a slight shuffle when he walked. After the war, in 1919, Macmillan served in Ottawa, Ontario, Canada, as an *aide-de-camp (French expression meaning helper)* to Victor Cavendish, 9th Duke of Devonshire, the then Governor General of Canada and his future father-in-law. He returned to London in 1920, where he joined the family publishing firm Macmillan Publishers, as a junior partner. Macmillan married Lady Dorothy Cavendish, the daughter of the 9th Duke of Devonshire, on 21 April 1920, and although they had four children and 46 years of marriage together, it wasn't a traditional marriage. His wife, Dorothy, carried on a lifelong affair with Tory backbencher Robert Boothby (an open secret in political and journalistic circles) but he was unwilling to pursue a divorce that would most likely have ended his political career, and so

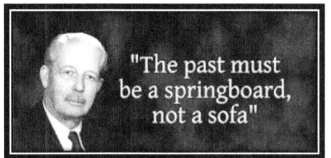

Macmillan and Dorothy lived largely separate lives. Although tempted to join the Liberal Party, Macmillan, calculated that they were in decline and instead decided to join the Conservative Party. In the 1924 General Election, he became the Conservative MP for Stockton-On-Tees, but in the face of high regional unemployment he was defeated in the May 1929 General Election by a majority of 2,389 Labour 18,961 votes, Macmillan Unionist 16,572 and Liberal's 10,407. He did return to the House of Commons again as MP for Stockton in the October 1931 General Election, picking up the Liberal votes for a majority of 11,031 (Macmillan, Conservative 29,199, Labour 18,168, no Liberal candidate stood). Macmillan spent the 1930s on the backbenches, and in March 1932 he published 'The State and Industry' following on from an earlier pamphlet named 'Industry and the State' (co-produced with Robert Boothby). Macmillan was a strong believer in social reform, but his left-wing views were unpopular with the Conservative Party leadership. He was also highly critical of the foreign policies of Stanley Baldwin and Neville

Chamberlain and so remained a backbencher until 1940, when Winston Churchill invited him to join the government as Parliamentary Secretary to the Ministry of Supply. In 1942, Macmillan went to North Africa where he filled the new Cabinet post as Minister at Allied Headquarters, and on 14 September 1944, he was appointed Chief Commissioner of the Allied Central Commission for Italy. He returned to England after the European war, and was Secretary of State for Air for two months in Churchill's caretaker government. Macmillan lost his seat in Stockton in the landslide Labour post-war General Election victory of July 1945, Labour 27,128, Macmillan 18,464 and the Liberals 3,718 (majority 8,664). But he returned to Parliament in the November of 1945 in a By-election victory in Bromley, with a 5,557 majority (Macmillan 26,367, Labour 20,810 and Liberals 5,990). In 1946, Winston Churchill asked Macmillan to join a committee to look into reshaping the Conservative Party. On 3rd October, Macmillan published an article in the *Daily Telegraph* where he suggested that the name should be changed to the "New Democratic Party", which was never implemented, and in the article he called for the Liberal Party to join Conservatives in an anti-socialist alliance. At the 23 February 1950 General Election, Macmillan was re-elected in Bromley with 23,042 votes to Labour's 12,354 and the Liberals 4,847. A General Election followed twenty months later on 25 October 1951, and Macmillan retained his Bromley seat with a majority of 12,125 (Macmillan 25,710, Labour 13,585). The Conservative's regained power and Macmillan became Minister of Housing & Local Government under Churchill, who entrusted him with fulfilling the pledge to build 300,000 houses per year (which was achieved a year ahead of schedule at the end of 1953). Macmillan was then made Minister of Defence from October 1954, with the major theme of his tenure at Defence being the ministry's growing reliance on the nuclear deterrent, resulting in 'The Defence White Paper' of February 1955, the White Paper announced the decision to produce the hydrogen bomb. Macmillan was briefly Foreign

Secretary from April to December 1955, and was then appointed Chancellor of the Exchequer on 20 December 1955. One of Macmillan's innovations at the Treasury was the introduction of Premium Bonds, which he announced in his Budget of 17 April 1956, although the Labour Opposition initially disparaged them as a 'squalid raffle', they proved an immediate hit with the public and £1,000 was won in the first prize draw in June 1957. With the onset of the Suez Crisis in November 1956, Macmillan was accused by the Labour Shadow Chancellor Harold Wilson of being

JOHN F KENNEDY WITH MACMILLAN

'first in, first out' by being at first, very supportive of the invasion, then instigating Britain's humiliating withdrawal. Britain's humiliation at the hands of the US caused deep anger among Conservative MPs, with Prime Minister Eden's political standing destroyed, he resigned on grounds of ill health on 9 January 1957. At the time the Conservative Party had no formal mechanism for selecting a new leader, and so on 10 January 1957, after taking advice from Churchill, the Queen appointed Macmillan as Prime Minister. Macmillan set out his premiership with an image of calm and style, although initially he was accused of cronyism when he appointed seven former Etonians to his Cabinet. Macmillan was the first Conservative Prime Minister to accept that countries within the British Empire should be given their freedom, and in 1957, the Gold Coast, Ghana, Malaya and North Borneo were granted their independence. In January 1958, Macmillan refused to introduce strict controls on money, with his economic policies resulting in an economic boom and a reduction in unemployment. This led to the Conservatives winning the 1959 General Election, increasing their majority from 67 to 107 seats. Macmillan was re-elected in Bromley, winning with a majority of 15,452 (27,055 votes to Labour's 11,603). In February 1959, he became the first British Prime Minister to visit the Soviet Union since the Second World

War, and he held talks with Soviet leader Khrushchev to ease tensions in East-West relations over West Berlin. During his time as Prime Minister, average living standards steadily increased while numerous social reforms were carried out, including the 1957 Housing Act, the 1960 Offices Act, the 1960 Noise Abatement Act and the Factories Act 1961. Macmillan also introduced a graduated pension scheme to provide an additional income to retirees, the establishment of a Child's Special Allowance for the orphaned children of divorced parents, and a reduction in the standard work week from 48 to 42 hours. But as the sixties progressed, Macmillan began to fear his Conservative party was in decline, and with the defeat in a By-election in April 1962 of a safe Tory seat in Orpington (a majority of 14,760 was lost with a swing of 26.3%), he became convinced of the need to act. He had lost faith in several members of his Cabinet, including his high-profile colleague and friend, Chancellor Selwyn Lloyd. On the evening 12 July 1962, he sacked Lloyd, and the following day (Friday 13th) six other cabinet members were sacked. Macmillan called them into his office one by one to confirm the news, and with one third of his 21 cabinet ministers being sacked, the press dubbed it the 'night of the long knives'. The report *The Reshaping of British Railways* (Beeching report) was published on 27 March 1963, with Macmillan's premise that the railways should be run as a profitable business, which led to the notorious Beeching Axe, destroying many miles of permanent way and severing towns from the railway network. On 27 July 1960, Macmillan had appointed John Profumo as British Secretary of State for War, an appointment which was to later cause a major scandal. At the country estate of Lord Astor on July 8, 1961, Profumo was introduced to 19-year-old London dancer Christine Keeler by Stephen Ward, an osteopath with

JOHN PROFUMO

contacts in both the aristocracy and the underworld. Also present at this gathering was a Russian military attaché, Eugene Ivanov, who was Keeler's lover. Profumo began an affair with Keeler, and rumours of their involvement soon began to spread. In March 1963, Profumo lied about the affair to Parliament, stating that there was "no impropriety whatsoever" in his relationship with Keeler. Evidence to the contrary quickly became too great to hide however, and 10 weeks later in June 1963 Profumo resigned admitting "with deep remorse" that he had deceived the House of Commons. The whole episode damaged the credibility of Macmillan's government and the affair became an attack not only on Profumo, but on the morality of Macmillan's government. Although Macmillan's reputation was partly rehabilitated by the successful negotiations in July 1963, between Great Britain, the United States, and the Soviet Union for the Nuclear Test-Ban Treaty, the Profumo affair directly contributed to Macmillan's departure from 10 Downing Street. A full report by Judge Alfred Denning into the Profumo Scandal was published on 26 September 1963, this combined with Macmillan suffering prostate problems that required surgery on 10 October, led to Macmillan resigning as Prime Minister on 18 October 1963 and retiring from politics in September 1964. Macmillan died at Birch Grove, the Macmillan family mansion on the edge of Ashdown Forest near Chelwood Gate in East Sussex, four days after Christmas in 1986 aged 92 years and 322 days. A public memorial service, attended by the Queen and thousands of mourners, was held on 10 February 1987 in Westminster Abbey.

Harold Macmillan facts:

Macmillan and Clement Attlee are the only British Prime Ministers to have been seriously wounded in battle.

During his early years as Prime Minister, Macmillan had been nicknamed 'Supermac', but after 'the night of the long knives' he acquired a new nickname...'Mac the knife'.

Macmillan left in his will £51,114, approx. worth £150,764 in 2020.

Macmillan was elected Chancellor of Oxford University in 1960, in the first contested election to be held since 1925.

Macmillan was a member of many clubs, commenting that the perfect combination for a club is '75% gentlemen and 25% crooks'.

Macmillan's only son, Maurice Macmillan was a Conservative MP from 1955 to 1984 and was Paymaster General in Alec Douglas-Home's 1970 – 1974 government.

Macmillan's memoirs include:
Winds of Change, 1914–1939 (1966);
The Blast of War, 1939–1945 (1967);
Tides of Fortune, 1945–1955 (1969);
Riding the Storm, 1956–1959 (1971);
Pointing the Way, 1959–1961 (1972);
At the End of the Day, 1961–63 (1973);
The Past Masters: Politics and Politicians, 1906–1939 (1975).

Peter Thorneycroft
1909 - 1994 (84 years old) Conservative

Chancellor of the Exchequer:
13 January 1957 -
6 January 1958
(11 months and 25 days)
Born
26 July 1909, Dunston, Stafford

Died
4 June 1994, age 84, London

Title: Baron Thorneycroft

Constituencies Represented as MP:
Stafford 1938 - 1945
Monmouth 1945 - 1966

Other Official Offices held:
President of the Board of Trade 1951 - 1957
Minister of Aviation 1960 - 1962
Secretary of State for Defence 1962 - 1964
Shadow Secretary of State for Defence 1964 - 1965
Shadow Home Secretary 1965 - 1966
Chairman of the Conservative Party 1975 - 1981
Member of the House of Lords 1967 - 1994

Prime Minister served with as Chancellor:
Harold Macmillan

Education:
Royal Military Academy, Woolwich and City Law School.

George Edward Peter Thorneycroft, Baron Thorneycroft, (26 July 1909 – 4 June 1994) was a Conservative MP from 1938 to 1966. He served as Chancellor of the Exchequer in Harold Macmillan's government between 1957 and 1958.

Thorneycroft was born in Dunston, Staffordshire, the son of Major George Edward Mervyn Thorneycroft a soldier and landowner, and his wife Dorothy Hope Franklyn. Thorneycroft went to Eton, but failing to distinguish himself he signed up for the Royal Artillery in Woolwich, where on 29 August 1929, he was commissioned as a second lieutenant. After just two years, Thorneycroft resigned his commission and studied law, he was called to the bar for the Inner Temple in 1933.

Thorneycroft entered politics by standing as a Conservative candidate in a By-election in Stafford, on 9 June 1938, winning with a majority of 4,408 (16,754 votes to Labour's 12,346). But just over a year later, with the outbreak of World War Two, Thorneycroft was re-commissioned into the Royal Artillery in his previous rank, on 30 August 1939. By 1942, he had returned to the Commons and played a role in the process of reforming Tory policy that would take place after the war. He served in Winston Churchill's caretaker government as Parliamentary Secretary at the Ministry of War Transport, but after the war he lost his seat in Stafford, in a closely fought contest. In the General Election on 5 July 1945, he lost by 793 votes (Labour 17,293 to Thorneycroft's 16,500), but he returned later that year in a By-election in the safe Conservative seat of Monmouth, winning on 31 October 1945 with a majority of 2,139 (21,092 votes to Labour's 18,953). Thorneycroft soon made his mark in the Commons as one of the new generation of Tories willing to embrace a new industrial strategy and revamped Conservatism. At the 23 February 1950 General Election, Thorneycroft was again returned in Monmouth with an increased majority of 4,231 (21,956 votes to Labour's 17,725) and again in the following General Election twenty months later on 25 October 1951, with a similar result, a majority of 4,523 - 22,475 votes to Labour's 17,952. With a Conservatives win, in his second spell as Prime Minister, Churchill promoted Thorneycroft to President of the Board of Trade, making him the youngest member of Churchill's Cabinet. After Anthony Eden became leader, he called a snap General Election on 26 May 1955, Thorneycroft was again returned in Monmouth with a slightly increased majority of 5,797 (22,970 votes to Labour's 17,173).

Thorneycroft stayed as President of the Board of Trade until 1957, when his support for Harold Macmillan in Macmillan's successful leadership contest for the premiership, led to his appointment on 13 January 1957, as Chancellor of the Exchequer.

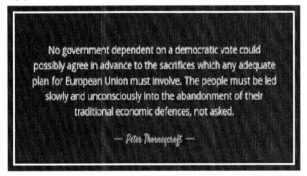

No government dependent on a democratic vote could possibly agree in advance to the sacrifices which any adequate plan for European Union must involve. The people must be led slowly and unconsciously into the abandonment of their traditional economic defences, not asked.

— Peter Thorneycroft —

In his position as Chancellor, Thorneycroft inherited the post-Suez mess, notably the continuing pressure on sterling, to which he responded by introducing sharp cuts in spending that had been set in train by Macmillan. He made tax cuts in his only Budget, but in the face of sterling's problems and inflation, he knew policy had to be tightened, and he won Cabinet support for raising the Bank Rate from 5 per cent to 7 per cent. Thorneycroft along with his juniors, Enoch Powell and Nigel Birch, wanted a restraint in expenditure with cuts in welfare but he found himself under attack from his own colleagues, notably the rising Health Secretary, Iain Macleod. Thorneycroft's relationship with Macmillan had deteriorated, and with a Cabinet determined to fight off cuts, Macmillan refused to support his Chancellor.

A Cabinet crisis ensued when Thorneycroft, Powell and Birch all resigned on 6 January 1958, and in his resignation speech Thorneycroft said:

"For twelve years, we have been attempting to do more than our resources could manage, and in the process we have been gravely weakening ourselves... I believe that there is an England which would prefer to face these facts and make the necessary decisions now. I believe that living within our resources is neither unfair nor unjust, nor, perhaps, in the long run even unpopular. There are millions of men and women in this country, in the Commonwealth, and in many other countries of the world who depend for the whole of their future on sustaining the value of our money... The simple truth is that we have been spending more money than we should".

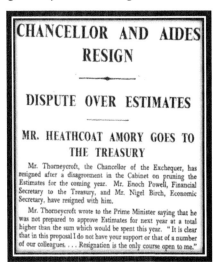

CHANCELLOR AND AIDES RESIGN

DISPUTE OVER ESTIMATES

MR. HEATHCOAT AMORY GOES TO THE TREASURY

Mr. Thorneycroft, the Chancellor of the Exchequer, has resigned after a disagreement in the Cabinet on pruning the Estimates for the coming year. Mr. Enoch Powell, Financial Secretary to the Treasury, and Mr. Nigel Birch, Economic Secretary, have resigned with him.

Mr. Thorneycroft wrote to the Prime Minister saying that he was not prepared to approve Estimates for next year at a total higher than the sum which would be spent this year. "It is clear that in this proposal I do not have your support or that of a number of our colleagues. ... Resignation is the only course open to me."

Macmillan retorted before heading off on a Commonwealth tour by saying: "It is always a matter of regret from a personal point of view when divergences arise between colleagues, but it is the team that matters and not the individual, and I am quite happy about the strength and power of the team". At the 8 October 1959 General Election, the Conservatives won their third consecutive victory and Thorneycroft was returned in Monmouth with a 6,257 majority (25,244 votes to Labour's 19,165). Thorneycroft did return to the Cabinet again in 1960, when he was appointed Minister of Aviation by Macmillan. In 1962, he was promoted to be Minister of Defence and retained the post when Macmillan's resigned and was replaced by Sir Alec Douglas-Home. In April 1964, the post was combined with the First Lord of the Admiralty, Secretary of

State for War and Secretary of State for Air, all three coming under the Secretary of State for Defence. At Defence, Thorneycroft played a pivotal role in the Sunda Straits Crisis, first supporting and then opposing the passage of the aircraft carrier HMS *Victorious* through the Indonesian-claimed Sunda Strait during the height of the Indonesia-Malaysia confrontation in August and September 1964. At the following General Election on

PETER THORNEYCROFT

15 October 1964, Labour ended the Conservative's thirteen years in government with a slender four seat majority. Thorneycroft was re-elected in Monmouth in a closely fought battle, winning with a reduced majority of 714 (22,365 votes to Labour's 21,921 and the Liberal's 6,764). He then served as Shadow Secretary of State for Defence under Alec Douglas-Home, before being made Shadow Home Secretary by Edward Heath in 1965. At the 31 March 1966 General Election, Labour increased their 1964 majority to 98 seats, and Thorneycroft lost his Monmouth seat to Labour's Donald Anderson with a majority of 2,965 (28,619 votes to 25,654), the first time the Conservative's had lost Monmouth since it became a new seat in 1918. Thorneycroft was raised to the peerage as a life peer as Baron Thorneycroft of Dunston in the County of Stafford, on 4 December 1967. In the following years, he returned to his earlier interest in trade diplomacy while developing a new range of interests in business. From 1968 to 1975, he was chairman of Sitpro (Simplification of International Trade Procedures) and from 1972 to 1975 chairman of the British Overseas Trade Board. His business interests included the chairmanships of Pye of Cambridge, Pirelli UK and Trusthouse Forte. After being out of politics for nine years, Thorneycroft made an unexpected return when newly elected leader of the Conservative party, Margaret Thatcher asked him to be party

Chairman. At the time the Conservative party was bitterly divided

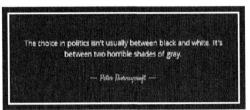

following the struggle for the leadership.

There had been discontinuity at Conservative Central Office with eight chairmen in twelve years, and defeat in four out of the five previous General Elections, which had left staff dispirited. Thorneycroft took drastic measures to streamline the organisation at Central Office, and to construct a cohesive team at senior level, employing Saatchi and Saatchi in the conduct of a General Election campaign in 1979, which was revolutionary in method and ultimately powerfully effective. After the success of the 1979 General Election, he stayed as part Chairman until 1981. After a long illness Thorneycroft died in London on 4 June 1994 aged 84.

Interesting Peter Thorneycroft facts:

Thorneycroft was appointed to the Order of the Companions of Honour (CH) in the 1980 New Year Honours.

He married twice and had a son by his first wife, and a daughter by his second.

Thorneycroft was an avid amateur watercolourist and held Exhibitions of his paintings.

Dereck Heathcote-Amory
1899 - 1981 (81 years old) Conservative

Chancellor of the Exchequer:
6 January 1958 -
27 July 1960
(2 years, 6 months and 22 days)

Born
26 December 1899, Mayfair,
London

Died
20 January 1981, age 81, Devon

Title: 1st Viscount Amory

Constituency Represented as MP:
Tiverton 1945 - 1960

Other Official Offices held:
Minister of State for Pensions 1951 - 1953
Minister of State for Trade 1953 - 1954
Minister of Agriculture and Fisheries 1954
Minister of Agriculture and Fisheries and food 1954 - 1958

Prime Minister served with as Chancellor:
Harold Macmillan

Education:
Christ Church, Oxford.

Derick Heathcoat-Amory, 1st Viscount Amory, 26 December 1899 – 20 January 1981) was a Conservative MP for Tiverton from 1945 to 1960, when he became a member of the House of Lords. He served as Chancellor of the Exchequer between 1958 and 1960 in Harold Macmillan's government.

Heathcote-Amory was born on 26 December 1899 in London, the second son of Sir Ian Murray Heathcoat Heathcoat-Amory, second baronet and his wife, Alexandra Georgina. He was educated at Eton College and at Christ Church, Oxford, where he achieved a third in modern history, after which he settled down to a business career in the family's textile business in Tiverton, Devon.

From leaving university to the start of the Second World War, Heathcote-Amory worked for John Heathcoat & Co, eventually becoming Managing Director. He was commissioned as a second lieutenant in the 11th (Devonshire) Brigade of the Royal Artillery (Territorial Army) on 31 July 1920, promoted to lieutenant in the 96th (Royal Devonshire Yeomanry) Field Brigade on 31 July 1922, and promoted to Captain on 1 September 1926. He was promoted to Major on 1 October 1935. In 1932, he was elected to the Devon County Council as Chairman of education. During the Second World War, he saw action at Salerno, and in 1944, he was responsible for training paratroopers for the Arnhem landings, insisting on taking part along with his trainees, he was wounded and captured during Operation Market-Garden (an unsuccessful World War II military operation fought in the Netherlands from 17 to 25 September 1944). After the war ended in 1945, Heathcote-Amory stood as a Conservative candidate in the 5 July 1945 General Election, in Tiverton East Devon, (a constituency previously held from 1868 to 1885 by his grandfather Sir John Heathcoat-Amory, 1st Baronet), he won the seat with an 8,285 majority (16,919 votes to Labour's 8,634 and Liberal's 7,418). Heathcote-Amory spent the next six years on the opposition benches, regaining his seat in Tiverton at the 23 February 1950 General Election, with a majority of 8,551 (20,606 votes to Labour's 12,055 and Liberal's 6,885), and again in the 25 October 1951 General Election when Winston Churchill regained power for the Conservatives. In the 1951 election Heathcote-Amory was returned with a larger majority in a two horse race with a 10,448 majority (24,532 votes to Labour's 14,084), and was rewarded by Churchill with a ministerial office as Minister of State for Pensions. He stayed as Minister for Pensions until 1953, then after a short period as minister of State at the Board of Trade (1953–1954), he joined the Cabinet as Minister of Agriculture, Fisheries, and Food on 28 July 1954. As economic conditions improved he carried through the final demolition of wartime rationing, a policy that considerably aided the Conservative Party's chance of re-election in 1955. When Churchill retired in April 1955, the new Prime Minister, Anthony Eden called a snap General Election on 26 May 1955, with the Conservatives improving their majority in the Commons to sixty seats. Heathcote-Amory was re-elected in Tiverton, with an almost identical majority to his 1951 victory, with 23,475 votes to Labour's 13,051 (majority 10,424).

Eden kept him as Minister of Agriculture, Fisheries, and Food throughout his premiership (1955–1957), as did Harold Macmillan on succeeding Eden in January 1957. A year later, Macmillan suffered a Cabinet crisis with the resignation of his Chancellor of the Exchequer, Peter Thorneycroft on 6 January 1958, after the Cabinet refused to agree to expenditure cuts deemed necessary to reduce inflation. Macmillan turned to Heathcote-Amory to try and restore business and party confidence in government policy. With only weeks to prepare for his first Budget, and under extreme scrutiny (not least from the previous team of Thorneycroft, Nigel Birch, and Enoch Powell), Heathcote-Amory produced a Budget that was a personal triumph. He did enough to get the economy moving after a period of sluggish growth, and continued to proclaim his adherence to Thorneycroft's war on inflation. He produced a second more expansive Budget in 1959, cutting both interest and purchase tax when growth was already surging ahead, and went a long way to ensure a Conservative re-election in the following October. At the 8 October 1959 General Election, the Conservatives had their third consecutive election victory, improving their majority to one hundred seats. Heathcote-Amory also improved his own majority in Tiverton up to 11,878 (21,714 votes to Labour's 9,836 and Liberal's 7,504). In his final Budget in 1960, Heathcote-Amory helped to prepare the way for the recession, credit squeeze, and major economic setbacks of 1961 to 1963, after presiding over a period of steady economic growth, low unemployment, and sustained business confidence. Having previously made it clear that he planned to retire at sixty, true to his word he stepped down in 1960, not just from the government but from his Commons seat as well. On his departure from the Commons in September 1960, he was made a viscount and succeeded his brother as fourth baronet in 1972. He devoted the rest of his life mainly to public service, most prominently as chairman of the Medical Research Council (1960–1961 and 1965–1969) and as British high commissioner in Canada (1961–1963). He died unmarried in January 1981, aged 81. The viscountcy became extinct upon his death and his younger brother succeeded him as Sir William Heathcoat-Amory, 5th Baronet.

Interesting Dereck Heathcote-Amory facts:

Heathcoat-Amory was an accomplished sailor, who famously had his yacht brought up the Thames to take him away after making Budget speeches when Chancellor of the Exchequer.

Heathcoat-Amory was the Chancellor of the University of Exeter from 1972 to 1981.

Heathcote-Amory left £491,305 in his will approx. worth £1,895,676 in 2020.

Selwyn Lloyd
1904 - 1978 (73 years old) Conservative

Chancellor of the Exchequer:
27 July 1960 -
13 July 1962
(1 year, 11 months and 17 days)

Born
28 July 1904, West Kirby,
Cheshire

Died
18 May 1978, age 73,
Oxfordshire

Title: Baron Selwyn Lloyd

Constituency Represented as MP:
Wirral 1945 - 1976

Other Official Offices held:
Minister of Supply 1954 - 1955
Minister of Defence 1955
Foreign Secretary 1955 - 1960
Leader of the House of Commons 1963 - 1964
Lord Privy Seal 1963 - 1964
Speaker of the House of Commons 1971 - 1976

Prime Minister served with as Chancellor:
Harold Macmillan

Education:
Magdalene College, Cambridge.

John Selwyn Brooke Lloyd, **Baron Selwyn-Lloyd**, (28 July 1904 – 18 May 1978), known for most of his career as **Selwyn Lloyd**, was a Conservative MP who served the Wirral from 1945 to 1976. Acted as both Foreign Secretary and Chancellor of the Exchequer in the late 1950's and 1960's.

Selwyn Lloyd was born on 28 July 1904 at Red Bank, West Kirby, Wirral, the third of four children, and only son of Welsh descendant John Wesley (Jack) Lloyd, a doctor and dentist and his wife, Mary. Lloyd was educated at Leas School, a local preparatory school overlooking the links of the Royal Liverpool Golf Club. At the age of fourteen he won a scholarship to Fettes College, Edinburgh. From Fettes he won a scholarship to Magdalene College, Cambridge, where he became President of the Union in 1927. He graduated with seconds in classics and history and a third in the second part of the law tripos in June 1928.

Selwyn Lloyd stood as a Liberal candidate in the 30 May 1929 General Election in Macclesfield, where he came third with 12,891 votes behind the Unionist 19,329 and Labour 13,911. After his failure in Macclesfield, he concentrated on his legal career on the northern circuit where he established a successful common-law practice, and was admitted to Gray's Inn in 1926, and was called to the bar in 1930. Lloyd's ultimate goal however, was for a political career, and he gained an apprenticeship by serving for ten years on the Hoylake urban district council, becoming the youngest-ever Chairman of the council at the age of 32. Nationally, he broke with the Liberals over the 1931 financial crisis, disappointed by the failure of the new party in 1930–1931 to establish a middle way, he was convinced of the necessity for a protective tariff. He was pessimistic about the long-term electoral prospects of the National Liberals and turned to the Conservatives, although he did not formally join the Conservative Party until he was selected as a Parliamentary candidate in 1945.

In January 1939, certain that war was inevitable, Lloyd was one of the principal organisers in raising a second line unit of the Royal Horse Artillery, in which he was commissioned as a second lieutenant. On the outbreak of war he went to the Staff College, Camberley, where he rose steadily through the military ranks. He was made a lieutenant-colonel on the general staff by 1942, and in the spring of 1943 he was posted to the newly formed Second Army. As a result, he was a close observer of General Bernard Montgomery during the preparations for D-day, in which he had important logistical planning duties. Lloyd was promoted brigadier in March 1945 and was with the first allied forces to enter Belsen. He was made a military OBE in 1943, a CBE in 1945, and was twice mentioned in dispatches. One of his last duties before returning to Britain to fight the 1945 General Election was to identify the body of Heinrich Himmler, shortly after his suicide. After the war, Lloyd stood as a Conservative candidate in Wirral in the 5 July 1945 General Election, and although Labour won a landslide victory, Lloyd entered Parliament with a healthy 16,625 majority (42,544 votes to Labour's 25,919 and Liberal's 14,302). In six years in opposition, Lloyd worked closely with Anthony Eden and R. A. Butler, both of whom sought his services when the Conservatives returned to power in October 1951. His most significant contribution in opposition however, was as the dissenting voice in the Beveridge broadcasting committee, his minority report of 1949 on the BBC's monopoly, made him in many people's eyes 'the father of commercial television'. He believed that it should not be in the power of a single body to provide broadcasting, and that competition would raise standards. At this time Lloyd again picked up on his legal career, taking silk in 1947 and becoming recorder of Wigan from 1948 to 1951. His legal and political experience made him a notable figure in the contentious debates on capital punishment at the time of the *Criminal Justice Bill* in July 1948. At the 23 February General Election, Lloyd was returned in Wirral with a reduced majority of 13,239 (29,232 votes to Labour's 15,993 and Liberal's 6,018) and at the snap General Election on 25 October 1951, he was again returned in a two horse race with an increased majority of 15,239 (36,631 votes to Labour's 17,392). The Conservatives were returned with a majority of seventeen seats, and Lloyd was surprised at being appointed Minister of State at the Foreign Office by Winston

Churchill. As Minister of State, Lloyd worked for three years on disarmament questions at the United Nations, and also on the issue of Sudanese self-determination. A treaty was signed in February 1953 which gave Sudan self-government for a period of three years, at the end of which, the country would decide on full independence. Lloyd's subsequent visit to Sudan was the most dramatic of his overseas missions as

COAT OF ARMS SELWYN LLOYD

Minister of State. Riots broke out when he was staying at the Governor-General's residence, on the site where General Gordon had been murdered, but Lloyd's contribution was vital in paving the way for full independence. Subsequently he served as Minister of Supply from October 1954, and in April 1955 he entered Anthony Eden's Cabinet as Minister of Defence. At the 26 May General Election, Lloyd held his seat in the Wirral with a large 17,051 majority (33,027 votes to Labour's 15,796), gaining valuable experience, firstly with Churchill and latterly with Eden, he attended more than one hundred Cabinet meetings before his promotion as Foreign Secretary in December 1955. On 21 March 1956, Lloyd obtained Cabinet approval for a policy of hostility against the President of Egypt, Nasser, who was seen as a threat to British interests in the Middle East. Part of his policy was the withdrawal of American and British financial aid for the Aswan High Dam, which would trigger Nasser's nationalisation of the Suez Canal. The Suez Crisis then began in earnest on 26 July 1956 when Nasser nationalised the Suez Canal. Lloyd's belief was that, although Nasser's action presented a serious threat to oil supplies to Western nations, a solution should be sought through negotiation rather than by the military action Eden favoured. British and French paratroopers landed at dawn on 5 November 1956, and Lloyd was given a rough ride in the House of Commons. On 7 November the United Nations General Assembly passed a resolution calling for withdrawal of British, French and Israeli forces. Lloyd's initial position was that Britain was not prepared to withdraw their forces until they had been replaced by

a peacekeeping force acceptable to Britain. The Americans met this idea with extreme hostility, insisting on total British withdrawal. On 3 December 1956, Lloyd made a statement announcing British withdrawal to a very hostile House, which was followed by angry scenes. The House of Commons held a No Confidence debate on Suez, on 5 December, with the government going on to win the confidence vote on 6 December, by 327 votes to 260, but Eden still resigned as Prime Minister citing ill health in January 1957. Harold Macmillan was appointed Prime Minister and retained Lloyd as Foreign Secretary, although Lloyd offered to resign in May 1957, citing unfavourable publicity which his pending divorce might attract, but his offer was declined. After the Suez debacle, Lloyd played a significant role in the major summits, and in the restoration of Britain's battered international reputation. At the 8 October 1959 General Election, Lloyd received his biggest majority in the Wirral, with a 21,002 majority (39,807 votes to Labour's 18,805). And in a 1960 Cabinet reshuffle, Macmillan made Lloyd Chancellor of the Exchequer, therefore he became one of only nine men to have run both the Foreign Office and the Treasury. As Macmillan's third Chancellor, Lloyd told Macmillan on his appointment, that he would be an orthodox Chancellor on taxation and public expenditure. In the first of his two Budgets in April 1961, he introduced the 'regulator', which allowed the government to vary taxes by 10 per cent (a variation on the percentage of the current rate, not a 10 per cent change in the tax itself) without recourse to a Budget, which was an example of his willingness to try new ideas. His second and last Budget in April 1962, was altered on the eve of its delivery, when the Cabinet refused to endorse his plans for the abolition of the old Schedule A tax on owner occupation. But he carried on with raising of the surtax starting point on earned income from £2000 to £5000. However, the 'pay pause' (a freeze

Politics is the best game in town.

— *Selwyn Lloyd* —

in wages) he had introduced in the sharply deflationary July measures of 1961 was particularly unpopular with nurses and teachers, who had a large measure of public support and contributed to a series of By-election reverses for the government. On 13 July 1962, in what became known as the 'Night of the Long Knives', Macmillan dismissed seven cabinet ministers, including Lloyd. Lloyd refused Macmillan's offer of a peerage as he was still intent on continuing his career in the Commons. As a senior back-bencher, Lloyd undertook an inquiry into the Conservative Party Organisation, and the 'Selwyn Lloyd report' marked the beginning of his rehabilitation in the senior ranks of the party. When Macmillan resigned from the premiership due to ill health on 18 October 1963, Lloyd played a key part in influencing the succession in favour of Alec Douglas-Home. After Home became Prime Minister, it was no surprise when Lloyd was recalled to the Cabinet as Lord Privy Seal and Leader of the House of Commons. After the Conservative defeat in the General Election on 15 October 1964, Lloyd held his seat at

Wirral with a 14,639 majority (32,084 votes to Labour's 17,445 and Liberal's 14,574) and continued to serve in the shadow cabinet, first under Sir Alec Douglas-Home, and from July 1965, under Edward Heath. At the 31 March 1966 snap General Election, Labour increased its majority from four seats to ninety-eight, and Lloyd was returned in the Wirral with a reduced majority of 9,853 (31,477 votes to Labour's 21,624 and Liberal's 12,313), continuing on the backbenches for the duration of the

CHANCELLOR JOHN SELWYN LLOYD

Labour government. At the 18 June 1970 General Election (the first in which people could vote from the age of 18) there was a surprise victory for the Conservative party under Ted Heath with a majority of thirty-one, Lloyd's majority again rose in the Wirral to 16,458 (38,452 votes to Labour's 22,605 and the Liberal's 9,276). In 1971, Lloyd became Speaker of the House of Commons voted in by 294 votes to 55, a position he would hold for over five years. At the first of two General Elections that occurred in 1974, the Labour and Liberal Parties broke with convention by contesting the Speaker's seat, Lloyd though was returned in the Wirral at the first election on 28 February 1974 with a majority of 15,847 (38,452 votes to Labour's 22,605 and Liberal's 14,123) which resulted in a hung Parliament. At the second General Election of the year on 10 October 1974, Lloyd in what turned out to be his last General Election, was returned in the Wirral with a 13,488 (35,705 votes to Labour's 22,217 and Liberal's 12,345). Lloyd retired as Speaker on 3 February 1976, when he was raised to the peerage and appointed to be the Steward of the Manor of Northstead. On 8 March 1976 Lloyd was created a life peer as Baron Selwyn-Lloyd, of Wirral in the County of Merseyside. He died at home of a brain tumour on 17 May 1978 aged 73.

Interesting Selwyn Lloyd facts:

In 1969 Lloyd was captain of the Royal Liverpool Golf Club in its centenary year, a course which he overlooked from his preparatory school.

Lloyd left £154,169 in his will, approx. worth £890,318 in 2020

Lloyd published two books, *Mr Speaker, Sir* (1976) and *Suez 1956: a Personal View*, which came out posthumously in 1978.

He received honorary degrees from the universities of Cambridge, Liverpool, Oxford, and Sheffield, and became an honorary fellow of his old college, Magdalene.

In March 1951, at the age of forty-six, Lloyd married his secretary at Westminster, Elizabeth, (his wife was twenty-three years his junior), they had one daughter, Joanna. Selwyn Lloyd and Elizabeth divorced in 1957.

Selwyn Lloyd left £154,169 in his will approx. worth £904,520 in 2020

Reginald Maudling
1917 - 1979 (61 years old) Conservative

Chancellor of the Exchequer:
13 July 1962 -
16 October 1964
(2 years, 3 months and 4 days)

Born
7 March 1917, North Finchley,
Middlesex
Died
14 February 1979, age 61,
Hampstead, London

Title: None

Constituencies Represented as MP:
Barnet 1950 - 1974
Chipping Barnet 1974 - 1979

Other Official Offices held:
Parliamentary Secretary to the Ministry of Civil Aviation 1952
Economics Secretary to the Treasury 1952 - 1955
Minister of Supply 1955 - 1957
Paymaster General 1957 - 1959
President of the Board of Trade 1959 - 1961
Secretary of State for the Colonies 1961 - 1962
Home Secretary 1970 - 1972

Prime Minister served with as Chancellor:
Harold Macmillan and Alec Douglas-Home

Education:
Merton College, Oxford.

Reginald Maudling, (7 March 1917 – 14 February 1979) known as Reggie, was a Conservative MP from 1950 to 1979. He was in several Cabinet's and held the post of Chancellor of the Exchequer from 1962 to 1964. He also a business man and held directorships in several British financial firms.

Maudling was born at 53 Westbury Road, North Finchley, London, on 7 March 1917, the only child of Reginald George Maudling, consulting actuary, and his wife, Elizabeth Emilie Pearson. Maudling spent his early years at Bexhill, Sussex, where his parents had moved due to the German air raids on the capital. And after the family's return to London, Maudling won scholarships to Merchant Taylors' School in Hertfordshire and Merton College, Oxford, where he obtained a first class degree in Greats (Literae Humaniores) in 1938, and going on to read for the Bar.

Six days after the outbreak of war, on 9 September 1939, Maudling married Beryl Laverick at Worthing register office (they went on to have a daughter and three sons). In 1940, Maudling was called to the bar (Middle Temple), however, he had already volunteered for active service and was commissioned in RAF intelligence. He subsequently became Private Secretary to Sir Archibald Sinclair, Secretary of State for Air, and served in the air staff secretariat. The experience strengthened his resolve for a political career, and he became convinced that after the war a new closer co-operation between government and industry was going to be vital. On the conclusion of war, Maudling stood as a Conservative candidate in the 5 July 1945 General Election, but although getting a healthy 22,623 votes he lost out to William Williams of Labour, with a majority of 6,569 (Labour 29,192 and Independent Nationalist 1,919). In November 1945, Maudling became the first staff member of the Conservative Parliamentary Secretariat, later the Conservative Research Department, servicing the parliamentary party's finance committee and was economic adviser and speech-writer for Winston Churchill and Anthony Eden. Under the guidance of Rab Butler, Maudling and his colleagues enabled the Conservatives to recapture the political middle ground by committing the party to build on, and not reverse, the post-war settlement. Namely, managing the economy on Keynesian principles, guaranteeing full employment, and providing universal, state secondary education, health care, and social security. Maudling stood as the Conservative candidate

REGINALD MAUDLING

in Barnet in the 23 February 1950 General Election, turning around a Labour majority of 682 to win with a 10,534 majority (32,953 votes to Labour's 22,419 and Liberal's 6,441), and in the snap General Election twenty months later on 25 October 1951, Maudling increased his majority to 13,152 (35,527 votes to Labour's 22,375 an Liberal's 4,463). The new Prime Minister, Winston Churchill, appointed Maudling as Parliamentary Secretary to the Ministry of Civil Aviation in April 1952, and in the November, aged thirty-five, he became Economic Secretary to the Treasury. Maudling worked closely over the next two and a half years with his mentor, Rab Butler, deputising for the Chancellor at the World Bank and International Monetary Fund meeting. At the 26 May 1955 General Election, Maudling again won the seat in Barnet with a 10,729 majority (33,136 votes to Labour's 19,373) and the new Prime Minister, Anthony Eden, promoted Maudling to become Minister of Supply and a Privy Councillor, a position from which he supported the Suez invasion. When Harold Macmillan became the new Prime Minister in January 1957, Maudling refused to continue at the Ministry of Supply and also rejected an offer of the Ministry of Health, so Macmillan appointed Maudling to the post of Paymaster General and spokesman in the House of Commons for the Ministry of Fuel and Power. After nine months impressing as Paymaster General, Macmillan brought Maudling into the Cabinet on 17 September 1957, where he acted as a Minister without Portfolio. At the 8 October 1959 General Election, Maudling was returned in Barnet with his largest ever majority, 13,399 (33,136 votes to Labour's 19,737) and Macmillan appointed him as President of the Board of Trade. As President Maudling was responsible for introducing the government's proposals to help areas of high unemployment. This was achieved by paying grants to companies to create new plants in deprived areas, and also by the government taking over unused land for development. On 9 October 1961, with continual rows between ministers over British decolonisation, Macmillan appointed Maudling as Secretary of State for the Colonies in place of Iain Macleod, where he chaired constitutional conferences that hastened independence for Jamaica, Northern Rhodesia (Zambia), Kenya, and Trinidad. Faced with opposition in the Cabinet to his plans for Northern Rhodesia (Zambia), he threatened to resign before eventually pushing through his independence constitution. Maudling was keen to return to economic policy, and seized his opportunity when Macmillan made it clear in private that he supported a voluntary incomes policy. Maudling promptly made his case in public, and three weeks later on 13 July 1962, at the age of forty-five he was appointed Chancellor of the Exchequer in Macmillan's "Night of the Long Knives" attempt to revitalise his Cabinet. As Chancellor, in November 1962, Maudling cut purchase tax and gave special help to areas of high unemployment, and in January 1963 he cut bank interest rates. In his 1963 Budget, Maudling aimed at "expansion without inflation" with a growth target of 4%, and he was able to remove income tax from owner-occupiers residential premises, while abolishing the rate of duty on home-brewed beer. By 1963, during the Profumo affair, there was talk, of Maudling succeeding Macmillan as Prime Minister, but he was poorly received at the Conservative Party conference and following Macmillan's resignation, Alec Douglas-Home was appointed as Prime Minister. Maudling retained his post as Chancellor under Douglas-Home, and by 1964 the economic recovery was fast becoming a boom and needed restraining, but his Budget increased duties by only £100 million. Maudling pressed for an early election, but Douglas-Home's delayed it until October, which destroyed hopes of agreeing an incomes policy

with the unions, and the trade deficit grew bigger than forecast. At the 15 October 1964 General Election, Maudling had a prominent role at the helm of the party's daily press conferences and he was re-elected at the election in Barnet with a reduced majority of 8,517 (25,537 votes to Labour's 17,024 and Liberal's 10,172). But with the Conservative government's defeat at the polls, Maudling relinquished the Chancellorship. When Douglas-Home resigned on 16 October 1964, after putting in place a system in which the leadership was directly elected, Maudling contested the leadership against Edward Heath and Enoch Powell. Maudling received 133 votes against Heath's 150 with Powell gaining 15 votes. Although Maudling was neither personally nor politically close to Heath, he still served as his Deputy Leader, and was also a prominent member of the Shadow Cabinet, however, his influence declined and his support for an incomes policy went against party policy. At the General Election on 31 March 1966, which resulted in a Labour landslide, Maudling was returned in Barnet with his lowest majority of 5,486 from the nine eventual General Elections he stood in (24,833 votes to Labour's 19,347 and Liberal's 8,539). After Enoch Powell had been sacked from the Shadow Cabinet in 1968 for his controversial *Rivers of Blood* speech, Maudling was moved from the position of Shadow Commonwealth Secretary to become Shadow Defence Secretary until 1969. At the General Election on 18 June 1970, there was a surprise victory for the Conservatives under Edward Heath, with Maudling slightly improving his majority in Barnet to 8,679 (26,845 votes to Labour's 18,166 and Liberal's 6,329). Maudling was appointed as Home Secretary on 20 June 1970, with the most pressing of problems was tackling the troubles in Northern Ireland. Maudling made a statement in the House of Commons following the 30 January 1972 Bloody Sunday massacre of thirteen people in Londonderry, in which he agreed

> # For God's sake bring me a large Scotch. What a bloody awful country.
>
> Reginald Maudling

MAUDLING QUOTE ON VISITING NORTHERN IRELAND

with the British army's statement that the Parachute Regiment had fired only in self-defence, (which turned out to be untrue) and resulted in Bernadette Devlin the sitting MP for Mid-Ulster (who had attended the march), after having been refused a point of order, walk down from the opposition benches to the floor of the House and slap Maudling causing a melee and Parliament having to be suspended. Maudling concluded that civil war in Northern Ireland could be averted only by suspending devolution and transferring responsibility to a Secretary of State, and in March 1972 William Whitelaw became Northern Ireland secretary. Maudling continued as Home Secretary and introduced community service as an alternative to prison, but on 18 July 1972 he resigned when the Metropolitan Police, for whom he was responsible, began investigating John Poulson, a former business associate who was subsequently jailed for corruption. When seats were redistributed for the February 1974 General Election, the Greater London parts of the old constituency of Barnet moved to the new Borough Constituency of Chipping Barnet. Maudling won the 28 February 1974 seat in Chipping Barnet with a majority of 9,911 (22,094 votes to Labour's 12,183 and Liberal's 11,714). Maudling did not return to the front bench under Heath, and it was a surprise when Margaret Thatcher appointed him Shadow Foreign Secretary in 1975. Invariably, their personalities and politics clashed, and he was sacked on 19 November 1976. Maudling died at the Royal Free Hospital in London from kidney failure and cirrhosis of the liver, on 14 February 1979 aged 61.

Interesting Reginald Maudling facts:

Maudling was portrayed by Irish actor Michael Culkin in the BBC-produced 2018 limited television series *A Very English Scandal*.

Maudling's daughter, Caroline Maudling, was a journalist in the 1960s.

Maudling left £140,690 in his will, worth approx £207,226 in 2020.

Maudling's parting shot on leaving Parliament was "hired by Winston Churchill, fired by Margaret Thatcher".

There has been a tradition of ministers leaving their successors a jokey private note for when they take over office. In 1964 when Reginald Maudling handed over the Treasury to Jim Callaghan he left a note saying: "Good luck, old cock. Sorry to leave it in such a mess!"

James Callaghan
1912 - 2005 (92 years old) Labour

Chancellor of the Exchequer:
16 October 1964 -
30 November 1967
(3 years, 1 month and 15 days)
Born
27 March 1912, Portsmouth,
Hampshire
Died
26 March 2005, age 92,
Ringmer, East Sussex

Title: Baron Callaghan of Cardiff

Constituencies Represented as MP:
Cardiff South 1945 - 1950
Cardiff South East 1950 - 1983
Cardiff South and Penarth 1983 - 1987

Other Official Offices held:
Parliamentary Secretary to the Ministry of Civil Transport 1947-50
Parliamentary Secretary to the Admiralty 1950 - 1951
Home Secretary 1967 - 1970
Secretary of State Foreign and Commonwealth Affairs 1974-76
Prime Minister 1976 - 1979
First Lord of the Treasury 1976 - 1979
Minister for the Civil Service 1976 - 1979

Prime Minister served with as Chancellor:
Harold Wilson

Education:
Portsmouth Northern Grammar School.

Leonard James Callaghan, Baron Callaghan of Cardiff, (27 March 1912 – 26 March 2005), known as **Jim Callaghan**, was an MP from 1945 to 1987. He was Chancellor from 1964 to 1967, Prime Minister from 1976 to 1979 and Leader of the Labour Party from 1976 to 1980.

Callaghan was born in Portsmouth, England, on March 12, 1912. His father, James Callaghan, was a chief petty officer in the Royal Navy. In 1921, when Callaghan was nine, his father died of a heart attack, aged only 44, plunging the family into poverty and forcing them to rely on charity. Their financial situation was improved in 1924 when the first Labour government was elected and introduced changes which allowed Mrs Callaghan to be granted a widow's pension of ten shillings a week. This was granted on the basis that her husband's death was partly due to his war service. Callaghan attended Portsmouth Northern Grammar School (now Mayfield School) and gained the Senior Oxford Certificate in 1929. Unfortunately, the family could not afford the entrance to university and so instead he sat the Civil Service entrance exam.

At the age of 17, Callaghan left to work as a clerk for the Inland Revenue at Maidstone in Kent. While working as a tax inspector, he joined the Maidstone branch of the Labour Party and the Association of the Officers of Taxes (AOT), a trade union for those in his profession, and within a year, he became the office secretary of the union. In 1932, he passed a Civil Service exam which enabled him to become a senior tax inspector, as well as becoming the Kent branch secretary of the AOT. In 1933, he was elected to the AOT's national executive council and in 1934, he was transferred to Inland Revenue offices in London. Following a merger of unions in 1936, Callaghan was appointed a full-time union official, and to the post of Assistant Secretary of the Inland Revenue Staff Federation (IRSF) resigning from his Civil Service duties. With the outbreak of World War II he applied to join the

Royal Navy in 1940, but was initially turned down on the basis that a Trade Union official was deemed to be a reserved occupation. He was finally allowed to join the Royal Navy Volunteer Reserve as an Ordinary Seaman in 1942. While he trained for his promotion, his medical examination revealed that he was suffering from tuberculosis (an infectious disease usually caused by bacteria), so he was admitted to the Royal Naval

CALLAGHAN IN THE ROYAL NAVY

Hospital Haslar which was in Gosport, near Portsmouth. After he recovered, he was discharged and assigned to duties with the Admiralty in Whitehall. He was assigned to the Japanese section and wrote a service manual for the Royal Navy 'The Enemy: Japan'. He then served in the East Indies Fleet on board the escort carrier HMS

Activity and was promoted to the rank of Lieutenant in April 1944. Whilst on leave from the Navy, Callaghan was selected as a Parliamentary candidate for Cardiff South, and in 1945, he served on HMS *Queen Elizabeth* in the Indian Ocean. After VE Day, he returned to the UK to stand in the 5 July 1945 General Election in Cardiff South, and was returned as a Labour MP with a majority of 5,944 (17,489 votes to Conservative's 11,545). In 1947, Callaghan was appointed Parliamentary Secretary to the Ministry of Transport before moving to be Parliamentary and Financial Secretary to the Admiralty in 1950, where he was a delegate to the Council of Europe resisting plans for a European army. Callaghan was elected to the Shadow Cabinet every year while the Labour Party was in opposition from 1951–1964. He was elected as MP in the Cardiff South East constituency at the 23 February 1950 General Election (a seat he held until it was abolished in 1983), with a 5,895 majority (26,254 votes to

Conservative's 20,359 and Liberal's 4,080) and he was also returned in the following General Election twenty months later, on 25 October 1951, with a majority of 4,499 (28,112 votes to Conservative's 23,613). He was Parliamentary Adviser to the Police Federation from 1955–1960 when he negotiated an increase in police pay. At the 8 October 1959 General Election, Callaghan scraped through in Cardiff South East with a slim 868 majority (26,915 votes to the Conservative's 26,047) and was appointed Shadow Chancellor in November 1961. When Labour leader Hugh Gaitskell died in January 1963, Callaghan ran to

succeed him, but came third in the leadership contest behind Harold Wilson and George Brown. At the General Election on 15 October 1964, Callaghan was returned again in Cardiff South East with a much increased majority of 7,841 (30,129 votes to Conservative's 22,288) and the new Prime Minister, Harold Wilson, appointed him as Chancellor of the Exchequer. The new Labour government was immediately faced with a deficit of £800 million, which contributed to a series of sterling crises. A possible solution was to devalue the pound against other currencies to make imports more expensive (which meant more inflation), but exports cheaper. On 11 November 1964, when Callaghan gave his first Budget he announced increases in income tax, petrol tax and the introduction of a new capital gains tax. The Budget also contained social measures to increase the state pension and the widow's pension. An electioneering Budget on St David's day (March 1) 1966, included the promise of a decimalised currency, which was followed by a General Election on the last day of March, in which

Labour won with an overall majority of ninety-six seats. Callaghan's stock was high, and he was again returned in Cardiff South East with another large majority of 10,837 (29,313 votes to Conservative's 18,476 and Liberal's 3,829). By the summer of 1966, the pressure on sterling was acute but Wilson and Callaghan were still determined to resist devaluation. On 12 July 1966, the Cabinet rejected the devaluation option and agreed to a tough package of deflation and austerity instead. In the autumn of 1967, Callaghan was elected treasurer of the Labour Party with an automatic seat on the national executive. However, due to several factors including international crises and dock strikes, by November 1967, the financial pressures had become altogether overwhelming. On 16 November, Callaghan, with Wilson's backing,

> A leader must have the
>
> courage to act against an
>
> expert's advice
>
> James Callaghan

recommended to the Cabinet that sterling should be devalued by just under 15 per cent. This was agreed and then implemented at 14 per cent on 18 November 1967. A package of measures including defence cuts, restrictions on hire purchase (credit) and higher interest rates was also agreed. Callaghan immediately resigned as Chancellor and became the new Home Secretary on 30 November 1967. In 1968 Callaghan presented to Parliament the Race Relations Act making it illegal to refuse employment, housing or education on the basis of ethnic background. The Act extended the powers of the Race Relations Board at the time, to deal with complaints of discrimination and unfair attitudes. On 12 August 1969, the 'Battle of the Bogside' erupted in Derry, Northern Ireland, resulting in three days of fierce clashes in the Bogside district between the RUC and thousands of

Catholic/nationalist residents. On 14 August 1969, Callaghan as Home Secretary was responsible for sending troops to Northern Ireland after a request from the Ulster Unionist Government. At the 18 June 1970 General Election, the Conservatives had a surprise victory, and Callaghan's majority was halved in Cardiff South East to 5,455 (26,226 votes to Conservatives 20,771 and Liberal's 2,585). While in opposition between 1970 and 1974, Callaghan held the positions of Shadow Home Secretary (1970-1971), Shadow Secretary of State for Employment (1971-1972) and Shadow Foreign Secretary (1972-1974). After Edward Heath failed to get a majority at the 'who rules' General Election on 28 February 1974, Harold Wilson and the Labour Party were returned to power and Callaghan was appointed Foreign Secretary. Callaghan had retained his seat in Cardiff South East with a 7,146 majority (20,641 votes to Conservatives 13,495, Liberal's 3,800 and Plaid Cymru 1,254). In the second General Election to be held in 1974 (10 October) Callaghan improved his majority to 10,718 (21,074 votes to Conservative's 10,356, Liberal's 8,006 and Plaid Cymru 983). As Foreign Secretary Callaghan had responsibility for renegotiating Britain's terms of membership of the European Economic Community (EEC), and when Harold Wilson resigned in 1976, Callaghan defeated Michael Foot for the leadership of the Labour Party by 176 votes to 137 (a 39-vote majority) and consequently became the Prime Minister. Callaghan's government
lost its majority of seats in Parliament on his first day in office, forcing him to rely upon the support of the Liberal Party through 1977 to 1978 and then the Scottish National Party for the remainder of the government. It is for this reason that the 1979 referendum on the devolution of powers to Scotland was produced, which was narrowly defeated by the Scottish voters. In 1977, Callaghan and his Chancellor of the Exchequer, Denis Healey, controversially began imposing tight monetary controls. This included deep cuts in public spending on education and health. Callaghan's time as Prime Minister also saw the

introduction of the Police Act of 1976, which formalised Police complaints procedures, the Housing (Homeless Persons) Act of 1977 which established the responsibility of local authorities to provide housing to homeless people and the Education Act of 1976, which limited the number of independent and grant-maintained schools in any one area.

With Britain's economy performing badly, wage restrictions for public sector workers caused a wave of strikes across the winter of 1978 to 1979 which became known as the 'Winter of Discontent', causing Labour's standing in the opinion polls to

CALLAGHAN'S MEMOIRS

slump dramatically. On 28 March 1979, the Conservative leader, Margaret Thatcher called for a vote of no confidence in Callaghan's government, which was passed in the House of Commons by one vote, 311 to 310, forcing Callaghan to call a General Election. The election was held on 3 May 1979 and the Conservatives ran a campaign on the slogan 'Labour Isn't Working' resulting in a 5.2% swing from Labour to the Conservatives (the largest swing since the 1945 election). The result of the election was a parliamentary majority for the Conservatives of 43 seats. Callaghan retained his own seat with a majority of 8,701 (23,871 votes to Conservatives 15,170 and Plaid Cymru's 628) and he continued as Labour leader until he resigned on 15 October 1980. In 1983, Callaghan became Father of the House as the longest continually serving member of the Commons. In his last General Election on 9 June 1983, Callaghan was returned in Cardiff South and Penarth with a majority of 2,276 (17,448 votes to Conservative's 15,172, Liberal's 8,816 and Plaid Cymru 673).

He was made a Knight of the Garter in 1987, and stood down at the 1987 General Election after 42 years as an MP. Shortly afterwards, he was elevated to the House of Lords on 5 November 1987 as a life peer with the title Baron Callaghan of Cardiff. Callaghan died on 26 March 2005 at Ringmer, East Sussex, one day before his 93 birthday. He died as the longest-lived former UK Prime Minister, having beaten Harold Macmillan's record 39 days earlier. He died just 11 days after his wife (Audrey) of 67 years and was survived by his son and two daughters.

Interesting James Callaghan facts:

Callaghan is the only Parliamentarian to have the honour of holding the four offices of Chancellor of the Exchequer, Home Secretary, Foreign Secretary and Prime Minister.

On 5 April 1976, at the age of 64 years and 9 days, Callaghan became Prime Minister—the oldest Prime Minister at time of appointment since Winston Churchill.

Callaghan would become the last British Prime Minister to be an armed forces veteran and the only one ever to have served in the Royal Navy.

Callaghan published his autobiography 'Time and Chance' in 1987.

Callaghan played rugby union before the Second World War for Streatham RFC in the position of lock.

Callaghan's daughter, Margaret Jay, Baroness Jay of Paddington was a Labour MP and Leader of the House of Lords.

Roy Jenkins
1920 - 2003 (82 years old)
Labour/SDP/Liberal Democrats

Chancellor of the Exchequer:
30 November 1967 -
19 June 1970
(2 years, 6 month and 21 days)
Born
11 November 1920, Abersychan, Wales
Died
5 January 2003, age 82,
East Hendred, Oxfordshire
Title: Baron Jenkins of Hillhead

Constituencies Represented as MP:
Southwark Central 1948 - 1950 (Labour)
Birmingham Stechford 1950 - 1977 (Labour)
Glasgow Hillhead 1982 - 1987 (SDP)

Other Official Offices held:
Chair of the Fabian Society 1957 - 1958
Home Secretary 1965 - 1967 and 1974 - 1976
Deputy Leader of the Labour Party 1970 - 1972
President of the European Commission 1977 - 1981
Leader of the Social Democratic Party 1982 - 1983
Leader of the Lib Dems in the House of Lords 1988 - 1997

Prime Minister served with as Chancellor:
Harold Wilson

Education:
Balliol College, Oxford.

Roy Harris Jenkins, Baron Jenkins of Hillhead, (11 November 1920 – 5 January 2003) was a Member of Parliament from 1948 to 1987 for two different parties. He served as Chancellor of the Exchequer and Home Secretary in the Wilson and Callaghan Labour Governments. He was also President of the European Commission from 1977 to 1981, He was an MP for the Labour Party, Social Democratic Party (SDP) and the Liberal Democrats.

Jenkins was born at Greenlands, Snatchwood Road, Abersychan, Monmouthshire, on 11 November 1920. The only child of Arthur Jenkins, assistant miners' agent and Labour MP for Pontypool, and his wife, Harriet (Hattie), a music shop assistant and subsequently magistrate and county councillor. Jenkin's father, Arthur, represented the Labour party as an MP from 1935 to 1946 and was a strongly militant socialist. During the General Strike of 1926 he was arrested on disputed charges, hauled before the magistrate and sent to prison for nine months (serving three). Jenkins junior worshipped his father who after leaving prison went on to be Parliamentary Private Secretary to the leader of the Labour Party (Clement Attlee), and finally a junior minister in the post-war Attlee government. Jenkins was educated at Pentwyn Primary School, Abersychan County Grammar School and University College, Cardiff, before going on to study Politics, Philosophy and Economics (PPE) at Balliol College, Oxford in 1938, attaining First-Class Honours (one of only four awarded that year) in the summer of 1941.

Jenkins was commissioned in the summer of 1942 into the West Somerset yeomanry, which, together with the Leicestershire yeomanry, supplied artillery support for the guard's armoured division. He served as a lieutenant with a domestic battery for a little under two years, before being summoned through a War Office direction to join the code breakers working at Bletchley Park. Although not being a mathematician, or even a dedicated puzzle solver, the 23-year-old Jenkins lacked the talents of some of his to his more highbrow colleagues working at Bletchley, which at first intimidated him, but he acquitted himself well and more than justified the faith placed in his mental ingenuity. After the war, Jenkins stood as a Labour candidate in the 5 July 1945 General Election, getting a good response in the predominantly Conservative area of Solihull, gaining 21,647 votes but losing out

to British Army officer Sir Martin Lindsay who received 26,696 (majority 5,049). Jenkins then worked as an apprentice amateur merchant banker for the Industrial and Commercial Finance Corporation. In 1947, Jenkins edited a collection of Clement Attlee's speeches, published under the title *Purpose and Policy* from which Attlee then granted Jenkins access to his private papers so that he could write his biography. The biography was published in 1948 (*Mr Attlee: An Interim Biography*). On 29 April 1948, Jenkins stood in a By-election as a Labour candidate in Southwark Central, which he won and entered Parliament with a 4,121 majority (8,744 votes to Conservative's 4,623). At 26-years-old he was the 'Baby of the House' (the unofficial title given to the youngest member of a parliamentary house). At the 23 February 1950 General Election, Jenkins stood for Labour in the newly formed constituency of Birmingham Stechford, where he was returned with a 12,378 majority (33,077 votes to Conservative's 20,699 and Liberal's 2,789) even though he stood (and won) in the subsequent eight General Elections in Stechford, this was to be his largest majority. At the quickly followed General Election on 25 October 1951, Jenkins retained his seat with a 10,971 majority (34,355 votes to Conservative's 23,384). In 1951, the

JENKINS IN THE ARMY

democratic socialist political magazine, *Tribune,* published his seven-thousand-word pamphlet *Fair Shares for the Rich,* in which Jenkins advocated the abolition of large private incomes by taxing them, graduating from 50 per cent for incomes between £20,000 and £30,000 to 95 per cent for incomes over £100,000. He also proposed further nationalisations on which he said: "Future nationalisations will be more concerned with equality than with planning, and this means that we can leave the monolithic public corporation behind us and look for more intimate forms of ownership and control". Between 1951 and 1956, Jenkins wrote a weekly column for the Indian newspaper *The Current*, in which he advocated progressive reforms such as equal pay, the decriminalisation of homosexuality, the liberalisation of the obscenity laws and the abolition of capital punishment. In 1954, Jenkins published '*Mr Balfour's Poodle'*, a short account of the House of Lords crisis of 1911 that culminated in the Parliament Act 1911. At the 26 May 1955 General Election, Jenkins was again re-elected in Birmingham Stechford with a slightly reduced majority of 6,740 (23,358 votes to Conservatives 16,618). Jenkins by this time had become a keen writer, and wrote a biography of the Victorian radical, Sir Charles Dilke, which was published in October 1958. In July 1959, Penguin published Jenkins' *The Labour Case*, timed to anticipate the upcoming election in which he set out a list of necessary progressive social reforms: the abolition of the death penalty, decriminalisation of homosexuality, abolition of the Lord Chamberlain's powers of theatre censorship, liberalisation of the licensing and betting laws, liberalisation of the divorce laws, legalisation of abortion, decriminalisation of suicide and more liberal immigration laws. At the 8 October 1959 General Election,

> The permissive society has been allowed to become a dirty phrase. A better phrase is the civilised society
>
> Roy Jenkins

Labour were defeated to the Conservatives third consecutive General Election victory, with Jenkins being returned in Stechford with a 2,923 majority (21,919 votes to Conservative's 18,996). In May 1960, Jenkins joined the Campaign for Democratic Socialism, a Gaitskellite pressure group designed to fight against left-wing domination of the Labour Party, and in July 1960 he resigned from his frontbench role in order to be able to campaign freely for British membership of the Common Market. At the 15 October

1964 General Election, Labour finally broke thirteen years of Conservative rule when Harold Wilson led them to a four-seat majority. Jenkins improved his majority in Stechford to 5,388 (22,421 votes to Conservative's 17,033) and accepted the position of Minister of Aviation, which although not in Cabinet, meant he was in charge of his own department. Jenkins was also sworn of the Privy Council on 24 October 1964, and the following year on 23 December 1965, Harold Wilson appointed him as Home Secretary. When Labour won the 31 March 1966 General Election, Jenkins who had been re-elected in Stechford with an improved majority of 11,871 (24,597 votes to Conservative's 12,727) carried on as Home Secretary, pushing through a series of police reforms which reduced the number of separate forces from 117 to 49. Jenkins also introduced two-way radios to the police, increasing the possession of Metropolitan police radios from 25 to 2,500, and provided similar numbers of radios to the rest of the country's police forces. Jenkins also provided the police with more car radios making the police more mobile and reactive, but reduced the amount of time they spent patrolling the streets.

Jenkins Criminal Justice Act 1967, introduced more stringent controls on the purchase of shotguns and introduced majority verdicts in juries in England and Wales. His Act was also designed to lower the prison population by the introduction of release under licence, easier bail, suspended sentences and earlier parole. Between 1965 and 1967, Jenkins presided over the reformation of divorce laws, the legal treatment of homosexuals was made much less oppressive, abortion on demand accepted within legal and medical limits, and the traditional theatrical

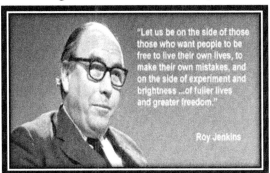

"Let us be on the side of those those who want people to be free to live their own lives, to make their own mistakes, and on the side of experiment and brightness ...of fuller lives and greater freedom."

Roy Jenkins

censorship exercised by the Lord Chamberlain was abolished. Accusations were aimed at Jenkins of creating a 'permissive society' but he justified the actions by saying he had just introduced 'civilised standards'. Following the devaluation crisis of November 1967 and James Callaghan's resignation as Chancellor of the Exchequer, Wilson turned to Jenkins as his Chancellor to try and restore stability to sterling at after devaluation. Jenkins took on the role of Chancellor on 30 November 1967, pursuing deflation by including cuts in public expenditure and increases in taxation in order to ensure that resources went into exports rather than domestic consumption. Jenkins warned in the House of Commons in January 1968 that there was "two years of hard slog ahead". Rather than view the situation as a poisoned chalice, Jenkins took on the challenge with the view that it was better to start at the bottom of the market and work your way up. In his March 1968 Budget, Jenkins restored prescription charges (which had been abolished when Labour returned to office in 1964) and postponed the raising of the school leaving age to 16 from 1971 to 1973. Housing and road building plans were also heavily cut, and he raised the taxes on drinks and cigarettes (except on beer), purchase tax, petrol duty, road tax, a 50 per cent rise in Selective Employment Tax and a one-off Special Charge on personal incomes. In the lead up to the 1970 General Election, Jenkins received some criticism for not following the traditionally cynical strategy of a 'giveaway' Budget just before an election, although Jenkins's third and final Budget in April 1970 released £150 million into the economy it was seen as insufficient. At the 18 June 1970 General Election, there was a surprise victory for the Conservatives under Edward Heath, although Jenkins retained his seat in Stechford with a 6,711 Majority (22,559 votes to Conservative's 15,848 and National Democratic's 1,483). After the 1970 defeat, Jenkins stayed as Shadow Chancellor of the Exchequer and was elected to the deputy leadership of the Labour Party in July 1970. At this time Jenkins appeared to be the natural successor to Harold Wilson, with an opportunity to become Prime Minister. It did not take long however, for events to turn entirely, and transform Jenkins political future. Edward Heath announced in 1971 that Britain would apply to join the European Economic Community (EEC) which caused a split in the Labour party. Labour issued a three-line whip to all its MPs requiring them to vote against the government. This totally misfired. when no fewer than sixty-nine Labour MPs, led by Jenkins, joined the bulk of the government supporters in the 'aye' lobby, while another twenty abstained, it gave Heath a comfortable majority of 112 in favour of the United Kingdom joining with Europe. Although Jenkins was re-elected as Deputy Leader on 17 November 1971 (defeating Michael Foot by 140 votes to 126) he found his pro-European position untenable and resigned from the shadow cabinet, and as deputy leader in April 1972. He did return to the Labour fold when he was appointed as shadow home secretary in November 1973, and after the Labour victory in the 28 February 1974 General Election, he started his second stint as Home Secretary. Jenkins had been re-elected in Birmingham Stechford with a 10,232 majority (23,704 votes to Conservative's 13,472 and Liberal's 7,221) and at the following 10 October 1974 election, the second General Election that year, Jenkins slightly increased his majority to 11,923 (23,075 votes to Conservative's 11,152 and Liberal's 5,860). In June 1975, Jenkins led a cross-party campaign for a 'yes' vote in the June 1975 European referendum, which returned a successful 'yes' vote by 17,378,581 against 8,470,073. On 5 January 1977, Jenkins became the first British President of the European Commission stating he wanted to "build an effective united Europe". In Jenkins last year as President of the

'GANG OF FOUR'

Commission it was dominated by Margaret Thatcher's fight for a rebate on Britain's contribution to the EEC budget and by this time, he had stated that he would not stand as a Labour candidate again. With the anti-European position of the James Callaghan government, Jenkins was the prime mover behind the formation of the Social Democratic Party (SDP). Along with three Labour politicians David Owen, Bill Rodgers, and Shirley Williams. Jenkins had gradually grown estranged from his political roots and decided to speculate on the formation of a new centre party. Becoming known as the 'Gang of Four' Jenkins joined Owen, Rodgers and Williams in issuing the Limehouse Declaration which brought a call for the "realignment of British politics" forming the Social Democratic Party (SDP) on 26 March 1981, which started off with fourteen former Labour MPs and one former Conservative member. Jenkins delivered a series of speeches setting out the SDP's alternative to Thatcherism, and argued that the solution to Britain's economic troubles lay in the revenue from North Sea oil, which he said should be invested in public services. He then stood in Warrington as an SDP candidate on 16 July 1981, in a By-election, in which he was narrowly defeated by Labour to a majority of 1,759 (Labour 14,280, Jenkins SDP 12,521 and Conservative's 2,102). The following year on 25 March 1982, Jenkins again stood in a By-election as an SDP candidate, this time in Glasgow Hillhead where he gained 33.4% of the vote to win with a majority of 2,038, gaining the seat from the Conservatives (Jenkins 10,106 votes to Conservative's 8,068 Labour's 7,846 and SNP 3,416). Jenkins was elected leader of the SDP beating David Owen in a leadership contest with 55.7% of the vote-26,256 to 20,864. At the 9 June 1983 General Election, Jenkins held on to his Glasgow Hillhead seat with a reduced majority of 1,164 (14,856 votes to Labour's 13,692, Conservative's 9,678 and SNP 2,203). He then faced a

fresh leadership challenge from David Owen in 1983, but rather than face him in an open challenge, Jenkins chose to retire from the party leadership, leaving Owen to be elected unopposed. Despite the SDP gaining 11.6 per cent of the national vote, its representation in the Commons decreased from twenty-nine to six and the following years effectively marked Jenkin's withdrawal from front-line politics. This was partly due to ill health, when towards the end of 1984, he underwent a prostate operation, which had complications that did not clear up for more than two years. Jenkins did stand in his last General Election on 11 June 1987 in Glasgow Hillhead, but was defeated by Labour's George Galloway by a majority of 3,251 Labour 17,958, Jenkins 14,707, Conservative's 6,048 and SNP 2,713). From 1987, Jenkins remained in politics as a member of the House of Lords as a life peer, with the title Baron Jenkins of Hillhead of Pontypool in the County of Gwent. Also in 1987, Jenkins was elected Chancellor of the University of Oxford winning a contest against the political historian Lord Blake and his own old Balliol contemporary Edward Heath. Jenkins was also leader of the Liberal Democrats in the Lords from 1988 until 1997, and became a personal guide and political mentor to future

Prime Minister Tony Blair. Jenkins was a prolific political writer and famously wrote many political biographies, including a biography of William Gladstone (1995) which won the 1995 Whitbread Award for Biography, and a highly acclaimed biography of Winston Churchill (2001). Jenkins died of heart failure aged 82 at his home, St Amand's House, East Hendred, Oxfordshire, on 5 January 2003 (he had undergone a heart bypass operation at the Wellington Hospital in St John's Wood in the autumn of 2000). Jenkin's funeral took place in the village church, and he was buried in the village churchyard which was attended by Tony Blair and his wife Cherie. Blair paid tribute by saying Jenkins was "one of the most remarkable people ever to grace British politics". A memorial service was subsequently held in Westminster Abbey.

Interesting Roy Jenkins facts:

In 1991 Jenkins' memoirs, *A Life at the Centre*, was published by Macmillan, who paid Jenkins a £130,000 advance.

In 1993, he was appointed to the Order of Merit and his book *Portraits and Miniatures* was published. The main body of the book is a set of 6 biographical essays (Rab Butler, Aneurin Bevan, Iain Macleod, Dean Acheson, Konrad Adenauer, Charles de Gaulle), along with lectures, articles and book reviews.

Jenkins left £611,269 in his will, approx. worth £988,354 in 2020.

Jenkins was married to Mary Jennifer (Jennifer) Morris for 58 years and they had three children, 2 boys, Charles and Edward, and a daughter, Cynthia.

Jenkins was the President of the Royal Society of Literature from 1988 until his death in 2003.

Jenkins in total wrote 19 books.

Iain Macleod
1913 - 1970 (56 years old) Conservative

Chancellor of the Exchequer:
20 June 1970 -
20 July 1970
(31 days)

Born
11 November 1913, Skipton,
Yorkshire
Died
20 July 1970, age 56,
London

Title: None

Constituency Represented as MP:
Enfield West 1950 - 1970

Other Official Offices held:
Minister of Health 1952 - 1955
Minister of Labour and National Service 1955 - 1959
Secretary of State for the Colonies 1959 - 1961
Leader of the House of Commons 1961 - 1963
Chancellor of the Duchy of Lancaster 1961 - 1963
Shadow Chancellor of the Exchequer 1965 - 1970

Prime Minister served with as Chancellor:
Edward Heath

Education:
Gonville and Caius College, Cambridge.

Iain Norman Macleod, (11 November 1913 – 20 July 1970) was a Conservative MP for Enfield West from 1950 until his death in 1970. He was a Cabinet minister who served as Chancellor of the Exchequer for thirty-one days until his untimely death in July 1970.

Macleod was born on 11 November 1913, at Clifford House, Skipton, Yorkshire, the second child and eldest of three sons of Norman Alexander Macleod a doctor, and his wife and second  *cousin, Annabella. Macleod at first attended St Ermysted's, Skipton's grammar school, before being sent in 1923 to St Ninian's, a Dumfriesshire preparatory school, which served as a feeder for the fee-paying Fettes College in Edinburgh. During his four years at St Ninian's and five at Fettes, Macleod developed an enduring love of literature, especially poetry, which he read and began to write. In 1932, Macleod proceeded to Gonville and Caius College, Cambridge, where he read modern history, but steered clear of student politics. Macleod soon found out he enjoyed the night life, financing his playboy lifestyle largely through gambling, especially at the bridge table. Macleod founded the Cambridge bridge club with himself as President, and spent a great deal of his time in Crockford's and other West End gaming clubs. It was through bridge, rather than his academic studies, that he honed his intellect and developed his formidable powers of memory and concentration.*

It was also at bridge that Macleod met the chairman of Thomas De La Rue, a firm which specialised in printing playing cards and banknotes. Following Macleod's graduation in 1935, with a lower second, De La Rue gave him office work at £3 a week. Macleod's interest though was the nightlife. He became a professional bridge player, becoming an England international by 1936, and co-inventor of the Acol bidding system in 1937. His nights at the table often left him too tired to work during the day and in 1938, he was relieved of his day job. Macleod then enrolled at the Inner Temple in a short-lived attempt to read for the bar. His life in this period was vibrant, apolitical, and comfortably supported by his bridge earnings. This all came to an end with the outbreak of World War Two, when Macleod joined the Royal Fusiliers as a private. After being commissioned as a subaltern in the Duke of Wellington's regiment in April 1940, he was sent to France to join the retreating British expeditionary force. He was involved in setting up a road block Near Neufchatel, when a German armoured car burst through spreading debris, from which a log fractured Macleod's thigh. Macleod was evacuated to a hospital in Exeter, from which he eventually emerged with a slight, but permanent limp. Once again fit for duty, he served as a staff captain with the 46th Division in Wye. One night in 1941, a drunk Macleod demanded that his friend and senior officer, Alan Dawtry, play stud poker with him. Dawtry declined and retired to his room, whereupon Macleod drew his revolver and fired several shots through Dawtry's door. Fortunately, Dawtry wasn't hit, and they remained good friends. In 1943, Macleod entered the Staff College, Camberley, for advanced officer training, where he encountered a hard-working environment and first-class competition which made him realise the extent of his abilities, and gave him a newfound sense of purpose and political ambition. Macleod graduated from Camberley in 1944, and as a Major, he landed in France on Gold Beach on D-Day, 6 June 1944, as Deputy Assistant Quartermaster-General of the 50th (Northumbrian) Infantry Division, a first line TA formation.

Surviving D-Day, Macleod served in France until his division returned to Yorkshire in November 1944. His final army posting was in Norway in 1945 and he was demobilised from the British Army in January 1946. Macleod secured an interview with David Clarke, the director of the Conservative parliamentary secretariat, which was a new organisation whose main function was to produce debating briefs for the parliamentary party. Macleod impressed and was recruited and in due course found himself writing briefing papers for Conservative MPs on Scottish affairs, labour and health. In 1946 Macleod won Conservative endorsement for the newly created seat of Enfield West, where he bought a house which was paid for through his continued expertise at the bridge table and the writing of a weekly bridge column for the *Sunday Times*.

> JOHN FITZGERALD KENNEDY DESCRIBED HIMSELF, IN A BRILLIANT PHRASE, AS AN IDEALIST WITHOUT ILLUSIONS. I WOULD DESCRIBE THE PRIME MINISTER AS AN ILLUSIONIST WITHOUT IDEALS.
>
> - IAIN MACLEOD -

At the 23 February 1950 General Election, Macleod won the Enfield West seat with a 9,193 majority (20,588 votes to Labour's 11,395 and the Liberal's 3,638). He was elected alongside an influx of new Conservative MP's including Enoch Powell, Angus Maude and Edward Heath, who formed the One Nation group, advocates of a social and conciliatory toryism ('Tory', not 'Conservative', was Macleod's description of himself). Macleod and Maude were mainly responsible for the group's manifesto, *'One Nation'*, in 1950. At the 25 October 1951 General Election the Conservative's overturned Labour's five seat majority and Winston Churchill again became Prime Minister, Macleod was returned in Enfield West with a slightly increased majority of 10,225 (22,351 to Labour's 12,126) and became Chairman of the backbench Health and Social Services Committee. He made his mark in his new role in a debate on the *National Health Service Bill* on 27 March 1952. Macleod spoke after Aneurin Bevan, the architect of the National Health Service (NHS) and one of the opposition's finest orators. After Bevan had finished his forceful speech, Macleod stood up and retorted 'I want to deal closely and with relish with the vulgar, crude and intemperate speech to which the House of Commons has just listened'...Churchill was in the chamber, having come in to hear Bevan, and was preparing to leave when

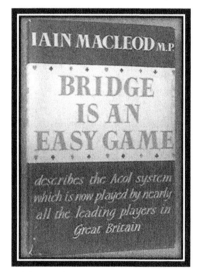

Macleod began, his attention captured, Churchill stayed and listened attentively to Macleod's speech. Macleod's discourse was a feat of argument, with deft handling of interjections including Bevan's, stating that a debate on the NHS without Bevan would be like *Hamlet* 'with no one in the part of the First Gravedigger'. His speech made such an impact with facts and figures gained from his time in the research department, that on 7 May 1952, Macleod was summoned by Churchill to Downing Street to find himself appointed Minister of Health.

Although he did not sit in Cabinet Macleod was clearly up and coming, and the first of his contingent to achieve ministerial rank and a privy councillorship. With his promotion, Macleod's career as a bridge player came to an end when he published his successful *Bridge is an Easy Game* in 1952. He stayed as Minister for Health until the 26 May 1955 General Election, when the Conservatives were re-elected under the leadership of the new Prime Minister Anthony Eden. He retained his seat in Enfield West, increasing his majority again, to 11,518 (22,021 votes to Labour's 10,503) with Eden promoting Macleod who was still only forty-two to a place in Cabinet as Minister of Labour. The London busmen's strike of 1958 brought Macleod into a prolonged confrontation with the general secretary of the Transport and General Workers' Union, Frank Cousins. During the seven weeks it took to reach a settlement, Macleod gained a reputation for toughness and became a national figure. He was appointed to the Steering Committee to decide on the Conservative's political strategy in the run-up to the 1959 election. At the 8 October 1959 General Election, Macleod increased his majority in Enfield West for the fourth consecutive General Election, regaining the seat with a 13,803 majority (24,861 votes to 11,058). Harold

IAIN MACLEOD

Macmillan, who had taken over Eden as Prime Minister in January 1957 after the Suez crisis, appointed Macleod as Secretary of State for the Colonies on 14 October 1959. Macleod had no previous experience in overseas policy and indeed had never set foot in a colonial territory, but his lack of experience enabled him to think colonial policy afresh. He saw Nigeria, British Somaliland, Tanganyika, Sierra Leone, Kuwait and British Cameroon become independent. In October 1961, Macmillan replaced Macleod as Colonial Secretary with Reginald Maudling, and Macleod replaced his old mentor Rab Butler as Leader of the House of Commons and Chairman of the Conservative Party. He was also given the sinecure post (an office, carrying a salary or otherwise generating income, that requires or involves little or no responsibility, labour, or active service) of Chancellor of the Duchy of Lancaster, a slightly less prestigious office than the other sinecures of Lord Privy Seal or Lord President of the Council. When Macmillan resigned and was replaced by Alec Douglas-Home in October 1963, it halted Macleod's ministerial career, as he refused to serve in Cabinet under Douglas-Home.

With Macleod's ministerial career stalled, other employment soon came his way. His friend and fellow Conservative MP Ian Gilmour, owner of *The Spectator*, offered him the paper's editorship, which he accepted, and he was also appointed as a non-executive director with Lombards Bank. At the 15 October 1964 General Election, which ended thirteen years of Conservative government, Macleod was re-elected in Enfield West with a majority of 10,727 (19,612 votes to Liberal's 8,845 and Labour's 8,853). After the

WE NOW HAVE THE WORST OF BOTH WORLDS – NOT JUST INFLATION ON THE ONE SIDE OR STAGNATION ON THE OTHER SIDE, BUT BOTH OF THEM TOGETHER. WE HAVE A SORT OF 'STAGFLATION' SITUATION.

- IAIN MACLEOD -

election defeat, Macleod joined the shadow cabinet and set out to reconstruct his political career. When Douglas-Home resigned on 16 October 1964, Edward Heath took over as leader of the Conservative party and appointed Macleod as shadow Chancellor of the Exchequer. Although Macleod was no economist, his favoured project was tax reform and he planned to abolish Selective Employment Tax and cut personal income tax, while not increasing indirect taxes. At the 31 March 1966 General Election, in which Labour increased its seats, Macleod was returned in Enfield West with a majority of 10,157 (20,675 votes to Labour's 10,518 and Liberal's 7,202). Macleod continued as shadow Chancellor, where he made proposals for a national lottery, and in 1967 he helped to found the homeless charity 'Crisis' which was in response to the shocking Ken Loach film *Cathy Come Home*, which had been shown the previous November highlighting the plight of homeless people. In the General Election on 18 June 1970, Macleod was returned in Enfield West with a majority of 11,962 (21,858 votes to Labour's 9,896, Liberal's 4,820 and the National Front's 1,175) and the Conservatives claimed a surprise thirty-one seat victory. The new Prime Minister Edward Heath appointed Macleod as Chancellor of the Exchequer on 20 June

1970, but on 7 July after his one and only major speech on the economy as Chancellor, Macleod experienced severe abdominal pain and was taken to St George's Hospital where he underwent an operation for a ruptured pelvic diverticulum. He returned to 11 Downing Street on 19 July, after what had appeared to be a satisfactory recovery, but late in the evening of the 20th he suffered a heart attack and died aged 56, in 11 Downing Street. He was buried on 24 July 1970 at Gargrave, Yorkshire, a few miles from his Skipton birthplace.

Interesting Iain Macleod facts:

Macleod met Evelyn Hester Mason in September 1939 whilst he was waiting to be called up for army service and she interviewed him for a job as an ambulance driver. They married on 25 January 1941 and had a son and a daughter, Torquil and Diana, who were born in 1942 and 1944.

Macleod left £18,201 in his will, approx. worth £287,929 in 2020.

Macleod was credited with inventing the phrase 'the nanny state' which he referred to in the 3 December 1965 edition of *The Spectator* when he said, "what I like to call the nanny state".

Macleod was, the only Chancellor to have never delivered a Budget due to his untimely death, until Sajid Javid in 2020.

Macleod's daughter Diana Heimann was a UK Independence Party candidate at Banbury in the 2005 General Election.

Macleod was one of the great British bridge players. He won the Gold Cup in 1937, with teammates Maurice Harrison-Gray (Capt), S. J. Simon, Jack Marx (bridge) and Colin Harding, he also authored a 154-page book, *Bridge is an Easy Game* in 1952.

Anthony Barber
1920 - 2005 (85 years old) Conservative

Chancellor of the Exchequer:
25 July 1970 -
4 March 1974
(3 years, 7 months and 8 days)
Born
4 July 1920, Kingston upon Hull,
Died
16 December 2005, age 85, Suffolk

Title: Baron Barber

Constituencies Represented as MP:
Doncaster 1951 - 1964
Altrincham and Sale 1965 - 1974

Other Official Offices held:
Economic Secretary to the Treasury 1959 - 1962
Financial Secretary to the Treasury 1962 - 1963
Minister of Health 1963 - 1964
Chairman of the Conservative Party 1967 - 1970
Chancellor of the Duchy of Lancaster 1970

Prime Minister served with as Chancellor:
Edward Heath

Education:
Oriel College, Oxford.

Anthony Perrinott Lysberg Barber, Baron Barber, (4 July 1920 – 16 December 2005) was a Conservative MP from 1951 to 1974. He served as Chancellor of the Exchequer in Edward Heath's Cabinet from 1970 to 1974.

Barber was born in Bornholm, Northfield, Kingston-Upon-Hull on 4 July 1920 to John Barber and his wife Musse. Barber's father was a managing director of a confectionary firm in Doncaster, his mother was Danish, and he had two brothers; Noel who became a novelist/journalist and Kenneth who was a banker.
Barber was educated at Retford grammar school in Nottinghamshire with the intention of training as a solicitor, but his plans were curtailed in 1939 by the start of World War II.

In early 1940, Barber was commissioned into the Royal Artillery and stationed in France, but he returned to Britain with the retreat from Dunkirk. He was then transferred to the RAF as a pilot in the photographic reconnaissance unit. In 1942, on a mission flying over France, Barber had to bail out and was taken as a prisoner of war in Stalag Luft III, from where he tried to escape on several occasions, on one of his attempts he reached as far as Denmark before he was recaptured. Barber then spent the rest of the war devoting himself to gaining a first-class law degree through the help of the International Red Cross. Upon cessation of hostilities and the war ending, Barber returned to England where he continued his education with a two-year degree in philosophy, politics and economics at Oriel College, Oxford. He graduated with a second-class law degree and was called to the bar by the Inner Temple in 1948. Barber went on to specialise as a barrister in taxation before standing at the 23 February 1950 General Election, as a Conservative candidate in Doncaster. In a closely fought contest, Barber lost out to future Labour Minister Ray Gunter by 24,440 votes to 23,571, a majority of 878. On 5 September 1950, Barber married Jean Asquith who had stood as a Conservative candidate in the 1950 General

Election, Jean had stood and lost in Hemsworth. Twenty months after the 1950 General Election, a snap election was called by the Labour government in an attempt to increase their slim majority of just five seats on 25 October 1951. Barber again faced Gunter in Doncaster, this time though reversing the 1950 result with a 384 majority (25,005 votes to Gunter's 24,621) on an 82% turnout. In government, Barber was Parliamentary Private Secretary to George Ward who was the Undersecretary for Air from 1952 to 1955 and at the 26 May 1955 General Election, Barber again went head-to-head with Ray Gunter in Doncaster, emerging victorious in anther closely fought campaign with a 1,660 majority (24,598 votes to Gunter's 22,938). From 1955 to 1958, Barber was a junior whip under Edward Heath, after which he was appointed as Parliamentary Private Secretary to the Prime Minister, Harold Macmillan. At the General Election on 8 October 1959, Barber faced a new Labour candidate (Ted Garrett) and managed to increase his majority to 3,586 (26,521 votes to Labour's 22,935) and was rewarded with promotion to the Treasury, serving first as Economic Secretary, and from July 1962 as Financial Secretary. With the appointment of Alec Douglas Home as Prime Minister in October 1963, Barber was installed in the Cabinet as Minister of Health and sworn to the Privy Council. Barber served as Minister for Health for twelve months before he lost his seat in Doncaster to the Labour candidate, Harold Walker, at the 15 October 1964 General Election by 23,845 votes to 22,732 (majority 1,201). Barber's absence from Parliament was short-lived though as on 4 February 1965 he won the safe Conservative seat in an Altrincham and Sale By-election with a majority of 8,543 (20,380 votes to Labour's 11,837 and Liberal's 7,898). With the Conservatives in opposition from 1964 to 1970, Barber built up a successful business career as a director of British Roads and Chairman of his father-in-law's company Redfearn National Glass. On the political front during this period, Barber led Edward Heath's successful campaign to become the Conservative party leader to replacing Douglas Home in July 1965. At the 31 March 1966 General Election, Barber was again returned in Altrincham and Sale with a 6,837 majority (24,376 votes to Labour's 17,899 and Liberal's 8,891). Barber was rewarded for his efforts in Heath's leadership challenge by being appointed as the Conservative party chairman in 1967. Barber's hard-working ethos and problem-solving skills came to the fore in the build up to the June 1970 General Election (the first election where 18-year olds could vote). The Conservatives were behind in the polls leading up to the election, but Barber and Heath's plans for entry into the European Economic Community (EEC), and their desire to revive the British economy gave them a surprise victory with a thirty-one-seat majority. Barber was returned in Altrincham and Sale with an increased majority of 11,233 (27,904 votes to Labour's 16,671 and Liberal's 7,875) and Heath appointed Barber as the Duchy of Lancaster, with responsibility for negotiating Britain's entry into Europe. Unfortunately, things took a turn with the sudden death of the newly appointed Chancellor Iain Macleod, after only a month in position. Barber returned from Brussels and reluctantly accepted Heath's offer of the Chancellorship on 25 July 1970, giving rise to Labour leader Harold Wilson remarking that Barber's appointment was the first time he realised Edward Heath had a sense of humour. In his first Budget in March 1971, Barber announced the replacement of purchase tax with the introduction of value added tax (VAT), which was to be implemented from April 1973 (initially at a rate of 10% reduced to 8% a year later) while he reduced the basic rate of income tax. He also imposed charges for entry to museums and art galleries and ended free milk for primary school children, for which Margaret Thatcher as Secretary of State for Education at the time was blamed. With unemployment rising, Barber announced in his 1971 Budget large reductions in taxation, and in his 'dash for growth' he stated that his Budget would add 10% to the UK's growth in two years. Events soon proved him wrong though when inflation soared, increased by the newly floated pound and the

1973 oil crisis. This period became known as the 'Barber Boom' where the economy grew rapidly but at an unsustainable pace, it meant the balance of payments went into a heavy deficit. By late 1973 Barber imposed cuts in public spending,
increased surtax and introduced statutory prices to try and combat rising inflation. The incomes policy he imposed created tensions with the trade unions, which ultimately led to the 1974 miners' strike, a three-day week
and ultimately the Conservative defeat in the next General Election. From 1 January 1974, commercial users of electricity were limited to three specified consecutive days and were not permitted to work longer hours. With industrial unrest and the economy flattening, Heath called a General Election for February 1974. Barber stood in Altrincham and Sale, in what was to be the last General Election he would stand in, on the 28 February, winning with a majority of 8,696 (26,434 votes to Liberal's 17,738 and Labour's 15,550), but with the Conservative defeat Barber was made a life peer in Heath's dissolution honour's list and entered the House of Lords as Baron Barber of Wentbridge, and consequently he did not stand in the second General Election of 1974 in October. Still only fifty-four, Barber returned to business with his political reputation tarnished due to rising inflation and a record balance of payments deficit after he left office. Barber became Chairman of the Standard Charter Bank a post he held until 1987, and he was also director of BP from 1979 to 1988. Barber kept a low profile in the House of Lords, but he did publish a memoir 'Taking the Tide' in 1996. Towards the end of his life, Barber suffered from Parkinson's disease and died aged 85 on 16 December 2005, in Ipswich hospital from bronchopneumonia.

Interesting Anthony Barber facts:

Barber left £83,583 in his will, approx. worth £127,631 in 2020.

He was married twice, with two daughters from his first marriage.

Denis Healey
1917 - 2015 (98 years old) Labour

Chancellor of the Exchequer:
4 March 1974 -
4 May 1979
(5 years, 2 months and 1 day)

Born
30 August 1917, Mottingham

Died
3 October 2015, age 98,
Alfriston

Title: Baron Healey

Constituencies Represented as MP:
Leeds South East 1952 - 1955
Leeds East 1955 - 1992

Other Official Offices held:
Secretary of State for Defence 1964 - 1970
Deputy Leader of the Opposition 1980 - 1983
Shadow Foreign Secretary 1959 - 1961, 1970 - 1972 and 1980 - 1987

Prime Minister's served with as Chancellor:
Harold Wilson and James Callaghan

Education:
Balliol College, Oxford.

Denis Winston Healey, Baron Healey, (30 August 1917 – 3 October 2015) was a Labour MP for Leeds from 1952 to 1992. He served as Chancellor of the Exchequer from 1974 to 1979, and as Secretary of State for Defence from 1964 to 1970. Healey remains the longest-serving Defence Secretary to date, serving 5 years, 8 months and 3 days.

Healey was born at Tower House nursing home, Mottingham, Kent, on 30 August 1917, the elder son of William Healey an engineer, and his wife, Winifred Mary (Winnie) a schoolteacher. When Healey was five, the family moved to Keighley in Yorkshire where Healey senior had been appointed principal of Keighley Technical School. Healey won a scholarship to Bradford Grammar School when he was eight, and in the following years he became an avid reader but had little interest in politics at this stage. As time progressed, he acquired a passion for painting, music, film, and the theatre, and at nineteen, in 1936 he won an exhibition in classics to Balliol College, Oxford. As tensions in Europe intensified, Healey got more involved in student politics and joined the Communist party in 1937. As Healey explained in his memoirs, "Only the Communist party seemed unambiguously against Hitler." Healey graduated with a double first degree in classical moderations and in Greats in 1940.

He then went on to serve in the Second World, with his military career began mundanely, as he was checking travel arrangements at Swindon station. But after operations training in Scotland in 1942, his expertise in logistics saw him given the job of beachmaster at Anzio, south of Rome, in the allied invasion. He was mentioned in dispatches twice during that campaign and was promoted to Major for his

HEALEY IN THE ARMY

excellent contributions in the landings he was appointed a military MBE in 1945. After the war, Healey concentrated on a move towards politics and stood as a Labour candidate in the Pudsey and Otley constituency in the July 1945 General Election, where he was narrowly defeated by Malcolm Stoddart-Scott the Conservative candidate, by a majority of 1,651 (22,755 votes to 21,104 with the Liberal's on 5,592). After the defeat, Healey had the option of staying in the army, going back to Oxford to take up

a senior scholarship at Merton College or take the lowly paid position of Labour Party international secretary. Keen on pursuing a political career, Healey chose the latter, with his task being to try and rebuild relationships between the Labour Party and socialist parties in Europe, and helping to re-establish the Socialist International. In May 1947 a pamphlet, written by Healey, called 'Cards on the Table' was published, in which he bluntly pointed out the facts of the postwar international scene, making it clear that co-operation with the United States was based not on ideology but on practical grounds. He dismissed as unrealistic, the idea that Britain could pursue an independent policy as leader of a socialist European bloc. 'Cards on the Table' was an important step in Healey's progression, giving notice to the Labour hierarchy and helping set the scene for the revolution in foreign policy, which culminated two years later in the setting up of the North Atlantic Treaty Organisation (NATO). Healey didn't stand for Parliament again until 7 February 1952, when at the age of thirty-four, he was asked to stand in a By-election as the Labour candidate in the safe seat of Leeds South East. Healey won the election with a 7,199 majority (17,194 votes to Conservative's 9,995). Healey's entry into Parliament coincided with thirteen years of Conservative government, but he worked his way up in the Labour party and was a good friend of fellow Leeds MP and Labour leader Hugh Gaitskell. In the 26 May 1955 General Election, Healey won in the recreated Leeds East constituency (a seat he would hold until 1992) with a majority of 4,939 (26,083 votes to Conservative's 21,144). In 1959 he won a place in the shadow cabinet becoming the party's second-line spokesman on foreign affairs. He retainied the Leeds East seat in the October 1959 General Election with a 4,785 majority (28,707 votes to Conservative's 23,922). Two years later he was given responsibility for colonial and Commonwealth issues, and after the untimely death of Gaitskell in 1963, the new party leader, Harold Wilson, made him the chief opposition spokesman on defence. Following Labour's victory in the 15 October 1964 General Election, in which Healey had won the Leeds East seat with a majority of 8,006 (29,480 votes to the Conservative's 21,474) he was made Defence Secretary and given a seat in the Cabinet. He won again in Leeds East at the 31 March 1966 General Election, with an improved majority of 11,277 (30,073 votes to Conservative's 18,796). Healey's task as Defence Secretary was to try and make the department's workings more rational while maintaining the United Kingdom's security obligations, which included fighting an undeclared jungle war in Borneo. Healey also had to scrap ineffective and wasteful projects and cut back defence spending in line with Cabinet decisions. Healey's six years as Defence Secretary was seen as a big success to the extent that when Labour left office in 1970, Britain was spending more on education than on defence. With Labour's defeat in the 18 June 1970 General Election, Healey retained his seat in Leeds East with a reduced majority of 7,715 (28,827 votes to Conservative's 21,112) and became Shadow Foreign Secretary as well as getting elected to the party's national executive committee (NEC). When Roy Jenkins resigned as shadow chancellor over Labour's commitment to a referendum on Europe, Healey replaced him on 19 April 1972. After the 28 February 1974 General Election, Labour formed a minority government and the new Prime Minister, Harold Wilson, appointed Healey as the Chancellor of the Exchequer. Healey was returned in Leeds East at the February 1974 election with

a majority of 10,514 (25,550 votes to Conservative's 15,036 and Liberal's 9,906) and again in the second General Election to be held in 1974, on 10 October with a majority of 12,311 (24,745 votes to Conservative's 12,434 and Liberal's 6,970). The period immediately after the referendum on membership of the European Communities in June 1975 (resulting in a two-to-one victory for the 'yes' campaign) enabled Wilson to curb the influence of the left and allowed Healey to establish a more effective counter-inflation policy. Healey had long believed that Britain was living dangerously above its means, and as Chancellor he planned to be more cautious. His actions weren't universally accepted within the Labour party, but with inflation at 26.9 per cent a year in August 1975, he managed to reduce it to 12.9 per cent by July 1976, but he paid a price by being voted from Labour's national executive. On 16 March 1976, Wilson resigned as Prime Minister and party leader, and Healey stood in the following leadership election on 25 March 1976, he received thirty votes in the first round against five opponents (Michael Foot, James Callaghan, Roy Jenkins, Tony Benn and Anthony Crosland). In the second ballot on 30 March 1976, Healey came third with thirty-eight votes against James Callaghan (141) and Michael Foot (133).

Healey subsequently dropped out and Callaghan went on to be elected leader in the final ballot with 176 votes to Foot's 137. The International Monetary Fund (IMF) balance of payment crisis began in March 1976, with a loss of confidence in sterling (balance of payments is the difference between all money flowing into the country in a particular period e.g. a quarter or a year, and the outflow of money to the rest of the world). For the next nine months, Healey tried in vain to satisfy the markets that the British economy was back under control, but on 27 September 1976, the first day of the Labour conference in Blackpool, sterling was in free fall. Two days later Healey announced that the UK would make a formal application to the IMF for support amounting to $3.9 billion. Healey

EMERGENCY BUDGET **1976**

eventually persuaded his cabinet colleagues to accept the IMF terms and all the economic indicators began to move in the right direction. Healey came out of the whole episode in a positive light, receiving a standing ovation at the Labour party conference of 1977, as opposed to the tough time he had received at the 1976 conference when he was voted off the National Executive. But trouble lay ahead in the shape of the 'winter of discontent' of 1978–1979, Callaghan, against Healey's advice delayed the upcoming General Election until the spring of 1979. The trade union's revolt against incomes policy gathered pace and the government lost control of events, resulting in opposition leader Margaret Thatcher bringing about a vote of no confidence on 28 March 1979, which the government lost by one vote, 311 to 310. The result was a decisive General Election victory for the Conservatives on 3 May 1979, with a majority of forty-three seats. Healey was made a Companion of Honour in the dissolution honour's list and retained his seat in Leeds East with a 10,536 majority (26,346 votes to Conservative's 15,810 and Liberal's 4,622). Callaghan stayed as Labour leader until the party conference in Blackpool in October 1980, with Healey as the favourite to take over, winning the first ballot on 4 November 1980 with 112 votes to Michael Foot's 73, with John Silkin and Peter Shore eliminated on 38 and 32 votes. In the second ballot on 10 November 1980, Healey was surprisingly beaten by Foot by ten votes (139 to 129) but was returned unopposed as deputy leader.

The following year Tony Benn challenged Healey for the post of deputy leader, and in an acrimonious contest, Healey only just prevailed by a small margin of 50.4% to Benns 49.6%. Healey who had been appointed shadow Foreign Secretary in December 1980, lost support within the Labour party with his opposition to the party's endorsement of unilateral British nuclear disarmament. At the 9 June 1983 General Election, Healey accused Thatcher of "glorying in slaughter" after the Falklands war and had to withdraw the remark, he retained his seat in

Leeds East with a 6,095 majority (18,450 votes to the Conservative's 12,355 and Liberal's 10,884) and remained as shadow Foreign Secretary.

After the 11 June 1987 General Election, which was the last election he would stand in, Healey won Leeds East with a majority of 9,526 (20,932 votes to the Conservative's 11,406 and Liberal's 10,630) but he retired from the shadow cabinet, and in 1992 stood down after 40 years as a Leeds MP. He was made a life peer as Baron Healey, of Riddlesden, West Yorkshire in 1992. In the Lords he made the occasional speech on defence, international affairs, and economic issues. Healey died of cancer of the liver at his home in Alfriston on 3 October 2015 of cancer of the liver aged 98.

Interesting Denis Healey facts:

Healey was famed for his notably bushy eyebrows.

In the 1970's the popular impressionist Mike Yarwood coined the catchphrase "Silly Billy" in his impression of Healey. Healey had never used the phrase, but he adopted it and used it frequently.

Healey married Edna May Edmunds on 21 December 1945, having met Oxford University before the war. The couple had three children, one of whom is the broadcaster, writer and record producer Tim Healey.

Healey is the only Chancellor to have appeared on the popular BBC One comedy programme the *Morecambe and Wise Show*.

Healey's autobiography was published in 1989 titled '*The Time of My Life*'.

As well as having a puppet on the satirical television puppet show 'Spitting Image' Healey appeared as himself in season 1 episode 12.

In 1993 Healey was paid £50,000 for "making scrambled egg with smoked salmon" for a Sainsbury's television advert.

Healey appeared on *The Dame Edna Experience* with a song and dance number "Style" alongside James Bond actor Roger Moore.

Geoffrey Howe
1926 - 2015 (88 years old) Conservative

Chancellor of the Exchequer:
4 May 1979 -
11 June 1983
(4 years, 1 month and 8 days)
Born
20 December 1926, Port Talbot, Glamorgan
Died
9 October 2015, age 88, Idicote, Warwickshire
Title: Baron Howe of Aberavon

Constituencies Represented as MP:
Bebington 1964 - 1966
Reigate 1970 - 1974
East Surrey 1974 - 1992

Other Official Offices held:
Solicitor General for England and Wales 1970 - 1972
Second Lord of the Treasury 1979 - 1983
Secretary of State for Foreign and Commonwealth Affairs 1983 – 1989
Deputy Prime Minister 1989 - 1990
Leader of the House of Commons 1989 - 1990
Lord President of the Council 1989 - 1990

Prime Minister served with as Chancellor:
Margaret Thatcher

Education:
Trinity Hall, Cambridge.

Richard Edward Geoffrey Howe, Baron Howe of Aberavon, (20 December 1926 – 9 October 2015), known from 1970 to 1992 as Sir Geoffrey Howe, was a Conservative MP from 1964 to 1992, and was Margaret Thatcher's longest-serving Cabinet minister. He held the posts of Chancellor of the Exchequer, Foreign Secretary, Leader of the House of Commons, Deputy Prime Minister and Lord President of the Council. He was at Foreign Office for the second longest period of the twentieth Century.

Howe was born on 20 December 1926, at Glasfryn, Port Talbot, Glamorgan, the elder son of Benjamin Edward Howe, solicitor and coroner and his wife, Eliza Florence. Howe's sister, Barbara, died in infancy before he was born and his brother, Colin became a surgeon at Guy's Hospital in London. Howe was educated at three independent schools: Bridgend Preparatory School in Bryntirion, followed by Abberley Hall School in Worcestershire and after winning an exhibition, Winchester College in Hampshire. While at Winchester during the wartime years, Howe developed both his interest in law and his political ambitions as a Conservative as well as a lifelong enthusiasm for hill-walking. With the outbreak of World War II, Howe served in the Royal Signals for his national service from 1945 until 1948, spending much of the time in Kenya and Uganda. Howe then went on to Trinity Hall, Cambridge from 1948 to 1951, and received a first in part one of the Law tripos. He also became politically active, chairing the Cambridge University Conservative Association and serving on the committee of the Cambridge Union.

Upon leaving Cambridge, Howe was called to the bar by the Middle Temple in February 1952, his early practice was mainly in personal injury and negligence cases, taking briefs from the steelworkers' union and working on the Wales and Chester circuit. As well as his law practice, Howe stood as a Conservative candidate in the safe Labour seat of Aberavon, firstly in the 26 May 1955 General Election where he lost to a majority of 16,297

(Labour 29,003 votes to Howe's 12,706) and also in the 8 October 1959 General Election, again losing to Labour with a 17,638 majority (Labour's 30,397 votes to Howe's 12,759). He was however, developing a reputation as a leading Conservative thinker of the younger generation. In 1951 he was one of the founders of the Bow Group (named after the Bow and Bromley Constitutional Club), which sought, in his words, "to make the Tory Party fit for *Observer* and *Guardian* readers to live in". The Bow Group, which Howe chaired in 1955, produced a stream of pamphlets from its magazine, *Crossbow*, which Howe edited

from 1960 to 1962. He finally got a candidacy for a winnable seat when he stood in the 15 October 1964 General Election in Bebington (Wirral, Merseyside), and won in a closely fought contest, with a majority of 2,209 (26,943 votes to Labour's 24,743 and the Liberal's 7,765). In Parliament he became a chairman of the backbench committee on social services, being quickly recognised for promotion to the front bench as opposition spokesman on welfare and labour policy. At the 31 March 1966 General Election, Howe lost his seat in Bebington to a 3.85% swing to labour, losing to a 2,337-majority (Labour 30,545 votes to Howe's 28,208). He spent the next four years out of the Commons, however, he increased his reputation, particularly in areas where the law and politics overlapped, and he became legal correspondent for the Sunday Telegraph. Howe continued in his pursuit of a political career while being appointed a QC in 1965. He then stood in Reigate in the 18 June 1970 General Election in Reigate (Surrey), where he was comfortably returned to Parliament with a 13,029 majority (28,462 votes to Labour's 15,433 and the Liberal's 8,952) and was appointed Solicitor General in Edward Heath's government and as customary was knighted. Howe was responsible for the Industrial Relations Act 1971, that tried to stabilise industrial relations by forcing concentration of bargaining power and responsibility to the formal union leadership, using the courts, but it caused immediate retaliatory union strikes. Howe was promoted in 1972 to Minister of State at the Department of Trade and Industry, with a seat in the Cabinet and Privy Council membership. At the 28 February 1974 General Election, Labour won with the narrowest majority recorded, three seats and Howe won the boundary changed seat of East Surrey with a 9,845 majority (23,563 votes to Liberal's 15,544 and Labour's 6,946). At the following October General Election, Howe retained his seat with an increased majority of 9,845 (22,227 votes to Liberal's 12,382 and Labour's 7,797). After the Conservatives' second defeat of 1974, Howe who was not close to Margaret Thatcher voted for Heath in the first Conservative leadership ballot, and after Heath's defeat and withdrawal, Howe himself stood in the second round but gained just nineteen votes. However, this period proved a decisive turning-point in his career, when Thatcher appointed him as Shadow Chancellor in February 1975, beginning nearly fifteen years when his fortunes would become inextricably tied to those of Thatcher. In opposition, Howe masterminded the development of new economic policies embodied in the mini manifesto *The Right Approach to the Economy,* and when he criticised Labour Chancellor Denis Healey over the IMF loan in 1978, Healey famously retorted with the comment "it was like being savaged by a dead sheep". With the Conservative victory in the 3 May 1979 General Election in which Howe was re-elected in East Surrey with a much-increased majority of 19,400 (28,266 votes to the Liberal's 8,866 and Labour's 7,398) and he was appointed Chancellor of the Exchequer in the Thatcher government. Howe's plan as Chancellor which he homed in opposition, was an ambitious programme of radical policies intended to restore the public finances, reduce inflation and free the economy. The development of a medium-term financial strategy, with the shift from direct to indirect taxation, the abolition of exchange controls and the creation of tax-free enterprise zones. Howe set the tone in his first Budget on 12 June 1979, when he cut the top marginal rate of income tax from 83 to 60 per cent (while eliminating the counter-productive rate of 98 per cent on unearned income) and reduced the basic rate from 33 to 30 per cent, financing this by creating a new rate of VAT of 15 per cent, up from the previous rates of 8 and 12.5 per cent. The period from late 1979 to spring 1981 was spent trying to get public

THATCHER AND HOWE

spending under control in the face of rising unemployment and sharply falling output. Interest rates also remained high, and the growth of wages and prices showed no real signs of coming down. In his two-hour Budget speech in March 1980, Howe concentrated on getting control of the public finances. Successive plans were announced to reduce public spending which had continued to rise. In July 1980, it proved impossible to deliver the £2 billion of savings for which the Cabinet had agreed, and Howe was forced into a mini budget in autumn 1980. In his second Budget in March 1981, Howe raised duties significantly, with duty on petrol increased by 20p per gallon, duty on a packet of 20 cigarettes increased by 13p, duty on beer increased by 4p, duty on spirits increased by 60p and duty on wine increased by 12p. The leader of the Opposition Michael Foot said of the Budget "This is a budget to produce over three million unemployed". In a letter to *The Times* from 364 economists, including five of the six surviving Treasury chief economic advisers, it argued that 'there is no basis in economic theory or supporting evidence for the Government's present policies. They will deepen the depression, erode the industrial base of our economy and threaten its social and political stability'. In the spring of 1982, as economic confidence began to improve, and with interest rates already three points lower than at their peak of 16 per cent the previous autumn, public spending and borrowing had started to move in a favourable direction, which allowed Howe to announce some modest tax reliefs for individuals and businesses in his final Budget in March 1983. The economy slowly climbed out of

BARON HOWE

recession, however, unemployment which was already extremely high, was pushed to a 50-year high of 12% by 1984. At the General Election on 9 June 1983, the Conservative's increased their majority of seats in the House of Commons from 43 seats to 141 and Howe was returned in East Surrey with a majority of 15,436 (27,272 votes to the Liberal's 11,836 and Labour's 4,249). After the election, Thatcher promoted Howe, stating that she "wanted to promote Geoffrey for all he had done" and appointed him as Foreign Secretary on 11 June 1983. The Conservative government had aligned itself with the Cold War policies of President Ronald Reagan. It tripled Britain's nuclear strength by buying submarine missile systems from America and negotiated a deal with China to surrender Hong Kong in 1997. Thatcher's antipathy to a European union finally alienated Howe, with the immediate sticking point being the European mechanism to set exchange rates as a precursor to a common currency. Thatcher believed it would harm Britain's economy, but Howe said she was jeopardising Britain's future in Europe. Tensions led to a 1989 Cabinet shuffle. Thatcher named John Major as Foreign Secretary and demoted Howe to the largely ceremonial post of Deputy Prime Minister. Thatcher attended the European council meeting in Rome where she had declared for the first time that Britain would never enter a single currency, and when there were calls for greater central control in Europe she famously said in the Commons on 30 October 1990 "No, no no". Howe, the last

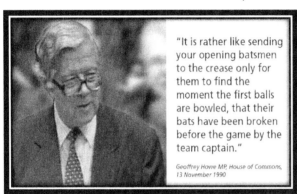

"It is rather like sending your opening batsmen to the crease only for them to find the moment the first balls are bowled, that their bats have been broken before the game by the team captain."

Geoffrey Howe MP, House of Commons, 13 November 1990

original member of the 1979 Thatcher government, quit the cabinet two days later on Nov 1, 1990. Howe's scathing resignation speech from the backbenches on 13 November 1990 would come to haunt Thatcher. On her approach to European negotiations, Howe told a hushed Commons: "It is rather like sending your opening batsmen to the crease, only for them to find that their bats have been broken before the game by the team captain." Howe went on to finish his speech by saying "That is why I have resigned. In doing so, I have done what I believe to be right for my party and my country. The time has come for others to consider their own response to the tragic conflict of loyalties with which I have myself wrestled for perhaps too long." Howe's final words are now regarded as a starting gun for the leadership contest that ousted Thatcher less than a fortnight later. Howe retired from the House of Commons in 1992, and was made a life peer on 30 June 1992 as Baron Howe of Aberavon, of Tandridge in the County of Surrey. In the Lords, Howe continued to speak on a wide range of foreign-policy and European issues, and led opposition to the Labour government's plans from 1997 to convert the second chamber into a largely elected body. Howe retired from the House of Lords on 19 May 2015, and died at the age of 88 on 9 October 2015 following a suspected heart attack.

Interesting Geoffrey Howe facts:

Howe published his memoirs *Conflict of Loyalty* in 1994.

Howe married Elspeth Rosamund Morton Shand on 28 August 1953, and they had three children, Cary (*b*. 1955), and twins Amanda and Alec (*b*. 1959).

Howe's wife Elspeth served as deputy chairman of the Equal Opportunities Commission from 1975 to 1979, and in various other capacities from 1980. She was later made Chair of the Broadcasting Standards Commission. In the 1999 New Year's Honours she was appointed a Commander of the Order of the British Empire (CBE). Lady Howe was a Justice of the Peace in Inner London from 1964 until her retirement from the Bench in 2002.

Baroness Howe of Idlicote and her husband Geoffrey, were one of the few couples who both held titles in their own right.

Howe's dramatic resignation speech in the House of Commons in November 1990 formed the basis of Jonathan Maitland's 2015 play *Dead Sheep*.

While Chancellor, Howe named his dog 'Budget'.

Howe enraged trade unions and the opposition by banning trade union membership at GCHQ in Cheltenham when he became Foreign Secretary.

Nigel Lawson
Born 1932 - Conservative

Chancellor of the Exchequer:

11 June 1983 -
26 October 1989
(6 years, 4 months and 16 days)

Born
11 March 1932, Hampstead, London

Title: Baron Lawson of Blaby

Constituency Represented as MP:
Blaby 1974 - 1992

Other Official Offices held:
Financial Secretary to the Treasury 1979 - 1981
Secretary of State for Energy 1981 - 1983
Second Lord of the Treasury 1983 - 1989
Member of the House of Lords Lord Temporal 1992 - incumbent

Prime Minister served with as Chancellor:
Margaret Thatcher

Education:
Westminster School, London
Christ Church, Oxford.

Nigel Lawson, Baron Lawson of Blaby, (born 11 March 1932) is a Conservative politician who represented Blaby as an MP from 1974 to 1992. He served in the Cabinet of Margaret Thatcher from 1981 to 1989, six of them as Chancellor.

Lawson was born on 11 March 1932, to a wealthy Jewish family in Hampstead, London. His father, Ralph Lawson was the owner of a commodity-trading firm in the City of London, while his mother, Joan Elisa (Davis), was also from a prosperous family of stockbrokers. Lawson was educated at two independent schools; Beechwood Park School in Markyate (nr. St Albans) Hertfordshire, followed by Westminster School in London. He then attended Christ Church, Oxford. At Oxford Lawson gained a first-class honours degree in Philosophy, Politics and Economics.

After leaving Oxford, Lawson carried out his National Service as a Royal Navy officer, during which time he commanded the fast-patrol boat HMS *Gay Charger*. Upon completion of his National Service, he began a career as a journalist, initially at the *Financial Times* in 1956 writing the Lexicon column. He progressed to the positions of City editor of *The Sunday Telegraph* in 1961 – where he introduced his friend Jim Slater's *Capitalist* investing column – and then editor of *The Spectator* from 1966 to 1970. At the General Election on 18 June 1970, Lawson stood as the Conservative candidate in Eton and Slough, losing out to Labour's Joan Lester in a closely fought contest, with Lister receiving 24,903 votes to Lawson's 21,436 votes for a 2,667 majority, the Liberal candidate Peter Naylor came third with 3,407 votes. Lawson had to wait until the first of two General Elections in 1974 before he entered Parliament. At the first election on 28 February, Lawson stood as the Conservative candidate in Blaby, Leicestershire, winning with a majority of 12,298 (26,892 votes to G Broad, Liberal 14,594 and D.E.Lack, Labour 13,749). At the second General Election of 1974 on 10 October, Lawson received a majority of 12,161 (25,405 votes to M.F.Fox Labour 13,244 and

D. Inman 12,290). While in opposition, Lawson worked on securing legislation for the automatic indexation of tax thresholds to prevent the tax burden being increased by inflation (typically in excess of 10% per annum during that Parliament). At the General Election on 3 May 1979, the Conservatives came to power under the leadership of Margaret Thatcher and Lawson was re-elected in Blaby with an increased majority of 20,640 (33,221 votes to Keith

Hill, Labour 12,581 and D.Inman, Liberal 12,290). In Thatcher's first ministry, Lawson was appointed to the post of Financial Secretary to the Treasury dealing in such measures as the ending of unofficial state controls on mortgage lending, the abolition of exchange controls and the publication of the 'Medium-Term financial Strategy'. The document set the course for both the monetary and fiscal sides of the new government's economic policy. In a Cabinet reshuffle of September 1981, Lawson was promoted to the position of Secretary of State for Energy. In this role his most significant action was to prepare for what he saw as an inevitable full-scale strike in the state-owned coal industry over the closure of deep coal mines, whose uneconomic operation accounted for the coal industry's business losses and the consequent requirement for state subsidy. Lawson became a key proponent of the Thatcher Government's privatisation policy. During his tenure at the Department of Energy, he set the course for the later privatisations of the gas and electricity industries, and on his return to the Treasury he worked closely with the Department of Trade and Industry in privatising British Telecom, British Airways, and British Gas. At the General Election on 9 June 1983, Thatcher and the Conservative's increased their parliamentary majority from 43 seats to 144. Lawson was re-elected in Blaby with a 17,116 majority (32,689 votes to Richard Lustig, Liberal Alliance 15,573 and C.Wrigley, Labour 6,838). After the election, Lawson was promoted to the position of Chancellor of the Exchequer in succession to Geoffrey Howe. As Chancellor, Lawson's main focus was concentrated on tax reform, and in his first Budget on 13 March 1984, he reformed corporate taxes through a combination of reduced rates and reduced allowances. Lawson stated at the start of his Budget that "There will be no letting up in our determination to defeat inflation. We shall continue the policies that we have followed consistently since 1979. These policies provide the only way to achieve our ultimate objective of stable prices. To abandon them would be to risk renewed inflation and much higher unemployment. As a result of our determined

efforts, inflation is at its lowest level since the 1960s. Economic recovery is well under way and employment is growing". In his Budget on 19 March 1985, Lawson stated that his Budget had two themes: "to continue the drive against inflation and to help create the conditions for more jobs", while continuing the trend of shifting from direct to indirect taxes, by reducing National Insurance contributions for the lower-paid, and extending the base of value added tax. Lawson's reputation as Chancellor continued to grow and in his 18 March 1986 Budget, Lawson said "we can now look back to five solid years of growth at around 3 per cent a year. Even more important, 1985 was the third successive year in which we secured the elusive combination of steady growth and low inflation – the first time this has been achieved since the 1960s. In 1985 as a whole, output grew by a further 3½ per cent. I expect 1986 to be a further year of steady growth with low inflation. Indeed, with output forecast to rise by 3 percent, and inflation to fall to 3½ percent, 1986 is set to register our best overall performance in terms of output and inflation for a generation". The course taken by the UK economy from this point is described as "The Lawson Boom" an analogy of

NIGELLA AND NIGEL

the phrase "The Barber Boom" which describes the period of rapid expansion under Chancellor Anthony Barber, in the Conservative Government of Prime Minister Edward Heath. In his 17 March 1987 Budget, which led up to the General Election, Lawson said "Nineteen eighty-six was

dominated by the sudden collapse of the oil price. Our own economy was affected not only directly, as a major oil producer and exporter" he continued "the setting for this year's Budget is more favourable than it has been for very many years. We are now entering our seventh successive year of steady growth, and the fifth in which this has been combined with low inflation. The public finances are sound and strong, and unemployment is falling. These are the fruits of the Government's determination, in bad times as well as good, to hold firmly to our policies of sound money and free markets". At the 11 June 1987 General Election, Thatcher and the Conservative's won their third consecutive election with another large majority of 102, Lawson was re-elected in Blaby in what was to be the last General Election he would stand in, winning with his largest ever majority of 22,176

(37,732 votes to Richard Lustig, Liberal Alliance 15,556 and James Roberts, Labour 9,046). Lawson continued as Chancellor and in his 15 March 1988 Budget, he said "I am reliably informed that my Budget speech last year was the shortest this century. My Budget speech this year is likely to have a different claim to a place in the history books—not, the House will be glad to learn, as the longest Budget speech this century, but as the last untelevised Budget speech". His Budget speech did take almost two hours though due to continuous interruptions and protest from opposition members. Scottish National Party MP, Alex Salmond, was suspended from the House and several MPs voted

LAWSON AS CHANCELLOR

against the amendment of the law bill (which is typically agreed by all members of the House). Lawson said in his statement "I have announced a £2½ billion increase in public expenditure plans for 1988–89, with resources allocated to programmes up by over £4½ billion. This means that, over the coming year, we will be spending at least £1,100 million more on health than in the year now ending, at least £900 million more on education, and at least £500 million more on law and order". Lawson was opposed to the 'Community tax' and disagreed with Thatcher on the issue of exchange rate mechanism, and the re-employment by Thatcher in 1989 of Sir Alan Walters as her personal economic adviser. These issues increased tensions between Lawson and Thatcher, and although both agreed to a steady rise in interest rates to restrain demand, it had the effect of inflating the headline inflation figure. Lawson felt that the differences between him as exchange-rate monetarist and the views of Walters (who continued to favour a floating exchange rate) were making his job impossible and he resigned on 26

October 1989. On 1 July 1992 he was given a life peerage as Baron Lawson of Blaby, of Newnham in the County of Northamptonshire.

Interesting Nigel Lawson facts:

Lawson has been married twice, having children from both marriages, first marriage to Vanessa Salmon in 1955 (dissolved in 1980), produced four children (2 boys and 2 girls). Lawson's second marriage was to Therese Maclear, married in 1980, dissolved in 2012, producing 2 children (1 boy and 1 girl).

Lawson's first daughter from his first marriage is food writer and television cook Nigella Lawson. His second daughter, Thomasina, sadly died from breast cancer in 1993 aged 32.

In 2013, Lawson advocated Britain leaving the EU. He argued that 'economic gains [from leaving the EU] would substantially outweigh the costs. In the 2016 EU referendum, he supported Leave and was appointed chairman of the Vote Leave campaign.

Lawson has published the best-selling *The Nigel Lawson Diet Book* (1996) and his memoir *The View from No.11: Memoirs of a Tory Radical in 1992.*

Lawson is involved with the climate change denial movement and believes that man-made global warming has little or no impact. He became chairman of a new think tank, the Global Warming Policy Foundation on 23 November 2009.

In 2008, Lawson published a book, *An Appeal to Reason: A Cool Look at Global Warming*. He states that the impact of Global Warming will be relatively moderate rather than apocalyptic.

John Major
1943 - Conservative

Chancellor of the Exchequer:
26 October 1989 -
28 November June 1990
(1 year, 1 month and 3 days)

Born
29 March 1943, St Helier, Carshalton,
Surrey

Title: Sir John Major

Constituency Represented as MP:
Huntingdon 1979 - 2001

Other Official Offices held:
Lord Commissioner of the Treasury 1984 - 1985
Parliamentary Under-Secretary of State for Social Services 1985 -
1986
Minister of State for Social Security 1986 - 1987
Chief Secretary to the Treasury 1987 - 1989
Secretary of State for Foreign Affairs and Commonwealth Affairs
1989 - 1990
Prime Minister 1990 - 1997

Prime Minister served with as Chancellor:
Margaret Thatcher

Education:
Rutlish Grammar School (left school at sixteen).

Sir John Major, (born 29 March 1943) was the Conservative MP for Huntingdon from 1979 to 2001, he served as Chancellor of the Exchequer in the Margaret Thatcher government, and was Prime Minister and Leader of the Conservative Party from 1990 to 1997.

John Major was born on 29 March 1943, at St Helier Hospital and Queen Mary's Hospital for Children in St Helier, Surrey, the son of former music hall performer Tom Major-Ball and Gwen Major (née Coates). He began attending primary school at Cheam Common School from 1948, and in 1954 he passed the 11+ exam which enabled him to go to Rutlish Grammar School, in Wimbledon. He left school on the eve of his sixteenth birthday in 1959 with three O-levels and joined the Brixton Young Conservatives.

After leaving school Major had a variety of jobs, including working as a clerk in insurance and working in the garden ornaments business. In 1962, after caring for his ill mother, he was unemployed for a short while, a situation which he described as 'degrading'. He found work in December 1962, working at the London Electricity Board, and at the age of 21, he stood as a Conservative Councillor in the Larkhall ward at the Lambeth London Borough Council election in May 1964, losing out to Labour. In 1965, he moved jobs and went into banking, and through his work he was sent for a long secondment in Jos, Nigeria in December 1966, where he cultivated his hatred for racism. While in Nigeria in 1967 he was involved in a serious car accident, damaging his leg, and led him to being flown home. After finally recovering Major stood again as Councillor in the May 1968 Lambeth London Borough Council election, this time for the Ferndale ward. Although a Labour stronghold Major took the third seat available winning by 70 votes (991 to 921) and after being elected he took a big interest in housing matters. In February 1970, Major became Chairman of the Lambeth Housing Committee, but at the 1971 Lambeth London Borough Council election, he lost his seat as Labour took all three seats back from the Conservatives. Major, undeterred, still had political ambitions and was selected as the Conservative candidate for the Labour dominated St Pancras North constituency, where he fought in both the February and October 1974 General Elections losing on both occasions to majorities of 6,835 (Labour 14,761 to Major's

7,962 and the Liberal's 4,825) and 7,553 (Labour 14,155 to Major's 6,602 and Liberal's 3,428). He was still determined for a career in politics and applied for selection to the safe Conservative seat of Huntingdonshire in December 1976. He won selection and started working part-time in 1978 so that he could devote more time to his constituency duties. At the 3 May 1979 General Election, Major was returned as MP for Huntingdonshire with a large 21,563 majority (40,193 votes to Labour's 18,630 and the Liberal's 12,812). He became Secretary of the Environment

ON THE CAMPAIGN TRAIL

Committee and also assisted with work on the Housing Act 1980, which allowed council house tenants the 'Right to Buy' their homes. In 1981, Major was appointed as a Parliamentary Private Secretary, and then as a junior whip in 1983. After boundary changes, he was returned in the 9 June 1983 General Election for the Huntingdon ward with a majority of 20,348 (34,254 votes to the Liberal's 13,906 and Labour's 6,317). He was promoted to Treasury Whip in October 1984 and also in the same month, he narrowly avoided the IRA's Brighton hotel bombing, having left the hotel only a few hours before the bomb went off. In September 1985, Major was made Parliamentary Under-Secretary of State for the Department of Health and Social Security, before being promoted to become Minister of State in the same department in September 1986. At the 11 June 1987 General Election, Major was again returned for Huntingdon with an increased majority of 27,044 (40,530 votes to SDP's 13,486 and

Labour's 8,883) and on 13 June he was promoted by Margaret Thatcher to the Cabinet as Chief Secretary to the Treasury, gaining respect due to his ability to keep spending down. In a surprise re-shuffle on 24 July 1989, Major was appointed Foreign Secretary, succeeding Geoffrey Howe, a position he only spent three months in as he was appointed Chancellor of the Exchequer after Nigel Lawson's resignation in October 1989. Major presented only one Budget (the first Budget ever to be televised live) on 20 March 1990, and announced it as '*a Budget for savings*' introducing the Tax-Exempt Special Savings Account (TESSA) while increasing taxes on alcohol, cigarettes and petrol. In 1990, with opposition in the Conservative Party growing against Margaret Thatcher and two By-election defeats, there were doubts about a Conservative victory in an upcoming election. With a forced leadership election, Margaret Thatcher

MAJOR ON HIS SOAP BOX

resigned as Conservative Leader and Prime Minister after the first leadership ballot, and stood behind Major in the second ballot. On 27 November 1990, the second ballot was held with 187 votes being the winning target. Major fell two votes short with 185, but he polled far enough ahead of both Douglas Hurd and Michael Heseltine to secure their immediate withdrawal. With no remaining challengers, Major was formally named Leader of the Conservative Party that evening and was duly appointed Prime Minister the following day. His new Cabinet was substantially different from Thatcher's, and served to demonstrate that Major was looking for moderation on Europe and the desire to build a 'classless society'. One of Major's first policy decisions was to abolish the notorious Community Charge or Poll Tax and replace it with a Council Tax, paid for partly by a rise in VAT. In 1992, the Conservatives were widely expected to lose the General Election to Neil Kinnock's Labour Party so Major decided to take his campaign onto the streets, famously delivering many addresses from an upturned soapbox as in his Lambeth days. Major's "common touch" approach stood in contrast to the Labour Party's seemingly slicker campaign, and it seemed to resonate with the electorate, along with a hard-hitting negative advertising campaign focusing on the issue of Labour's approach to taxation. Major won a second period in office at the April 9, 1992 General Election, albeit with a smaller parliamentary majority of just 21 seats (down from a majority of 102 seats at the previous election) but the Conservatives won over 14 million

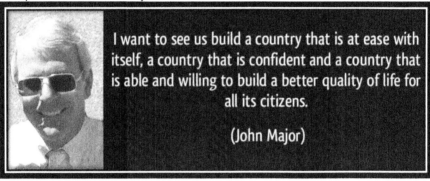

I want to see us build a country that is at ease with itself, a country that is confident and a country that is able and willing to build a better quality of life for all its citizens.

(John Major)

votes, which was the highest popular vote ever recorded. Major himself was returned in Huntingdon with an improved majority of 36,230 (48,662 votes to Labour's 12,432, Lib Dems 9,386 and the Liberal's 1,045), but his premiership was soon hit by a recession, with inflation hitting 10.9% and unemployment rising to three million. With the UK's commitment to the European Exchange Rate Mechanism (ERM) constraining its ability to cut interest rates and thereby stimulate the economy, the UK was forced to withdraw from the ERM in September 1992. On 16 September 1992, a day which would come to be known as 'Black Wednesday', billions of pounds were wasted in a futile attempt to defend the value of sterling. The upheaval caused by the day's events was such that Major came close to resigning as Prime Minister. The UK was ultimately forced out of the ERM because it could not prevent the value of the pound from falling below the lower limit specified by the ERM. The disaster of 'Black Wednesday' left the Government's economic credibility damaged and after seven months had passed, it led to Major sacking Norman Lamont as Chancellor of the Exchequer and replacing him with Kenneth Clarke. At the 1993 Conservative Party Conference, Major began the "Back to Basics" campaign, which he intended to

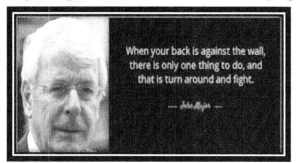

be about the economy, education and policing, but a series of sexual and financial scandals (given the catch-all term 'sleaze') hijacked the campaign and hit the Conservative party over the subsequent years. In 1994, Major's government set up the National Lottery, which up until then, all forms of gambling and lotteries in the UK had been severely restricted, however European legislation meant that lotteries from other EU countries would be able to operate in the UK. So, Major's government set up a British lottery with the money being raised going to good causes within the country. On 22 June 1995, tired of the continual threats of leadership challenges, Major resigned as Leader of the Conservative Party and announced that he would contest the resulting leadership election, telling his opponents that "it is time to put up or shut up". He continued to serve as Prime Minister whilst the leadership was vacant. John Redwood resigned as Secretary of State for Wales to stand against him, and on 14 July 1995, a vote was held, with Major winning by 218 votes to Redwood's 89 with 12 spoiled ballots and 10 abstaining. This was easily enough to win, and no further challenges were forthcoming. In March 1996, Major had to deal with a serious public health scare following a scientific announcement of a possible link between bovine spongiform encephalopathy (BSE, colloquially referred to as 'mad cow disease') and a form of Creutzfeldt–Jakob disease (vCJD), a serious and potentially fatal brain disease in humans. A huge cattle slaughter programme was introduced in a bid to restore faith in Britain's beef industry. In May 1996, with an EU ban in place on British beef, Major decided to withhold British

cooperation on all EU-related matters until the beef situation had been resolved (the ban on British beef was not lifted until August 1999). The economy had picked up after leaving the Exchange Rate Mechanism, and, under Major, the beginning of Britain's longest period of continuous economic growth began. He also began work on engaging with the IRA to move towards a peaceful end to the conflict in Northern Ireland, his work leading the way for the Good Friday Agreement in 1998. In 1997 Major knew he would have to call a General Election by May, even though Labour were ahead in the polls, and so on 17 March he announced that the election would be held on 1 May 1997. At the Election Labour under Tony Blair won by a landslide, winning 418 seats to the Conservatives 165 with the Liberal Democrats increasing their seats to 46. The Conservative Party suffered the worst electoral defeat by a ruling party since the Reform Act of 1832. Major himself was re-elected in his own constituency of Huntingdon with a reduced majority of 18,140 (31,501 votes to Labour's 13,361, Lib Dems 8,390 and the Referendum Party 3,114), but the election defeat left the Conservatives without any MPs in Scotland or Wales for the first time in history. Major stood down but served as Leader of the Opposition for a further seven weeks until the leadership election to replace him was underway. His resignation as Conservative Leader formally took effect on 19 June 1997 with the election of William Hague. Major still remained active in Parliament in the following years, regularly attending and contributing in debates until he eventually stood down from the House of Commons after 22 years as an MP at the June 2001 General Election. After leaving Parliament, Major actively engaged in charity work, becoming President of Asthma UK and a Patron of the Prostate Cancer Charity, Sightsavers UK, Mercy Ships, Support for Africa 2000 and Afghan Heroes. In the 1999 New Year Honours List, Major was made a Companion of Honour for his work on the Northern Ireland peace process, and on 23 April 2005, he was bestowed with a knighthood as a Companion of the Order of the Garter by Queen Elizabeth II.

Interesting John Major facts:

Major became the first British Prime Minister to subject himself to a leadership election while in office, which he comfortably won on July 4, 1995.

Following the death of Diana, Princess of Wales in 1997, Major was appointed a special guardian to Prince William and Prince Harry with responsibility for legal and administrative matters.

Major is a long-time cricket enthusiast and in 2005 he was elected to the Committee of the Marylebone Cricket Club (MCC).

Major was the youngest British Prime Minister of the 20th century, at 47 he was the youngest Prime Minister since Lord Rosebery some 95 years earlier.

Major's one and only Budget was the first to be televised live.

In 1999 he published his autobiography, covering his early life and time in office. He also wrote a book about the history of cricket in 2007 - *More Than a Game: The Story of Cricket's Early Years* and a book about Music Hall (*My Old Man: A Personal History of Music Hall*) in 2012.

In 2008 Major won the British Sports Book Awards (Best Cricket Book) for *More Than a Game: The Story of Cricket's Early Years*.

In 2013 the town of Candeleda in Spain named a street (*Avenida de John Major*), after him, as he has holidayed there since 1989.

On 20 June 2008, Major was granted the Freedom of the City of Cork and he was also granted the Outstanding Contribution to Ireland award in Dublin on 4 December 2014.

Major married Norma Johnson (now Dame Norma Major) on 3 October 1970 at St Matthew's Church, Brixton. Norma was a teacher and a member of the Young Conservatives. They met on polling day for the Greater London Council elections in London and became engaged after only ten days. They have two children: a daughter, Elizabeth (born November 1971) and a son, James (born January 1975).

As well as his love for cricket, Major is also a supporter of Chelsea Football Club.

There is a large John Major Suite at The Oval, home to Surrey County Cricket Club; the venue also contains a painting of Major.

Major has been depicted on screen by Keith Drinkel in *Thatcher: The Final Days* (1991), Michael Maloney in *Margaret* (2009) and Robin Kermode in *The Iron Lady* (2011).

Major's father was a former circus performer/vaudeville manager.

Norman Lamont
Born 1942 - Conservative

Chancellor of the Exchequer:

28 November 1990 -
27 May 1993
(2 years, 6 months)

Born
8 May 1942, Lerwick, Shetland,
Scotland

Title: Baron Lamont of Lerwick

Constituency Represented as MP:
Kingston–upon-Thames 1972 - 1997

Other Official Offices held:
Parliamentary Under Secretary of State for Energy 1979 - 1981
Minister of State for Trade and Industry 1985 - 1986
Minister of State for Defence Procurement 1985 - 1986
Financial Secretary to the Treasury 1986 - 1989
Chief Secretary to the Treasury 1989 - 1990
Second Lord of the Treasury 1990 - 1993

Prime Minister served with as Chancellor:
John Major

Education:
Fitzwilliam College. Cambridge.

Norman Stewart Hughson Lamont, Baron Lamont of Lerwick, (born 8 May 1942), is a former Conservative MP, who served the Kingston-upon-Thames constituency from 1972 to 1997. He served in John Major's government from 1990 until 1993, as Chancellor of the Exchequer (two and a half years).

Lamont was born in Lerwick, in the Shetland Islands (an island chain north of Scotland) the son of the islands' surgeon, Daniel Lamont and his wife Helen. Daniel was awarded an OBE for his services on the Shetland Islands where he was stationed in the Second World War. Lamont was educated at Loretto School, Musselburgh, Scotland and read Economics at Fitzwilliam College, Cambridge, where in 1963 he was President of the Conservative Association of Cambridge, and in 1964 was President of the Cambridge Union.

After graduating, Lamont continued his political interests by taking a position as a research assistant to Duncan Sandys, a Tory Member of Parliament. Lamont worked as a staff researcher for the Conservative Party from 1966 to 1968 and stood in the 18 June 1970 General Election in Kingston upon Hull East, but lost to future Labour Deputy Prime Minister, John Prescott, to a majority of 22,123 (36,859 votes to 14,736). From 1968 to 1979, Lamont worked as a merchant banker for the investment banking firm N.M. Rothschild and Sons and in between he stood in a By-election on 4 May 1972 in Kingston-upon-Thames, winning with a majority 6,787 (16,679 votes to Labour's 9,892 and the Liberal's 3,601). Lamont turned thirty, four days after his election victory and was the youngest Conservative Member of Parliament at that time. At the two General Elections of 1974, he increased his majority on his By-election victory, firstly to a 10,307 majority in February 1974 (23,006 votes to the Liberal's 12,699 and Labour's 11,369) and to an 8,414 majority at the October election (20,680 votes to Labour's 12,266 and the Liberal's 9,580). Lamont was on the opposition benches until Margaret Thatcher came to power in

May 1979, with a Parliamentary majority of forty-three seats. Lamont received what would be his highest majority gained in Kingston-Upon-Thames, 13,544 (24,944 votes to Labour's 11,400 and the Liberal's 6,771) and was appointed Parliamentary Under Secretary of State for Energy on 7 May. He stayed as Under Secretary for just over two years, until 14 September 1981, when he was appointed as Minister of State for Trade and Industry. At the General Election on 9 June 1983, Lamont was re-elected in Kingston-Upon Thames with an 8,872 majority (22,094 votes to Liberal's 13,222 and Labour's 4,977) and stayed as Minister of State for Trade until 2 September 1985, when he was appointed Minister of State for Defence Procurement, a position he would hold until the May of the following year, when on 21 May 1986, he was promoted to the position of Financial Secretary to the Treasury. At the General Election on 11 June 1987, Lamont was re-elected in Kingston-Upon-Thames with an 11,186 majority (24,198 votes to Liberal's 13,102 and Labour's 5,676) and on 24 July 1989, he was again promoted, this time as Chief Secretary to the Treasury under Nigel Lawson's Chancellorship. When Lawson resigned in October 1989, Lamont stayed as Chief Secretary under the new Chancellor John Major. Lamont accepted Major's decision to join the European Exchange Rate Mechanism (ERM) at a central parity of 2.95 Deutschmarks to the Pound, and shortly afterwards he successfully managed Major's election campaign to succeed Margaret Thatcher as party leader and Prime Minister. Lamont succeeded Major as the Chancellor of the Exchequer on 28 November 1990, and in his first Budget on 19 March 1991, Lamont said "I intend to carry forward my predecessor's work. My central economic aim is to bring inflation down and keep it down. Beyond that, my objective is to encourage enterprise by creating a broadly based tax system that allows markets to do their job with the minimum of distortion and Government interference. Although there is no scope this year for an overall reduction in taxes, my Budget today will include measures to help business through the recession in the short term and to encourage it to invest for the longer term". On 16 May 1991, Lamont famously stated in Parliament that "Rising unemployment and the recession have been the price that we have had to pay to get inflation down. That price is well worth paying" the comment caused a furore at the time, and is still used in debate today. In Lamont's second Budget, which came just before the General Election in 1992, the Budget cleverly forced Labour into opposing the introduction of a lower rate of income tax, branding them the

party of high taxation. Lamont called it a Budget for recovery by introducing a new 20% income tax band on the first £2,000 of taxable income. At the General Election on 9 April 1992, which resulted in a fourth consecutive victory for the Conservative's, Lamont was re-elected in Kingston-Upon-Thames with a 10,153- vote majority (20,675

LAMONT AS CHANCELLOR

votes to Lib Dems 10,522 and Labour's 7,748). But trouble lay ahead when on September 16, 1992, a collapse in the pound sterling forced Britain to withdraw from the European Exchange Rate Mechanism (ERM). The UK was forced out of the ERM because it could not prevent the value of the pound from falling below the lower limit specified by the ERM. The day became known as 'Black Wednesday'. In Parliament the next day John Smith, the Labour leader, derided Lamont and Major's government's economic policy. He said: "The real lesson of the ERM crisis was that 'before you can have a strong currency you need a strong economy'." Lamont saw Black Wednesday as a way for economic policy to be rebuilt "out of the ashes" and when asked at a press conference in Washington a fortnight later why he was so cheerful, he replied: "Well, it is a very beautiful morning, but it is funny you should say that. My wife said she heard me singing in the bath this morning." The remark did not go down well with the British public, and neither did the answer which he gave to the question the following Spring, during a Newbury By-election; "Which do you regret more, singing in the bath when forced to withdraw from the ERM, or talking prematurely of green shoots last autumn?" to which Lamont replied "Je ne regrette rien" (I regret nothing). Three weeks after the government's big loss in the By-election, on 27 May 1993, Lamont resigned saying in his resignation speech to the House "To give up being Chancellor of the Exchequer in the circumstances in which I did is bound to be an uncomfortable experience, but I have also been a Treasury Minister for almost

LAMONT AND DAVID CAMERON

seven years, a longer continuous period than anyone else this century. Indeed, I have been the only person ever to have held the three offices of Financial Secretary, Chief Secretary and Chancellor of the Exchequer". He continued "There is something wrong with the way in which we make our decisions. The Government listen too much to the pollsters and the party managers. The trouble is that they are not even very good at politics, and they are entering too much into policy decisions. As a result, there is too much short-termism, too much reacting to events, and not enough shaping of events. We give the impression of being in office but not in power. Far too many important decisions are made for 36 hours' publicity" and he finished by saying "Today, when I walked through Westminster Hall and up the stairs into the Lobby, I felt exactly the same pride and excitement as when I first entered this House 21 years ago. I look forward with anticipation to the great parliamentary events and battles that lie ahead." After his resignation, Lamont became a staunch euro-sceptic and became one of the first leading politician to raise the prospect of Britain withdrawing from the European Union. At the

JOHN MAJOR AND LAMONT

1997 General Election Lamont's constituency of Kingston upon Thames was split up and he was adopted as the Conservative candidate for the new seat of Harrogate and Knaresborough in Yorkshire. The move was seen as an attempt to parachute in an outsider against a local teacher, the Liberal Democrat candidate, Phil Willis. In the General Election on 1 May 1997, to the disillusionment of the Conservatives, it led to a massive tactical voting campaign in the constituency, with Willis winning the seat with a 6,236-vote majority (Willis 24,558, Lamont 18,322 and Barbara Boyce, Labour 4,151). Lamont was not recommended for a peerage in John Major's resignation honours, but the following year William Hague recommended him, and Lamont was made a life peer as Baron Lamont of Lerwick, of Lerwick in the Shetland Islands, on 24 July 1998. Lamont said of his time as Chancellor and the three Budget's he gave: "I have been privileged to present three Budgets. All three achieved the objectives that I set for them. The first [1991] drew the sting of the poll tax; the second [1992], by introducing the 20p income tax band, helped us to win the election; the third [1993], unpopular though it undoubtedly was, made a significant step toward reducing our budget deficit." He is the only person ever to have been Financial Secretary, Chief Secretary and Chancellor. After leaving the House of Commons, in addition to his membership of the House of Lords Economic Affairs Committee, he has a dozen or so directorships or consultancies that keep him busy and includes his work for Balli, a private Anglo-Iranian industrial and trading company, which has led to his being chairman of the British-Iranian Chamber of Commerce. In late 2008, Cameron asked Lamont, together with fellow former chancellors Geoffrey Howe, Nigel Lawson and Kenneth Clarke, to provide him with strategic political and economic advice as Britain's banking and fiscal position worsened.

Interesting Norman Lamont facts:

On the crisis of 'Black Wednesday' Lamont understated it by saying "It has been a difficult day".

In June 2007, Lord Lamont became Honorary Patron of the Oxford University History Society.

A 1997 Treasury analysis estimated that 'Black Wednesday' cost the UK £3.3 billion, based on exchange rates at which currency reserves were sold then rebuilt.

In 1993, Lamont was at the ITV Comedy Awards being shown on television to present an award, when the comedian Julian Clary made a risqué joke about him, which resulted in 'public outrage'

THERE ARE GOING TO BE NO DEVALUATIONS, NO LEAVING THE ERM. WE ARE ABSOLUTELY COMMITTED TO THE ERM. IT IS AT THE CENTRE OF OUR POLICY. WE ARE GOING TO MAINTAIN STERLING'S PARITY AND WE WILL DO WHATEVER IS NECESSARY, AND I HOPE THERE IS NO DOUBT ABOUT THAT AT ALL.
- NORMAN LAMONT -

according to the newspapers who launched an unsuccessful campaign to have Clary banned from television.

After Lamont resigned John Major said in his memoirs about Lamont: "'It was a stilted series of exchanges that illustrated the chill that had descended upon our relationship.... "Yes, Prime Minister." "No thank you, Prime Minister." "I wish to leave the Cabinet" were the only words he spoke. He turned and left. We have never spoken since." Lamont has since said "'Grass grows over the battlefield. We had to talk when the Black Wednesday papers were released under the Freedom of Information Act in 2005, we've had lunch since."

Speaking in May 2020, Lamont said of the Covid 19 crisis and the subsequent furlough scheme that the scheme had lulled "people into a false sense of security" and that many do not realise "their jobs have disappeared or are about to disappear, or that their firm is in serious trouble" continuing "Some sectors will bounce back, but not necessarily back to where they were before".

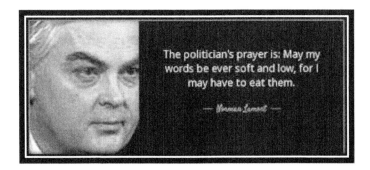

The politician's prayer is: May my words be ever soft and low, for I may have to eat them.

— Norman Lamont —

Lamont married Rosemary White in 1971, when he was a Rothschild financier and she was a researcher on the magazine House and Garden. They had two children Hilaire and Sophie. Lamont and Rosemary divorced in 1999.

Kenneth Clarke
Born 1940 - Conservative

Chancellor of the Exchequer:
27 May 1993 -
2 May 1997
(3 years, 11 months and 7 days)

Born
2 July 1940, West Bridgford,
Nottinghamshire

Title: Baron Clarke of Nottingham

Constituency Represented as MP:
Rushcliffe 1970 – 2019

Other Official Offices held:
Minister of State and Health 1982 - 1985
Paymaster General 1985 - 1987
Chancellor of the Duchy of Lancaster 1987 - 1988
Secretary of State for Health 1988 - 1990
Secretary of State for Education and Science 1990 - 1992
Home Secretary 1992 - 1993
Second Lord of the Treasury 1993 - 1997
Secretary of State for Justice 2010 - 2012
Lord High Chancellor of Great Britain 2010 - 2012
Father of the House of Commons 2017 - 2019

Prime Minister served with as Chancellor:
John Major

Education:
Gonville and Caius College, Cambridge.

Kenneth Harry Clarke, Baron Clarke of Nottingham, (born 2 July 1940), often known as **Ken Clarke**, is a Conservative politician who served in government with three different Prime Ministers, Margaret Thatcher, John Major and David Cameron. He served the constituency of Rushcliffe from 1970 until 2019. He served as Home Secretary from 1992 to 1993 and Chancellor of the Exchequer from 1993 to 1997. A member of the Conservative Party, he was Member of Parliament for Rushcliffe from 1970 to 2019 and was Father of the House of Commons between 2017 and 2019. The President of the Tory Reform Group since 1997, he identifies with economically and socially liberal views.

Clarke was born in West Bridgford, Nottinghamshire on 2 July 1940, and was christened with the same name as his father, Kenneth Clarke senior, a Nottinghamshire mining electrician who later had a small shop repairing watches. Clarke's mother was called Doris and taught him to read before he attended school. At five year old, Clarke attended Aldecar Infant School before moving on to Langley Mills Boys School at seven. At an early age Clarke was an avid reader of the Daily Mail, taking a keen interest in the Atlee government at the time and became absorbed in politics. At the age of nine, he kept a scrapbook on the 1950 General Election and announced in school that he intended to become an MP. On 1 June 1950, the Clarke family moved to Bulwell and Clarke attended Highbury Primary School, after passing the 11-plus examination he won a scholarship to Nottingham High School, where he spent almost eight years, before passing an examination in history to attend Gonville and Caius College, Cambridge where he became President of the Cambridge Union. Clarke left Cambridge in 1963 with a second class law degree and an overdraft of £3,000 (approx. worth £64,000 in 2020).

Upon leaving Cambridge, Clarke worked on the Midland Circuit as a barrister, living in Olton, a suburb in Solihull and commuting by steam train into work. Clarke also began looking for a Conservative candidature and was selected in the safe Labour seat of Mansfield in 1964. With only a few months preparation for the 15 October 1964 General Election, Clarke set about actively campaigning in Mansfield and received a respectable 10,021 votes against Labour's Bernard Taylor who received 29,055 and Reginald Strauther, Liberal 6,628. Clarke was readopted in

Mansfield for the General Election on 31 March 1966, in which he was again beaten by the new Labour candidate Don Concannon by 28,849 votes to 9,987 with Reginald Strauther (Liberal) coming third with 6,628 votes. After the election, Clarke became the new Conservative candidate for Rushcliffe in Nottingham, a seat that Labour had won at the General Election with a slim majority of 380. Clarke set about campaigning to be elected for Parliament, and in the lead up to the 1970 General Election he had support in Rushcliffe from Conservative leader Edward Heath, who Clarke described as "Being stiff and awkward and quite unable to communicate with any member of the public". At the 18 June 1970 General Election, Clarke, at the age of twenty-nine, was elected in Rushcliffe with a majority of 6,168 (30,996 votes to incumbent Labour candidate Antony Gardner's 24,798 and the Liberal's 4,180) and was then appointed Parliamentary Private Secretary to Geoffrey Howe. The Conservatives were in power from 1970 to 1974, but as they were heading for a defeat in the 1974 General Election, Clarke said in his biography that "the real problems turned on Ted Heath's own personality and style of government". At the 28 February 1974 General Election, Clarke was re-elected in Rushcliffe, increasing his majority significantly to 17,709 (29,828 votes to Labour's 12,119 and the Liberal's 11,719). In opposition, but unable to live on his salary as a government whip, Clarke went back to his practice as a barrister in Birmingham, working all hours to balance both jobs. In the second General Election of 1974, on 10 October, Clarke was re-elected in Rushcliffe with a majority of 14,943 (27,074 votes to Labour's 12,131 and the Liberal's 10,300). With the defeat of the Conservatives at the election, Clarke campaigned for Geoffrey Howe in the leadership campaign, but he wasn't surprised when Margaret Thatcher, who was seen as an outsider, won the contest. Clarke served on the opposition benches until the Conservative's won the 3 May 1979 General Election, with a 43 seat majority. He was re-elected in Rushcliffe with a large 22,484 majority, 34,196 votes to Labour's 11,712 and the Liberal's 9,060. He was then appointed by the new Prime Minister, Margaret Thatcher as Under Secretary of State for Transport. He was informed by phone, and when he explained to Thatcher that he knew nothing about the politics of transport, she simply said "My dear boy, you'll soon pick it up" and hung up. He served for three years at Transport, before being promoted to Minister of State for Health on 5 March 1982. At the 9 June 1983 General Election, Clarke was re-elected in Rushcliffe, with another large majority of 20,220 (Clarke 33,253, Liberal's 13,033 and Labour 7,290). After three years of attempting to bring reforms to the NHS, Clarke was given a full Cabinet position in September 1985 as Minister of State for Employment. Clarke said that although he had political differences with Thatcher (especially on Europe) they shared the same robust debating style and that she was the most impressive Prime Minister he had worked with. At the 11 June 1987 General Election, he was re-elected in Rushcliffe with a similar majority as he had in 1983 with 20,839 (Clarke 34,214 votes, SDP 13,375 and Labour 9,631). After a brief spell as Chancellor of the Duchy of Lancaster in 1987, he was appointed Secretary of State for Health on 25 July 1988, where he opposed Thatcher's idea of compulsory health insurance and produced a

White Paper 'Working for Patients' in January 1989. The White Paper proposed some of the most significant reforms in the history of the NHS and introduced a split between the bodies who provided care and those who purchased it, creating an internal market in the NHS. In the final weeks of Thatcher's government, Clarke was the first Minister to advise Thatcher to resign after her victory in the first round of the November 1990 leadership contest. At the 9 April 1992 General Election, he was re-elected in Rushcliffe with a 19,766 majority (34,448 votes to Labour's 14,682 and the Lib Dems 12,660). He had been appointed as Secretary of State for Education and Science in November 1990, working closely with the new Prime Minister, John Major, who then appointed him as Home Secretary on 10 April 1992. After the crisis of 'Black Wednesday', Major sacked Norman Lamont and appointed Clarke as the Chancellor of the Exchequer on 27 May 1993. As Chancellor, Clarke enjoyed great success, he reduced the basic rate of income tax from 25% to 23 % and there was a notable fall in unemployment. In his Budget in November 1994, which was introduced as a 'Budget for jobs' he committed the government to reduce spending by £24bn over 3 years. The Labour leader, Tony Blair, in response said it would be remembered as the "VAT on fuel Budget". In his 1996 Budget, Clarke announced it as "A Budget for lasting prosperity" and in the lead up to the 1997 General Election, he said it was a "Rolls Royce recovery-built to last", Blair responded by saying it was the "last gasp Budget of a government whose time is up". At the 1 May 1997 General Election, Labour under Tony Blair won a landslide victory, and Clarke received what would be his lowest majority in Rushcliffe of 5,055 (Clarke 27,558, Labour 22,503 Lib Dems 8,851 and Referendum Party 2,682). With John Major stepping down as Conservative leader, Clarke stood in the ensuing leadership election, topping the first and second round votes but losing to William Hague in the third and final ballot by 90 votes to 72. At the 7 June 2001 General Election, he was returned to Parliament in Rushcliffe with a 7,357 majority (25,869 votes to Labour's 18512, Lib Dems 7,395 and UKIP 1,434). After the Conservatives second successive election defeat, William Hague stepped down as party leader and Clarke again ran for the leadership. He eventually lost out to Iain Duncan Smith in a membership ballot on 11 September 2001, by 155,933 votes to 100,864. Clarke was again re-elected in Rushcliffe at the 5 May

MAJOR AND CLARKE - BUDGET TIME

2005 General Election, with a 12,974 majority (Clarke 27,899 votes to Labour's 14,925 and Lib Dems 9,813). He again stood in the Conservative leadership election when Michael Howard stepped down in 2005, but he was eliminated in the first ballot with 38 votes, and David Cameron went on to be

the new leader. The Conservative's had suffered their third consecutive General Election defeat and David Cameron promised a new 'modern compassionate' Conservative party with an end to 'Punch and Judy politics in Westminster'. At the 6 May 2010 General Election, the Conservatives received a large swing in votes but still fell 20 seats short of an outright majority. Clarke improved his majority in Rushcliffe to 15,811 (27,470 votes to Lib Dems 11,659, Labour 11,128 and UKIP 2,179) and was appointed by the new Prime Minister, David Cameron, as Lord Chancellor, Secretary of State for Justice. In June 2010, Clarke signalled an end to short prison sentences after warning it was "virtually impossible" to rehabilitate any inmate in less than 12 months. In his first major speech after taking office, he indicated a major shift in penal policy by saying prison was not effective in many cases, which could result in more offenders being handed community sentences. Following the 2012 Cabinet reshuffle, Clarke was moved from Justice Secretary to Minister without Portfolio. It was also announced that he would assume the role of roving Trade Envoy with responsibility for promoting British business and trade interests abroad. In the 2014 Cabinet reshuffle, after more than 20 years serving as a Minister, it was announced that Clarke had stepped down from government, to return to the backbenches. He was honoured with appointment as a Companion of Honour, upon the Prime Minister's recommendation, in July 2014. His total time as a government minister is the fifth-longest in the modern era after Winston Churchill, Arthur Balfour, Rab Butler, and The Duke of Devonshire. At the 7 May 2015 General Election, Clarke in what was to be his last election in Rushcliffe, was re-elected with a majority of 13,829 (28,354 votes to Labour's 14,525, UKIP's 5,943 and the Green's 3,559). Clarke who was opposed to Brexit, joined 20 other rebel Conservative MPs to vote against the Conservative government of Boris Johnson on 3 September 2019. Subsequently, all 21 were advised that they had lost the Conservative whip and were expelled as Conservative MPs, requiring them to sit as independents if they decided to run for re-election in a future election. Clarke retired from the House of Commons at the 2019 General Election, and on 4 September 2020 he was created Baron Clarke of Nottingham, *of West Bridgford in the County of Nottinghamshire*. He made his maiden speech in the House of Lords on 28 September 2020.

Interesting Kenneth Clarke facts:

Clarke is an avid fan of Jazz music, as well as cricket and football.

During his ministerial career, he became known for wearing brown suede Hush Puppies, but he said he never wore Hush Puppies - but instead owned handmade shoes from Crockett and Jones.

Clarke's memoir, *Kind of Blue*, was published in October 2016.

Gordon Brown
Born 1951 – Labour

Chancellor of the Exchequer:
2 May 1997 -
27 June 2007
(10 years, 1 month and 26 days)

Born
20 February 1951, Giffnock,
Renfrewshire

Title: None

Constituencies Represented as MP:
Dunfermline East 1983 - 2005
Kirkcaldy and Cowdenbeath 2005 - 2015

Other Official Offices held:
Shadow Chief Secretary to the Treasury 1987 - 1989
Shadow Secretary of State for Trade and Industry 1989 - 1992
Shadow President of the Board of Trade 1989 - 1992
Shadow Chancellor of the Exchequer 1992 - 1997
Second Lord of the Treasury 1997 - 2007
Prime Minister 2007 - 2010
First Lord of the Treasury 1997 - 2010
Minister for the Civil Service 2007 - 2010

Prime Minister served with as Chancellor:
Tony Blair

Education:
University of Edinburgh.

James Gordon Brown, (born 20 February 1951) is a Labour politician who was an MP in Scotland and served as the Chancellor of the Exchequer from 1997 to 2007 in Tony Blair's Cabinet. He was also Prime Minister and Leader of the Labour Party from 2007 to 2010.

Brown was the son of Elizabeth Brown and John Brown, who was a Labour Party supporter and Church of Scotland minister. Born in Giffnock, Renfrewshire, Scotland, the Brown's moved to Kilkady when Gordon was three. The family of five (elder brother John and younger brother Andrew) lived in a manse (clergy house). Brown was educated first at Kirkcaldy West Primary School and then Kirkcaldy High School. At the age of 16 he won a scholarship to the University of Edinburgh (he was the youngest student to

enter the university since World War II), where he immersed himself in student politics, eventually becoming chair of the university's Labour club. While competing in an end-of-term rugby union match, he received a kick to the head and suffered a retinal detachment leaving him blind in his left eye. He graduated from Edinburgh with a First-Class Honours MA degree in history and became the youngest ever Rector of Edinburgh University in 1972. He then stayed on to obtain his PhD in history. From 1976 to 1980 Brown was employed as a lecturer in politics at Glasgow College of Technology, he also worked as a tutor for the Open University.

At the May 1979 General Election, Brown stood as the Labour candidate in Edinburgh South, and although gaining 15,526 votes he lost out to the Conservative candidate Michael Ancram (17,986) to a majority of 2,460. Brown was then appointed in Scottish TV as a journalist and editor in the current affairs department from 1980 to 1983. In 1982 Brown completed a doctorate in history at Edinburgh, his dissertation was titled *'The Labour Party and Political Change in Scotland, 1918–1929'.*

In his second attempt to be elected to Parliament, Brown was successful as he stood in Dunfermline East as the Labour

candidate in the 9 June 1983 General Election, defeating the Liberals into second place with a majority of 11,301 (18,515 votes to 7,214 with the Conservative's 6,764 and SNP 2,573). In Parliament he soon became friends with another new MP, Tony Blair, and the two of them soon found themselves at the forefront of the campaign to modernise Labour's political philosophy, replacing the goal of state socialism with a more pragmatic, market-friendly strategy. After Labour lost the June 1987 General Election, where Brown increased his own majority to 19,589 (25,381 votes to Conservative's 5,792, Liberals 4,122 and SNP 3,901) he served in Labour's shadow cabinet, first as Shadow Chief Secretary to the Treasury from1987 to 1989, and then as Shadow Trade and Industry Secretary. At the 9 April 1992 General Election, Brown was again re-elected in Dunfermline East with a 17,444 majority (23,692 votes to Conservative's 6,248, SNP's 5,746 and the Liberal's 2,262), but it was Labour's fourth successive electoral defeat. Brown was named Shadow Chancellor of the Exchequer by John Smith, the then Labour Party leader. When Smith died in May 1994, Brown didn't contest the leadership, deciding to make way for Blair in what became known as the 'Granita pact' (Granita being a North London restaurant), where it was rumoured that the pair forged an agreement for Brown to not run for the Labour leadership, in exchange, Blair is claimed to have vowed to hand over the reins of power to Brown in his second term as Prime Minister. Brown did subsequently say in his book, *My Life, Our Times*: "The Granita discussion merely confirmed what he had already offered and I had already agreed. The only new point was Tony's overture that he wanted to show that, unlike the Tories

under Mrs Thatcher, Labour was not a one-person band but a partnership. As we walked out of the restaurant towards his home, he emphasised the word 'partnership' again and again, telling me it represented a new departure for British politics."

Brown did eventually succeed Blair as Prime Minister, but not until mid-way through Blair's third term in 2007. Blair won the Labour leadership election in 1994 and after the landslide General Election victory on 1 May 1997, Brown retained his Dunfermline East seat with a majority of 18,751 (24,441 votes to SNP's 5,690, Conservative's 3,656 and the Lib Dems 2,164) and he took the office of Chancellor of the Exchequer. As Chancellor he became a formidable force, his 'Spending Review' in 2000 outlined a major expansion of government spending, particularly on health and education, tackling child poverty and getting a better deal for pensioners. He gave the Bank of England its operational independence and blocked any desire to take Britain into the Euro while introducing the minimum wage. At the 7 June 2001 General Election, Brown won the Dunfermline East seat for the last time before it was abolished in constitutional changes with a 15,063 majority (19,487 votes to SNP's 4,424, Conservative's 2,838 and Lib Dems 2,281). Brown then imposed a windfall profits levy on the privatised utilities and later raised national insurance contributions to bring in extra money for the NHS, and in doing so, he showed that progressive governments were able to make tax rises that weren't unpopular. Talks of Britain adopting the Euro led to Brown bringing in the 'five economic tests', the criteria of which had to be met before entry into a monetary union was considered. After regular reviews Brown stated that the decision not to join had been right for Britain and for Europe. Brown had a strong interest in international economics, serving as the United Kingdom's governor of

the International Monetary Fund and as chair of the organisation's primary decision-making committee, he was instrumental in brokering a European agreement in 2005 that would double foreign aid to developing countries. At the May 2005 General Election, Labour won its third consecutive election victory, although the majority fell from 167 to 66 seats, Brown was returned in the Kirkcaldy and Cowdenbeath seat with a majority of 18,216 beating the SNP into second place (24,278 votes to SNP's 6,062, Lib Dems 5,450 and Conservative's 4,308). After the Iraq war and a poor showing for Labour at local elections, pressure was building on Tony Blair as Prime Minister and on 7 September 2006, Blair stated that he would step down within a year. Brown subsequently pledged his support for Blair, and Blair in turn later backed Brown to succeed him as Labour Party leader and Prime Minister. Brown faced no opposition in the campaign to succeed Blair as Labour Party leader, and on June 27, 2007, three days after he officially became Labour Party leader, Brown became Prime Minister. He pledged to make reform of the National Health Service a major priority, to retain the various public-sector reforms that had been implemented by Blair, and to "wage an unremitting battle against poverty." Brown as Prime Minister was severely tested when in early October 2008, the world's financial system was on the brink of systemic collapse. Despite the announcement of a multi-million pound bail-out, major British banks were about to go bust. Wall Street suffered the worst week in its history. Stocks on the Dow lost 18% of their value in five days, London and Frankfurt were down 21% on the week. Japan's Nikkei index crashed 24%, and the 10 October 2008 became known as 'Black Friday'. By the end of 'Black Friday', John Gieve, the then deputy

Governor of the Bank of England, said HBOS and RBS had 'run out of money'. After a long weekend of talks, Brown's Government and the Bank of England announced a bail-out package offering £500 billion of support to banks, averting a global economic meltdown. Brown later stated that if the bailout had failed he would have been forced to resign. Brown's premiership introduced neighbourhood policing in every area, a legally-enforceable right to early cancer screening and treatment, and the world's first ever Climate Change Act, which was implemented in autumn 2008.

In April 2009, British forces withdrew from Iraq and he worked with his Irish counterpart Brian Cowen to negotiate the devolution of policing and justice powers in Northern Ireland. With Labour doing poorly in the 2008 local elections, and in the 2009 European elections, Brown called for a General Election on 6 May 2010 (the first time the three main party leaders had taken part in a series of televised debates). A feature in the build up to the election was when Brown was caught on microphone describing a voter he had just spoken to in Rochdale as a "bigoted woman", Brown later visited the voter at her home to apologise saying he was a "penitent sinner". The election resulted in a large swing to the Conservatives, and Labour lost its 70-seat majority. However, none of the parties achieved the 326 seats needed for an overall majority, with the Conservatives winning 306 seats (20 short of a majority), Labour 258 and the Liberals 57. This was only the second General Election since the Second World War to return a

hung Parliament (the first being 1974). Brown announced on the evening of Monday 10 May that he would resign as Leader of the Labour Party, knowing that a deal between the Conservatives and the Liberal Democrats was imminent, and so on Tuesday 11 May, Brown announced his resignation as Prime Minister, marking the end of 13 years of Labour government. Brown had won his seat in Kirkcaldy and Cowdenbeath at the 2010

GORDON BROWN

election with a majority of 23,009 (29,559 votes to SNP's 6,550, Lib Dems 4,269 and Conservative's 4,258). When Brown stood down in Kirkcaldy the Labour majority was lost to the SNP (Scottish National Party) at the 2015 General Election with a 34.6% swing. Brown stayed on in Parliament, serving as a Labour backbencher, and on 14 July 2012, United Nations Secretary-General Ban ki-moon named Brown as UN Special Envoy for Education. On 1 December 2014, Brown announced that he would not be seeking re-election to Parliament, and he stood down at the General Election in May 2015. The Office of Gordon and Sarah Brown was set up in 2018 to establish their work and to facilitate their ongoing involvement in public life. This includes their charitable work which has raised over £3.5 million pounds to support good causes both locally and internationally.

Interesting Gordon Brown facts:

'The Deal' is a 2003 British television film that depicts the Blair-Brown deal, the actor David Morrissey won the award of Best Male Actor at the Royal Television Society Awards for playing the part of Gordon Brown.

Brown was the first Prime Minister from a Scottish constituency since the Conservative Sir Alec Douglas-Home in 1964.

Brown was Britain's longest serving modern Chancellor of the Exchequer after being appointed in May 1997, until he took over as Prime Minister in June 2007.

Brown was the sixth post-war Prime Minister, of a total of 13, to assume the role without having won a General Election.

Brown was the youngest ever Rector of Edinburgh University in 1972.

Brown was one of only five Prime Ministers that had not attended either Oxford or Cambridge University.

Brown is the author of several books including *'Beyond the Crash: Overcoming the First Crisis of Globalisation'*, *'My Life, Our Times'* and in 2021 *'Seven Ways to Change the World'*.

At the age of 49 Brown married Sarah Macaulay in a private ceremony at his home in North Queensferry, Fife, on 3 August 2000.

Brown's constituency name of Dunfermline East was something of a misnomer as it never actually included any part of the town of Dunfermline. Cowdenbeath was the largest town in the constituency.

Alistair Darling
Born 1953 – Labour

Chancellor of the Exchequer:
28 June 2007 -
11 May 2010
(2 years, 10 months and 14 days)

Born
28 November 1953, Hendon,
Middlesex

Title: Baron Darling of Roulanish

Constituencies Represented as MP:
Edinburgh Central 1987 - 2005
Edinburgh South West 2005 - 2015

Other Official Offices held:
Chief Secretary to the Treasury 1997 - 1998
Secretary of State for Social Security 1998 - 2001
Secretary of State for Work and Pensions 2001 - 2002
Secretary of State for Transport 2002 - 2006
Secretary of State for Scotland 2003 - 2006
Secretary of State for Trade and Industry 2006 - 2007
Second Lord of the Treasury 2007 - 2010

Prime Minister served with as Chancellor:
Gordon Brown

Education:
University of Aberdeen.

Alistair Maclean Darling, Baron Darling of Roulanish, (born 28 November 1953) is a Labour Party politician who served as MP in Edinburgh from 1987 to 2005. He was Chancellor of the Exchequer under Gordon Brown from 2007 to 2010. He was one of only three people to have served in the Cabinet continuously from Labour's landslide victory at the 1997 General Election, until their defeat at the 2010 General Election, the other two were Gordon Brown and Jack Straw.

Darling was born in London, the son of a civil engineer, Thomas, and his wife, Anna MacLean. He is the great-nephew of Sir William Darling, a Conservative/Unionist Member of Parliament for Edinburgh South from 1945– 1957, who had served as Lord Provost of Edinburgh during the Second World War. Darling was educated at Chinthurst School, in Tadworth, Surrey, then in Kirkcaldy and at the private Loretto School in Musselburgh. He attended the University of Aberdeen, from where he graduated in 1976 as a Bachelor of Laws (LLB). He became the President of Aberdeen University Students' Representative Council.

DARLING AGED **5**

Darling's first involvement in politics was as a supporter of the International Marxist Group, before he joined the Labour Party in 1977, at the age of 23. In 1978, Darling became a solicitor and in 1984, he was admitted to the Faculty of Advocates (a body of independent lawyers who practise law as Advocates before the Courts of Scotland). He entered politics in 1982 when he was elected Councillor to the Lothian Regional Council, and served as Chairman of the Transport Committee from 1986 to 1987. At the 11 June 1987 General Election, at the age of thirty-four, Darling stood as the Labour candidate in Edinburgh Central, winning in a closely fought contest with a majority of 2,262 (16,502 votes to the Conservative's 14,240, Liberals 7,333 and the SNP 2,559). Within a year, he had joined the Opposition Home Affairs Team, and in 1992 he was appointed Opposition Spokesman on the City and Financial Services on Neil Kinnock's front bench. At the 9 April 1992 General Election, Darling was re-elected in Edinburgh Central with a very similar majority to the previous election of 2,126 (15,189 votes to Conservative's 13,063, SNP 5,539 and Lib Dems 4,500).

A YOUNG DARLING

After the election Darling became a spokesman on Treasury Affairs and in 1996 he was promoted to Tony Blair's Shadow Cabinet as the Shadow Chief Secretary to the Treasury. Of his entry into Parliament and the ten years in opposition Darling said "The first ten years in Parliament was a huge training ground. How you perform there, how you behave, how you react to your own backbenchers who are also in opposition matters an awful lot." At the 1 May 1997 General Election, Labour swept to a landslide victory and Darling increased his majority in Edinburgh Central significantly to 11,070 (20,125 votes to Conservative's 9,055, SNP 6,750 and Lib Dems 5,605) returning to Parliament as a Cabinet minister as Chief Secretary to the Treasury. In 1998, Darling was promoted to the post of Secretary of State for Social Security, where he worked until the 2001 General Election. At the 7 June 2001 General Election, Darling was re-elected in Edinburgh South with an 8,142 (14,495 votes to Lib Dems 6,353, Conservative's 5,643, and SNP 4,832) and with the Department of Social Security being abolished it was replaced with the new Department for Work and Pensions, which also took employment away from the education portfolio. Darling fronted the new department until 2002 when he was moved to the Department for Transport. As Secretary of State for Transport

Darling oversaw the creation of Network Rail, the successor to Railtrack, which had collapsed in controversial circumstances. He also procured the passage of the legislation, the Railways and Transport Safety Act 2003, which abolished the Rail Regulator and replaced it with the Office of Rail Regulation. Darling was also responsible for the Railways Act 2005 which abolished the Strategic Rail Authority, a creation of the Labour government under the Transport Act 2000. In 2003, when the Scotland Office was folded into the Department for Constitutional Affairs, he was appointed Scottish Secretary in combination with his Transport portfolio. At the 5 May 2005, General Election changes to constituency boundaries meant that the Edinburgh Central seat was abolished and therefore Darling stood in the newly created seat of Edinburgh South West, in which he won with a majority of 7,242 (17,476 votes to Conservative's 10,234, Lib Dems, 9,252 and SNP 4,654). On 5 May 2006, he was appointed as Secretary of State, until 28 June 2007, when Tony Blair gave way to Gordon Brown as Prime Minister and Darling took Brown's place as Chancellor of the Exchequer. In September 2007, there was a run on the British bank, Northern Rock, and although the Bank of England and the Financial Services Authority have jurisdiction in such cases, ultimate authority for deciding on financial support for a bank in exceptional circumstances rested with Darling as the Chancellor. The 2007 subprime mortgage financial crisis had caused a liquidity crisis in the UK banking industry, and Northern Rock was unable to borrow as required by its business model. On 14 September 2007, Darling authorised the Bank of England to lend Northern Rock funds to cover its liabilities and provided an unqualified taxpayers' guarantee on the deposits of savers in Northern Rock to try to stop the run. Northern Rock borrowed up to £20bn from the Bank of England, while Darling was criticised for becoming sucked into a position where so much public money was tied up in a private company. Darling said later in a 2018 interview, that the country was hours away from a breakdown of law and order if the bank had not been bailed out. Darling gave his first Budget speech on 12 March 2008, which was labelled *'Stability and opportunity: building a strong, sustainable future'* and he increased taxes on alcohol, cigarettes and high-polluting cars, while raising Child Benefit to £20 a week from April 2009. Winter fuel payments for pensioners would also be increased and all long-term recipients of Incapacity Benefit would have to attend work capacity programmes from April 2010. In an interview in August 2008 Darling said "The economic times we are facing

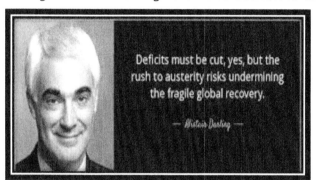

are arguably the worst they've been in 60 years. And I think it's going to be more profound and long-lasting than people thought." His blunt warning led to confusion within the Labour Party.

However, Darling insisted that it was his duty to be "straight" with people. In October 2008, there was a major intensification of the financial crisis, triggered by the previous month's collapse of the United States *Lehman Brothers* investment bank. Darling and Prime Minister Gordon Brown responded with a rescue package for British banks, and an international campaign to persuade other governments to adopt similar measures in support of their banks. During the following months, the British example was followed by other European countries and similar measures were adopted by the United States. Those actions were followed by stabilisation of the financial system, but many British banks continued to suffer serious financial difficulties. A programme of additional support for the banks was adopted, and by April 2009, five of the nine largest British banks had been taken partly or wholly into public ownership, in addition to the

2007 nationalisation of Northern Rock. Darling delivered his second Budget speech on 22 April 2009 named *'Building Britain's Future'* he said" the Budget will continue to help people through the global recession, and prepare Britain for the opportunities of the future". To stimulate the motor industry, he introduced a £,2,000 scrappage allowance for a car more than 10 years old, if

it was traded in for a new car and if it had been in the car buyer's ownership for the previous 12 months. £1,000 of this was to be provided by the government, and £1,000 by a motor manufacturer. Darling stated that the income tax rate on those earning more than £150,000 was to increase from 45% to 50% from the April of the following year, and personal tax allowance of those earning over £100,000 was to be withdrawn from the following April. Pension tax relief was restricted for those on incomes over £150,000 from April 2011, and was gradually tapered to the same 20% rate received by most people. Darling increased Fuel duty by 2% from the September and 1% above indexation every April for the following four years. He also increased tobacco duty by 2% from 6pm on Budget day and alcohol duties rose 2% from midnight. With a General Election due in 2010 Darling announced in his third (which would be his final Budget) on 24 March 2010, that the deficit was not as big as predicted, and there would be a crackdown on tax evasion. Planned petrol rises would be staggered, first time buyers stamp duty would be cut, a green investment fund would be founded and that 20,000 university places would be pledged. Darling also increased the tax on strong cider, with Conservative leader David Cameron accusing Darling of stealing Tory policies on stamp duty and the extra tax on strong cider, while dismissing the Budget as "a political dodge not an economic plan". At the 2010 General Election, although Darling was re-elected in Edinburgh South West with an increased majority of 8,447 (17,473 to Conservative's 11,026, Lib Dems 8,194 and SNP 5,530) Labour lost 91 seats resulting in a hung Parliament and the formation of a Conservative/Liberal Democrats coalition government. Darling had stood in what was

Alistair Darling

to be his last General Election and his seat in Edinburgh at the General Election of 2015 was won by the SNP with a 23.2% swing (majority 8,135). Following the 2010 General Election defeat Darling announced that he intended to leave frontbench politics and served as

the opposition's Shadow Chancellor until October 2010, when he retired from the Shadow Cabinet saying he would concentrate on his constituent's in Edinburgh South West.

In 2012, Darling launched the official *Better Together* cross-party campaign to keep Scotland within the United Kingdom, ahead of a referendum on independence scheduled for 18 September 2014 which the "No" side won with 55.3% of the vote. Darling was nominated for a peerage in the 2015 Dissolution Honours, becoming Baron Darling of Roulanish and taking his seat in the House of Lords on 10 December 2015. On 28 July 2020, Lord Darling retired from the House of Lords, citing distance and the COVID-19 pandemic.

Our goal is to make finance the servant, not the master, of the real economy.

Interesting Alistair Darling facts:

Darling's grandfather had been a Liberal candidate and his great uncle, Sir William Young Darling, was Lord Provost of Edinburgh during the war, before serving as Tory MP for Edinburgh South for 12 years.

Three of Darling's four junior ministers at the Treasury were female (Angela Eagle, Jane Kennedy and Kitty Ussher) which led the press to dub his team, "Darling's Darlings"

Darling had sported a beard throughout his political career, but shaved it off in August 1997. He insisted it was his own choice and nothing to do with any pressure from party image-makers – despite stories that Labour leaders wanted high-profile figures to get rid of 'suspicious' facial hair.

Darling married former journalist Margaret McQueen Vaughan in 1986 and the couple have a son, Calum, born in 1988 and a daughter, Anna, born in 1990.

Darling published a political memoir in 2011, 'Back From the Brink' which covered the financial crisis of 2007 – 2008.

In August 2014, Darling took part in Salmond & Darling: The Debate and Scotland Decides: Salmond versus Darling, were televised debates with First Minister Alex Salmond on the pros and cons of Scottish Independence. Opinion polling ahead of the broadcast suggested that the general public expected Salmond to win, but a snap poll conducted by ICM stated Darling won the debate by 56% to 44%.

Darling was born in London but always proudly declares himself as Scottish, and only ever represented the Edinburgh constituencies throughout his political career.

George Osborne
Born 1971 - Conservative

Chancellor of the Exchequer:
11 May 2010 -
13 July 2016
(6 years, 2 months and 3 days)

Born
23 May 1971, London
Title: 13 May 2010: appointed to
the Privy Council of the United Kingdom,
giving him the honorific style of "The
Right Honourable" for life.

Constituency Represented as MP:
Tatton 2001 - 2017

Other Official Offices held:
Shadow Chief Secretary to the Treasury 2004 - 2005
Shadow Chancellor of the Exchequer 2005 - 2010
Second Lord of the Treasury 2010 - 2016
First Secretary of State 2015 - 2016

Prime Minister served with as Chancellor:
David Cameron
Education:
Magdalen College, Oxford.

George Gideon Oliver Osborne, (born **Gideon Oliver Osborne**; 23 May 1971) is a Conservative politician who served as MP in Tatton from 2001 to 2017. He served as David Cameron's only Chancellor of the Exchequer from 2010 to 2016, and as First Secretary of State from 2015 to 2016.

Osborne was born on 23 May 1971, in Paddington, London, the son of Sir Peter Osborne, 17th baronet of Ballintaylor, a cofounder of the upmarket fabric and wallpaper designer Osborne & Little. His mother is Felicity Alexandra Loxton-Peacock, the daughter of Hungarian-born Jewish artist Clarisse Loxton-Peacock (née Fehér). At the age of 13, in what he described as a rare act of rebellion, he dropped his given name, Gideon, in favour of George (and added it officially to his name by deed poll). Osborne was educated at two independent schools: Norland Place School, Colet Court and St Paul's School. In 1990, he was awarded a demyship (a form of scholarship) at Magdalen College, Oxford, where in 1993 he received a 2:1 bachelor's degree in Modern History.

Upon leaving Oxford, Osborne intended to pursue a career in journalism and was shortlisted for, but failed to gain a place on *The Times*' trainee scheme. He then applied to *The Economist*, but was unable to gain a position, before he finally gained some freelance work on the 'Peterborough' diary column in *The Daily Telegraph. In 1994, Osborne* joined the Conservative Research Department becoming the head of its political section and between 1995 and 1997 he worked as a special advisor to Douglas Hogg the Minister of Agriculture, Fisheries and Food. In the run-up to the 1997 General Election, Osborne worked on John Major's campaign team while still considering a career in journalism. Between 1997 and 2001 he worked for William Hague, Major's successor as Conservative Party leader, as a speechwriter and political secretary. He helped to prepare Hague for the weekly session of Prime Minister's Questions and under the subsequent leaderships of Michael Howard and David Cameron, he remained on the Prime Minister's Questions team. Osborne decided to stand for Parliament, and at the 7 June 2001 General Election, he stood as the Conservative candidate in Tatton (Cheshire) winning the seat with an 8,611 vote majority (19,860 votes to Labour's 11,249 and the Lib Dems 7,685) to

become (at that time) the youngest Conservative MP in the House of Commons, having just turned thirty. Osborne soon impressed in Parliament and in September 2004 he was appointed to the shadow cabinet, as Shadow Chief Secretary to the Treasury by the Conservative leader Michael Howard. At the 5 May 2005 General Election, Osborne increased his majority in Tatton to 11,741 (21,447 votes to Labour's 9,716 and the Lib Dems 9,016) and was promoted to Shadow Chancellor of the Exchequer by Howard. When Howard announced he was stepping down after the election, there was talk of Osborne standing as leader, but he decided instead to serve as David Cameron's campaign manager, and he kept the Shadow Chancellor's position when Cameron was elected leader in December 2005. With the Conservative's having lost three consecutive General Elections, Cameron and Osborne set about modernising the Conservative party. Together they wanted to rid the party of its right-wing image and its reputation for not caring about public services, or people with average and below-average incomes. They planned to modify the party's long-standing ambitions to cut taxes. Osborne promised to stick to the Labour government's spending plans on health and education and to delay tax cuts until they could be afforded. In 2007 he did commit the party to reducing inheritance taxes, but this was to be offset by a levy on wealthy foreigners living in Britain. Osborne used the 2008 financial crisis as a way of attacking Labour's financial policies, stating that Labour had mismanaged the economy, with his attacks helping to give the Conservative's a lead in the polls running up to the 2010 General Election. At the 6 May 2010 General Election, Osborne was re-elected again in Tatton with an improved majority of 14,487 (24,687 votes to the Lib Dems 10,200 and Labour's 7,803) and when Cameron became Prime Minister at the head of a Conservative–Liberal Democratic coalition government on May 11, he appointed

OSBORNE AND DAVID CAMERON

Osborne Chancellor of the Exchequer, making him at 38 years and 11 months old, the youngest person to hold office of Chancellor for more than 120 years. Two of Osborne's first acts was the setting up the Office for Budget Responsibility and commissioning a government-wide spending review, which concluded in autumn 2010 setting limits on departmental spending until 2014 - 2015. In his first Budget on 22 June 2010, officially known as *'Responsibility, freedom, fairness: a five-year plan to re-build the economy'* Osborne dubbed it an "emergency Budget" and that its purpose was to reduce the national debt accumulated under the Labour government. After the financial crisis of 2008 – 2009 Osborne had set himself a target of reducing the UK's deficit, and in October 2010, he introduced a five-year austerity plan that would reduce spending, and by 2013, the government announced it had reduced public spending by £14.3 billion. The plan included cuts to welfare entitlements, public-sector layoffs of up to 500,000 employees and a stepped-up introduction of the raising of the age of pension entitlement from age 65 to 66. In his second Budget on 23 March 2011, officially called *'A strong and stable economy, growth and fairness'* Osborne forecast that borrowing had fallen to £146 billion in 2011, £122 billion in 2012 and £29 billion by 2015–16. The national debt was estimated at 60% of current national income, rising to 71% in 2012 before starting to fall back to 69% by 2015. Opposition Leader, Ed Miliband responded by saying that the Government was going "too far, too fast" to reduce the deficit. In his third coalition Budget on 21 March 2012, Osborne announced that the personal

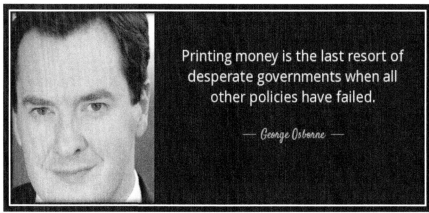

Printing money is the last resort of desperate governments when all other policies have failed.

— George Osborne —

tax allowance would rise from £8,105 to £9,205 making up to 24 million people better off, he cut the top rate of income tax from 50% to 45% and from April 2013 people over 65 years of age would not get an enhanced personal income tax allowance, known as the age allowance. HM Revenue and Customs estimated that 4.4 million pensioners would become worse-off in real terms by up to £83 in 2013–14, Miliband in reply said; the coalition government's Budget "failed the fairness test" and that cutting the top rate of income tax to 45% from 50% showed it was a "millionaire's Budget which squeezes the middle" and that the Budget was an "omnishambles Budget". In his fourth Budget on 20 March 2013, Osborne again raised the personal allowance that each UK employee was entitled to earn before income tax was levied to £10,000 from 2014, and he announced a reduction of the rate of corporation tax, a freeze of the rate of fuel duty, and the cancellation of the duty escalator on beer, while predicting that the UK would not enter recession again in 2013. In his Budget on 19 March 2014, Osborne announced the introduction of a new and highly secure £1 coin. The proposed new coin was set to be bi-metallic with 12 sides, and adopt new Royal Mint technology to protect against counterfeiting (the government introduced the new coin on 28 March 2017). Osborne stated in his Budget "I can report today that the economy is continuing to recover – and recovering faster than forecast. We set out our plan and together with the British people, we held our nerve. We're putting Britain right, but the job is far from done. Our country still borrows too much". He finished his Budget statement by saying "With the help of the British people we're turning our country around. We're building a resilient economy. This is a Budget for the makers, the doers, and the savers". The Budget on 18 March 2016, was the sixth and final budget of the Conservative–Liberal Democrat coalition government which would lead into the General Election on 7 May 2015. Osborne said in his Budget statement that "Compared to five years ago: Inequality is lower. Child poverty is down. Youth unemployment is down. Pensioner poverty is at its lowest level ever. The gender pay gap has never been smaller. Payday loans are capped. And zero hours contracts regulated". He finished by saying "We have provided clear decisive economic leadership – and from the depths Britain is returning. The share of national income taken up by debt – falling. The deficit down. Growth up. Jobs up. Living standards on the rise. Britain on the rise. This is the Budget for Britain. The Comeback Country". At the General Election in May 2015, the Conservatives defied the polls and were elected with their first outright win for 23 years with a small overall majority of 12 seats. Osborne was re-elected in Tatton in what would be his last election with his highest majority to date of 18,241 (26,552 votes to Labour's 8,311, UKIP's 4,871 and the Lib Dems 3,850) and he was reappointed Chancellor of the Exchequer and was also appointed First Secretary of State. In his second Budget of 2015

on July 8, which was the first fully Conservative budget since that presented by Kenneth Clarke in 1996. Osborne said "The Budget today puts security first. The economic security of a country that lives within its means. The financial security of lower taxes and a new National Living Wage (£9 an hour by 2020 for 25+ year olds). The national security of a Britain that defends itself and its values. A plan for working people…
One purpose. One policy. One nation".
The Budget increased funding for the National Health Service, with efforts to increase productivity, more apprenticeships and cuts to the welfare budget. In response, the Conservative led Local Government Association, on behalf of 375 Conservative,

OSBORNE AND THERESA MAY

Labour and Liberal Democrat-run councils, said that further austerity measures were "not an option" as they would "devastate" local services. They said that local councils had already had to make cuts of 40% since 2010, and couldn't make any more cuts without serious consequences for the most vulnerable. In his March 16 2016 Budget, which would turn out to be his last one, Osborne introduced a sugar tax on soft drinks from 2018, raising around half a billion pounds which was to be used to fund after-school activities such as sport and art. He also raised the tax-free allowance for income tax to £11,500, as well as lifting the 40% income tax threshold to £45,000. Following the UK's vote to leave the European Union in June 2016, Osborne pledged to further lower corporation tax to "encourage businesses to continue investing in the UK". Osborne had already cut the corporation tax rate from 28% to 20%, with plans to lower it to 17% by 2020. When David Cameron resigned as Prime Minister on 13 July 2016, Osborne also resigned saying "it had been a privilege to hold the job, others will judge - I hope I've left the economy in a better state than I found it." Osborne returned to the backbenches and in September 2016, he launched the Northern  Powerhouse Partnership, a body bringing together business leaders and politicians to promote regional devolution. Osborne announced he would be standing down as the MP for Tatton in April 2017, a day after the 2017 General Election was declared. He did not rule out returning to the Commons at some point. "It's still too early to be writing my memoirs", he wrote in a letter to his constituency party, and did not "want to spend the rest of my life just being an ex-Chancellor. I want new challenges". Osborne was announced on 17 March 2017 as the next future editor of the *London Evening Standard*, a position which commenced on 2 May and which he held until March 2021, becoming an investment banker at Robey Warshaw in April 2021.

Interesting George Osborne facts:

Osborne was portrayed by Sebastian Armesto in the 2015 Channel 4 television film *Coalition*.

Osborne married Frances Howell, author and elder daughter of Lord Howell of Guildford, a Conservative politician, on 4 April 1998. The couple have two children (Luke and Liberty) both born in Westminster. George and Frances divorced in September 2019.

In April 2021, Osborne announced his engagement to his former adviser Thea Rogers.

Osborne was awarded the 2015 *British GQ* Politician of the Year award.

Philip Hammond
Born 1955 - Conservative

Chancellor of the Exchequer:
13 July 2016 –
24 July 2019
(3 years and 12 days)

Born
4 December 1955, Epping, Essex

Title: Baron Hammond of Runnymede

Constituency Represented as MP:
Runnymede and Weybridge 1997 - 2019

Other Official Offices held:
Shadow Chief Secretary to the Treasury 2005 and 2007 - 2010
Shadow Secretary for Work and Pensions 2005 - 2007
Secretary of State for Transport 2010 - 2011
Secretary of State for Defence 2011 - 2014
Secretary of State for Foreign and Commonwealth Affairs 2014 - 2016
Second Lord of the Treasury 2016 - 2019

Prime Minister served with as Chancellor:
Theresa May

Education:
University College, Oxford.

Philip Hammond, Baron Hammond of Runnymede, (born 4 December 1955) a Conservative politician who was MP for Runnymede and Weybridge from 1997 to 2019. He served as Chancellor of the Exchequer in Theresa May's Cabinet from 2016 to 2019, Foreign Secretary from 2014 to 2016 and Defence Secretary from 2011 to 2014.

Hammond was born in Epping, Essex, the son of a civil engineer. He was educated at Shenfield School (now Shenfield High School) in Brentwood, Essex before he went on to read Philosophy, Politics and Economics at University College, Oxford, where he was an Open Scholar, graduating in 1977 with a first-class honours degree.

Hammond joined the medical equipment manufacturers Speywood Laboratories Ltd in 1977, becoming a director of Speywood Medical Limited in 1981. He left in 1983, and from 1984, served as a director in Castlemead Ltd. On the political front, Hammond was the Chairman of the Lewisham East Conservative Association for seven years from 1989, and was also a political assistant to Colin Moynihan, then Minister of Sport. His first attempt to enter Parliament came when he stood as the Conservative candidate in a By-election on 9 June 1994, in the safe Labour seat of Newham North East, losing out to Stephen Timms the Labour candidate who had a majority of 11,838 (14,688 votes to Hammond's 2,850). From 1993 to 1995, he was a partner in CMA Consultants and, from 1994, a director in Castlemead Homes. Hammond pursued a varied business career and over a 20-year period his professional interests ranged from property to energy and health care. He also gained overseas work experience, undertaking assignments for the World Bank in Latin America, and for two years from 1995 until his election to Parliament in 1997, he served as a consultant to Malawi's government. At the 1 May 1997 General Election, Hammond stood in the newly formed constituency of Runnymede and Weymouth where he was elected with a 9,875 majority (25,051 votes to Labour's 15,176, Lib Dems 8,397 and Referendum Party 2,150). In Parliament, he served on the Environment, Transport and the Regions Select committee from 1997, until he was promoted by the Conservative leader, William Hague, as front

A YOUNG PHILIP HAMMOND

bench spokesman for Health. When Iain Duncan Smith became Conservative leader in September 2001, he appointed Hammond as the Trade and Industry spokesman, before he was transferred to Shadow Minister for Local Government and Regions in 2002. At the 5 May 2005 General Election, Hammond was re-elected in Runnymede and Weybridge with an increased majority of 12,349 (22,366 votes to Labour's 10,017 and Lib Dems 7,771) and was promoted to the Shadow Cabinet by the then

Conservative leader Michael Howard, as the Shadow Chief Secretary to the Treasury. Following the election of David Cameron as Conservative leader later in 2005, Hammond became the Shadow Secretary of State for Work and Pensions, but he was moved back to the role of Shadow Chief Secretary to the Treasury in Cameron's reshuffle following Gordon Brown's accession to the premiership. At the 6 May 2010 General Election, Hammond again increased his majority in Runnymede and Weybridge to 16,509 (26,915 votes to the Lib Dems 10,406, Labour's 6,446 and UKIP's 3,146) and was appointed as Secretary of State for Transport in the Conservative/Liberal coalition government on 10 May 2010. The following year after Liam Fox resigned as Defence Secretary, Cameron turned to Hammond to fill the position and he was appointed as Secretary of State for Defence on 14

October 2011. As Defence Secretary, Hammond oversaw much of the British troop withdrawal from Afghanistan. He also established himself as a leading figure on the right of the party, advocating significant cuts to welfare spending, opposing same-sex marriage, and declaring that he would rather see the United Kingdom leave the EU if reforms were not initiated. When William Hague resigned as Foreign Secretary in July 2014, Cameron again

turned to Hammond to fill the vacant position. At the 7 May 2015 General Election, Hammond more than doubled his majority from when he was first elected in Runnymede and Weybridge in 1997 to 22,134 (29,901 votes to Labour's 7,767, UKIP's 6,951 and Lib Dems 3,362). After Britain voted to leave the European Union (Brexit) in June 2016, Cameron resigned as Prime Minister and was replaced by Theresa May on 13

HAMMOND AT A PARTY CONFERENCE

July 2016. May's first Cabinet appointment's made for a sweeping change, with nine of Cameron's ministers either being sacked or resigning from their posts. Hammond filled one of the vacated posts, that of George Osborne as Chancellor of the Exchequer. As Chancellor, although he was in support of Brexit, Hammond warned that there would be serious economic damage if an exit agreement wasn't reached. In his first Budget on 8 March 2017, (the last Budget to be held in Spring until 2020), Hammond forecast borrowing would total £58.3bn in 2017-18, £40.6bn in 2018-19, £21.4bn in 2019-20 and £20.6bn in 2020-21. During his hour-long speech he highlighted diesel cars, income tax, education and the seemingly inevitable, alcohol. He also announced that stamp duty would be removed for first-time buyers of properties under £300,000. Two years after the previous election, Theresa May called a snap General Election for

8 June 2017, in an attempt to secure a larger majority, to "strengthen [her] hand" in the forthcoming Brexit negotiations. Hammond was re-elected in Runnymede and Weybridge with a majority of 18,050 (31,436 votes to Labour's 13,386, Lib Dems 3,765 and UKIP's 1,675) but the Conservatives made a net loss of 13 seats from their original 17 seat majority. Hammond presented an Autumn Budget on 22 November 2017, and in terms of Brexit, he announced he was putting aside £3 billion, with more available if needed. He said: "We have already

THERESA MAY AND HAMMOND

invested almost £700m in Brexit preparations and today I am setting aside over the next two years a further £3bn and I stand ready to allocate further funds." Brexit Britain will "look forward, not backwards, to meet challenges head on and to seize opportunities for Britain", he added.

"No one should doubt our resolve!" As time moved on and Britain and Europe failed to agree a deal on Brexit, Hammond delivered another Budget speech on Monday, 29 October 2018, (the first time since 1962 that the Budget had been delivered on a day other than a Wednesday), in which he said "I can report to the British people, that their hard work is paying off and the era of austerity is finally coming to an end." He continued "Our economy continues to confound those who talk it down and we continue to focus resolutely on the challenges and opportunities that lie ahead as we build a new relationship with our European neighbours, a new future outside the European Union." On 23 July 2019, Hammond wrote to the Prime Minister, Theresa May, submitting his resignation shortly before her own resignation saying "I believe that your successor must be free to choose a Chancellor who is fully aligned with his policy position". On 3 September 2019, Hammond led 20 other rebel Conservative MPs

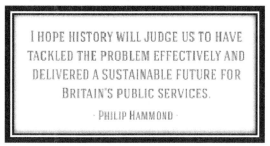

I HOPE HISTORY WILL JUDGE US TO HAVE TACKLED THE PROBLEM EFFECTIVELY AND DELIVERED A SUSTAINABLE FUTURE FOR BRITAIN'S PUBLIC SERVICES.

- PHILIP HAMMOND -

to vote against the Conservative government of Boris Johnson. The rebel MPs voted with the Opposition against a Conservative motion, which subsequently failed. Effectively, they helped block Johnson's "no-deal" Brexit plan from proceeding on 31 October. Consequently, all 21 were advised that they had lost the Conservative whip, expelling them as Conservative MPs and requiring them to sit as independents. Hammond did not contest the 2019 General Election, as he would be a "direct challenge" to the Conservative

party. If he or the other rebel MPs had decided to run for re-election, the party would have blocked their selection as Conservative candidates. Hammond later suggested that "the Conservative Party has been taken over by unelected advisors, entryists and usurpers who are trying to turn it from a broad church into an extreme right-wing faction", and that "it is not the party I joined." Despite his fall out with the new party leadership over Brexit, Hammond was offered a life-peerage in February 2020. Lord Hammond now once again sits as a Conservative, although this time in the Upper Chamber. In July 2020, it was revealed that Hammond had taken up a paid role as an advisor to Saudi Arabia's Minister of Finance.

Interesting Philip Hammond facts:

Hammond was educated at Shenfield School in Essex where he shared a classroom with Richard Madeley, later of Richard and Judy fame.

As a Philosophy Politics and Economics (PPE) student at Oxford University, Hammond met then Geography student Theresa May. They were acquaintances but never close.

Hammond married Susan Carolyn Williams-Walker on 29 June 1991. The couple have two daughters and a son.

Hammond sometimes had the nickname 'Spreadsheet Phil'

Hammond is a financial backer behind the Sugar Hut, a kitschy nightclub in his home town of Brentwood that shot to fame through ITV reality show The Only Way Is Essex.

Hammond was said to be the second richest Conservative member in the Cabinet. He has a net worth of £8.2m and is thought to have made his millions from stakes within health care and nursing homes development along with consultancy work.

When he was Defence Secretary, Hammond announced in 2011, that women would be allowed on Submarines. Women began their service on Submarines in 2013.

According to some reports, in his youth, Hammond used to set up and run discos.

Hammond said of the relationship between Prime Minister and Chancellor "I think all Prime Ministers want to spend more money than most Chancellors think is prudent."

Sajid Javid
Born 1969 - Conservative

Chancellor of the Exchequer:
24 July 2019 -
13 February 2020
 (6 months and 21 days)

Born
5 December 1969, Rochdale

Title: None

Constituency Represented as MP:
Bromsgrove 2010 - present

Other Official Offices held:
Economic Secretary to the Treasury 2012 - 2013
Financial Secretary to the Treasury 2013 - 2014
Secretary of State for Culture, Media and Sport 2014 - 2015
Secretary of State for Business, Innovation and Skills 2015 - 2016
Secretary of State for Housing, Communities and Local Government 2016 - 2018
Home Secretary 2018 - 2019
Second Lord of the Treasury 2019 - 2020

Prime Minister served with as Chancellor:
Boris Johnson

Education:
University of Exeter.

Sajid Javid, (born 5 December 1969) is a Conservative politician who is current MP for Bromsgrove. He served as Home Secretary from 2018 to 2019 and was Boris Johnson's Chancellor of the Exchequer from 2019 to 2020. He has been Member of Parliament for Bromsgrove since 2010. He was the first British Asian to hold one of the Great Offices of State in the UK.

Javid was born in Rochdale, one of five sons, but was mainly raised in Bristol. Javid's family were from the tiny village

of Rajana near Toba Tek Singh, Punjab, from where at 17 his father migrated to the UK in the 1960s looking for work, eventually becoming a bus driver. After attending Downend School, a state comprehensive near Bristol, at the age of 14 he went to see his father's bank manager and arranged to borrow £500 to invest in shares, and became a regular reader of the Financial Times. His goal was to work in the City, so he passed maths O-Level and rejected his school's suggestion that he become a TV repair man. Javid went on to attend Filton Technical College from 1986 to 1988, before enrolling in Exeter University, where he read Economics and Politics from 1988 to 1991.

Upon the conclusion of his studies, Javid embarked on a career in investment banking in business and finance. In 1992, aged 25, he moved to New York City in America and became the youngest Vice President at Chase Manhattan Bank. He later moved to Deutsche Bank where he became a senior manager by the age of 40, helping to build its business in emerging market countries. Javid left Deutsche Bank as a senior Managing Director in the summer of 2009 to concentrate on a political career, in which he "wanted to give something back through politics". On 6 February 2010, Javid entered a selection contest held by the Bromsgrove Conservative Association after the resignation of sitting MP Julie Kirkbride, he received over 70% of the votes cast by its members, and was announced as the official Conservative & Unionist Party Parliamentary Candidate for the 2010 General Election. At the 6 May 2010 General Election, Javid was elected to Parliament with a majority of 11,308 (22,558 votes to Labour's 11,250, Lib Dems 10,124). Once in Parliament, Javid began to make his mark and was named as the Newcomer of 2010 by the ConservativeHome blog. He made swift progress

SAJID JAVID

with positions in the Treasury, firstly as Economic Secretary to the Treasury from September 2012 to October 2013, and then Financial Secretary to the Treasury from October 2013 to April 2014. Javid became the first cabinet minister of South Asian descent when David Cameron appointed him as Culture, Media and Sport Secretary on 9 April 2014, and in January 2015, Javid was awarded the Politician of the Year award at the British Muslim Awards. At the General Election on 7 May 2015, Javid was re-elected in Bromsgrove with an improved majority of 16,529 (28,133 votes to Labour's 11,604 and UKIP's 8,163) and on 12 May 2015, he was appointed as Secretary of State for Business, Innovation and Skills. After being appointed as Business Secretary, Javid said that there would be "significant changes" to strike laws under the new Conservative government, announcing that strikes affecting essential public services will need the backing of 40% of eligible union members under new government plans. In the build up to Brexit, Javid who was seen as a Eurosceptic said, "with a heavy heart" that he voted Remain. In June 2016, following David Cameron's resignation as Prime Minister, the Secretary of State for Work and Pensions Stephen

Crabb announced that he would be standing in the July 2016 Conservative leadership election, on a "joint ticket" with Javid. If Crabb became Prime Minister, Javid would have become Chancellor of the Exchequer. Crabb withdrew from the contest after receiving 34 votes to Theresa May's 165 in the first round of voting amongst Conservative Members of Parliament. In July 2016, Javid was appointed Secretary of State for Communities and Local Government by the new Prime Minister, Theresa May. At the snap General Election on 8 June 2017, Javid was re-elected in Bromsgrove with a very similar majority to his 2015 victory with a 16,573 majority (33,493 votes to Labour's 16,920 and the

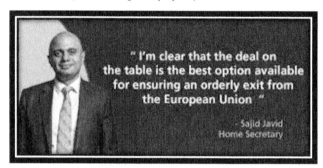

Lib Dems 2,488) and in January 2018, he gained the additional portfolio of Housing in England to his role as Communities Minister. In the role, he focused on increasing housing supply, including delivering a new generation of affordable council housing. As Communities Secretary, Javid launched a wide-ranging programme of leasehold and commonhold reform, targeting rogue managing agents as well as the exorbitant service charges faced by many leaseholders across England and Wales. On 30 April 2018, Javid was appointed as Home Secretary following Amber Rudd's resignation for misleading MPs over the Windrush scandal, Javid started his role saying he's determined to fix the injustices of the Windrush scandal and launched a consultation. On his appointment as Home Secretary, Javid became the first person from an Asian background to hold one of the Great Offices of State in the UK. He lifted the cap on immigration for NHS doctors and nurses and planned a crackdown on the number of low-skilled migrants coming to the UK, ready for when Britain left the EU. Javid used an exceptional power as Home Secretary to issue a licence for a child with acute epilepsy to be treated with medical Cannabis oil, and also launched a new panel to consider applications from patients seeking to use cannabis oil, while announcing a review of medicinal cannabis. Following advice from the Chief Medical Officer and the Advisory Council on the Misuse of Drugs, Javid announced that medicinal cannabis would be available for prescription on the NHS, although he clarified the position by saying that prescribing medicinal cannabis was not a step towards

legalisation for recreational use. Javid stood in the Conservative leadership contest, when Theresa May stepped down and was one of ten Conservative MP's nominated. Javid survived the first four ballots, before being eliminated on 20 June 2019, with 34 votes,

BORIS JOHNSON AND JAVID

leaving Boris Johnson, Jeremy Hunt and Michael Gove as the three remaining candidates. When Boris Johnson became Prime minister on 24 July 2019, he immediately appointed Javid as the Chancellor of the Exchequer in the new Cabinet. Upon his appointment, Javid 'tweeted' that he was looking forward to working at the Treasury to prepare the United Kingdom for leaving the EU, and he planned to overhaul the Treasury's approach to Brexit, beginning with "significant extra funding" to get Britain ready to leave with or without a deal. Tensions between 10 Downing Street and Treasury had come to a head during August 2019, when the Prime Minister's Chief Special Adviser, Dominic Cummings, dismissed one of the Chancellor's aides, Sonia Khan without Javid's permission and without informing him. Javid "voiced anger" to Johnson over the dismissal of Khan. In November 2019, following questions of a rift between Johnson and Javid, Johnson gave his assurance that he would retain Javid as Chancellor after the 2019 General Election. At the election on 12 December 2019, Javid increased his majority

significantly in Bromsgrove to 23,106 (34,408 votes to Labour's 11,302 and Lib Dems 6,779) but by February 2020, it was reported that in the forthcoming Johnson reshuffle, although Javid would remain in his role as Chancellor, Rishi Sunak would stay on as Chief Secretary to the Treasury in order to "keep an eye" on Javid. On 13 February 2020, following a meeting with the Prime Minister on the day of the reshuffle, Javid resigned as Chancellor of the Exchequer. During the meeting, Johnson had offered that Javid could keep his position on the condition that he fire all of his advisers at the Treasury, with them being replaced with individuals selected by 10 Downing Street. Upon resigning, Javid told the Press Association that "no self-respecting minister would accept those terms". Javid had been due to deliver his first Budget on 11 March 2020, in which he was expected to include increased spending on infrastructure, public services and the environment. But on the day of his resignation, he was immediately replaced by his deputy, Rishi Sunak. Javid became the first Chancellor in 50 years to not deliver any Budget since Iain Macleod in 1970, and his time as Chancellor, 204 days, represented the second-fewest days in office since the Second World War. In his first speech to Parliament on returning to the backbenches after his resignation, he said that he felt he still had "more to give" in regards to his political future.

Interesting Sajid Javid facts:

On 26 January 2020, a 50p coin to mark Brexit was unveiled by Javid, bearing the inscription 'Peace, prosperity and friendship with all nations' with the new leaving date of 31 January.

In 2013, Javid was influential in getting the beer duty escalator abolished and cutting beer duty for the first time in over a half-century. In his honour, a commemorative beer was brewed called "Sajid's Choice" and was served in the Strangers' Bar at the House of Commons and also sold locally in Bromsgrove.

Javid is a Senior Fellow at Harvard Kennedy School (Mossavar-Rahmani Center for Business and Government).

Javid is an active local campaigner in Bromsgrove and has campaigned for fairer school funding, an upgrade the train station, improvement of road and transport services, better local NHS services for residents and the creation of more opportunities in the town.

Since being first elected in 2010, Javid has held six annual Jobs Fairs and four Pensioners Fairs.

Javid met his future wife, Laura, while doing a summer job at Commercial Union. He said they sat opposite each other and shared a stapler, they have four children.

Javid, has described himself as a non-practising Muslim.

Rishi Sunak
Born 1980 - Conservative

Chancellor of the Exchequer:
Assumed Office
13 February 2020

Born
12 May 1980, Southampton

Title: None

Constituency Represented as MP:
Richmond 2015 - present

Other Official Offices held:
Chief Secretary to the Treasury 2019 - 2020
Second Lord of the Treasury 2020 - present

Prime Minister served with as Chancellor:
Boris Johnson

Education:
Winchester College
Lincoln College, Oxford
Stanford University

Rishi Sunak, (born 12 May 1980) is a Conservative Member of Parliament for Richmond and has been Chancellor of the Exchequer in Boris Johnson's government since February 2020. He was previously Chief Secretary to the Treasury from July 2019 to February 2020. He has been the (MP) for Richmond in North Yorkshire since 2015.

Sunak was born on 12 May 1980, in Southampton, Hampshire, the eldest of three children to to Yashvir and Usha Sunak. His father Yashvir was born in Kenya and his mother Usha was born in Tanzania. His father was an NHS family GP and his mother ran her own local chemist shop. Sunak said his parents sacrificed a great deal so he could attend good schools, firstly he attended Winchester College, an all-boys' public boarding school, where he was head boy and the editor of the school paper. He then studied Philosophy, Politics and Economics at Lincoln College, Oxford, graduating with a First in 2001. In 2006, he obtained an MBA from Stanford University, where he was a Fulbright scholar.

While living, studying then working in California, Sunak met Akshata his now wife, with whom he has two daughters, Krishna and Anoushka. Sunak worked as an analyst for investment bank Goldman Sachs between 2001 and 2004. He then worked for hedge fund management firm The Children's Investment Fund Management (TCI), becoming a partner in September 2006. He left in November 2009 to join former colleagues at new hedge fund firm Theleme Partners, which launched in October 2010. Sunak was also a director of investment firm Catamaran Ventures, owned by his father-in-law, Indian businessman N. R. Narayana Murthy. During his time at the university, Sunak undertook brief work experience at Conservative Campaign Headquarters, but it wasn't until October 2014 that he became actively involved in politics, when he was selected as the Conservative candidate for Richmond (Yorks). Sunak took over the Richmond seat from previous Conservative leader William Hague, and in the safe Conservative seat he was elected to Parliament in the 7 May 2015 General Election with a majority of 19,550 (27,774 votes to UKIP's 8,194, Labour's 7,124 Lib Dems 3,465). During the 2015–2017 Parliament he was a member of

the Environment, Food and Rural Affairs Select Committee. Sunak campaigned for Britain to leave the EU in 2016 saying: "I have spent my business career working around the world, investing in countries like the US, India and Brazil. I have also helped British companies expand internationally. My own experience convinced me that not only can our businesses thrive in these exciting markets, but that they must." He continued by saying: "The country will be 'freer, fairer and more prosperous' if the public vote 'out' on the June 23 referendum". After the Brexit victory, Sunak was re-elected in Richmond in the 2017 General Election on 8 June with an improved majority of 23,108 (36,458 votes to Labour's 13,350 and the Lib Dems 3,360). He voted on three occasions for Theresa May's withdrawal agreements, but when May resigned, he supported Boris Johnson in the 2019 Conservative Party leadership election. At the 12 December 2019 General Election, Sunak again increased his majority in Richmond to 27,210 (36,693 votes to Labour's 9,483, Lib Dems 6,989 and the Green party 2,500) and was appointed by Johnson as Chief Secretary to the Treasury on 24 July 2019, and a member of the Privy Council the following day. In the weeks leading up to a February 2020 reshuffle, a number of briefings in the press had suggested that a new economic ministry led by Sunak might be established to reduce the power and political influence of the Treasury. Sunak was considered to be a Johnson loyalist and favoured by his chief advisor, Dominic Cummings. By February 2020, it was reported that Sunak would stay on as Chief Secretary to the Treasury, for Cummings to "keep an eye" on Chancellor Savid Javid. After a meeting with the Prime Minister, Javid resigned as Chancellor and on 13 February 2020, Johnson appointed Sunak as the new Chancellor of the Exchequer. Sunak's promotion came at a time when the Covid 19 pandemic was about to hit, and in his first Budget on 11 March 2020, he announced an allocation of £12 billion to mitigate the economic impact of the pandemic and £6

billion of new funding in the period of Parliament to support the NHS. He finished his Budget statement by saying it was "A people's Budget from a People's Government". In July 2020, Sunak unveiled a plan for a further £30 billion of spending which included a stamp

SUNAK AND FAMILY

duty holiday, a cut to VAT for the hospitality sector and he created a job retention bonus for employers. He also created

the 'Eat Out to Help Out scheme'. 'Eat Out to Help Out' was announced to support and create jobs in the hospitality industry. The government subsidised food and soft drinks at participating cafes, pubs and restaurants at 50%, up to £10 per person. The offer was available from 3 to 31 August on Monday to Wednesday each week. In total, the scheme subsidised £849 million in meals. In his second Budget 0n 3 March 2021, Sunak said in his Budget

statement: "We have announced over £280 billion of support, protecting jobs, keeping businesses afloat, helping families get by. Despite this unprecedented response, the damage coronavirus has done to our economy has been acute. Since March, over 700,000 people have lost their jobs. Our economy has shrunk by 10% - the largest fall in over 300 years. Our borrowing is the highest it

SUNAK AS CHANCELLOR

has been outside of wartime. It's going to take this country – and the whole world – a long time to recover from this extraordinary economic situation. But we will recover." In the Budget he announced that the deficit had risen to £355 billion in the fiscal year 2020/2021, the highest in peacetime. The Budget included an increase in the rate of corporation tax from 19% to 25% in 2023, a five-year freeze in the tax-free personal allowance and the higher rate income tax threshold, while extending the furlough scheme until the end of September. Sunak was the first Chancellor to raise the corporation tax rate since Labour's Denis Healey in 1974. In an Ipsos MORI poll in September 2020, Sunak had the highest satisfaction score of any British Chancellor since Healey, back in April 1978. On 4 March 2021, Sunak unveiled a new fraud taskforce to clamp down on criminals who have exploited the government's Covid support schemes. By March 2021, the total spending by the Treasury for pandemic support had topped £407bn.

Interesting Rishi Sunak facts:

Sunak has said that in his spare time he enjoys keeping fit, cricket, football and movies.

Born in Southampton, Sunak supports Southampton FC, and one of his most prized possessions is a birthday card signed by the whole Southampton team for his 18th birthday.

Sunak is a Hindu, and has taken his oath at the House of Commons on the *Bhagavad Gita* since 2017 and is teetotal.

Sunak's wife, Akshata, is a director at her father's investment firm Catamaran Ventures and manages her own fashion label.

Sunak has been a school governor, a board member of a large youth club, and volunteered his time to education programmes that spread opportunity.

Sunak's favourite drink is Coke, to which he commented that he has seven fillings to prove it.

As a child Sunak was a big fan of Star Wars and has an extensive collection of light sabres and Star Wars Lego.

Sunak's billionaire father-in-law has been described by Time magazine as "father of the Indian IT system".

Sunak turned forty on 12 May 2020. He has been described as the 'Prime Minister in waiting'.

Sunak is 1.7m or 5' 6" tall.

Chancellors of the Exchequer – A Concise History

Printed in Great Britain
by Amazon